The Art of Teaching Dance Technique

by
Joan Schlaich
and
Betty DuPont

National Dance Association
an association of the
**American Alliance for Health, Physical Education,
Recreation and Dance**

The American Alliance for Health, Physical Education, Recreation and Dance is an educational organization designed to support, encourage, and provide assistance to member groups and their personnel nationwide as they inititate, develop, and conduct programs in health, leisure, and movement-related activities. The Alliance seeks to:

- Encourage, guide, and support professional growth and development in health, leisure, and movement-related programs based on individual needs, interests, and capabilities.
- Communicate the importance of health, leisure, and movement-related activities as they contribute to human well-being.
- Encourage and facilitate research which will enrich health, leisure, and movement-related activities and to disseminate the findings to professionals and the public.
- Develop and evaluate standards and guidelines for personnel and programs in health, leisure, and movement-related activities.
- Coordinate and administer a planned program of professional, public, and government relations that will improve education in areas of health, leisure, and movement-related activities.
- To conduct other activities for the public benefit.

Copyright © 1993
2nd Printing, October 1996
American Alliance for Health, Physical Education,
Recreation and Dance
1900 Association Drive, Reston, Virginia 20191

ISBN 0-88314-544-8

Contents

Chapter 3

Chapter 4

Chapter 5

Chapter 6

Chapter 7

Chapter 8

"*A technique class should help students create instruments capable of doing any movements.*"

Photograph by Niki, Deganit Kathzir

Preface

Why is it that in some dance classes students seem to become dancers while in others they make the motions but make no progress? This is the question that motivated us some years ago to start investigating the techniques, thoughts and methods of teachers we saw who were producing skilled dancers in their technique classes. How, we wondered, were these teachers different from others who might be equally proficient as dancers and who seemed to work just as hard in their classes? What makes a good teacher of modern dance technique? Can any reasonably good dancer learn to be one?

This book is the result of our searching for answers to these questions. It puts readers in touch with the thinking and methods of some of the outstanding teachers of modern dance in this country. Much of the material is drawn from our interviews of eleven teachers we know to be excellent and from observations of their teaching.

The interviews ranged from one to three hours in length. Although we had a basic set of questions asked all teachers, we made no effort to limit the interviews to those topics only. Often the teachers took very different approaches to answering the same question. A transcript of the taped interview was sent each interviewee for any corrections or additions.

We do not claim that these are the *only* expert dance teachers or even the *most* expert ones. They are just *some* of the expert teachers we know about and could make contact with and observe.

In years past modern dance classes in college and high school programs often were taught by someone who had taken two or maybe three semester classes in dance from one teacher. Nowadays, such classes are apt to be taught by dancers who have studied a variety of dance forms from a variety of teachers or have studied intensely with one artist. As with most skills, dance is better taught by those who are good at it. As with other arts, it should be taught by artists.

Although all of the artists included in this book teach modern dance, much of what they say and do applies to other dance forms as well. We believe any teacher of dance will find the book interesting and helpful. It aims specifically to help dance students or others who are skilled dancers learn to become dance technique teachers.

Joan Schlaich and Betty DuPont
California State University
Long Beach, California

Acknowledgments

We are deeply grateful to the eleven technique teachers who shared their thoughts with us and invited us to observe their teaching. We hope their abiding commitment to dance pervades the text as it did their interviews. Their cooperation and encouragement made this book possible. A brief biography of each follows.

We also wish to thank Eric Ruskin and Mark Uranker who talked with us so frankly about the life and trials of dance musicians. We appreciate the helpful suggestions from three high school dance teachers, Kathleen Owens, Barbara Noel, and Leanne Lacazotte. We owe special appreciation to Patricia Knowles and her students at the University of Illinois, Urbana. They gave us valuable input from their use of a preliminary draft as a text.

The Artist/Teachers

The eleven teachers interviewed and observed for this book have taught extensively throughout the United States and internationally as well. They have taught in studios and in universities as guest teachers, as regular faculty, and as artists-in-residence. The brief biographies that follow will identify the teachers as artists rather than list their many teaching experiences.

CAROLYN BROWN danced with the Merce Cunningham Dance Company as a principal dancer and as Cunningham's partner from 1953 through 1972. She has choreographed for (among others) Juilliard Dance Ensemble, Maryland Dance Theatre, and Ballet Theatre Contemporain in France. She writes and lectures about dance, has produced and directed a film, *Dune Dance,* and is the recipient of an honorary degree, Doctor of Fine Arts, from Wheaton College, a John Simon Guggenheim Fellowship, and numerous National Endowment for the Arts choreography grants.

VIOLA FARBER, director and choreographer for her own company since 1968, was a lead dancer with the Merce Cunningham Dance Company for twelve years. She also performed with Katherine Litz and Paul Taylor. Her works have been commissioned for Repertory Dance Theatre of Utah, Manhattan Festival Ballet, Nancy Hauser Dance Company, and others. She was artistic director of the Centre National de Danse Contemporaine, Angers, the national center for modern dance in France. She taught and choreographed in England and chairs the Dance Department at Sarah Lawrence College.

ELLEN GRAFF, former member of the Martha Graham Dance Company, has also performed with the companies of May O'Donnell, Pearl Lang, Sophie Maslow, and John Butler. She has appeared in Broadway musical theatre, in film, and on national television shows such as the Carol Burnett Show. She is assistant professor of dance at Barnard College and a doctoral candidate at New York University.

BETTY JONES, a founding member of the José Limón Dance Company, received international recognition for her portrayal of Desdemona opposite Limón's Othello in his *The Moor's Pavane*. Currently she is performing, teaching, and co-directing (with husband Fritz Ludin) the Dances We Dance Company in Honolulu, Hawaii. In 1990 they reconstructed Limón's *There Is a Time* for the Maly Opera Ballet in Leningrad.

GLORIA NEWMAN, founder and artistic director of the Gloria Newman Dance Theatre in Southern California, choreographed for her company and for others. She presented more than fifty residency/concert tours from New York to San Francisco. She received five National Endowment for the Arts choreography grants and other awards for her contributions to dance from the Los Angeles Dance Alliance, the California Dance Educators Association, and the Orange County Arts Alliance. She was on the dance faculty at California State University, Long Beach from 1972 until her death in 1992.

MARCIA SAKAMOTO, once co-director of Dance Project (now The Dance Place) in Washington, D.C., also founded and directed the former Moving Space School and Company in Berkeley, California. She has appeared in her own work as well as that of Gladys Bailin, Lynn Dally, and Betty Walberg, with whom she also collaborated in two film projects: *Bridge of Dreams* and *Sonata in F Minor*.

JEFF SLAYTON began his professional career with the Merce Cunningham Dance Company and later was a principal dancer with the Viola Farber Dance Company. For six years he was artistic director and choreographer for Jeff Slayton and Dancers based in Southern California. He has received several National Endowment for the Arts grants and choreographed for (among others) the New Dance Ensemble, Colorado Repertory Dance Company, and DancArtCompany. He is on the dance faculty at California State University, Long Beach.

CLAY TALIAFERRO was formerly a principal dancer and guest artist with the José Limón Dance Company and its assistant artistic director. He has also performed with the companies of Donald McKayle, Lotte Goslar, Anna Sokolow, Stuart Hodes, and Emily Frankel. He has choreographed widely, including for his own company, The Theatre Dance Trio.

DAN WAGONER, choreographer and artistic director for his own New York based company, Dan Wagoner and Dancers, since 1969, has toured nationally and internationally. He formerly danced with the companies of Martha Graham, Paul Taylor, and Merce Cunningham. He has created dances for companies in the United States, Canada, and Great Britain, where from August 1989 until December 1990 he was artistic director of the London Contemporary Dance Theatre.

ETHEL WINTER, soloist for over twenty years with the Martha Graham Dance Company, was the first dancer after Graham to perform several of her famous roles. Often a soloist with the Sophie Maslow Company, she also has appeared with the New York City Opera and in Broadway shows, television, and summer stock. She has choreographed for her own dancers and for Batsheva Dance Company in Israel. She lectured, performed, and taught in London to help establish the London Contemporary Dance School.

MARTHA WITTMAN, formerly a member of the Juilliard Dance Theatre, the Ruth Currier Dance Company, and the Anna Sokolow Dance Company, has taught at Bennington College in Vermont since 1959. She choreographs extensively and has had a long professional association as a choreographer with the Dances We Dance Company. Awards received to support new choreography include the Doris Humphrey Fellowship, National Endowment for the Arts grants, and faculty grants from Bennington College.

Introduction

A successful dance technique class is one in which most students improve in movement skills (technique) and artistry. It takes the help of a demanding teacher for such improvement to occur. Even professional dance performers take class regularly under the watchful eye of a knowing teacher. There probably has not been a successful self-taught dancer since Isadora Duncan. There is, therefore, a great need in the dance world for good teachers, teachers who can help their students achieve technical improvement and the ability to dance.

If you dance well and enjoy it and you want to become a teacher of dance, this book is for you. It will help you discover whether or not you have the personal qualities needed for successful teaching. It will give you an understanding of what takes place in a good dance class and what part students play in their relation to the teacher.

The joy in teaching dance technique is seeing students change, seeing bodies that were awkward and hesitant learn to move beautifully with control. This is the joy for students also, getting better, making progress they can see and feel.

It has been said that sooner or later most dancers become teachers. Many start teaching without any preparation for that exacting task. Usually they copy a favorite teacher—often the current or most recent one—without giving the actual techniques involved much thought. This book offers guidance from eleven experts, people acknowledged to be exceptional teachers.

This is not a step-by-step book on what to teach. There are no lists of exercises or techniques. It is assumed that those wishing to teach modern dance have spent many years in dance classes themselves, perhaps with a variety of teachers. Such persons have a great backlog of materials to draw from in teaching. They have no need of lists of foot exercises, back warm-ups, or ways to vary pliés. They need help with HOW to teach—not WHAT to teach. They can be helped by studying techniques and beliefs of successful teachers, teachers whose students learn to dance.

Every class has three elements, a teacher, content (activities of some sort), and students. The first three chapters of this book set standards of quality for each of these elements. Once readers have a picture of the ideal teacher, the ideal class, and ideal students, they should have a sense of what they are trying to achieve when becoming dance teachers.

The text then continues with practical steps in teaching, class planning, presenting material, making corrections, and providing dance accompaniment. The final chapter gives some of the thoughts and philosophies of the expert teachers on whose experience this book is based.

The appendices contain ideas on some of the more routine aspects of teaching such as class organization and grading. Many apply only to classes in schools.

"A technique class should develop an underlying sense of performance in students. . . . Good classes are aesthetic as well as training experiences."

Technique class, California State University, Long Beach

Photograph by Niki, Deganit Kathzir

CHAPTER 1

Important Qualities in a Technique Teacher

There are some parallel qualities found in all outstanding teachers of dance technique. These include not only mastery of the materials of the class, but also personal qualities and beliefs about dance, themselves, and their students. Occasionally a new teacher can clearly be seen to have a natural gift for teaching. Most are not so blessed, but by understanding what makes some truly great teachers so special, they may gain the tools to work toward joining those who are known as some of the best teachers in the country.

Love of Movement and Teaching

A love of movement is a basic requirement. Marcia Sakamoto expanded that in saying, "The dance teacher must be curious about movement and not be satisfied with one formula or get in a rut. The dance teacher must keep growing, keep being stimulated."

There must be a deep concern for others and satisfaction in the development of students. To be really successful, teaching itself must be exciting and stimulating. Gloria Newman described the need for "a trained eye, a creative mind, a passion for the medium, and a touch of the missionary."

Clay Taliaferro said he tries to share his own enthusiasm with students to teach them to work tirelessly and still want more.

Basic Knowledge of Dance

Knowing the basic skills of dance plus having "physical" knowledge of movement is the only way to have a "good eye," the ability to give meaningful corrections. The teacher must know what to look for. It must be clear when the student is not performing the movement correctly and what it will take to correct the problem.

Our expert teachers demonstrated an uncanny ability to see problems the instant they occurred. It appeared that they saw everyone in the class all of the time. There was an incredible awareness of detail. They would stop and straighten out problems before allowing the class to continue and were very precise about what they wanted and how students should move differently to make corrections. Yet they did not overcorrect.

Dance teachers must have extensive training with a broad awareness of movement possibilities. A technique teacher should have danced intensively, concentratedly. The ability to demonstrate beautifully is an asset, not essential but very helpful. However, the ability to demonstrate competently is essential.

This means the teacher of dance must have been trained by good teachers throughout the years of study. It is important to catch problems when the dancer is young before they become bad habits, which are more difficult to break later as the body becomes less supple.

In addition, a teacher of dance must understand the anatomy of the body, how to prevent injuries in dance, and both the possibilities and limitations of the body.

Supportive Attitude

A positive atmosphere results from the instructor being supportive of student efforts. Students must be permitted to make mistakes, to know that it is acceptable to fail while working toward accomplishing the movement. It is more rewarding to teach dancers who err as a result of "going for the movement" than those who are afraid to try. Which end of this scale students tend to use is often determined by the attitude of the teacher.

Dan Wagoner noted, "I try to create a space where the people taking the class can feel as free as possible to be themselves, to not feel inhibited. One lends them the dignity that they're here because they have chosen to be and that they are going to work as well as they can and as hard as they can. By giving students that expectation they often, I think, go beyond themselves and truly learn."

Ethel Winter talked about the need to be patient, particularly as students reach the inevitable plateaus and are discouraged. She concluded, "I take from Eric Fromm's book, *The Art of Loving*. I think it fits for the art of anything. He uses discipline, concentration, patience, and supreme concern. I talk to students about dance with those four things because they *are* of supreme concern. Teachers should have supreme concern for the instrument with which they are working."

A sense of humor may help students over the rough spots as may words of encouragement.

Clear Communication

Clarity is one of the most critical attributes of a talented technique teacher. Instructions to students must be absolutely clear, as must corrections. A problem the authors have seen many times with beginning teachers is that they see a movement is being performed incorrectly but do not know what to say to help the student make the correction.

Dan Wagoner explained, "I think that learning movement, gaining control of one's body, and gaining a craft of movement and technique are very difficult. So the teacher must be clear about what is expected and what the movement is—and give some clues about energy release and how to actually do it. That's what is important. To help a student learn technique, one must be as clear as possible in presenting the material and try to help students know exactly what is expected of them."

Musicality

A strong sense of musicality in the presentation of material (carefully counted and phrased and precisely executed) and in the communication with the accompanist is essential. Students must be instructed to listen to the music, dance with it, feel the rhythm.

Musicality is evidenced in movement phrases. Whatever the qualities, there are supporting rhythms that make them logical and interesting. As Martha Wittman said, "The key to executing a movement well often lies within its rhythm."

This is further expanded by Betty Jones. "Within each movement is the rhythm of that particular movement, the energy flow. I sometimes compare it to calligraphy, its sweep and attack, thick or wispy. It has to do with dynamics and the amount of energy, the finding of the inherent elasticity or rhythm, in a particular movement." One key to inventing

*"A teacher should be very aware that
you can only push so much.
You want to make a race horse, not a work horse."*

—**Ethel Winter**

Ethel Winter in "Suite of Three," choreographed by E. Winter

The Art of Teaching Dance Technique

interesting movement phrases is a musicality that responds to rhythm of movement, with or without accompaniment.

Focusing Beyond Technique

Successful teachers are able to get beyond just the physicality of technique in their teaching.

Viola Farber stressed the need for an "ability to teach technique without forgetting that it is about dancing, and that it isn't just about being in the right place at the right time—that technique is in the service of dancing."

In talking about technical skill and quality, Clay Taliaferro said, "I try never to separate them, never to allow the student to forget that technique simply facilitates dance. *Dance* is the priority and not the separate muscles."

The focus should be beyond shapes or position, to developing an artistry. Without this bridge to the quality of movement, dance becomes an exercise class.

Other Comments on Teacher Qualities

The following are some informative comments from the expert teachers that cross the preceding categories and will give readers additional information about the qualities of a good teacher.

Ethel Winter, in discussing the need for the teacher to be aware of injuries to students, said, "A lot of them won't stop when they should, and it seems a shame, particularly with young people, as they create a chronic injury that is unnecessary. I think a teacher should be very aware that you can only push so much. You sometimes have to push students, but when they are aching and paining too much it is not worth it because you really want to make a race horse, not a work horse."

Viola Farber felt a teacher should "realize that no one can learn everything at once . . . not expect the same thing of every student."

Ellen Graff: "I think it's possible to both entertain and teach, but when you start to teach you just cannot let students do anything they wish. You must insist that they master certain things, and that they learn something about what the body is doing."

Martha Wittman: "To be a teacher rather than just a collector of different ways of moving, you have to have some kind of personal belief or vision."

Carolyn Brown, in responding to the question, "What are the qualities you consider important in a technique teacher?" gave the following comprehensive statement:

"I'd like to answer your question indirectly by referring to four extraordinary teachers I've had—my mother, Margaret Craske, Antony Tudor, and Merce Cunningham. My mother, Marion Rice, who was trained in the Denishawn school, was my teacher for fifteen years. It isn't really technique so much as the experience of dance that is important for her. She communicates a sense of joy and love of dancing and a belief in its spiritual power, and although she certainly teaches technique, that is not what I remember most. Of course, she wanted our little feet pointed, legs turned out from the hips and tummies in, and all the usual kinds of things, but the overall way she got at it was through developing a love for dancing and for music. She particularly stressed an awareness of music. From the very beginning we were taught to listen to it, to feel it, to respond to it.

"The teacher who has probably had the strongest influence on my own teaching, or let's say, whose teaching I most aspire to, is Margaret Craske, with whom I studied for twenty years. Like my mother, she too was always saying, 'Listen to your music!' Miss Craske, it seems to me, was a pure classicist, an inspired teacher of classical ballet. She *really* taught! (There is a world of difference between giving a class and teaching a class!) Miss Craske taught her students very, very carefully how to do particular things in order to accomplish certain other things, and she explained why they work. There are rules to be learned and applied, particularly in relation to the placement of the body, which really work, which free the dancer and allow the movement its full expressivity. Miss Craske was strict and demanding but never personally cruel. She had a sharp analytic eye. If a student failed to execute a difficult or complicated step or phrase, she was able to pinpoint that dancer's specific problem. She was like a good diagnostician, and she was able to prescribe the cure in clearly stated physical terms. Although she analyzed movement in an almost scientific way, it was never cold or dry. Miss Craske was always after dancing with a capital 'D.' She was trying to develop quality, sensitivity, depth of expression and musicality, but from the inside out, from the movement itself. She was truly generous and unstinting in her willingness to help any dancer who seriously sought her advice.

"For the first twelve years that I studied with Miss Craske, I also studied with Antony Tudor. What a combination! They complemented

Carolyn Brown in Merce Cunningham's "Story," 1965

Photograph by Jack Mitchell

"Technique is not an end in itself."
—Carolyn Brown

each other wonderfully because Tudor was *extending* the same technique, the same Cecchetti material, but extending it in a creative, adventuresome way. He too had a great gift for analyzing movement, but he had a complicated personality which sometimes got in the way of his teaching. The most exciting aspect of his technique class was the sense of discovering with him new ground. He made beautiful phrases, exciting phrases which were distinguished by subtle, complex and profound musicality. Learning to dance this material pushed us beyond our own capabilities.

"Merce Cunningham, with whom I studied for twenty years (the same years I worked with Miss Craske), taught by doing, by his own daily devotion to his work. He taught through example, through his passionate presence, his fierce discipline and almost fanatical dedication. He inspired rather than explained. And by watching him, I learned about 'musicality' without music, and I discovered how dancing, unaccompanied, unsupported by a rhythmical beat, can be 'musical.' In all the years that I worked with him, he rarely corrected, criticized, or encouraged. When he did, it made a strong, lasting impression.

"I think these four teachers are really after the same thing; all of them ultimately focus *beyond* technique. Technique, after all, is not an end in itself. But each one goes about it in a different way. Each one of these people has been deeply touched by a spiritual quest, whether it was through Christianity, Meher Baba, or Zen Buddhism, and this involvement has surely affected their perception of dance."

Reflections

The expert teachers observed had several areas of total commonality. All were completely clear in giving instructions and making corrections. It was not enough for students just to *do* the movement. There was a *right* way to do it and there was constant correction to see that the movement was precisely what the instructor wanted. Such teaching requires a high degree of awareness of detail and a "good eye."

In all classes observed, movement phrases were interesting and varied. Faculty showed enormous facility in inventing movement.

The length of the class seemed irrelevant. The classes observed varied from sixty-five minutes to two hours in length, yet all were well taught. Good teachers hold the interest and focus of the students for very lengthy classes and can also accomplish a great deal in relatively short classes. Difficult as it is, an excellent class can be taught in thirty to forty minutes, when the school day is structured so that this is all the time possible.

None of the teachers observed was a "cheerleader." Many were low key but very intense. They were enthusiastic, but never hypernoisy or shouting. They were not giving themselves a class but taking time to watch their students carefully. No class was an ego trip for the teacher.

All instructors observed had their students "dancing," not doing exercises. No one harangued the class about performance, but by example and by many subtle clues students were encouraged to really "dance."

All had the full attention and respect of their students. They had the ability to make students want to work hard. The corrections observed were not of the vague variety, "You're doing that incorrectly," but rather clearly isolated the error and explained how the body could move differently in order to correct the mistake.

One big difference between effective and noneffective teachers is that the latter teach material and the former teach students. Those who teach material simply present the movement but do not have an awareness of the total class response or of the individuals within the group. They just forge ahead without observing that the students are not keeping up with them, or are far ahead and bored. Those who teach to their students stop when the class is not clear on the movement, make corrections before allowing the class to go on, and have an eye for catching the mistakes of each dancer. They are *teaching*, not just giving a class.

SUMMARY

Important qualities in a technique teacher are:

1. A love of movement that leads to
    a. Experimentation, not staying with one "formula"
    b. Understanding movement possibilities
    c. Being creative, adventuresome
2. A trained eye
    a. The ability to spot problems and give meaningful corrections
    b. An awareness of detail
3. Interest in people that results in
    a. "A touch of the missionary"

b. An excitement in watching someone grow
  c. Concern for students
4. A physical knowledge of movement
  a. A trained body: should have danced intensively, concentratedly
  b. The ability to demonstrate clearly and well
  c. The ability to create beautiful and exciting phrases
5. Knowledge of the mechanics of the body
6. Ability to create a positive atmosphere for learning by being
  a. Patient
  b. Supportive
  c. Able to make students want to work hard
7. Ability to communicate clearly
8. Musically knowledgeable, possessing
  a. Rhythm and musicality
  b. A sense of phrasing
9. Ability to teach "dancing" (not just technique) with artistry
10. Ability to plan a purposeful class
11. Understanding that
  a. No one can learn everything at once
  b. The same thing can't be expected of all students
  c. A sense of humor helps students over rough spots
12. A vision, personal beliefs about dance and movement

SUGGESTED PROJECTS

1. Recall and describe instances in recent classes you have taken or watched where teachers have demonstrated any three of the following important qualities:

Sense of humor	Trained eye	Creative ability
Supportive behavior	Trained body	Experimentation
Concern for student	Patience	Musicality

2. With the teacher's permission, observe a beginning level class. Select two or three students who appear to be progressing well within the class and specify how the teacher contributed to their progress.

CHAPTER 2

Content Considerations for a Technique Class

In order to teach effectively, you must understand just what you are trying to accomplish. Expert teachers are very clear on what is important in a technique class, based on their years of experience. By heeding their advice, you can make faster progress toward becoming a successful teacher.

Two concurrent activities are vital in a technique class, training (the development of skill) and dancing (learning to perform). Gloria Newman expressed it thus: "A technique class should be anatomically sound and aesthetically motivated."

Developing Dance Skills

A technique class should help students create instruments capable of doing any movements. In the words of Marcia Sakamoto, "Students should, within their structure and capabilities, extend themselves completely in all the traditional and accepted technical forms."

To be successful in developing skill a technique class needs to include the following:

1. Emphasis on correct body alignment and mechanics

Proper use of the body figures in every movement every day in a dance class. Most teachers would agree with Betty Jones who explained that she starts first on getting the body aligned and has a difficult time moving on if someone is still much off balance. "Efficiency of body mechanics, of necessity, requires an alignment which approaches mechanical balance, so I work a great deal on centering, specifically the three big weights of the body (head, chest, and hips) centered over each other." For excellent technical information on this subject, see the chapters on body structure and correct body use in Arnheim's book on dance injuries.*

2. Logical progressions from warm-ups to complex phrases

The technique class should be structured so it moves from warm-ups into increasingly more difficult and strenuous kinds of exercises, never pushing the student to do something until the body is ready. There needs to be a reasonable balance between warm-ups, exercises to develop strength, flexibility, and endurance, and the movement phrases that deal with articulation and intention of movement.

3. Varied actions that work all body areas

Since dance includes all parts of the body, it is necessary that all parts be trained, "including the brain," adds Martha Wittman. "It is terribly important for teachers to help students develop open minds as well as open hip sockets."

4. Work involving the basic elements of dance

Every dance class deals with time (rhythm), movement through space, and energy (dynamics). Students should be aware of different aspects of time and space and energy from the very beginning. "There should be a lot of rhythmical work," Wittman explained, "some experience of space and different speeds in space—some sense of energy flow and time."

5. Emphasis on good work habits

A dancer must learn to work regularly and effectively. Carolyn Brown spelled this out when she noted that a technique class is a time to develop good habits, mental habits as well as physical ones. "You have to do hundreds of pliés, tendus, grand battements, turns, jumps, falls, etc. to develop consistently good physical habits so that the mind and the body learn to work as one."

Jeff Slayton noted the need for consistency from day to day. Only with the supervision of a trained teacher will movements be performed correctly class after class.

---

*Arnheim, Daniel D. *Dance Injuries, Their Prevention and Care* (3rd ed.). Princeton, NJ: Princeton Book Company, 1991.

6. Corrections and accurate demonstrations

The two vital factors of corrections and accurate demonstrations in a technique class are dealt with in separate chapters later in the book.

Developing a Sense of Performance

Viola Farber's statement, "Technique is in the service of dancing," leads logically to the conclusion that "dancing" should be part of a technique class. Jeff Slayton reminds students that their class exercises are *dancing* exercises. He encourages them to try for technical correctness, but still *dance*. He finds many students think technique is separate from dancing, so he tells them, "Technique is something to free you to dance rather than to hold you back." He also stresses the importance of involving the entire body. When students are doing a foot exercise, for example, they should be "aware of what the top of the body is doing, that it is still but it's dancing. It's alive!"

What do these expert teachers do in class to develop a sense of performance in students? How do they help students learn to perform as they learn technique?

Stressing the artistry of movement

"It is important for me to keep my mind on the fact that no matter what the level, it's art," said Dan Wagoner. "It may be slow, awkward art, but it's something that's very special to me and I hope will be special to them." In class he addressed his students as dancers, "Do it again, please, dancers." And he told them, "You are dancing right now."

From Betty Jones: "I go after the musicality and artistry. I feel the artistry is a very important part of their dance training whether they are beginners or whatever level, up to professional." And again, "The idea of quality, the area beyond merely executing a step, is taught immediately to all levels. Working beyond the physical into a more spiritual and artistic realm is very important to a dancer. All great dancers have gone beyond the physical. Here again, balance is sought."

Working on quality and a sense of communication

"At all times I want them to feel a sense of communication and a reason for an exercise—not just a physical display," observed Ethel Winter. "I really go up the wall when students plié and their eyeballs go up to the heavens or a blank stare appears. Ben Belitt, the poet, calls it 'the terrible gift of the gaze.' So many of my expectations are in relation to performing while dancing. I do tell them to smile. Just because you enjoy a phrase doesn't mean you're not seriously working."

Clay Taliaferro finds that in a technique class even the most advanced students need to be reminded that technique is really about quality and feeling. In class he admonished, "Use your body to speak, not just for gymnastics." He wants students to be aware of compositional resources within a technique class. Parts of his classes seem like a dance in quality and mood.

Martha Wittman said, "I like to think that classes are more like dances." But she acknowledged they don't always go that way due to the need for explanations and corrections.

Encouraging inner understanding

Marcia Sakamoto believes a technique class should give students a deeper, fundamental understanding of what motion is all about. Otherwise, they are just learning routines. She advised, "If you haven't learned anything in a technique class about how to approach space and time, about how to create a myriad of dynamic sensations—kinetic sensations—then why are you doing technique? It is only one means to becoming a performer." In class she told her students, "You aren't shaping space clearly," and their performance quality greatly improved.

In a similar vein Gloria Newman said, "I am interested in building the dancer's technique with a strong inner awareness of the source of movement and its applications...in developing their ability to perform the phrases with a sense of individual focus."

Using aesthetically pleasing phrases for class work

The choice of material used for teaching affects the performance quality of students in the class. When movements fit logically and physically together so there is a natural flow, students perform with more assurance.

Combinations that are inventive, subtle, eloquent, or aesthetically pleasing in some other way seem to inspire students. Undoubtedly, the use of artistic material, even in beginning classes, greatly enhances the development of a sense of performance in students.

"Technique is really about quality and feeling."
—Clay Taliaferro

Clay Taliaferro in "Old Dancing, Arranged," choreographed by C. Taliaferro

Photograph by Les Todd

Other Important Elements

Many factors contribute to the success of a technique class by aiding students in the development of skill and a sense of performance.

Focus

A dance class should be organized and have some specific focus. It should be clear from the beginning of class to the end why certain things are done and where the class is headed. There should be some physical reason for whatever occurs whether it concerns dynamics or space or time. There should be a reason for doing any particular movement.

Pacing

A well-paced class keeps students alert mentally and physically. Marcia Sakamoto says she likes to keep things moving in a technique class. "Once the bodies have energized, they need to stay energized. They don't need to lift and drop and lift and drop during those periods when I talk a lot, so I try to say what I have to say as quickly as I can."

In practice the other teachers agreed. The authors used a stopwatch to get an approximate check on nonmovement time, when students were listening to directions or corrections, or watching demonstrations. The vast majority of these talk-times were thirty seconds or less. Very few went to two or three minutes in length, and there were no long sessions of listening without movement.

Even so, the technique classes observed varied greatly as to the total amount of nonmovement time, time when most of the class was not moving. This does not include walk-throughs or practice periods. The chart on the following page shows the times recorded by one person watching thirteen different classes. Two teachers were timed twice with different classes.

It is evident from the chart that the need for talking or showing varies greatly with different classes and different teachers. Even the teachers timed twice talked much more in one class than the other.

From this limited analysis we cannot relate nonmovement time per se to pacing as none of these classes seemed to drag or bore the students. Probably it is not the total amount of talk that counts, but the quality, and teachers at this level of experience express themselves very effectively. Even the teachers we observed who had the longest total non-

Nonmoving Time in Dance Technique Classes

Class Length	Approximate Nonmoving Time	
	Minutes & Seconds	Percent of Total
1. 100 minutes	8:54	8.9
2. 90 minutes	9:24	10.4
3. 80 minutes	11:54	14.9
4. 105 minutes	15:55	15.0
5. 100 minutes	18:15	18.3
6. 120 minutes	29:00	24.2
7. 90 minutes	22:55	25.4
8. 90 minutes	23:35	26.0
9. 90 minutes	26:30	29.4
10. 65 minutes	19:15	29.6
11. 95 minutes	30:20	31.9
12. 90 minutes	31.36	35.0
13. 70 minutes	24:40	35.3

movement time kept their classes paced so that muscles stayed warm. When there were a lot of comments, they were made quickly and concisely. The flow of the class was not interrupted.

Diversity

A diversity of material in a technique class can lead students to use their bodies more efficiently under different circumstances. It also makes a class more interesting so that students stay alert. Even within a single class, good teachers achieve diversity by using a variety of rhythms, changing dynamics from one phrase to the next, and using irregular directional patterns and unusual movement combinations.

Asked if he repeated a lot when teaching an ongoing class, Clay Taliaferro said, "Yes, but I try to repeat using different space, using different focuses, and using different rhythms very often."

Carolyn Brown noted that she also varies much of the material. "I give different brushes, extensions, back exercises, ronde de jambes, etc. and combine them in different ways—all with the intent of developing strength, clarity, resiliency, and good alignment in the body and flexibility in the mind."

Challenge

It seemed important to all the teachers that the students be challenged. During classes the authors often heard advice such as: "Take a chance!" "Don't be so cautious!" "Add a turn, if you can." When students were trying a difficult movement, Viola Farber exclaimed, "Go for it. Try it. Otherwise you'll never do anything except what you already can do!"

Good teachers continually introduce new elements to provide a challenge and stimulation. To help her students make progress Ellen Graff tries to walk the fine line between giving them material that is too difficult (frustrating) or too easy (boring). "It's like walking a tightrope," she remarked, "holding the carrot in front of them—just a little bit more than they can reach at that point."

Several teachers increased the speed of a phrase to make it more challenging. Others would make the pattern more complex by adding turns, increasing the movement range, or changing the counts. Such complexities demand mental as well as physical exertion so student concentration increases with the challenge. In every class most of the students could, with practice, meet the challenge and achieve reasonable success with the material.

Space

Expert teachers show skill in getting the utmost in movement from a large class in a small amount of space. Whether students are dancing in center space, moving straight or diagonally across the floor or around the room, they need to be well spaced and aware of each other. Teachers sometimes have half or a third of the class practice at a time to give students more space to move.

Most dance spaces have mirrors, but teachers sometimes face classes away from them. According to Viola Farber, "Mirrors are helpful if the class is large. I would prefer sometimes to have mirrors and sometimes not. I hate that thing of people dancing for the mirror. I think it's awful to have to rely on a mirror to know what you're up to."

Atmosphere

There should be a positive feeling in a class so students know they are welcome, not, in Dan Wagoner's words, "just lucky that the teacher is allowing them to be there." Along the same vein, Ethel Winter explained that she wants students to feel free enough to make mistakes. "It's easier to correct a real mistake than something that is sort of half baked. If students really go all out, then you have something to correct, so I like them to feel quite free in class even though I am very strict in a way."

In all of the classes observed students worked with concentration. There was no "freeness" in the sense of side conversations or half-hearted efforts. Some of the teachers encouraged students to ask questions or made humorous comments to relax the class. However, the atmosphere was one of serious concentration on the work at hand by teachers and students.

Music

Accompaniment that supports the dance movement in rhythm and mood contributes immensely to the quality of a dance class. Most dance teachers prefer having a qualified musician accompany class. This allows a certain spontaneity. When there is no musician, teachers use tapes or records with movements selected to fit the available music as well as suiting the purpose of the class. A later chapter deals with dance accompaniment.

Reflections

Most modern dance teachers would agree on the basic ingredients of a technique class: proper preparation of the body, training of all body areas in a variety of ways, and performing more complex movement phrases. Even when these basics are well done, however, other factors seem to determine whether a class is ordinary or really exceptional.

Number one is pacing, keeping the class moving at an appropriate speed. The teacher can have perfect warm-ups and great material, but if the class drags, the effect is lost. Boredom seems fatal to a dance class. Equally fatal is the opposite extreme where the class leaps along without sufficient repetitions or pauses for absorption of material. Pacing depends on judgment and sensitivity.

The best classes have a continuity, a logical flow from phrase to phrase. Each step is a preparation for the next, and a movement taught early in class may appear in different sequences later on. There is a building within the class of related elements, not a hodgepodge of disconnected patterns.

Ellen Graff, Graham dancer, 1962

"...walk the fine line between material that is too difficult (frustrating) or too easy (boring)."
—Ellen Graff

The Art of Teaching Dance Technique

There is an ever-present "danciness" in good classes. From the simplest warm-ups through complicated, challenging combinations every movement is executed with a sense of performance, a total participation of the entire body. Good classes are aesthetic as well as training experiences.

SUMMARY

1. A technique class should concentrate on the development of dance skill by including:
     a. Emphasis on correct body alignment, efficient mechanics
     b. Logical progressions from warm-ups to developmental exercises to more complex movement phrases
     c. Varied physical actions that work all body areas needed for integrated dancing, including the brain
     d. Work involving the basic elements of dance, time (many rhythmic activities) and space and dynamics
     e. Emphasis on good work habits, both physical and mental
     f. Corrections and accurate demonstrations, two factors dealt with in separate chapters
2. A technique class should develop an underlying sense of performance in students by:
     a. Stressing the artistry of movement
     b. Working on quality and a sense of communication
     c. Encouraging inner understanding
     d. Using aesthetically pleasing phrases for class work
3. Other important elements in a technique class include:
     a. Focus, a main goal for the class and a reason for each movement in the class
     b. Pacing, keeping the class moving at an appropriate speed for learning and interest
     c. Diversity, variety from class to class and within each class

    d. Challenge, the presentation of material appropri-
       ately difficult for these particular students
    e. Space, making the best use of the space available
       to accomplish a maximum of things
    f. A positive atmosphere
    g. Suitable accompaniment

SUGGESTED PROJECTS

1. Observe a dance technique class, and list elements of the class described in this chapter (itemized in the summary) that made an important contribution to its success.

2. Time a class. With the teacher's permission, use a stop watch to record all times when students are not moving. What percentage of the class was nonmoving time? How does this compare with the text chart on time?

CHAPTER 3

What Is Expected From Students

Ellen Graff summarized many points made by others in saying, "I expect students to be disciplined, to concentrate, and to be able to focus their energy on what's happening right there and then. They should be able to drop everything that is happening outside so that when they walk into the studio it is a place where they work and not where they worry about what they are having for dinner, or something else. I expect them to make progress, and I expect to see a difference in them from one month to another month. I expect, and I don't always get it, but I still expect them to watch what's being done and reproduce it. I expect them to be able to utilize general corrections and not have to be individually told everything, so that if I make a general correction I expect to see some difference in the class from that."

Commitment

When asked what he expected from students, Dan Wagoner responded, "Commitment, complete commitment." Viola Farber told her class, "I want you to do it, but it's more important that *you* want to do it."

Self-discipline and motivation were frequently mentioned as expectations from students. Betty Jones described a situation where a student asked why she hadn't been getting any criticism recently. "Until you make that alignment change, I can't go any further, " Betty answered. And a quote from Ellen Graff, "I expect them to be there to work. I don't expect to have to entertain them, so I expect them to be motivated when they come in, to want to learn."

Another viewpoint from Carolyn Brown: "The desire to please, unfortunately, is something we're all very vulnerable to, and I think learning to work for oneself is a lesson that some of us never, ever learn. We always do whatever we do for someone else or someone else's approval. But since dancing gives so little back to us in any material sense, particularly in modern dance, its real reward is in the doing, and if we dance for any other reason than the experience of dancing, we're in trouble." Clay Taliaferro commented, "More and more as I teach, I expect students to dance for themselves—not for me." And, "I expect one hundred percent participation on their level."

The statement came up several times that students are expected to give themselves to the moment, to what is being taught and, as Jeff Slayton phrased it, "to leave their daily problems in the corner with their dance bags and say, 'For this hour and a half, it's dancing I'm interested in,' so that all those other things are not in the way of the work." Taliaferro also expects his students to carry things too far sometimes, so that they know their limitations—rather than doing things too small, making them too big. Martha Wittman says, "I expect and hope for a love of movement and dancing that will extend beyond the technique class."

Responsibility

Most of our interviewees referred to the need for students to be responsible for applying *all* corrections made, including general comments and individual corrections made to other students. This was particularly clear in Gloria Newman's class where, as she was making general corrections, every student was observed working on that correction in his/her own body. There was total attention on the movement. Marcia Sakamoto reinforced this expectation by never moving on to new material until students had worked through the corrections she had given.

In observing classes, the authors noted the concentration expected of students. Gloria Newman exemplified this by singling out a student at various times in the class and asking that person to dance the phrase while counting it out loud at the same time. Martha Wittman also asked students to count the phrase they had just completed when their rhythm was clearly off. In both cases all students instantly focused strongly on clarifying the counts for themselves. Wittman asked a few times in class that students show her what they remembered of a phrase they had worked on in a previous class. Betty Jones frequently asks students questions about the movement and also the rhythm.

In class Clay Taliaferro advised, "Make yourself step on the beat. You're responsible for that." He also tells students that they are responsible for a long phrase themselves and should not watch someone else to get it from them. And Marcia Sakamoto said, "They are really responsible for their own training. I simply present the class and assist them to the best of my ability to understand what I'm trying to do. In that sense I demand a lot from them." Taliaferro summed it up by stating that students must be "responsible and accountable."

Trust

Students must have confidence in the instructor and be willing to try what *this* material is although it may be very different from their past experiences. They must be able to work in the way the teacher expects — to quote Viola Farber, "to give themselves, while they are there, totally to what's being done." Carolyn Brown tells students, "If your head is full of other ideas when somebody is trying to teach you, you're not going to learn anything and you're wasting your own time and the teacher's."

Reflections

All teachers interviewed expect a serious, focused student who is giving full attention to the work of the class. And in all cases these instructors received exactly that from their students. The range of classes we observed was from beginners through quite proficient students, yet the concentration was as intense with the beginners as it was with the more advanced. The ability to get students to focus their energy to the work of the class certainly is one of the attributes that separates the excellent teacher from those less effective.

Sometimes putting responsibility on the student for remembering counts or phrases from earlier work is a very effective tool for getting their absolute attention.

All teachers want to work with an open-minded student who comes to class to learn, who has commitment and self-discipline.

SUMMARY

Qualities that are expected from students:

1. Self-discipline
    a. Concentration
    b. Focus
    c. Self-motivation, a desire to learn
2. Ability to make progress by utilizing corrections
3. Love of movement and dancing
4. Trust
    a. Confidence in the instructor and willingness to work in the way the instructor requests
    b. Being open-minded

SUGGESTED PROJECT

Immediately after taking a technique class, evaluate your participation by answering the following questions.

1. Did you concentrate on class activities?
2. Were you disciplined and attentive?
3. Did you perform all movements presented to the best of your ability?
4. Did you apply all corrections given in class to your own body?
5. Were you following students in front of you instead of memorizing counts and phrases for yourself?
6. Did you feel enjoyment in taking the class?

CHAPTER 4

Planning

Planning is essential to achieve the kind of ideal technique class described in Chapter 2. All of the teachers interviewed plan in advance for each dance class. Even though they are teachers of long experience, not one goes to class vaguely waiting for inspiration to strike. All of them follow a basic class structure they have worked out which includes preparing the body, training the body, and performing combinations, but they have no set series of warm-up patterns they use without change in every class.

Need for Planning

One reason for planning is to set goals, long-term goals for a semester or series of classes and more specific goals for an individual class. With an ongoing class Clay Taliaferro establishes his priorities with the group during the first week. Then he devises his daily plans to achieve this progression. Teachers find they cannot use the same goals and plans with different classes.

In addition to setting goals in terms of progressions in technique, teachers also consider student weaknesses when deciding on class goals. Viola Farber explained, "A lot of what I give in class has to do with what I think is lacking in a majority of the students, things most of the people in the class need to work on." Jeff Slayton also noted that each class is planned for that specific group of students, centering on something they need to work on. Marcia Sakamoto sometimes makes a mental note of some weakness during class; then instead of making an immediate correction she will devise a correction in her plans for the next class.

A second reason for planning is to select or compose material, to make the movement choices basic to carrying out the class purpose. Gloria Newman observes that some teachers want to teach everything they know every class! But there is a limit to how much students can absorb, so the teacher has to make choices, has to plan. Marcia Sakamoto warns against movements that do not contribute to the class purpose. She says, "It's not enough just to throw a bunch of movements together to fill up an hour and a half." It takes time to build a logical series of movements and set them to exact counts, but that is part of planning. As Carolyn Brown declared, "By preparing the combinations before class I can be sure of the counts, not only for the students, but for the pianist as well."

Amount of Planning

The amount of planning varies from teacher to teacher and from class to class. Beginning teachers need to plan much more carefully than experienced teachers. Carolyn Brown said that when she first started teaching in the Cunningham studio she planned "every last twitch of the fingernail." That seems ridiculous to her now, but it does point up the fact that even experienced performers need to plan carefully when they first turn to teaching.

Many beginning teachers find it helpful to write out their teaching plan along with working it out in movement. Planning on paper helps some dancers get organized and teach a better class. Most use an outline form with some notes on teaching ideas and class organization such as the format shown in the sample in Appendix A.

Beginning teachers should also plan more material than they expect to use. Because of their inexperience in pacing a class they are more apt to race along and run out of material than have too much. And beginners tend not to stop as much for corrections as experienced teachers. Those new to teaching should plan additional combinations, just in case.

Gifted, experienced teachers may do less planning before class partly because they are able to plan on demand, as they teach. Explained Viola Farber, "I don't plan a whole class ahead much because I like to be able to deal with whatever is happening at the moment, and I can't if I have a rigid idea about what I'm going to do. I have an idea of the kind of thing I'm going to do, but I don't really plan a whole class from beginning to end." Carolyn Brown says she does not make detailed plans now because she likes to have flexibility, room for change and for following the needs of the students on that particular day.

Betty Jones expressed admiration for José Limón's ability to think in class and choreograph the phrase right there. "I would love to do a little more of that myself," she mused, "to be spontaneous enough to allow it to come." There seems to be general agreement that the ability to choreograph on demand in class is a rare skill!

These experienced teachers say it takes thinking time and studio time to plan a class. Mental planning for Martha Wittman includes recalling what particular things students had trouble with the previous week and deciding what order things will fall in. "Then," she adds "I need to go and spend some time in the studio by myself to prepare some things, to elicit them out of my own body. With longer sequences, I try to prepare them pretty fully ahead of time."

Studio time should include warm-up time for the teacher according to Jeff Slayton who avoids injury by warming up before planning his class on himself. Dan Wagoner allows a half hour warm-up period before he starts composing and working on movements for class. His favorite time for planning is the hour or so just before class (others agreed), but this is not always possible with busy schedules and busy studios. Even so, Gloria Newman notes that she tries to have some quiet time, if only a few minutes, just before class to recall the plan and get focused in, so to speak.

Sources of Movement Materials

Teaching involves a lot of composing for our expert teachers. All of them devise movements and combinations for specific classes. Gloria Newman explains why she tends not to use the same materials over and over: "The movements become too familiar to me. I'm not interested in rote teaching. I think by keeping myself alive in terms of finding new ways of approaching, I can keep my students alive, too " Betty Jones agrees, saying she likes to take time to create new phrases as that is important for student growth as well as mine—perhaps more so for mine."

Jeff Slayton's combinations may be newly made for that class or part of something choreographed previously for a class or even a performance. "There are certain things I have made up that I like, and they stay with me, " he said. But he noted that even these will be changed to fit a situation. Dan Wagoner states that he likes working on new material but he also will use phrases from dances or from previous classes that were especially nice. "I don't know why," he explained, "but certain phrases stick with me." From Betty Jones: "There are certain patterns of movement or nice phrases that I like to share." Others also reuse or extend on materials that seemed to work previously.

Concerning sources of material, Martha Wittman believes anything that will work and help the situation should be utilized in class. "I think anyone who starts to teach has that feeling of wanting to invent everything. It's good in that it makes us always try to find something new," she explained, "but sometimes an excerpt from a piece of choreography may seem a good challenge for a particular class. Sometimes if something needs to be worked out in a piece of choreography, I'll try it out in a technique class." She also uses phrases from other choreographers' works. "It's a wonderful way to break habits of rhythm, space, and energy that the teacher and class have become overconditioned to."

Clay Taliaferro rarely does an exact movement phrase from a dance in technique class except where the technique class is leading into a repertory class. Then he uses actual choreographic material because "it helps to remind the students of where the technique is leading." Viola Farber notes that her class material varies a lot because "often what I give in class has to do with what I'm involved with choreographically, what I'm concerned with making for the company at that time."

One major source of materials for beginning teachers will be the classes they took as students. They tend to use what they like and what seems appropriate from their student years, past and present. Experienced teachers also do this, feeling free to draw on their total background of movement and even look for new ideas from other teachers. Said Gloria Newman: "I think it's important for teachers to watch other teachers so they won't be so closed."

Contents of a Dance Class Plan

Plans vary in content just as classes and teachers vary, but the plan always includes warming up, training in dance skills, performing of phrases, and cooling down. (The Arnheim book on dance injuries noted on page 12 has helpful material on warm-ups and cool-downs as a means of preventing dance injuries.)

Basic Structure

As a general rule the plan fills in the basic class structure or format used by the teacher for technique classes. Teachers refer to this again and again. Marcia Sakamoto says her "drills are variations on a theme from day to day. Thus students are familiar with the materials but not the way they are going to be put together."

Carolyn Brown varies much of the material within her basic structure. She commented that "I know there are certain things which have to be done in every class every day. There are a variety of ways to present that material, and I can improvise on them endlessly."

Viola Farber rarely teaches the same thing twice. "I teach the same *kind* of thing," she explained, "but I always try to change how I get at it so students have to attack it in a fresh kind of way." Jeff Slayton's classes follow a pattern in which the starting order is usually the same (two back exercises, something for the feet, an arm exercise, another back exercise, then pliés) but he puts in something different for each class — not different enough to be confusing, just enough to keep the class alert.

Gloria Newman gave a more detailed description of the basic structure she follows in planning a class.

1. Warming up
    Back exercises (including upper torso)
    Joint actions (feet, ankles, knees, shoulders, elbows,
        hands)
    Torso circles and twists (rib actions)
    Brushes (including transfer of weight)
    Pliés (plus body actions and variations)
    Relevés
    Battements (in place and including shifting space
        and facings)
2. Preparations for combinations
    Short phrases focusing on specific movement
        concepts to be enlarged on later
3. Performing lengthier, more challenging phrases
4. Special feature
    Patterns requiring rhythmic speed, quick coordina-
        tion, and jumps
5. Warming down

Martha Wittman's plan for every class includes areas that deal with being in one place, that deal with the legs, with turning, with jumping, and with movement in space. This is the rough structure that becomes more particularized as time goes on. In her planning she varies these materials, changes their rhythm, speed, and/or space. "Otherwise," she says, "I would find the situation for both myself and the students too repetitive and boring."

Repetition

There are other views on the value of repetition. Betty Jones feels that repetition of material is important, but hopefully not to the point of boredom. Gloria Newman expressed mixed feelings about making every class different. "I know," she said, "that we can concentrate and work more deeply when we are familiar with the movement, and that sometimes repetition serves to enrich the quality of the movement." On the other hand, she notes the dangers of repetition in that students may repeat mistakes and create habit patterns in approaching movement. Jeff Slayton recalled watching a class in which the first forty minutes were a memorized routine of techniques without a pause. "I wonder," he mused, "how many classes or how many months pass before it becomes so automatic students really don't know what they're doing any more or why they're doing it?"

Logical Progressions

A large element of planning for these teachers is developing logical progressions of movement in which early class drills especially prepare students for the complex combinations that follow. Said Carolyn Brown, "What I plan before class are the long phrases and combinations at the end of class, and I prepare for these in the beginning of the class." She further explained how she gives bits and pieces of the combination that might present technical difficulties for students in simple slow exercises early in the class. Every teacher interviewed referred to this same process in their planning, leading up to complicated phrases with logical progressions of movement

Jeff Slayton observed that in planning his classes, he sometimes starts by making a combination that suits the class purpose and designs supportive exercises later. Other times he starts with exercises he knows are needed and builds the phrase from them. Either way, early warm-up parts of his classes lead up to the complicated combinations that come later. This integrated type of planning makes the purpose of the class evident throughout. Every part contributes to the goal.

Themes

Sometimes classes are developed around a theme so the planning centers on this theme or concept. Marcia Sakamoto described basing a whole class on a concept recently. "I wanted them to understand the center body in relation to outness, that is, reaching and stretching," she explained "So we simply started stretching to the ceiling, to the side, and then we stretched in all kinds of directions. We stretched and returned, stretched and returned, doing the whole warm-up on different ways of stretching. I devised a phrase that included stretches in many different directions and a phrase moving across the floor also. It was exciting to see the life that came into the center body during this class."

Jeff Slayton told how he might center a class on turns, for example. He puts different turns in a lot of the exercises—quarter turns, half turns, whole turns, spiral turns—and builds the class up to a complicated turning phrase.

Carry-over Material

Some dance plans contain carry-over materials from one class to the next. Many teachers like to start with a pattern and add to it in succeeding classes so there is a continuity. This presents a need for remembering on the part of students and makes them deal with more complexities each class.

Variety

"I always like to give something that is entirely new," said Viola Farber. Similarily, Clay Taliaferro says he sometimes "goes to left field with new material." Dan Wagoner occasionally likes to include elements not so usual in technique class, such as contact with another dancer, supporting another dancer, passing, manipulating the space so students have to deal with space as well as doing the step.

Jeff Slayton said, "Sometimes I give students something that I can't prepare them for necessarily, perhaps acting a little, something that has a bit of style and requires a kind of focus." He also suggests following a complex exercise with a simple one to give students a sense of security and ease their minds. When she is meeting a class daily, Martha Wittman plans to work a few materials of very different nature during a week and drop in and out of things.

Teaching Techniques

Considering how to teach a particular class or movement is another function of planning. For Wittman, planning how to teach may involve knowing the physical structure behind the action. "With some materials," she explained, "I occasionally run to the anatomy book to try to identify more clearly where an action is happening "

Gloria Newman made a point of the need to try different approaches in class. If students have been unable to get a skill, she will plan another way of doing it. "It's so easy to fall prey to habit," she noted. "It helps to challenge me if I can think of other ways." Furthermore, she believes students need to see that there are many ways of approaching the same material, all with great excitement and enthusiasm.

Special Situations

The first meeting with a new class takes some special planning since the students are unknown. Ethel Winter solves this by planning a class with a little of everything. That way she can size up her new students in a variety of moves. Jeff Slayton says he may make his first class with a new group a little too hard for them, "so I know what I 'm up against."

Master classes offer special problems. "There is no way of planning," observed Viola Farber, "when you don't know who will be there. It's absolutely hopeless to teach technique in one session. I just try to get students to move around, change directions, and change speeds." She added, "I enjoy master classes."

Clay Taliaferro plans for a master class but notes, "I must then be willing to throw that away and get down to the actual offering of material for this particular body of people in front of me for this time." He further remarked that most anything you do in class with people you never have worked with before will be accepted because it is different and there is an exotic appeal.

Master class teachers should prepare variations on the same material from simple to complex. That way they are ready for whatever level the class turns out to be.

"To be a teacher rather than just a collector of different ways of moving, you have to have some kind of personal belief or vision."
—Martha Wittman

Martha Wittman, Bennington College

Photograph by Josef Wittman

Studio classes call for different planning from university classes. Ellen Graff explained, "I think you have to be a little looser and more spontaneous because in a studio class you don't know who's going to show up that day. You have to be more ready to go with the people who are there. If you do something on Monday in a university class, you know you can take it to the next step at the next class." Marcia Sakamoto noted that in university classes she could gear each class around people because she could expect to see the same students every class. She might plan to emphasize one idea during the entire class. In studio teaching, however, she plans a well-rounded class each day so students who come only once a week have a total experience and not just part of a series.

Using the Plan

All our expert teachers warn there must be some flexibility in following a plan. As Ethel Winter put it, "Sometimes the class will take a different direction than I have planned, and I have to go with that." As an experienced teacher, she finds she can go in many directions from her basic plan. "But," she adds, "it's good to plan, because then you have something to change!"

Clay Taliaferro commented on how often he discards a plan or changes it mid-class. "I plan in order to throw it away, to cleanse my mind, more or less." And again, "I plan it, I begin the class, then decide I can't give this work to these people now." Viola Farber referred to similar experiences, saying, "If I see there is something that the class ought to be working on, I stop and I make something that just deals with that. So I have to stay alert as well as the students." And "Even after years and years of teaching, sometimes I make something I think will be fun and it turns out to be terribly difficult for everybody. Something else I think will be difficult, everybody gets in a snap." Either situation, of course, calls for a change of plans. The teacher must adapt and work with the reality of the situation.

Reflections

Planning is most evident to the students in the organization of a dance class. A planned class shows a logical progression. It may be that each pattern builds on the previous one, moving from simple to more complex. It may be that the class has some central focus such as turning or reaching. It may be that early simple patterns appear again in the complicated phrases at the end of the class. In every case students can pretty well do what is expected because they have been carefully prepared in earlier sections of the class.

In a planned class there are no waiting periods while the teacher composes movements or tries to establish counts for a sequence. Patterns have been worked out and set to exact counts before class. Planning helps pacing.

Planned classes are more varied and interesting. They avoid monotonous repetitions of the same material every class. This helps keep the students alert and receptive. The planned class has a purpose that students can recognize and respond to with a feeling of accomplishment.

Planning gives teachers, especially beginners, a sense of security and gives their classes a sense of direction.

SUMMARY

1. Planning is needed in order to:
   a. Set long-term goals for a series of classes
   b. Determine the purpose or goals for an individual class
      Based on needs (weaknesses) of students
      Based on technical progressions to be achieved
   c. Select or compose material, make movement choices
   d. Consider teaching techniques to be used
2. Amount of planning time depends on:
   a. Experience of teacher
      More detailed plans for beginners
   b. Thinking time needed
   c. Studio time needed and/or available
3. Sources of movement material drawn on in planning include:
   a. Movements composed specifically for this one class
   b. Movements taught previously which are appropriate for this class

4. Planning a dance technique class may include:
    a. Selecting or composing movements to fill in the basic class structure or format used for most classes
    b. Selecting or composing a logical progression in which warm-up movements specifically prepare students for complex combinations that follow
    c. Selecting or composing movements to support a theme or central concept for the class
    d. Selecting or composing movements to add to patterns taught previously
    e. Setting movements to exact counts
    f. Devising interesting variations on standard exercises
    g. Composing phrases and combinations of some complexity
    h. Deciding *how* to teach the movements selected
5. Special situations that affect planning:
    a. First day classes for a continuing group
    b. Master classes
    c. Studio classes where students may be different each class
6. Use of the plan in teaching may call for:
    a. Adjusting movements to suit skills of the students
    b. Digressing to meet an evident class need
    c. Being flexible in omitting unneeded sections of the plan

SUGGESTED PROJECT

In the next three technique classes you take, watch for elements of planning listed below. Describe the use of one observed for each class.

Logical progressions

Warming up and cooling down effectively

Variations on standard exercises

Phrases that use movements taught earlier in class

Movement sequences clearly presented to exact counts

Material carried over from one class to the next

CHAPTER 5

Presenting Material

As noted in Chapter 4, most of the teachers interviewed prepare students for complex phrases at the end of class by introducing individual movements or sections earlier, for example, in the warm-up. Others build a class around a particular movement theme and repeat that specific thematic material throughout the class.

Ellen Graff explains, "Let's say that I'm beginning to work on tilts in a class. I'll try to do that in the floor work and again in a standing position. I'll try to pinpoint several places during the class to use that in combinations, to use it coming across the floor in some way so we can work on it in different guises."

In the classes we observed, most teachers prepared the class by teaching parts of a phrase in the early part of a class or in previous classes and then incorporating those movements in a long combination. Jeff Slayton taught some long phrases that challenged students to think and remember. He said nothing while they moved. His demonstrations and explanations were so careful and clear that virtually all students understood. There was a completely logical development throughout Slayton's class. Movements would reappear in different combinations and he would sometimes remind the dancers that they had done a particular section of a long phrase as an isolated warm-up.

Betty Jones presents new material in several different ways. "Sometimes I throw out a phrase swiftly and let everyone catch as much as they can. Some people can learn better from seeing the complete phrase and falling into the rhythm of it. Others need each movement analyzed, so I break it down part by part and build it back up. Both ways are valid and will present some challenges to both types of learners.

Eventually, the slower learner speeds up as he/she understands movement better and sees it more clearly."

All teachers observed presented movement experiences in such a way that student "movement vocabulary" was constantly expanding. Phrases through space moved from a basic pattern into add-on variations and additions so that the phrase was developed each time it was repeated. If something didn't work or a great idea occurred to the teachers it could be changed. The final phrase might therefore be something very different from what the instructor had in mind when planning the class. There is space for spontaneity. Students never were taught "routines" where a set sequence was taught as a whole with no sense of the development possibilities within the movement phrase.

Demonstration

In a discussion on the role of demonstration, Dan Wagoner stated, "I demonstrate each exercise very carefully. I just simply start at the beginning of a phrase and demonstrate about the first four movements so they begin to see. Is it slow? Is it fast? What is the quality? Then I'll repeat from the beginning and go on and show the first part up to wherever I feel there is a breath or a seam in the phrase and have them try to get that, and then go on to the second part. I try to show it as clearly as I can on my own body; they ask questions and then we continue clear through it. Then I ask them to watch and I do it with the accompaniment to see if it's going to work and to check the tempo — and for them to see what the movement is like. Then if they want to ask more questions they can. I usually divide them into groups and the first time through it's like a rehearsal."

In answer to the question of how much demonstration is needed throughout the class, he continued: "I think I demonstrate a lot, partly because sometimes I'm trying to find the placement for myself and to work on it and to see what it feels like. I do think you have to be clear and that one should demonstrate the rhythm also. A lot of teachers mistake difficulty and unclarity for being demanding. I think students should learn to look and analyze quickly." Wagoner also addressed the problem of oververbalizing; "It's important to know that there are moves that cannot be precisely analyzed verbally— the weight is falling or suspended—funny little things in timing that if you analyze too much get sterile."

Marcia Sakamoto said she was testing the amount of talking

needed. "If I spoon feed them too much and break it down and explain everything verbally they begin to expect it, their heads are working and they're listening to me but they're standing still and getting cold — and they learn intellectually. So with advanced people, I often give them things very rapidly without much explanation. My thinking is that they probably begin to learn physically rather than mentally. So I show the phrase, usually only to one side, and then they do the full phrase on both sides. I show the whole thing again and tell them to watch for the moments they know they need help on. Sometimes we sort of `ping-pong' where I do, they do, I do, they do, and everytime I do it they watch for the moment they need. Then, after they get the whole phrase, if necessary I'll pick out certain places that we need to talk about or that they need to see in a different way."

She added that she finds she has to demonstrate the most when she has not demonstrated clearly the first time. But the demonstration is also to help her establish very clearly when in the phrase certain things occur. "If I give a good, clear demonstration and it's not a terribly complicated phrase, I often do it twice. And they get the gist of it."

In observing Sakamoto teach, it was evident that her demonstrations were exceptionally clear. Then she did not demonstrate, count, or talk while they moved. Her explanation: "I feel too many teachers, myself included, tend to perform as we teach. I realized I was doing that and it inhibited how well I could see what the students were doing. The advanced people need to learn how to perform at this point, and they can't if they're competing with me. So I give them *their* space. Beginners need to see and follow more. They don't have their own 'kinetic' yet. However, I don't move with them all the time because I don't want them to start imitating."

By not demonstrating unnecessarily she was able to use the time while students were dancing to move around and give individual corrections. Another technique Sakamoto used in presenting new material was demonstrating once facing them and once turned side-ward to the class.

Jeff Slayton said, "I try to show the movement at most three times, and then ask if it's clear. If it is not, I'll show it again and make sure they are watching. I'll say 'and' and I don't move. Then they know whether they've been watching or not. But if I do it with them, they're just following." Slayton also explained that, with beginners, you have to demonstrate more with full energy than is needed with advanced dancers. In his advanced class he many times demonstrated once

Betty Jones as Desdemona in José Limón's "The Moor's Pavane"

"I want to help students find their own unique way of moving."
—Betty Jones

forward, gave a brief verbal explanation, and then told them to do the pattern forward, side, side, back. They were able to do so as they had learned to watch and listen. He remarked, "I try to keep it *their* class, not mine."

In explaining why she demonstrated and then stopped while the students danced, Betty Jones observed, "In spite of needing and wanting the work for myself, I feel I'm cheating my students, dividing my attention between myself and them. Also, I feel they must take the initiative to understand, execute, and make the movement their own. Following doesn't do it. I want to help students find their own unique way of moving. Sometimes highly trained and exquisite teachers may invite imitation more than inspiration and the understanding of the work that went into their art."

Viola Farber said, "I realized that I often showed things about four times, and I discovered that people didn't really watch until the last time. I started showing something only once so they would learn to pick up quickly." She feels that when students study with the same person for a while they know the kind of thing they are doing and the teacher then has to dance with them less. She added, "They have to do what is given, but not try to imitate, so they learn to do things from the inside out rather than some kind of superficial 'copying' thing."

Martha Wittman agrees that the amount of demonstration should be held to a minimum so that students do not become "over-reliant on a teacher or assistant, but become engaged with the class and whatever is going on as directly as possible." She uses an advanced student as a demonstrator for beginning classes so that she is free to circulate about the class and make individual corrections. "Things can be said verbally that make things happen physically. But a good demonstration, by teacher or assistant, gives a clear indication of image or goal that most times words cannot replace." When Wittman demonstrated twice, it would be in two different parts of the studio.

Ethel Winter also uses a demonstrator. She finds that when she is giving a correction to one student, others stop moving if they do not yet have the movements deeply enough in the body. But with the demonstrator continuing, students will follow. Advanced students will internalize the movement so a demonstrator is not needed as much. She added that a demonstrator is needed less when the class is taught in a studio which has a wall of mirrors where the teacher can both demonstrate and see the class.

Taliaferro said that he demonstrates new material along with verbalization and imagery. "It's important to go through it with students at this point when they're first learning the material and then stop and watch them." When observed teaching a master class he went through a pattern three times. Then he stopped as he felt that he was demonstrating too regularly. He then switched to moving with them a little, stopping and watching for a while, then rejoining them later for a few measures.

The answer Carolyn Brown gave to her procedure for teaching/demonstrating was, "I prefer to give the materal, show it once or twice, teach it carefully by breaking it down and explaining how it can be done, and then let the dancers do it in their own way, not trying to copy the way I would do it, not trying to copy my style, mannerisms, etc. I would rather they find their own energy, do it for their own bodies."

The need for students to observe an accurate demonstration is explained by Ellen Graff. "Somewhere there's got to be that very direct and physical interaction, the student seeing the physical demonstration and also almost feeling it, feeling the energy vibrations or whatever it is that comes from a leg that is *really* straight and feet that are *really* pointed, and absorbing that. And once that's been absorbed then you can ask the student to give you a straight leg without physically demonstrating, as the student knows what it is."

Gloria Newman feels that demonstrations in class are important "because we learn by seeing and sensing." Concerning how much demonstration is needed in a class she answered, "I think it equally important to sketch and verbalize the intention and ask the dancers to color the movement. If the dancers merely copy, they lose their ability to explore their individual differences. I would rather they understand the essence of the movement than copy the design. I suppose my concern is in having seen dancers so set in one particular style that one is more aware of mannerisms than of the individual performing the movement."

A typical format for the use of demonstration was observed in Newman's class.

1. She demonstrated once at tempo while counting and the class watched.
2. Students marked it though with her once.
3. They went through it about four times while she watched.
4. She made general corrections and they marked it with her while she stressed places where there had been problems and made a few individual corrections.

5. They repeated the movement a number of times while she watched and gave some movement cues, not counting. The musician was trusted to keep the rhythm and the students were encouraged to listen to the music.
6. They might then move on to new movement sequences or, if there were still problems, they would re-mark with her and then perform it again while she watched.

Beginning-Advanced Students

The question presented to the teachers was, "Do you handle beginners differently from advanced students?"

"One thing that is not different is that no matter what the level of the class, my expectations within what's given in the class are the same," was Viola Farber's answer. She continued, "Obviously the material is different. I don't have beginners stand around in one place for a long time because they haven't got the stamina to concentrate for so long on one thing. A beginning class is just as serious as an advanced class. There isn't any point in trying to do anything less than well."

Carolyn Brown explained the range of approach for beginners through company members. "I think there is a world of difference in how one should approach teaching technique to beginning, intermediate, advanced, and company dancers. Briefly, I'd say that beginners need some basic information about how to stand, how to center their weight, and then how to move without tension in extremely simple ways without losing that sense of placement. Beginners need slow and simple stretching and strengthening exercises and then they need endless repetition of simple activities to give them self-confidence and to accustom their bodies to a variety of movement possibilities.

"The intermediate students need more of the same, but they need a bit more complexity, a compounding of movement elements. They need to work on smaller, quicker articulations of the feet and torso, as well as learning to jump and fall

"At the advanced level, one should attempt to explore the full range of movement possibilities in all their complexity and difficulty, working for extremes in adagio, slow motion, speed, height, fine articulation, completeness, variety of attack—the list is endless. The advanced dancer needs to be constantly challenged to grow.

"At the company level, it's a bit more complicated. Class has to correspond to the day-to-day needs of the company's work schedule. When the schedule of rehearsals or performances is heavy, only a basic, simple class is needed. When the company is not performing or rehearsing constantly, class can be a time to develop the potential of each dancer."

A vital component of teaching beginners was stressed by Ellen Graff. "I spend a lot of time with beginners on trying to focus them on what it is like to work in a way that is concentrated and disciplined, so that they can make progress, because without that they can repeat movement patterns forever and you won't see any progress. It's amazing to me how quickly you can see them progress once they've developed a capacity to work in class."

With beginners, Marcia Sakamoto keeps the count and directional changes simple but still keeps the pace moving rapidly. She stated that "Beginners are frightened about learning physically, but if I can capture them with the movement, they're willing to do it."

Many expressed the same viewpoint as Dan Wagoner. "The material is going to have to be slower for the beginning students, but I try to work as if they're there because they're going to be artists, that they're serious and committed to it. Once they realize you're behaving that way, they begin to feel the specialness of it." He talked about the need to get at good dance values, alignment, good use of muscle, those things that make for quality in movement. He reflected on his experience as an affiliate artist teaching beginners and concluded that many people are frightened by the subjective realm of dance, where "you do have to reveal yourself and that's not easy. It's often painful. In making a dance, or anything for that matter, you have to be willing to be vulnerable. For those who do make sense of it—it changes their whole life. They really begin to look at everything differently, and to think of themselves differently—and that's quite beautiful."

None of those interviewed denigrated the value of teaching students who are new to dance. Many shared Wagoner's experience of the rewards of finding that those students who persevered experienced dramatic changes in their perceptions and in their lives. And so there was another kind of value other than that associated with the excitement of teaching advanced dancers where the teacher can "throw material at them or test new movement on them for choreographic ideas," as Clay Taliaferro expressed it. Taliaferro has found he enjoys working with serious-minded beginning students who respect the discipline and the excitement of it.

Martha Wittman finds beginning dancers wonderful because they are usually enthusiastic, original, unconditioned. "What is difficult is that they don't know what they don't know. They need to be encouraged a lot and they need to have a vigorous physical experience in each class—lots of contrasts, changes of space and speed and energy." In a more advanced class she expects "to take basics for granted. These classes can become more choreographic, more about performance and endurance. More quality is expected." In an overall view, Wittman said she teaches dance as dance. More advanced and less advanced students take class differently. The more advanced generally "will work harder, see more, retain more, practice more."

Betty Jones teaches an advanced class so that "it is more complicated and challenging." Her approach parallels our other interviewees in that "quality, the area beyond merely executing a step, is taught immediately to all levels."

With an advanced class, Ethel Winter feels that you can "get to the refinement of a phrase. You are getting toward performance. Even though I try to get them to perform as beginners, real subtleties can come out more in an advanced class." With a beginning class she might say, "Now you have four counts and I am going to say a word." Then she says something such as "stretch," "turn," or "fall" (knowing she cannot teach a fall all at once but that they will fall and come up) and they respond in different ways.

Clearly, all expect the same discipline and focus from beginners as from advanced students but the material is different and the presentation of the material may be handled differently. As stated earlier, the amount and spacing of demonstrations will vary according to the level of the students in a class.

Individuality of Students

In response to the question of whether exact replication of material is desired or should students add something of themselves, Viola Farber answered, "I think in all dancing, no matter how precisely you do what someone else is doing, unless you put yourself into it, it's not very interesting. Yes, I want them to be on the right foot, to do things with the right rhythm, even to have whatever quality it is I've given them, but for every student that's going to be very different because we're all physically different, and in precision there still is a great deal of room for individuality."

Ethel Winter confirmed that "the spirit has to be there and they can give their own individual life to it. Counts don't mean that much. It is what you do in between the counts that, for me, makes a dancer. I may teach the same exercise but change the counts or change something in it so that they are just not little mice running around on a signal."

A balance is encouraged by Betty Jones. "Movement needs its own life and motivation and that's the individuality, but in order to progress there needs to be discipline. A precise performance without motivation, life, or truth is pure mechanics and not interesting to me in the least."

Support for the idea that the dancer must give something of self is added by Martha Wittman. "I think if one finds out what a particular action, activity, or physical situation is about, then there's no way you cannot contribute something of yourself."

Clay Taliaferro encourages "individuality within my framework, and I very often say, 'Now you do *you* within my framework, do it your way.' I like to stimulate and encourage individuality within limitations."

Ellen Graff looks for "precise performance of technique and within that there is a space for all the individuality in the world. If you're working between being here on one and there on two, there is a space to be very individual about what you're doing, but I still want you here on one and there on two."

Jeff Slayton agrees that he wants students to make movements their own within the structure of what he has given. "I don't want them to make it so much their own that it's not what I'm working on, but I don't want them to try to look like me. I want them to find out how to dance with *their* bodies."

Carolyn Brown feels that dancing reveals the dancer so each dancer can't help but be unique. She would like the dancers "to try to get the shape as I gave it as precisely as possible, and even more important, get the rhythm precisely. But even within the rhythm, there is the natural body rhythm unique to each person, and the way one attacks a phrase and the way one resolves it can be very individual. However, class is a time and place to attempt exactness of execution, not the time or place to practice self-expression."

Dan Wagoner summed up what it seemed all the others want: "I want them to be beautifully *individual* and do precisely what I say!" Wagoner talked about company members who remain individuals, but "they're able to bring the central aesthetic idea together and to show it, and then the individuality will illuminate it. They understand their own life in relationship to what they're doing and they illuminate it by being themselves. And that's true art, I think, in dance."

Jeff Slayton, California State University, Long Beach

"I don't want them to try to look like me. I want them to find out how to dance with _their_ bodies."
—Jeff Slayton

Photograph by Keith Ian Polakoff

Reflections

Many young teachers overdemonstrate, moving with the students all or most of the class time. Therefore they give few or no individual corrections and their students keep repeating and reinforcing mistakes. Although some of those observed did move with the class more than they expressed a need for, others were very stinting in the amount of demonstration and clearly let the students make the material theirs. Reactions from our interviewees address the difference between "imitating" the instructor or demonstrator and "learning," which is evidenced when there is no demonstration and students are on their own to move. Although beginners need to see more demonstration than do more advanced students, all interviewees felt that demonstrations must be limited so that students are actually learning the material and so that the teacher can move about the studio and give individual corrections.

Everyone we observed built the final phrases in a class by gradually adding on to material. A variation or addition was added only when students had experienced and understood the basic elements of the phrase. In contrast, beginning teachers frequently present an entire complex study through space to students at one time, with chaotic results! Teaching a section at a time and adding on allows the phrase to grow as the class is observed performing each section.

There was some commonality in techniques used to clarify material. Many have half of the class perform a phrase in center while the rest of the class watches, and then change. This gives a sense of performance. Others felt this took time when students should be moving, not standing and watching, so if the space was large enough for all students to move at once, phrases were always performed in unison.

From our observations we saw that most of these teachers demonstrated sometimes back to the students and other times facing them. If the teacher sorts out left and right sides when facing the class, there is the advantage of eye contact and the ability to spot errors quickly. Demonstrating back to the class seemed particularly counterproductive when there were no mirrors as time was wasted on stopping them later for group corrections that could have been caught as they marked the movements with the instructor had the instructor been facing them. Demonstrating back to the class seems necessary when the movement phrase incorporates turns or crossing the feet, as the movement and direction are confusing when the instructor is facing the class.

Several teachers speeded up the counts once students had learned the basic structure of a pattern. One teacher told students to complete a combination within four counts instead of in eight as they had learned the movements.

From our observations it seemed clear to us that the demonstration is the most critical phase of teaching new material. There is a sensitive line, but the problem universally appears to be too *much* not too little demonstration. The quality of the demonstration is also critical. A precise, accurate demonstration can save hundreds of words.

Clearly, dedication and discipline are expected whether students are beginners or advanced dancers. One of the more striking aspects of the classes we observed was that even rank beginners were expected to focus on the material and work very hard and with great seriousness. And, as a result, they did so.

No one wanted little robots, all looking exactly alike and mirror images of the teacher. The expectation was that the material would be performed exactly as the instructor presented it but that there is an individuality about everyone which could and should come through when performing in class or on stage. This does not mean class time should be for self-expression but rather that one reveals oneself when moving.

SUMMARY

1. To teach new material to a dance class, it is helpful to:
    a. Introduce movements in the warm-up and center work that will be incorporated into longer phrases in the final section of class.
    b. Build a class around a movement concept so that thematic material is repeated in different parts of the class.
    c. Stress the development of a movement vocabu- lary, rather than teaching "routines."
2. In determining when and how much to demonstrate, consider:
    a. If students keep imitating they are not learning.
    b. A qualified student demonstrator is sometimes helpful.
    c. Demonstrating at different angles to the class or in different parts of the studio clarifies movement for students.

d. Dancing with students all the time does not allow them to make the movement their own.

e. Limiting demonstration allows the instructor the freedom to make individual corrections which are essential for progress to occur.

3. When teaching classes at different levels, beginners and advanced, consider:

a. The approach is the same disciplined, focused, commitment to the art.

b. The material varies according to the ability of students to comprehend and perform the movement.

4. Students should be expected to:

a. Perform material as presented by the instructor, including precise counts.

b. Bring something of themselves to the movement.

SUGGESTED PROJECTS

1. Observe a technique class (could be one you are taking) and list movements and/or sequences taught during the class which were later seen as part of a phrase performed toward the end of the class.

2. As a student in a technique class, determine when you were prepared to perform a combination: After the first demonstration? The second? Third? Do the same for verbal explanations. When were you ready to follow directions?

3. Observe classes of at least two different technical levels. Record differences in range of movement, amount of repetition, complexity of movement, complexity of rhythm, and amount of explanation and demonstration.

CHAPTER 6

Making Corrections

Basic to making effective corrections is the teacher's ability to *see* what is wrong and *know* what will help. This refers back to the first chapter where teachers pointed out the need for a good eye and fundamental dance knowledge. In addition, communication seems to be a critical factor.

A correction may be one word ("Lift!") or a careful explanation. We noted four types of corrections being used:

Physical (or anatomical), dealing with correct use of the body
Facilitating, designed to make the movement easier or better
Rhythmic, dealing with counts and being on the right beat
Qualitative, to improve the aesthetics of the movement.

Our artist/teachers consider corrections an essential part of a technique class. They made an average of slightly over 21 per hour of teaching. About half were directed toward individuals and half to the whole class. The chart on the following page gives figures for each class as recorded by one observer. The fewest corrections noted were in a master class, the most in an intermediate college class. On an average these teachers tend to give a correction every 2.5 to 3 minutes during a technique class. Clearly they believe that student progress depends on effective corrections, as they devote a fair portion of class time to them.

Approaches to Making Corrections

"I try to stay as objective as possible," said Dan Wagoner. Along with objectivity he recommends being direct and specific, but some times he

Approximate Count of Corrections Made in Classes Observed

Class Length	Number of Corrections			Average Frequency	Average Per Hour
	Group	Individual	Total		
				every	
1. 100 minutes	13	4	17	6 min.	10
2. 90 minutes	10	10	20	4.5 min.	13
3. 100 minutes	13	11	24	4.25 min.	14
4. 90 minutes	7	14	21	4.25 min.	14
5. 95 minutes	13	20	33	3 min.	21
6. 90 minutes	23	8	31	3 min.	21
7. 120 minutes	16	25	41	3 min.	21
8. 105 minutes	10	33	43	2.5 min.	25
9. 90 minutes	19	18	37	2.5 min.	25
10. 70 minutes	12	18	30	2.25 min.	26
11. 90 minutes	29	14	43	2 min.	29
12. 80 minutes	24	14	38	2 min.	29
13. 65 minutes	11	21	32	2 min.	30

achieves his goal by being oblique. He recalled talking about the need for breakfast when a dancer looked weak in a sequence instead of criticizing the performance.

In the same vein, Gloria Newman remarked, "I try to keep corrections impersonal, although they seem very personal to students." She advises students to think of the body as an instrument. For example, "If you were a cello and I said you were playing the wrong note, you wouldn't cry. So if I tell you your rib is out just try to hear the right note and play it."

Jeff Slayton prefers the direct approach, saying something like, "This is the way to do the step" or "This is the way I want you to think about turning out your leg." This approach is quick and to the point. It was used often by the teachers, as they stressed the need for being exact and very clear.

Several recommended an analytical approach. "In relation to technique," observed Marcia Sakamoto, "it's not enough simply to make demands. If you don't let students understand how to arrive at the demands, there's no point in making them. " A similar comment came from Martha Wittman: "The best way is to get students to feel what they're doing *and* understand why they're doing it." Viola Farber noted that an analytical approach to making corrections can be very time-consuming, although there are dancers who have to understand everything intellectually before they can do it.

In several classes the teachers encouraged student questions as an approach to making corrections. Others never asked for questions but would answer those asked. This can be a time-consuming approach, and students who just want attention may delay the class with thoughtless questions.

No one recommended getting angry with students when correcting their dancing, but Farber indicated that this can be an effective approach. "I must say I never do it on purpose, but I have a temper, and sometimes you can shock people into pulling themselves together."

Some teachers feel that corrections may be easier to accept if the teacher is not always perfect. "I like to demonstrate that we are all fallible," said Clay Taliaferro, "that I, too, can fail the exercise." In her classes, Ethel Winter says, "I didn't clarify that, did I. I'm sorry." Then she repeats her correction, having accepted blame instead of placing it on the class. Other teachers also took this approach of sharing responsibility when things did not go well.

Many suggested using a variety of approaches. Jeff Slayton advised, "The main thing about corrections is that you try to be as clear as you can. If you see it doesn't work with a student, then you try another approach. I've learned how to say 'Turn out your leg' in many different ways." "What I try to do," said Marcia Sakamoto, "is to look at the person's body and what it seems to be feeling, then go from there." In the same vein Viola Farber observed, "For different types of students, different ways of dealing with them are effective. I think some people would just be incapacitated by having someone terribly angry at them. For other people, that works very well."

Techniques for Making Corrections

Betty Jones mentioned a favorite technique in saying, "I tend to wander around in class while students are doing exercises and make individual corrections." Every teacher observed moved among the students watching them from all sides as they practiced and making quick corrections as needed. Occasionally they touched a student to help with a correction. Said Martha Wittman, "Often touching someone will

"Even though you can force students into a certain exterior shape, if they can't feel it aesthetically or reproduce it, nothing is gained."

—Dan Wagoner

Dan Wagoner, Dan Wagoner and Dancers, New York

Photograph © 1986 by Johann Elbers

make something happen more easily than a word. For myself, I think it's better to minimize the verbal information so that students develop the kind of attention that comes from other senses, from sight and touch." Marcia Sakamoto expressed a similar idea. "Dance is a motion form," she observed, "and when I correct students verbally they make a static correction. If I can tactilely aid them in the process, then perhaps they'll feel it in a different way."

Teachers often ask before making corrections by touching students. As Carolyn Brown noted, "It's dangerous to move people very much, but there are certain kinds of positions that it's hard for some bodies to feel. If they've never experienced working the leg in the hip socket and have always lifted from the hip and thigh, it sometimes helps if I gently place their leg for them. Certainly it's not good to push, shove, or wrench their bodies, but after class I take them to a barre and then gently place the leg in the proper position, with leg and foot turned out, hip down, thigh turned over, so they can feel what that is. Often they exclaim, 'Oh! *That's* what you've been saying.' So it's a kind of revelation, and they might not have discovered it so quickly by themselves."

Other warnings were given in connection with touching students. Jeff Slayton advised telling students what to expect before physically moving them. This avoids the surprise of an unexpected adjustment. Dan Wagoner noted that even though you can force students into a certain exterior shape, if they can't feel it aesthetically or reproduce it, nothing is gained.

Ethel Winter questioned using touch to help correct placement in a plié because students tend to over-react and get out of line in a different way. When she does physically move students, she asks them to let her know if anything hurts. Ellen Graff declared, "I try not to push in any way as much as adjust where the body will allow itself to be taken. I'm not forcing."

Viola Farber explained that "If I move a student I do it very, very gently, and I only do it to people who I know have a little give there." She mentioned another method of touching she had seen used successfully, letting a student feel a motion on the teacher's body rather than the teacher moving the student.

Clay Taliaferro said he likes to call out to students while they are dancing a reminder of a particular correction they've been told to work on. Carolyn Brown mentioned the same technique as a way to make corrections without stopping the flow of the class, "but usually these are corrections I've already given either to the class as a whole or to the particular person."

"First of all," said Betty Jones, "I try to learn everyone's name, in order to make corrections while movement is being performed. There is instant awareness—or at least a better possibility of reaching someone." Most of the teachers used this quick correction technique of calling reminders as the students move. Sometimes they did it for an individual, often for the whole class.

Generalizing corrections is a common technique. Carolyn Brown makes general corrections directed to the whole class. She explained, "I may see that it's a particular person who needs this correction at the moment but know it's such a basic concept that all the students could benefit from hearing it." Betty Jones declared, "I like to involve everyone in a correction, keeping the whole class alert." She speaks loudly enough for everyone to hear when she stops the class to help an individual.

Martha Wittman tells her class, "Deal with the information with your own body while I'm helping someone else." "I'd like to give individual corrections," said Jeff Slayton, "but I try to teach students that when I give a correction to Susie, it's probably a correction for most people in the class so they shouldn't tune out when I'm talking to Susie." All the expert teachers seemed to use this technique. Thus, even though they dealt often with individual problems, they rarely lost the attention of the entire class.

Contrasting wrong and right ways of moving may point up a correction, Gloria Newman explained. "Sometimes I will demonstrate what they've done on myself and have students correct me. Or I may demonstrate the movement clarifying its source, path, and the intention of its rhythmic structure." She also may ask students to take part in the correction by trying both ways of doing a movement.

Ellen Graff does a lot of demonstrating of right and wrong on her own body, then asks, "Do you see the difference?" Or she may demonstrate physically with students to get them to try to feel the difference. "If I'm working on corrections with the way they are using their arms, for example, I may ask them to try leading from the elbow or leading from the wrist and note what that feels like. Then they do it from the back and feel the difference."

Clay Taliaferro says he sometimes has success by having students first make an overcorrection, for example, pushing the ribs into the back then relaxing to a corrected position. This helps students develop muscular control and get a feeling for correct placement.

"Images," said Ellen Graff, "can sometimes be extraordinarily effective in communicating what the body should feel like in doing a movement." She also favors images that have to do with the space around the body, its texture and feel.

Gloria Newman finds imagery helpful. "If I feel the dancers are placing too much emphasis on positions and poses instead of transitions," she remarked, "then I might relate it to a dot-to-dot book. You don't know what the picture is until you fill in the lines. As the dancer finds the path, the intention of the movement becomes visible." In class she told her students, "Plié like you're going to jump, not like it's the end of the world!"

Ethel Winter explained, "I think images are a good way to make corrections, not placement particularly, but in terms of what kind of an attack you want made or what quality you want—fluid—percussive—or whatever."

Imagery seems to be a matter of individual choice, not a basic element for making corrections. Some successful teachers use it, others avoid it. Although he has used images, Dan Wagoner thinks they get off the track sometimes, that his fantasy is not necessarily somebody else's fantasy. Jeff Slayton also has reservations about the use of images. "I guess it's just the way my mind works. I don't think in images. Dancing to me is an extremely physical thing and I like to give myself over to the movement rather than thinking about something to stick on top of it." In class he wants students to concentrate on the movement rather than on looking like something or being something else. "But," he concludes, "sometimes an image is the only way a student can understand."

Isolating the trouble area clarifies some corrections. When students were having difficulties with the arm movements in a phrase, Marcia Sakamoto had them practice only the arms. By limiting the movement she made it easier for students to concentrate on her correction.

When Jeff Slayton sees a student missing a sequence somehow, he may dance along side him/her until the student has made the correction by following him.

"Really difficult problems," observed Carolyn Brown, "have to be corrected after class or before, when there is sufficient time to explain and work on them slowly." Another reason for making corrections outside class was pointed up by one teacher who told a student, "I'll

> ***"Experiential learning is much more
> effective than immediate correction."***
> **—Marcia Sakamoto**

Marcia Sakamoto in "Bach Partita," choreographed by Gladys Bailin

The Art of Teaching Dance Technique

answer you later as that's been explained and I don't want to slow the class down."

Jeff Slayton often suggests to students that they do some exercise outside class to correct a problem showing up in class. He encourages students to stretch before and after class and sometimes makes individual corrections during this period if he notes poor alignment.

Marcia Sakamoto has recommended an alignment clinic to students who are not able to make corrections in class. She explained, "I'm thinking that experiential learning is much more effective than immediate voluntary correction because the incorrect habits are so set. In a technique class where students are trying to assimilate so many other things besides the correction, the habit can't help but return."

Martha Wittman summed up her thoughts on making corrections: "Any ways that a teacher can devise for more immediate seeing and translating back into the student's own body are important. Dancing with the music, if there is music, is more important than dancing to an instructor shouting."

Reinforcing Corrections

"What makes a correction effective," declared Viola Farber, "is if students take it and then realize that they're able to accomplish something they hadn't been able to accomplish before." Certainly success the student can feel is a powerful reinforcement for continuing the correction. Most teachers help this feeling of success along by letting students know when the correction is getting results. "Thank you!" exclaims Gloria Newman when a correction works. In other classes we heard, "That's better," "Very nice," "Pretty good," and similar supportive expressions.

Probably repetition is the most commonly used technique for reinforcing corrections. Again and again the authors saw teachers stop a class and repeat a general correction. They would not let students do a pattern incorrectly even for a few measures. Some commented on the need for repetition and the frustration for the teacher.

"There comes a point," said Marcia Sakamoto, "when you've made the same correction so many times that persons don't hear it anymore because they've been trying to make that correction. They become confused."

Farber recommended saying something over and over again, then added, "But after a while I really stop that, because I feel if *I'm* more interested in the student getting something correct than the *student* is, it's a little bit pointless."

Gloria Newman may let a correction rest and come back to it later. She explained, "I have found that many times the dancer's difficulty in making a correction is based on trying too hard, which creates too much tension in the body. This inhibits the ability to really see and experience the movement and commonly leads to frustration. The need then is to redirect the focus, energy, and/or attitude."

Jeff Slayton recalled advising individuals, "I've told you this several times. I'm not going to tell you again." Then he keeps an eye on them to see if they ever get it. "I haven't dropped such students from the class in my eyes. It just means that I've let them know I'm not going to help them until they start helping themselves."

He recalls one spectacular success with this technique. "I had a student once who stood in a model slouch for over a year, and suddenly that woman was dancing. I had tried every approach, then I realized she was listening to everything I said, thinking about it, trying it mentally, and one day she found it physically." Other teachers had similar stories of delayed success from a much-repeated correction.

Betty Jones recommends relating a correction to one made previously whenever possible. This builds on the basics already learned and reinforces previous corrections.

Reflections

The ability to make effective corrections may well be the one most distinctive difference between ordinary teachers and the experts. Students may have a good time doing interesting rhythmic movements in a class without effective corrections, but they will not improve technically, and they will not progress as dancers.

The technique for making the correction seems less important than the content of the correction, however it is made. Our expert teachers have developed an ability to perceive what is wrong and make a viable suggestion for improvement. These teachers are watching their students, not leading the action and taking class themselves.

SUMMARY

1. To make corrections a teacher must
    a. See what is wrong
    b. Communicate what will help
2. Types of corrections given to individuals or to the whole class
    a. Physical, concerning body use
    b. Facilitating, to aid movement
    c. Rhythmic
    d. Qualitative, concerning aesthetics
3. Importance of corrections is shown by their frequency
4. Approaches to making corrections
    a. Being objective
    b. Being direct
    c. Being analytical
    d. Encouraging questions
    e. Sharing responsibility
5. Techniques for making corrections
    a. Moving around speaking to individual students
    b. Touching students, moving them into position
       with care
    c. Calling out reminders as students move
    d. Generalizing an individual correction so it
       applies to the whole class
    e. Contrasting wrong and right
    f. Overcorrecting to find a correct position
    g. Using imagery to improve dance quality
    h. Isolating the trouble area
    i. Dancing briefly with students
    j. Working before or after class
6. Ways to reinforce corrections
    a. Letting students know when they have utilized a
       correction effectively
    b. Repeating corrections as needed
    c. Relating a correction to previous material

SUGGESTED PROJECTS

1. Observe a dance technique class and note the number of group and individual corrections made. How does that compare to numbers shown in the text?

2. From your experience in a technique class, give examples of two types of corrections from the list below. Recall the teacher's actual words as closely as possible.
>   Physical
>   Rhythmic
>   Facilitating
>   Qualitative

3. Observe a technique class and note two approaches to making corrections used by the teacher and two techniques for making corrections. Describe briefly. (See summary for list of approaches and techniques.)

CHAPTER 7

Music for Dance Technique Classes

Eric Ruskin and Mark Uranker, dance musicians at California State University, Long Beach, have extensive experience working with dance. They were interviewed concerning the skills necessary to create a class environment where instructor and musician work productively together. They discussed the qualities needed by the musician for successful operation, but first, they spoke of the qualities needed by technique teachers who want to have the best possible dance music in their classes.

Knowledge of Music

From a dance musician's viewpoint, a dance teacher should have:
1. At least a working knowledge of the music literature for dance, including Tchaikovsky, Stravinsky, Debussy, Copland, Dello Joio, and Cage
2. A basic historical knowledge of music from the Renaissance to the present
3. Familiarity with common musical terms, including measure, bar, time signature, ritard, staccato, tempo, and legato, and particularly those with a meaning different in music from in dance (such as adagio)
4. Familiarity with common dance forms, such as mazurka, polonaise, gigue, allemande, and pavane

With such knowledge of music the instructor can make helpful suggestions to the musician, such as, "I would like something in the style of…" and name a musician, a historical period, or a dance form.

Teaching Skills That Aid Musicians

Demonstrating clearly

Clarity of demonstration is essential. The musican needs to know just how the movement is supposed to look on the students, the tempo and dynamics, the quality and accents. To set the tempo and style for the musician, clear demonstration is more helpful than verbalization, but both are useful.

Eric Ruskin said, "I like to see the choreographic phrase. That's good enough for me. Then the teacher can say, `And!' and away we go."

Experienced dance musicians realize that the demonstration may be slower than the desired tempo (for clarity) or faster (so students get to move sooner) and they can "fine tune" as they go. However, the demonstration should approximate the actual tempo and style. As Mark Uranker explained, "It is helpful to know the correct tempo right at the beginning so that as the teacher is demonstrating I can be thinking about what I want to play that would be appropriate for the movement. Otherwise, if the actual tempo is never indicated until I hear, `Five, six, seven, eight,' I have only 2.45 seconds to come up with five minutes of music!"

Counting accurately

The teacher's counts should establish the meter (or meters) for the movement phrase. They should be "music" counts (evenly timed) not "dance" counts that pause when the dancer pauses as if the spaces between movements take no time. It is especially important to count out asymmetrical timing such as a combination of measures with three and five counts, for example.

Giving an appropriate starting signal

Both musicians and dancers appreciate a clear and emphatic signal to begin. Uranker pointed out that the accompanist needs just two points in time to verify the tempo, so "ready, and" or "seven, eight" are equally valid starting signals. "Five, six, seven, eight" also gives a precise tempo. If the demonstration has been clear and accurate, however, just the word "and" is sufficient.

Giving clear directions

Most instructors position themselves so the accompanist and the students can hear their directions. It helps the musician if these include how many repetitions there will be. However, calling out "One more time" will do if the teacher is not sure at the beginning how many repetitions will be needed—just so the musician has time to complete a phrase as the dancers complete their movement.

Focusing students on music

A dance teacher *never* should clap, snap fingers, slap the piano, or count while the musician is playing. Such actions are destructive as they annoy and distract the musician—and encourage students to listen to the clapping and not hear the music.

Uranker cautioned that "Often instructors watch a particular student and (although they do not know they are doing it) clap *that* person's rhythm. Then they look at a different student and clap *that* rhythm. Students are often not on the beat, so these instructors are speeding up and slowing down without realizing it. Furthermore, such clapping takes the responsibility for the rhythm away from the musician."

Dancers never will become musical if they hear clapping or a voice rather than listening to the music. The beat should be innate in their bodies. The goal is to prepare dancers for performance where there will not be someone in the wings clapping the beat. If the problem is that the accompanist is unable to keep an even tempo, that needs to be resolved by the instructor working with the musician in or out of class time. Beating out the tempo so that students are not aware of the music is not the solution.

The teacher can encourage students to focus on the music in many ways. One is by commenting on the music, pointing out when it is especially supportive of the movement. The teacher might ask for different styles of music for a movement sequence and explain which best "fits" with the movement.

Some faculty tell students they are making a duet with the music, paralleling but not exactly mirroring the sound. Viola Farber was quoted as saying to students, "Think of yourself as another instrument. Add your part to the fabric or texture of the music."

Some teachers stress listening to the music; then they ask the

"Think of yourself as another instrument. Add your part to the fabric or texture of the music."
—Viola Farber

Photograph by Lois Greenfield

accompanist to stop playing for a few measures and then pick up the beat again. The sound of feet landing broadcasts whether or not students know the count and are moving with it. They should be right on the beat when the accompanist comes back in. Uranker commented: "It's pretty ironic that you get students to listen to you by *not* playing!"

Keeping the class moving

A class that moves right along keeps the musician and the students alert and interested. When a teacher "explains a million things before each exercise" the class bogs down and becomes dull for everyone.

Helpful Teacher Attitudes

Teachers who consider musicians a valuable part of the teaching effort tend to be cooperative and appreciative. They recognize the skills involved, especially the difficulty of improvising musical material with barely time to think of what to play. Supportive teachers bring out the best in their accompanists.

Some teachers take time to talk with the accompanist a few minutes before class if they have some special plans for that day. Even more important, many talk with the accompanist after class. They discuss what things worked, what did not, and why. Conversations keep the channels open.

Sometimes musicians feel like furniture in the room, taken for granted. To get high quality dance music, it makes sense for the teacher to involve the musician, to remind students to listen to the music, and to praise excellence.

Overcoming Common Problems

Musicians have some helpful suggestions for the teaching problems most often seen with beginning teachers or those new to working with an accompanist.

Use regular rhythms

Teachers just starting to work with live music might do well to stay with regular measures and phrasing at first. Uranker's comment was, "I think they make life more difficult for themselves by having very strange rhythmic combinations when they could accomplish the same thing in square fours or eights, particularly with a beginning class."

Eric Ruskin added, "It's nice to have students get that four and eight feel in their bodies; it's such a human thing. Once they can feel that and not have to count eights any more, then they're ready to move on to fives, sixes, sevens, twelves."

Betty Jones made it clear she thinks the technique teacher needs a movement rationale for using irregular counts and phrases. They should not be arbitrary or due to counting incorrectly. Ruskin noted that an experienced accompanist may solve any problems with peculiar phrasing by making contrapuntal phrasing.

Vary meter and tempo

Musicians are equally disturbed by the opposite extreme of teachers using the same time signature and tempo for exercise after exercise. "It's surprising how many people do this," Eric Ruskin remarked. "They are just locked in and not thinking, but it kills a class." It also taxes the accompanist's ingenuity beyond reason and destroys the sense of spontaneity in a class. Even highly musical and experienced teachers sometimes become enamored of a meter and tempo in one phrase and then stay with that meter/tempo for the rest of the class while the accompanist desperately tries to think of yet *another* style to play in, or some way to break the cycle.

Overuse of threes by technique teachers is a huge problem for dance musicians. They say the music never gets sharpness anywhere with threes. Basically, it sounds like "down, up, up" no matter what the music. Teachers sometimes think they change things because the phrasing in one exercise is in eight measures and the next in five measures, but this does not help if the counts are all three to a measure at the same tempo. It is still monotonous! In addition, an occasional dance teacher will count in fours without realizing that there is an underlying three constantly, so that the count really is *one*, two, three; *two*, two, three; *three*, two, three; *four*, two, three.

Eric Ruskin found that one dance teacher actually did not know how to count in twos and fours and so used threes throughout all dance classes. He was able to help her with thinking in a different count mode and solved the problem of students and accompanist "overdosing" on threes.

Ask for help

Dance musicians find that some dance teachers seem embarrassed by their lack of knowledge of music and feel intimidated by working with an accompanist. The dance musicians interviewed pointed out that they are grateful when an instructor asks them for help as this can make both of their lives easier.

Observe experienced teachers

Watching experienced teachers is most helpful if the teacher being observed is exceptionally musical as well as experienced. The musician might suggest someone to watch and even help with ideas on what to watch for.

Be open-minded

Teachers who continue to have music problems in class should consider asking themselves some of the following questions:

1. Is my demonstration clear? Does it show what I want musically?
2. Am I taking some of the responsibility when the music is not working? Am I communicating clearly? Or am I getting angry at the accompanist rather than saying what I want?
3. Is my starting signal clear and in tempo?
4. Am I speaking loudly enough so the musician can hear my directions?

Qualities Needed by a Dance Musician

Anyone who is considering becoming a dance musician needs some basic skills, knowledges, and attitudes in order to succeed. Qualities dance teachers should look for when seeking to employ a musician include the following:

1. Skill as a classical pianist
2. Ability to improvise
3. Knowledge of music literature
4. Knowledge of traditional dance music, including ballet
5. Enjoyment of dance and working with students

With these qualities a musician is equipped to learn to be a dance musician. To be effective, dance musicians must love dance. If they are just in class because they need a job and do not like what they are doing, none of the other skills count for much. Those who love dance and are stimulated by working with young dancers can become valuable assets in a dance class and will some day have the satisfaction of looking back on hundreds of dancers they have helped educate.

Concerning skills, the ability to improvise is most critical. When employing a dance musician, given an either or situation, it might be wiser to choose a strong improviser over an accomplished performer.

Musicians who play for ballet classes as well as modern should have a repertoire of traditional ballet music so students will become familiar with the music (helpful when they attend ballet concerts). However, students must understand that the music has been altered to fit the exercise and that they are hearing, as Mark Uranker phrased it, "the Tchaikovsky-Uranker version, not the Tchaikovsky version." They could be encouraged to buy a recording of an authentic version. It should be noted also that sometimes ballet teachers say they want traditional music for class when what they really want is *appropriate* music.

Enhancing Skills as a Dance Musician

It is important for a musician to understand that perfection will not be achieved instantly. There are layers of proficiency, which could be ranked as:

1. Getting the right number of counts and the right tempo and phrasing
2. Getting the quality (a critical step)
3. Making music that enables the dancers to perform at their best levels
4. And finally, having an artistic duet with the dancers

Developing improvisational skills

There are books on keyboard improvising and keyboard harmony that are helpful in developing improvisational skill. However, where universities teach music improvisation, it generally is jazz improvisation, a useful addendum.

But the dance accompanist must be able to improvise in classical styles. The only way to become really proficient is to learn from someone who is an accomplished improviser, ideally a dance musician with extensive experience. You have to "learn by doing."

When Eric Ruskin started as a dance musician, he learned to improvise by copying composer's styles from records, from hearing other musicians play, and by asking questions of a musician with years of experience playing for dance. Mark Uranker enhanced his skills in improvising by studying composers, particularly their chord progressions. He practiced from scores, making the music his, making it part of his "palette."

It is particularly difficult to improvise to unusual meters or phrasing. Thinking of a seven as a three and a four may help. Studying the *Mikrokosmos* of Bartok will help with improvising in uneven meter. It may be that one is born to be a good improviser, that it is a gift to be nurtured. But the best way to improve at improvising is practice, practice, practice!

Taking dance classes

Some dance musicians have found it is essential to take dance classes, particularly in order to understand how to play for modern dance classes. Uranker said, "For me it was absolutely necessary to take modern dance classes. I didn't think it was until after I took them. When you're sitting at the piano you think, `Why can't they do that? That's so easy!' It's very humbling to try to do the movement yourself. You gain an understanding of the kinesthetic feeling you get when doing certain movements and you then have an empathy with the dancers. For me, taking class was essential, but I wouldn't have said that if I hadn't done it."

He found that when taking class he would imagine music that would help the dancers even more than what was being played. The aim is not to become a proficient dancer, but to understand what music is appropriate or not appropriate and what accents are important. Musicians often do not realize how difficult it is to lift the leg high and that the music can help get it up there.

Yet Eric Ruskin believes that, although taking dance classes might expedite the learning process, it is not absolutely necessary for musicians who have a good eye and a good empathy and who can dance in their own imagination.

Learning from other dance musicians

Beginning accompanists can get immeasurable help from experienced musicians, both by observing their classes and by talking with them. This is especially valuable for one who is "learning on the job" so suggestions can be applied immediately. In addition, it seems that accomplished musicians who never have tried to play for a dance class seldom understand what skills are needed.

Experimenting

Both Ruskin and Uranker point out that musicians need to "shock their brains out of a rut." It is so easy to get into a pattern of using the same kind of music day after day, especially if the dance teacher is doing the same kind of exercises.

For example, in one class Ruskin thought, "I'm going to play Bach with a kind of boogie-woogie feel." Then he wondered, "How many more pieces can I make in this style?" This was interesting for him as well as for the dancers. He did not, of course, stay with this mode throughout a full class.

In a class of advanced dancers, both of the musicians will sometimes play a three for a while, then a four, then back to the three, so the dancers learn to dance against the beat. This never should be tried with less experienced dancers; they would stop in their tracks when the accent shifted.

Asking for teacher suggestions

Musicians who ask the teachers they play for "What would you like to hear?" will probably get lots of ideas to increase their range and stimulate their imagination. Teachers who might hesitate to offer suggestions may well appreciate being asked for input.

Helping an Inexperienced Dance Musician

The inexperienced accompanist will be unaware of the type of music called for with specific movements. The teacher can be very helpful. As an example of helping with choice of style and type of music for battements, Ruskin noted the teacher might say, "I want something strong, a tango or a march, something that's got enough oomph to help get the leg up!" Asking for music in the style of Debussy (or some other composer) may clarify what is expected and offer an interesting challenge for the musician.

Dance teachers must realize that it is very difficult for even an experienced musician to play for a technique teacher for the first time. For a beginner, it is "unknown territory, very scary."

If the accompanist is floundering, some things to watch for are:

1. Is the musician watching/listening to the demonstration?
2. Is the musician noting the inner rhythm or only hearing the 1, 2, 3, 4 but not the smaller rhythmic values (1 and ah, 2 and ah, 3 and ah, 4 and ah)?
3. Is the repertoire too narrow? Does the musician need to develop different kinds of sounds?

Whatever the problem, the teacher should take steps to help. The teacher might ask, "Do you have a tango? Latin?" Or, hoe-down? Ragtime? Baroque? Impressionist music? Modernists (Stravinsky, Schoenberg)? Jazz? Bluegrass? Country? Pop? Western? Musical theatre? Something by Mozart? This means the teacher must be thinking of appropriate music while composing or demonstrating the phrase.

When the musician is having difficulties, it is *not* helpful for the teacher to say, "That's not what I want. Play something else." The musician must have some clues as to why the music did not work and what is missing or what is the particular style preferred.

Special Circumstances

Master classes

It helps the dance musician to talk with the master teacher for a few minutes before class if they never have worked together before. Some typical questions might be:

1. How do you let the accompanist know when to start?
2. Do you want a musical introduction to a phrase?
3. Do you demonstrate in tempo?
4. Are there particular styles you like? Don't like?
5. Is there anything else you want to tell me?

Synthesizers

The variety of sound possible with a synthesizer makes it an ideal alternate instrument for technique classes. Dancers will perform on stage to many more instruments than piano, and technique class serves as a good opportunity to hear additional sounds. The synthesizer can provide drums from East India, acoustic guitar, full orchestra with tympani and brass, harpsichord, and endless others.

Eric Ruskin uses the sequencer on his synthesizer when accompanying technique classes. "I'll turn on `record,' the dancers will go across the floor, and I'll play a drum. Then I will rewind it, change my sound to piano and play with the drums I just recorded. I add three or four layers and the texture is really thick! They love it!"

However, some think the synthesizer must be used judiciously. It may provide a "false energy" where the dancers are absolved of the responsibility for creating their own energy because the music is providing it on a grand scale. Also, the volume is generally fairly loud, and the instructor may be trying to shout over it and not be heard. Of course, the volume can be lowered, but some of the excitement of the sound is then lost.

A balance of piano and synthesizer provides a stimulating music environment for a modern dance class—and some ballet classes.

Musicians salaries

Securing a dance musician may come down to budget priorities. Oftentimes the salary range for a dance musician is hardly likely to entice excellent pianists/improvisers to consider working with dance. Recognition by the teacher of the need for good, supportive music for dance classes is the first step toward getting better payment and better qualified musicians.

Other dance accompaniment

It is most unfortunate when "live" music is not provided for dance technique classes, particularly modern and ballet. The usual alternatives are tapes, records, or percussion, mostly drums.

Recorded music has the obvious disadvantage that the teacher is stuck with counts, tempo, and phrasing as is. A broad library of tapes and records will help somewhat, but they still "box in" the instructor's ability to create musically varied phrases.

Records have the advantage that one may start anywhere and quickly. It is critical to have a record player with tempo control.

Tape players must have a counter to allow starting in various spots, but oftentimes the counter is inexact. A tempo control is an important feature to look for.

Drums can be exciting when used by an expert; they can be deadly used by a beginner. It is important to strive for variety of sound or the dancers become sluggish.

Both records and audiotapes created by dance musicians for dance classes may be purchased. Although still limiting, they do offer a great deal more variety than other recorded sound. It may be useful to have a dance musician record a "custom-made" tape, particularly if a warm-up is repeated in each class.

The spontaneity of movement invention is seriously hindered with use of recorded music. It is well worth battling to at least have an accompanist one or two days a week.

SUMMARY

1. Qualities in a dance technique teacher that contribute to a good working relationship with an accompanist:
    a. Knowledge of music
        Includes music literature, history, terms, and
            dance forms
    b. Teaching skills such as the ability to:
        Demonstrate clearly
        Count accurately
        Give an appropriate starting signal
        Give clear directions
        Focus students on the music
        Keep the class moving at an interesting pace
    c. Helpful attitude, cooperative and appreciative
2. Suggestions to help inexperienced teachers overcome problems in working with a musician:
    a. Use regular rhythms
    b. Vary meter and tempo
    c. Ask the musician for help
    d. Observe experienced teachers

      e. Be open-minded; share responsibility for problems
3. Qualities needed to be a dance musician
      a. Skill as a classical pianist
      b. Ability to improvise
      c. Knowledge of music literature and traditional dance music
      d. Enjoyment of dance and working with students
4. Ways to enhance skills as a dance musician:
      a. Develop improvisational skills
      b. Take dance classes
      c. Learn from other musicians
      d. Experiment
      e. Ask dance teachers for suggestions
5. Ways a teacher can assist an inexperienced musician:
      a. Help with choice of style and type of music
      b. Watch for causes of difficulties
6. Special circumstances involving class music
      a. Dealing with master classes
      b. Enhancing sounds with a synthesizer
      c. Increasing pay to attract better qualified musicians
      d. Using tapes, records, and/or drums in dance classes without a musician

SUGGESTED PROJECTS

1. Observe a modern dance technique class where an experienced dance musician is working with the technique teacher. Notice times when the music seems to work especially well. Why was the music effective in each instance?

2. Observe a dance technique class where there is no live music. Critique the use of records, tapes, or any other accompaniment.

3. Interview an experienced dance musician. Ask how the technique teacher can help (or hinder) the class accompaniment.

CHAPTER 8

Thoughts on Teaching Dance

The following ideas are based on conversations and interviews with the artist/teachers consulted in the preparation of this book.

What Is a Dance Teacher?

Dance teachers are an amalgam of all the training schools and all the rich experiences of their lives. Being moved deeply by a choreographer's work may be a spiritual influence on a teacher's work.

A fine teacher teaches not only the subject but also life itself, a discipline and joy in everything, approaching everyday tasks as an artist.

No dance teacher exists in a vacuum. They *come* from somewhere. Dance has evolved out of the things that people *do*. No one sat down and thought up a technique!

Good teachers have an opinion, an attitude, on the function of technique and on the progress of development. There must be a general core from which the technique is built.

In a well taught class there has to be something that personally comes from the teacher. It has to do with what he/she believes dance to be and his/her individual experience with dance. In the early days of modern dance the people who established vocabularies of movement had very strong personal beliefs.

There are teachers who dance so beautifully and articulately in class that their students understand much about dance just by watching, even though little explanation takes place.

Fine teachers can go beyond their own physical accomplishments or inadequacies.

Some rare artists teach by actually dancing along with the class, using full energy. They have such an appetite for moving that they transmit their passion for dance by a kind of osmosis. Students pick up on the drive and emulate the rhythm and shape as best they can, like children in a tribal ritual. Such teachers are rare, but very inspirational. Other teachers prefer that students find their own energy, do it for their own bodies.

One can think of a dance teacher as an energy bringing energy to the students. An outflow of energy helps students relate to the teacher.

Dance class is no place for a cheerleader. Students should produce their own excitement whether they are walking, skipping, hopping, running, or standing still.

Teachers bring out in their students a body intelligence that has always been there and that students can then use in their own ways.

Teachers who see every class as being different and interesting will not be bored. They continue to learn with their students. Perhaps it is that quality (the ability to see every class as being different) that makes an exceptional teacher.

Insistence on excellence, whatever the level, is one mark of an exceptional teacher. Students must not be allowed to stop when the work is not good enough.

Dance teachers loathe teaching "exercise" classes. People who come to class to trim up and don't want to be bothered with dance ideas are exhausting to teach for those who approach dance as an art form.

Teachers who have difficult bodies or have had a hard time technically tend to empathize with students who are struggling for a step and can't quite get the right feeling in the muscles to do it. Teachers who have had to struggle feel a generosity for students who struggle.

Students respond to teachers who like to work, who sometimes get excited in class about a phrase and what students bring to it.

Sometimes students excuse their poor efforts in class by saying, "I just want to teach. I don't have to be that good." This notion infuriates devoted teachers who feel that in some ways the teacher has to know more and have experienced more than the performer. There should not be lesser skill requirements for those who "just want to teach."

Some teachers of technique find they learned more about dance and movement from choreographers and choreography than from technique classes, perhaps because their understanding of dance heightens during choreographic undertakings, especially dancing in the works of top choreographers. Dancing makes sense to them in direct relation to the compositional process.

One has to have an ego to be a good dance teacher, but it is crucial how that ego is used. If it explodes in temperamental outbursts, nothing will be accomplished.

It is a paradox that some exciting, vital dance teachers confess to being utterly lazy when it comes to any other activity, such as walking a block to the store!

Great teachers are a continual inspiration. Says one teacher, "Hardly a week has gone by over my twenty-two years of teaching that I have not thought about some aspect of study learned from one or another of my fine teachers."

Exceptional teachers bring care and painstaking attention to the teaching of dance. They have a sense of the right order of exercises within a technique class, the special ability to make the next sequence beautifully happen because of what went before.

Superb instruction is revealed not in applause from students but rather in their lasting determination to know and respect quality.

A good teacher encourages a zest for further study.

Some teachers present classes that seem choreographed, that have such pacing, timing, and phrasing they almost teach themselves. The impossible becomes possible, if only temporarily! This is achieved primarily through movement rather than long explanations of theory.

Many dance teachers would agree with Gregor Piatigorsky, who said in an interview, "Teaching is the most difficult and demanding of professions. There are no prescriptions for a teacher to follow, because a teacher must deal with a total human being. There is a great deal of feeling involved."

On Being a Dance Student

Students who give themselves over to the movement will come through as individuals. If instead they try to copy each teacher and develop mannerisms, they will not come through.

Imitation of things seen and heard is a natural part of learning in a dance class, but students need also to get into the area of sensation, of feeling what is done, what part of the body is working, and what the activity is for.

Some prefer teaching without mirrors so students must get everything from their own sensations.

Students who perceive a technique class as a life situation in which they are using information, handling emotions, and dealing with situations tend to see themselves as dancers who are people. They transfer from other experiences the ability to handle frustration and failure, the will to try again with a new approach.

One teacher advises: "Try to approach everything you are doing in life, including your dancing, from an artistic standpoint. Think how beautiful a plié is as you practice! It will bring you much joy to be looking at life, yourself, and the others around you in a more beautiful way."

From the learner's perspective, no matter the teaching style, the successful dancer ultimately devotes energies toward the same things

—practice, repetition, and most importantly, calling on inner resources of intuition and intelligence.

Students who keep telling themselves they cannot do what the teacher is asking probably won't do it whether or not they can.

Serious beginners who want to move are most exciting to teach. They can change so much just learning to walk. If they respect the discipline and the newness of it, they are open, ready to learn, without preconceived notions to interfere.

How can students tell if they have had a good dance class? It takes more than being tired, though certainly there should be a sense of having really moved. Beyond that, each student should have a sense of achievement, of having accomplished at least one thing during the class. It may be something so small as going to relevé without wobbling. For some that is a great accomplishment!

It is astonishing that some people think they can learn technique from a book.

Dance students should be encouraged to be individuals. They've paid their money, bought the leotards, got themselves dressed and to class. Now they should do it for themselves, explore themselves within the framework of what has been asked for technically. It's a way of behavior in class where no one thinks of student-teacher but everyone just thinks of getting at the work.

When student and teacher are centered on a common goal and serve the same muse, they have an ideal relationship.

The visualization of movement, the seeing of a movement pattern, is crucial—not thinking about each step, but seeing the total picture and the rhythm of the movement. The muscles automatically coordinate to produce the concept and picture. The dancer's job is the refining and crystalizing of that picture.

One teacher's advice to students: "At the most negative moments in life, if you can hang on to a good alignment, it helps you get through. So when the landlord comes and says you've got to pay the rent, step right up into a nice first position, pelvis lifted, back long, and say, `I don't have it.' Modern dancers seldom have any money. They can't afford health insurance or fire insurance. In fact, they have no insurance except a good stance. You're paying your money now for class, so work on a good stance and that will be your insurance."

Working with different teachers has its advantages for students, as long as the teachers agree on such basics as placement and alignment. Students cannot become too rigid as sometimes happens when they study with only one teacher.

Ballet classes concentrate on pure technique. They are helpful for modern dancers.

At times all students need approval and support. But they have to learn to go all out on their own in the face of all kinds of negative things that seem to occur along the way.

Students working in different areas of Alexander, Feidenkrais, or Effort/Shape often gain another awareness of their bodies and seem to become more open and responsive to a variety of ways of teaching — also more sensitive in how they experience movement. Such studies may help them learn how to rest the body and renew energy when not actively dancing.

Many find they can ease muscle tightness through use of the constructive rest position devised by Lulu Sweigard, teacher at Juilliard. They feel that doing it daily brings the body into a more neutral position.

Sometimes a class in philosophy or Zen Buddhism helps students become more self-dependent in dance class.

Dancing is a very physical thing, and students need to give themselves over to the movement rather than thinking about how they look.

Beginning dance students can get a real education in dance appreciation partly by learning to enjoy moving without any self-consciousness or embarrassment.

Students should be encouraged to see as many different kinds of dance as possible, even though it would be impracticable to study too many different kinds of dance within a lifetime. They should also be encouraged to study other arts, history, the sciences—everything that will help them appreciate human efforts of all kinds.

On Being a Dance Teacher

Each teacher has a responsibility in shaping what the next generation of dancers will be like. So the teacher must think beyond materials to results.

Teaching dance is like rearing a child—a little help here, a little help there, but not hand-holding all the way.

Some teachers feel stage fright just before teaching, especially if it is a class of strangers such as a master class. Because they are about to expose themselves to total strangers, they feel incredibly nervous until they start giving and sharing their truths. But teachers who can present themselves without any pretense or cover stimulate individuality in their students. Believing in the honesty of their teacher is the first step students need to give wholly of themselves.

People can learn from a teacher who cares a good deal about dancing and is willing to share what can be known about it.

People who try to teach "just like" a favorite teacher may find themselves saying things and doing things not at all related to the students they are facing.

In a way, having their own studio gives some dance teachers a tremendous sense of freedom. They realize that students have a choice and need not stick with one assigned teacher as happens in so many school programs. Studio teachers can do what they consider best and not worry about being all things to every student.

Students need to be brought to some purity of feeling about movement.

Dancers need to be challenged beyond their imagination.

Some teachers will not let anyone take notes in their classes because they believe so strongly that what they are doing as a teacher is right only for this one time with this one group of students. Would-be teachers can learn from watching experienced teachers, but should not try to copy exact progressions and words with a different class.

When you're feeling frustrated because your students are not learning as much as you think they should, try to take the long view. Perhaps they will be there in three years if not now.

When students know a phrase thoroughly and are beginning to enjoy performing, it may increase their pleasure to have the teacher dance along with them, enjoying the movement as they do. Teachers usually can feel whether students are dancing with them or copying. Of course, teachers should not do this unless they are sufficiently warmed up so they will not be injured by suddenly dancing all out.

A teacher's worst nightmare is an overcrowded master class of students with mixed skills. The problem is how to move them so they don't kill each other!

Sometimes students will say, "That's my style," as a way of saying they don't want to change or go any further. Growing in dance is difficult, even painful, but the teacher must beware of letting students limit themselves by thinking they have only one style.

The teacher cannot give in to letting students do whatever they want to do. Dancing is hard work. It is very satisfying, but it is hard work!

Permissive teachers produce inadequate dancers. That is not to say that every student of a good teacher will be a good dancer.

Teachers should demand that students work at their optimum capacity and at the same time support students with a belief that they are capable of the work.

A good teacher watches for misunderstandings that interfere with communication in class. For example, one ballet student came to fear the stick the teacher used because the stick correction sometimes

Gloria Newman, director of Gloria Newman Dance Theatre

"*Dance teachers need a trained eye, a creative mind, a passion for the medium, and a touch of the missionary.*"
—Gloria Newman

seemed more like a whack than a touch. It was only years and many teachers later that the student could appreciate the value of the stick in aiding alignment.

Verbal changes in dynamics add to clarity. Words have rhythms and softness and hardness. They can fall or lift, resist or yield. Such verbal dynamics can make a point with students so they understand the movement more clearly.

The most difficult people to teach are those who do not want to move. Why do they take dance? Perhaps it's a fad, a trendy thing. Teachers must deal with their own anxiety and impatience when they try to teach such people.

When teaching adult beginners or anyone who is not going to continue in dance, it is important that the teacher approach dance in a serious way in order for such students to know what dance is, to give dancing its due, so to speak.

Teachers should be sure they are succeeding at teaching, not just at entertaining.

Dance students have the potential for becoming a good dance audience if the class develops appreciations along with skill.

Dance teachers should avoid overemphasizing minutiae to the point that fundamental skills are overlooked.

What Is Dancing?

Technique is not enough. By itself it is not dancing. Being able to do an array of steps technically well, even brilliantly, is still not dancing.

The mechanics of dance can be taught—how to jump, how to turn, etc. But how to make that dancing is a different problem, perhaps something that cannot be taught. Teachers can call attention to possibilities, but they cannot teach whatever it is that makes dancing full and makes it an art. Today students are more skilled than in years past. They can move quickly, get their legs very high. But the *other* thing does not happen any more than it used to—sensitivity to rhythm, phrasing, dynamics. It has to be inside students. It can be inside and maybe never get out unless they have some exposure, see some of the possibilities. Part of it has something to do with allowing yourself to put everything you are into what you do, not in a self-indulgent way, but something that is concentrated—and a little bit terrifying!

All that one has done is condensed into one moment of dance. One must be as assertive with dance as one is with life.

When the movement is clear, the person is clear. When dancers find out what a particular action is about, there is no way they can perform it without contributing something of themselves.

There is a basic pulse like the breathing. It rises and falls, gets faster or slower. The pulse, the body, the stretching, the contracting, the releasing—all of this is part of the basic body rhythm.

Sometimes with more advanced classes the teacher needs to emphasize that a leg up over the head and three turns is not necessarily art or even what is exciting to watch. There are other qualities and values besides the technical craft. The dancer must be vulnerable and revealing and illuminate the movement.

Do not separate dance as a special thing all by itself. It is life. It is exactly what one does.

Teachers can teach how to accomplish movements, but not always how to *dance* them. That comes from the inside. If the magic is not there, the teacher can only hope to produce an excellent technician, which is fine. But it is a joy to teach a real dancer who can accomplish the movements.

The teacher choreographs movement for class and wants it to look a particular way, but the instruments all come up different. Some are short and some are tall; some are heavy and some are thin. They've eaten differently and they dress differently, so they play the tune differently, and that's very beautiful. In fact, the movement is somehow different every time it is performed, even by the same person. That is an exciting thing about dance. It is of the instant, impermanent, and just as vulnerable and beautiful as the human creature.

No amount of good teaching can take the place of a natural affinity for movement and dance.

Movement starts with the idea to move, and the muscles repond to that idea. From the first faltering steps of a baby to the most complicated combinations of professional dancers, an idea or picture of the movement activates the muscle coordination. It is a matter of training, discipline, maturity, perseverance, plus innate ability and talent that go into making a dancer.

Teachers are not *using* dance to help students feel good or learn to cope or look better. They are *doing* dance in class. Their purpose is dance training, and that takes total involvement of each student. People may look better and feel better after dancing, but the dancing is the goal, not the therapy.

The teacher choreographs phrases for class as well as possible, assuming the performers (dance students) are going to commit themselves totally and do the best they can at that moment with what they understand. It's exciting, and frightening too, that so much is going to happen in ten minutes of one's life, but it is wonderful!

A favorite quote from Pierre Rameau's *The Dancing Master** written in 1725: "I shall then be told that one ought to possess a considerable aptitude to dance well. I agree; but goodwill will carry forward the least gifted, and I shall add further that such persons can dance passably well without any aptitude whatever, for dancing is no more than knowing how to bend and straighten the knees at the proper time."

---

*Rameau, Pierre. *The Dancing Master*. Paris, 1725, p. 12. Trans. C.W. Beaumont. A Dance Horizons Republication.

Sample Lesson Plan

Objectives: To learn to combine a movement phrase with falls.
To work on use of space and awareness of other dancers.

Movement To Be Taught	Teaching Reminders	Organization Accompaniment
Warm-up—Prances Increasing knee lift	Mirror students facing them so start L; they start R	8 counts
Review series of warm-ups taught in last two classes	Stress alignment	4's and 6's
Scallop pattern		Center floor
Scallop front, back and repeat	Clear pattern in space	8 counts
Side fall, recovery		8 counts
When phrase is clear, add arms	Curved arm	
Hop-leap-turn		Across studio
Step, hop, step, step, leap	Make eye contact with person ahead and then in back when turning	4 counts
Add walks with half turn		4 counts
Cool down movements		Center floor Quiet music

Note: This plan was written for a short high school class. Movements are sketchily described for the actual teacher's use and are not to be followed by anyone else. The plan is included here to give beginning teachers an idea how they might go about writing down their own plans.

Class Organization

Why organize

Basic to effective teaching is effective management. Unless class activities are carefully organized so there is minimum confusion, there will be neither time nor atmosphere for maximum learning.

Class procedures vary considerably depending on circumstances such as student age, class size, class locale, level of skill, class purpose, and the background of the students. Whatever the class, the teacher sees that any music or equipment the class will use is in place and ready to go in advance in a studio that is cleared and set for use. The goal is to be prepared and to establish procedures that facilitate good teaching.

Checking roll

Any time attendance is required or the teacher is responsible for the whereabouts of the students, roll checking becomes important. Many teachers check the roll as the students enter the studio; by doing it themselves, they can greet each student and learn names. If students check themselves in, the teacher can count the class later (easy to do when they are crossing the floor by fives or any number) to see that the actual number of bodies present agrees with the roll. If attendance affects the grade, the teacher must keep careful records in fairness to all students.

If attendance is required, staying the full class time usually is required also. The teacher must set whatever rules are needed concerning leaving the room, being tardy, or not participating and determine how these will affect the grade. Most want as few rules as possible, but situations differ. Whatever rules are made must be clearly understood and enforced fairly.

Suggested assignments for students not able to participate include doing some dance research in the library or taking notes in class such as writing down the movement phrase taught that day. Written work should be handed in at the end of the period.

Spacing concerns

In planning the class, the teacher thinks about where students will be and how they will move from one location to another easily, avoiding constant changes (such as up and down or to and from the barre) as well as the monotony of never changing. By learning to give brief, clear directions on changing location, the teacher can avoid many problems

If students are to move diagonally across the room from two corners, they need to know who goes to what corner, when to start, and what to do when they reach the opposite corner. If there are to be lines moving the length of the studio, the teacher sets the number of lines and may select who will lead each line.

In a large class, only fast-moving combinations should be used crossing the floor to minimize waiting. Combinations can be designed for performance in center floor with each student moving in his/her own limited space. The larger the class and less experienced the students, the more careful spacing plans must be. Perhaps doing some phrase in a single or double circle would be easier than getting a large group into lines. Circles keep everyone moving, and often that is an advantage. The traditional figure eight pattern achieves the same purpose because as soon as the last students clear the center, lead dancers start from the opposite corner.

The class must be spaced so everyone can see the teacher, who in turn can see every student. Most teachers bring the back row forward or turn the class around periodically so all can see the mirrors and/or have the responsibility for being in front sometimes. This is especially important during demonstrations. The teacher can also demonstrate in different parts of the room. If there are students who tend to be talkative, the teacher might move near them to demonstrate.

Time use

Classes usually have a set time schedule which the teacher should respect by starting and stopping on time. Whatever the length of the class, the teacher's plan should make good use of the time allowed. Even thirty-minute classes can accomplish much if there is no waiting around, especially if the class meets daily.

If students check in and go directly to the barre to start warming up there is time for center work, doing some combinations, and a little cool down. There is not time for long talks by the teacher. Corrections may be made without stopping the class or generalized for the whole class at once.

Injury care

Most institutions that offer dance classes have some standard policy concerning class injuries. There may be a school nurse or trainer available to students. The teacher needs to understand the legal implications of giving first aid or of prescribing any medication. They should ask the first day if any students have special health problems. A physician's permit may be requested.

Teachers often arrange to have ice available in the studio or dressing room. A small-sized freezer is relatively inexpensive. With ice frozen in a three-ounce paper cup, a student can tear off the paper and quickly apply ice to an injured area without disturbing the class. The Arnheim book on care and prevention of dance injuries referenced in Chapter 2 is recommended as a guide for students and teachers on caring for injuries.

Teachers need to watch that students do not start working too soon after an injury. Some injuries may allow students to take much but not all of the class, such as no jumps or leaps. Physician approval may be required if it is a questionable case. Liability could be a consideration.

The dance teacher should know about any clinics in the area that specialize in care for dance and/or sport injuries. Institutional policies on making referrals should be followed.

Dealing with Behavior Problems

Teachers who give an organized, challenging class will have few behavior problems whatever the age level. Some set a studio atmosphere for work by having students start warming up individually on entering the room. The need to concentrate when warming up and during class is emphasized. Chatting is discouraged. These instructors are teaching students how to take a dance class as well as teaching dancing. Working seriously is the only acceptable behavior in the dance studio.

Following are some teacher behaviors that often lead to student disruptive behavior:

1. Over-talking. Anything that leaves students inactive for very long leads to restlessness and poor behavior.

2. Confused directions.

3. Disconnected presentations. Long pauses while the teacher ponders what comes next can be deadly.

4. Teaching material that is too easy (boring) or two difficult (frustrating).

5. Talking to one student and ignoring the rest of the class.

6. Being unfair; having obvious favorites.

7. Being overly permissive, undemanding. When the teacher settles for sloppy skills, students feel they are wasting time.

8. Being a "personality teacher" who tries to keep student attention by showing off or being too friendly rather than by teaching effectively.

9. Being undiscriminating in selecting material that is not danceable or motivating. The teacher needs to set the tone of the class and strive for quality dance whatever the level

10. Failing to deal quickly and effectively with students who insist on being disruptive. This only encourages more such behavior.

Grading Dance Students

Dance teachers generally dislike assigning grades in a technique class. There are no scores or objective skill measurements to make grading easy in dance. However, most schools that give credit for dance classes require that teachers assign a grade to each student. Teachers should then:

1. Establish grading criteria for each class in terms of the goals of the class, the level of the students, and the requirements of the institution.

2. Give the criteria to the students in writing, if possible, so there is no misunderstanding about how the grade is decided.

3. Grade according to the criteria, being as objective and fair as possible.

In university classes for dance majors the grade often is based on the teacher's estimate of the skill level achieved. The students may perform a phrase they have learned which includes material covered to that point in the class, and the teacher scores each student's performance. Another method involves the teacher grading a few students during each class without the students knowing just who is being scored that day. Whatever the method, there should be several evaluations during a semester with teacher suggestions for improvement each time. The teacher may lower the skill grade due to excessive absences or failure to complete some assignments.

In high school or university classes where the skill level may be very mixed, teachers are more apt to grade on improvement in skill and effort put forth. Sometimes outside assignments such as attending dance concerts or reading assigned material may be considered along with attendance. Sometimes a written quiz is given covering vocabulary used in class or other dance information covered in class or reading assignments.

Whatever the requirements, they must be absolutely clear to the students. This makes grading easier for the teacher and curtails grade appeals from irate students.

Becoming an Effective Teacher

Dance students can start preparing to become effective teachers while they are still in college.

Keeping a notebook

Many experienced teachers highly recommend notebooks. After each class students should jot down items they noticed in class, some interesting variation, motivation, formation, or nice combination. It might be only one or two things per class, but they add up.

Teachers find it stimulating to look through their notes and recall good ideas which might trigger some new direction. Students also find that classes become more meaningful once they start noticing what is being done to motivate and educate. They become more aware of the teachable moment.

Many dance teachers continue looking for stimulating and refreshing ideas throughout their careers. They take classes, go to workshops and meetings, talk with other dance teachers, always gathering ideas for the notebook—probably a full-fledged file in a few years.

Volunteering

Teachers need to really like and enjoy students of the age they are teaching. That makes for understanding and better teaching. To discover the differences in behavior and learning at various ages, students can volunteer as teaching aides or assist in recreational programs. By thus participating in a variety of classes they may discover strong preferences that would influence their teaching choices.

Cooperating with others

Teachers who continually ask of themselves and of others, "Could I do that better?" are taking a giant stride toward genuine improvement.

Learning teachers can help each other by:

1. Timing classes with a stop watch to point up how much time is spent talking and how much dancing.

2. Videotaping classes so student-teachers see themselves in action.

3. Evaluating classes for each other. A form used by students in one teaching methods class is shown here.

Teaching Evaluation

Person evaluated ———————— Evaluator ————————
Class evaluated ———————— Date ————————

1. Class organization control, management	1	2	3	4	5
2. Logical progressions	1	2	3	4	5
3. Voice quality, projection	1	2	3	4	5
4. Time on task pacing, repetitions	1	2	3	4	5
5. Corrections individual, group	1	2	3	4	5
6. Demonstrations clear, accurate	1	2	3	4	5
7. Appropriate materials	1	2	3	4	5

Key: 1 = Needs much improvement; 2 = Needs some improvement;
3 = Effective; 4 = Very Effective; 5 = Outstanding.

EXAMPLES

SUGGESTIONS FOR IMPROVEMENT

Design of Electrical Services
for Buildings, 4th Edition

Design of Electrical Services for Buildings, 4th Edition

Barrie Rigby

Spon Press
Taylor & Francis Group

LONDON AND NEW YORK

First published 1974 by Chapman and Hall Ltd
Second edition published by 1982
Third edition published 1989
Reprinted 2001 by Spon Press

Fourth Edition published 2005
by Spon Press
2 Park Square, Milton Park, Abingdon, Oxon OX14 4RN

Simultaneously published in the USA and Canada
by Spon Press
270 Madison Ave, New York, NY 10016

Spon Press is an imprint of the Taylor & Francis Group

© 1974, 1982, 1989, 2005 Barrie Rigby

Typeset in Sabon by Keystroke, Jacaranda Lodge, Wolverhampton
Printed and bound in Great Britain by TJ International Ltd, Padstow, Cornwall

Every effort has been made to ensure that the advice and information
in this book is true and accurate at the time of going to press.
However, neither the publisher nor the authors can accept any
legal responsibility or liability for any errors or omissions that
may be made. In the case of drug administration, any medical
procedure or the use of technical equipment mentioned within
this book, you are strongly advised to consult the manufacturer's
guidelines.

British Library Cataloguing in Publication Data
A catalogue record for this book is available from the British Library

Library of Congress Cataloging in Publication Data
Rigby, Barrie.
    Design of electrical services for building / Barrie Rigby.— 4th ed.
        p. cm.
    Earlier editions were authored by Fred Porges.
    Includes bibliographical references and index.
    1. Buildings—Electric equipment. I. Porges, F. (Fred).
    Design of electrical services for building. II. Title.
    TK4001.R54 2004
    621.319¢24—dc22   2004002487

ISBN 0–415–31082–2 (hbk)
ISBN 0–415–31083–0 (pbk)

Contents

Preface to third edition

This book sets out to provide a basic grounding in the design of electrical services for buildings. It is intended for students of building services engineering in universities and polytechnics but will also be useful to graduates in mechanical and electrical engineering who are about to specialize in building services after obtaining a more broadly based, first degree. The emphasis throughout is on the needs of a design engineer rather than on those of an installation electrician or of an architect.

Engineering is one discipline, but with the increasing number of specialized first degree courses, the requirements for greater flexibility among engineers within industry have increased commensurably; many young graduates find themselves called on to work in fields not fully covered in their studies. In spite of the many opportunities which now exist for continuing professional education there is still a lack of books to bridge the gap between the theoretical texts and the unwritten experience of one's predecessors. It was in the hope of meeting this need that I originally wrote this book, and I believe the need still exists sufficiently to justify this new edition.

Opinions will always differ about the order in which the topics within the subject should be taken. I have retained the order of the previous editions, which was based on my own view that it is confusing to try to explain distribution without first saying to what the supply has to be distributed. Those who find a different order clearer may prefer to read the chapters out of sequence. A number of changes and additions have been made in this edition to keep up with the changes in practice; the section on hazardous areas has been expanded, the chapter on lighting has been considerably rewritten to bring the information on mercury and sodium discharge lamps up to date, and the chapter on lightning protection has been revised to take account of the new British Standard. To make this clearer, calculation examples have also been added. Sections have been added on the application of solid state electronics to fire alarms and to lift controls and the chapter on emergency supplies now includes uninterruptible power supplies. Elsewhere changes have been in terminology. Thus fused spur units have become fused connection units and earth leakage circuit breakers are now residual current circuit breakers.

There is a chapter on the form and function of the IEE Regulations, but I have not attempted any commentary on them. The intention of this book is to provide something more than a gloss on the regulations: A book which hopes to cover the complete design of an electrical installation must include many things not dealt with by regulations and should be free to follow its own methods and sequence. Once this was done there was nothing to be gained by covering the same ground a second time in the form of a commentary or explanation of the regulations.

The subject matter of this book is the design of electrical services in buildings and I have kept strictly to this. There are in practice many cases where the electrical designer relies on information and assistance from specialists in related but separate fields. This applies in particular to controls for heating and air conditioning, which are designed by specialists in that field and not by the consultant or contractor employed for the general electrical system. A description of them would, therefore, be out of place here. Many other services within a building include electrical equipment but the principles of motors, thermostats and controls are major studies of their own. Electric heating undoubtedly uses electricity but its design requires a knowledge of heating and ventilating. All these are topics which embrace more than the purely electrical work within a building and if they are to be dealt with properly they must have books of their own. Whilst appreciating that they may well form part of a complete engineering course I do not think they can all be covered in one book, and rather than treat them superficially and incompletely, I have left them out altogether.

I must again thank the many firms and organizations which have lent or given photographs for illustrations and to the staff of the publishers for help and guidance with the intricacies of revising an existing book for a new edition. In particular I would thank the editorial and production staff and Phillip Read at E. & F. N. Spon. On this occasion it is an added pleasure to be able to acknowledge the typing skills of Sonia Porges.

Fred Porges
Harrow

Preface to fourth edition

Much of what the late Fred Porges wrote as the preface to the previous edition still holds true. In this edition I have attempted to keep to the format of previous editions. With systems becoming more sophisticated, it is enough for the building services engineers to be reasonably aware of the systems in use, and the duties that they perform. Without the need for the engineer to be familiar with the intricacies of the electronic circuits. There are many building services design software packages on the market today, but the engineer still needs to know the basics of what they output and how the values are arrived at. The pace of change of legislation, introduction of European Standards, is ever increasing. I have left the academic parts of the book virtually unchanged, with the exception of changes in terminology. Other parts of the book have been completely overhauled to reflect modern practices and techniques. In particular I would thank the editorial and production staff at E. & F. N. Spon. I would also like to thank my dear wife and family for their support while I have been updating this book.

Barrie Rigby
Ulverston

Chapter 1

Accessories

Introduction

From the user's point of view the electricity service in a building consists of light switches, sockets, clock connectors, cooker control units and similar outlets. Such fittings are collectively known as accessories; this name came about because they are accessory to the wiring, which is the main substance of the installation from the designer's and installer's point of view. To them, the way the outlets are served is the major interest, but it is quite secondary to the user who is concerned only with the appearance and function of the outlet. In the complete electrical installation of a building the wiring and accessories are interdependent and neither can be fully understood without the other; a start has to be made somewhere however, and in this book it is proposed to consider accessories first.

Switches

A switch is used to make or interrupt a circuit. Normally when one talks of switches one has in mind light switches which turn lights on and off. A complete switch consists of three parts. There is the mechanism itself, a box containing it, and a front plate over it.

The box is fixed to the wall, and the cables going to the switch are drawn into the box. After this the cables are connected to the mechanism. To carry out this operation the electrician must pull the cables away from the wall sufficiently to give himself room to work on the back of the mechanism. He then pushes the mechanism back into the box and the length of cable that he had to pull out from the wall becomes slack inside the box. It is therefore important that the box is large enough to accommodate a certain amount of slack cable at the back of the mechanism.

Standard boxes for recessing within a wall are 16, 25, 35 and 47 mm deep. Sometimes the wiring is done not in the depth of the structural wall, but within the thickness of the plaster. For use with such wiring, boxes are made 16 mm deep (plaster depth boxes). It is often necessary to install wiring and accessories exposed on the surface of wall. For such applications surface boxes are made which are both more robust and neater in appearance than boxes which are to be recessed in walls and made flush with the surface, although they are made to similar depth. Typical boxes of both types are shown in Figure 1.1.

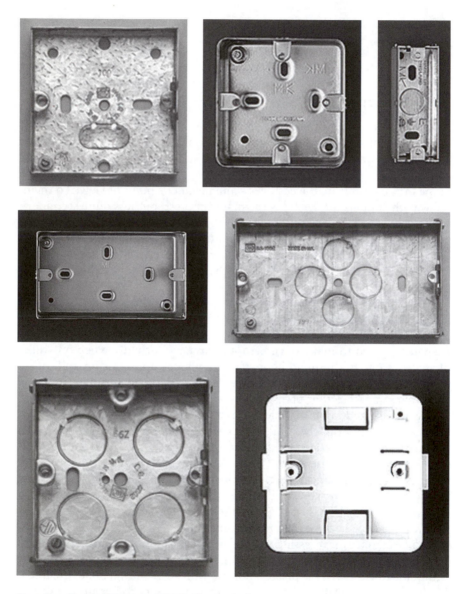

Figure 1.1 Boxes (Courtesy of M.K. Electric Ltd)

Rocker operated switches are illustrated in Figure 1.2. It has a rocker which is pivoted at its centre and which carries a spring-loaded ball. The ball presses on the moving contact and the combination acts like a toggle; the spring always forces the moving contact into one of its two extreme positions. The switch shuts when the bottom of the rocker is pressed and opens when the top is pressed. The advantages of the rocker switch are that it is easier to operate and that it is almost impossible to hold it half open, even deliberately. The disadvantages are that it is not so easy to see at a glance whether it is on or off and that it is more easily switched from one position to the other by an accidental knock.

Dolly switch

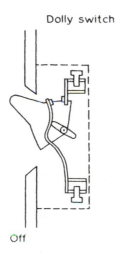
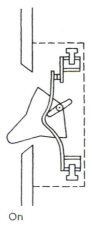

Off   On

Rocker switch

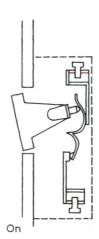

Off   On

Figure 1.2 Switch mechanisms

There is a maximum current which the contacts of any particular switch can make or break, and a maximum voltage that the contact gap can withstand. A switch must not be put in a circuit which carries a current greater than that which the switch can break. Most manufacturers make switches in standard capacities, the lower being rated at 5, 6, 15, or 20 A and the higher rating of 45 A for control of instantaneous shower units .

Discharge lights are an inductive load, and the induced voltage surge which occurs when an inductive load is broken must be taken into account in selecting a switch for, say, fluorescent lighting. It was for this reason that some of the older switches had to be de-rated when they were used for discharge lights, but switches in current production are suitable for inductive loads up to their nominal rating.

A 5 A rating is not as large as one might think at first sight. If ten tungsten lamps of 100 W 230 V each are controlled from one point, the total current to be switched is 4.35 A. However, discharge lights require control gear, power losses occur within the control gear. This must be taken into consideration when calculating the current taken by the discharge lights. The IEE Guidance Note 1 Selection and Erection of Equipment, and the IEE On-Site Guide recommends that the input current to a discharge light is calculated by (rated lamp watts × 1.8)/supply voltage. Alternatively the manufacturers data should be used which will yield a more economical value. For lighting schemes in larger buildings such as public buildings, it is often advisable to use switches higher than the lowest ratings.

When the switch is cabled and inserted in its box it needs a front plate over it. This is often a loose component with a hole which fits over the dolly or rocker and which is screwed to lugs on the box. Standard boxes always have lugs for that purpose. A switch with a separate front plate is called a grid switch. Alternatively the switch may be a plate switch, in which case the front plate is made as part of the switch and not as a separate piece. Both plate and grid switches are illustrated in Figure 1.3.

Grid switches are so called because with this type several mechanisms can be assembled on a special steel grid. This makes it possible for banks of any number of switches to be made up from individual mechanisms. Standard grids and front plates are available for almost any combination which may be required, and special boxes to take these assemblies are also available.

The standard switch boxes described so far are intended either to be fixed on a wall or to be recessed in it. Narrow boxes and switches are also made which can be recessed within the width of the architrave of a door. These are known as architrave switches. The grid switch shown in Figure 1.3 is of the architrave pattern.

Another type of switch is made which has no protruding lever or rocker, but is operated by a key which has to be inserted into the switch. This type of switch is very useful for schools and the public areas of blocks of flats. The caretaker has a key with which he can operate the lights but

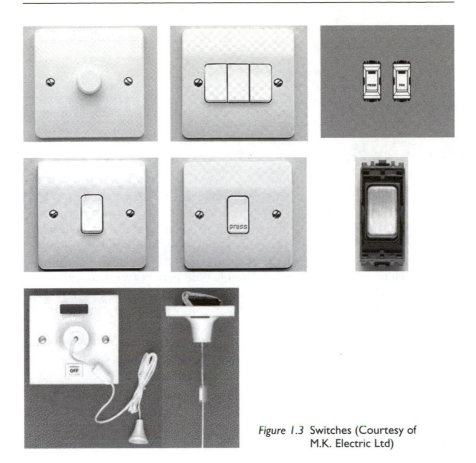

Figure 1.3 Switches (Courtesy of
M.K. Electric Ltd)

unauthorized persons cannot turn lights on or off. They are useful for simulating power failure on emergency lighting luminaires.

Safety regulations often make it impossible to use ordinary switches in certain zones in bathrooms. For such situations ceiling switches are made, operated from an insulating cord hanging from the switch. The cord rotates a cam through a ratchet. Thus when the cord is pulled the cam is turned through a fraction of a turn and when the cord is released the cam stays put. The switch has a fixed contact and a moving contact in the form of a leaf spring. In the off position the spring keeps the contacts open. A pull on the cord turns the cam and brings a lobe of the cam to press against the spring and close the contacts. The next pull on the cord brings the lobe off the spring and allows the contacts to open. Since each pull on the cord rotates the cam only part of a turn, the cam has several lobes around its circumference. The switch itself is on the ceiling and the cord hangs down to normal switch height.

Figure 1.4 Double pole switch (Courtesy of M.K. Electric Ltd)

In order that power equipment can be fully isolated it is often desirable to use a double pole switch. This expression means a switch which opens both the phase and neutral circuits. The mechanism is similar to that of an ordinary or single pole switch, but there are two contacts working side by side; the only difference being that both the phase and neutral are switched . A double pole switch is shown in Figure 1.4. Double pole switches are also made with a neon indicator and for putting in recessed boxes. Double pole pull-cord switches are used for local control of electric shower units in bathrooms and shower rooms.

There are certain very common applications of switches such as water heaters and fans. Some manufacturers, therefore, make double pole switches with the words 'Heater', 'Fan', 'Bath' or whatever other use is envisaged engraved on the front plate. The usual rating of double pole switches are 15, 20, 30, 45 and 60 A.

Socket outlets

A socket outlet is a female socket connected to the power wiring in the building and will accept the male plug attached at the end of the flexible cord of an appliance such as a vacuum cleaner, electric fire or electronic equipment.

The general arrangement of socket outlets is similar to that of switches. There is a box to house the outlet, the outlet itself and finally a front plate. In the case of socket outlets the front plate is usually integral with the outlet. In Great Britain the majority of socket outlets intended for domestic or commercial use are BS 1363 sockets, and are designed to accept 13 A plugs. These plugs have three rectangular pins and the sockets have three corresponding rectangular slots to take the pins. Each plug also has a fuse inside it, so that each appliance has its own fuse at the feeding end of its flexible cable or cord. This protects the cable or cord, and the fusing arrangements of the building wiring need protect only the permanent fixed wiring of the building.

However, there may be older installations still in existence and plugs and sockets for use with them are still being manufactured. The older fittings, all have round pins and sockets. They are rated at 2 A, 5 A and 15 A. The 15 A pattern is still used in the Republic of South Africa. The spacing of the pins and sockets are different for the different ratings. This makes sure that a plug of one rating cannot be inserted, even wilfully, into a socket of a different rating. Plugs and sockets rated at 2 and 5 A are available in both two and three-pin versions, but those of 15 A-rating are made only with three pins. The smaller-rated sockets are useful in situations where switching of reading lamps is required. The sockets are installed around the room in suitable locations, and a wall switch at the doorway controls the lighting socket circuit. The reading lamps are then all turned on together.

Two of the three pins are for the line and neutral cables, and the third one is for a separate circuit protective conductor. It should be noted that although a separate circuit protective conductor was not always provided on many older installations, it is essential with all present-day methods of wiring buildings.

Typical socket outlets are illustrated in Figure 1.5. It will be seen that they are available with and without switches. Unswitched sockets have the contacts permanently connected to the wiring and are, therefore, permanently live. The appliance to be connected is turned on as soon as the plug is pushed into the socket, and is disconnected when the plug is pulled out. If, however, a switch is incorporated in the socket outlet, the switch must be turned on before the line contact becomes connected to the supply. The switch mechanisms built into socket outlets for this purpose are of the same type as those used for lighting switches. It is possible to leave a plug half in and half out of a socket so that on older types of plug, parts of the bare pins are left exposed. If the socket is permanently live the exposed part of one of the pins is live and in this half-way position it could be touched by a small finger or a piece of metal. Newer types of plug have the rear end of the pins insulated so that the problem with older types of plug top has been alleviated. Also if an appliance connected to the plug is faulty and takes an excessive current arcing can occur as the plug is pushed in and out.

These hazards are avoided if the socket is not switched on until after the plug has been pushed in. Of course there is nothing to stop a householder switching the socket on first and pushing the plug in afterwards, and in fact many people do this. The switched socket outlets in a house are then left permanently switched on, so that the advantage of a switch is lost. However, people will not learn to use equipment properly if they are not provided with it, and it may perhaps be regretted that unswitched sockets are made at all.

A further refinement to a socket outlet is the addition of a neon indicator light which shows when the socket is switched on. This can be reassuring to mechanically minded people who find electricity difficult and feel happier if something visible happens when a switch is turned on. It is also convenient for seeing at a glance whether it is the power supply that has failed or the appliance connected to the plug, which has developed a fault.

13A unswitched   15A   2A standard fitting

13A twin-switched   13A non-standard (see earth pin)

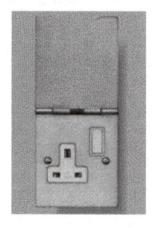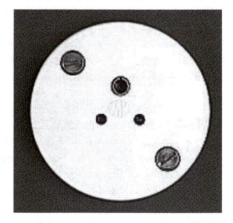

13A floor   2A conduit box fitting

Figure 1.5 Socket outlets (Courtesy of M.K. Electric Ltd)

Like switches, socket outlets can be recessed into a wall with the front flush with the face of the wall or they can be mounted completely on the surface. The socket outlets illustrated in Figure 1.5 are of both types.

Fused connection units

Fused connection units colloquially known as fused spur units are used for connecting a single permanently fixed appliance to the wiring. They are used, for example, for connecting fixed as opposed to portable electric fires, water heaters and other equipment of this sort. Electrically, they perform the same function as a socket and plug combination, the difference being that the two parts cannot be separated as the plug and socket can. They are often used when a fixed appliance is to be served from a ring main circuit serving socket outlets as well as the fixed appliance. Figure 1.6 shows some typical fused connection units.

Physically, they are similar to socket outlets and are connected to the wiring in the same way. They differ in that they have a fuse, which is accessible for replacement from the front, and in that they have no sockets for a plug to be pushed into. The outlet connection is permanently cabled, there being terminals for this purpose within the unit; the outlet cable is brought out of the unit either underneath or through the front. Like socket outlets, fused connection units can be switched or unswitched and can be with or without a neon indicator. The disadvantages are that it costs a little more and that unauthorized persons may be able to turn the appliance on and off, such as for an electric hand dryer in a public toilet. If this is a problem, then unswitched fuse spur units are available. They are used to connect mains-supplied equipment in bathrooms, such as electrically heated towel rails, in zones where connection of such equipment is permitted; the installation of mains-supplied socket outlets is prohibited in bathrooms and shower rooms in the UK.

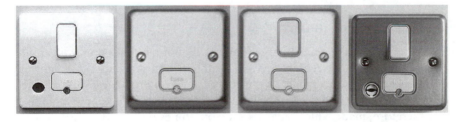

Figure 1.6 Fused connection units (Courtesy of M.K. Electric Ltd)

Figure 1.7 Shaver outlet (Courtesy of M.K. Electric Ltd)

Shaver outlets

The use of shaver outlets is described in Chapter 9. The outlet itself consists of a two-pin socket with a switch, the assembly being suitable for fitting into a standard deep box. Figure 1.7 shows a shaver outlet which has the assembly on the back of the front plate and is suitable for fitting into a box recessed in the bathroom wall. Some shaver outlets are unswitched, in which case the sockets are permanently live, as is the case with unswitched socket outlets. They are also available in switched versions with neon indicators. A shaver outlet fitted in a bathroom or shower room must comply with BS EN 60742, which incorporates a safety isolating transformer electrically isolating the output from the input. The output then is earth-free.

Cooker control unit

Electric cookers take a much larger current than most other domestic appliances. They therefore require heavier switches than those used for lighting or in socket outlets. Moreover, it is usually convenient to have a socket outlet near the cooker in addition to the cooker switch itself. Cooker control units are, therefore, made which have a 45 A (sometimes only a 30 A) switch with outgoing terminals for a permanent cable connection to the cooker and which also contain an ordinary 13 A switched socket outlet. The cooker switch is double pole, that is to say, on opening, it disconnects both phase and neutral lines, and the unit also has a substantial terminal for the circuit protective conductors.

Figure 1.8 Cooker control unit (Courtesy of M.K. Electric Ltd)

A cooker control unit is shown in Figure 1.8. Again units are available for both flush and surface fixing. The unit is mounted within easy reach, to the side of the cooker so that the operators can switch off the cooker quickly in an emergency without putting themselves in danger. The cable from the unit to the cooker is usually hidden in the wall and comes out at low level behind the cooker. A special flex outlet cover is made to fix on the surface of a box, which is let in flush with the wall to make a neat outlet from the wall to the cooker. The flex outlet is normally supplied as a loose piece with the cooker control unit.

Boxes

The use of boxes for housing switches and other accessories has already been described. The same boxes are used for conduit installations. When wiring is done by drawing cable through conduit, access must be provided into the conduit for pulling the cable in. Also where the paths of cables branch two or more conduits must be connected together. For both these reasons, a box of some sort is needed for use with conduit, and the type of box used is the same as that used for housing switches. As stated in the section on switches, boxes are available for recessing in walls, recessing within the narrow depth of plaster only or for fixing to the surface of walls. Where a large number of conduits is to be connected to the same box, the box is made longer in order to accommodate them side by side.

It can be seen in Figure 1.1 that the boxes have a number of circles on them. These are called knock-outs and their circumference is indented to about half the thickness of the parent metal. It is therefore easy for the electrician on site to knock out any one of them out in order to make a hole in the box. The hole so made is the right size to accept standard electrical conduit. It will be clear from the illustration that sufficient knock-outs are provided to make it possible to bring conduit into a box from any direction and in any position.

Figure 1.9 Cover plates

In addition to rectangular boxes of the sort illustrated, circular boxes are also made. These are useful for general conduit work and terminating wiring at points which are to take fittings.

When boxes are used for connecting lengths of conduit rather than for housing other accessories, they must have the open side covered with a blank plate. A typical plate is shown in Figure 1.9. Circular plates are also made for circular boxes. It should perhaps not need saying that when a box is recessed in a wall, the cover must be left flush with the surface of the wall so that it can be removed to give access to the cables inside the box. This is particularly important if the system is installed with the intention that it should be possible to rewire or add cables later.

Boxes have a wiring terminal which enables a cable to be connected to the metal of the box. This is used for connecting a circuit protective conductor. The purpose and use of earthing is discussed in Chapter 9. The importance of the earth terminal on the box arises when the accessory which is housed in the box has to be earthed through the box. This is particularly important when a plastic conduit system is used which necessitates the use of a separate circuit protective conductor. There must then be some means of connecting the circuit protective conductor to the accessory and this can become difficult if there is no suitable terminal in the box for making the connection. It is also recommended that an accessory requiring earthing, installed on a metallic conduit installation,m is provided with a lead between the earth terminal on the box and the accessory, if the box has adjustable tags such as on some knockout boxes.

TV outlets

Housing design today has to accept that every flat, maisonette or house will have a television which may require connection to an outdoor aerial. It

Figure 1.10 TV outlets (Courtesy of M.K. Electric Ltd)

was common to provide a communal aerial system which serves all dwellings on an estate from a single aerial. The chief reason for doing this is that it avoids the ugliness of a large number of aerials, all of different patterns, put up close to each other by different people. It has the further advantage that one powerful aerial erected in a carefully chosen position can give better reception than the aerials which individual occupiers install. This signal may be fanned out to individual dwellings through a mains supplied booster. Terrestrial channels may be accessed through satellite aerials.

If a communal aerial system is installed, it becomes necessary to run a television aerial cable from the aerial to an outlet in each dwelling, or hotel bedroom. There has to be a suitable terminal in the room, and this takes the form of a socket capable of accepting the coaxial plugs used on the end of aerial cable. An outlet of this kind is shown in Figure 1.10. Since a television set also needs a power supply, it is usual to provide a mains socket outlet near the aerial outlet. One manufacturer makes a combined unit having an aerial socket and 13 A socket outlet within one housing.

For radios which require both an aerial and an earth connection, special two-pin outlets are available. These can also be combined in a single unit containing the mains socket outlet as well as the two-pin outlet.

Telephone outlets

To avoid the need for a lot of surface cable fixed after a building is occupied, it is quite common to put in wiring for telephones as part of the services built into the structure as the building is erected. This wiring must, of course, be brought to suitable terminals in the positions at which the telephones are to

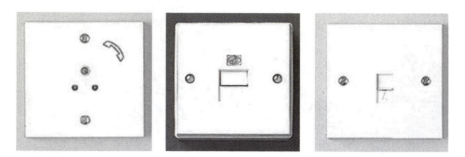

Figure 1.11 Telephone outlets (Courtesy of M.K. Electric Ltd)

be connected later. The only essential requirement is an opening through which standard telephone cable can be brought out neatly. A plate with a suitable outlet which fits into a standard box, is shown in Figure 1.11.

The more modern practice is to connect each telephone set to the permanent installation via a telecom socket and plug; in the UK, a BT pattern in used, which is slightly different to the US pattern. The socket forms part of a lid which screws onto a standard conduit box at the agreed outlet positions. An outlet of this kind is shown in Figure 1.11.

Clock connector

Special outlets are made to which electric clocks can be easily connected. A typical one is shown in Figure 1.12 and can perhaps be considered as a special-purpose fused-connection outlet.

It contains a 2 A fuse and terminals to which the cable from the clock can be connected. The fuse is needed because a clock outlet is usually connected to the nearest available lighting circuit. The fuse protecting the whole circuit will never be rated at less than 5 A, and may be as much as 15 A. The clock

Figure 1.12 Clock connector (Courtesy of
M.K. Electric Ltd)

wiring is not suitable for such a large current and must, therefore, have its own protection at the point at which the supply to it branches from the main circuit. The necessary protection is provided by the fuse in the connector. The front of the connector has an opening through which the clock cable can be taken out to the clock. In most cases, the clock connector is made flush with the wall and the clock is subsequently fixed over it. However, surface connectors are available, and in this case the clock would be fixed next to the connector with a short length of cable run on the surface of the wall between the clock and connector. With the development of quartz battery clocks, clock connectors are seldom used.

Lampholders and ceiling roses

In public buildings the luminaires are fixed as part of the electrical instal-lation. In housing, the choice of the lampshade or luminaire is usually left to the owner or tenant and is made once the dwelling is occupied. Plain lampholders are, therefore, provided which will accept ordinary 100 W and 150 W tungsten bulbs, and which usually have a ring or skirt to which a normal lampshade or similar luminaire can be attached. The top of the lampholder screws down to grip the flexible cable cord on which it is suspended from the ceiling. Typical lampholders are shown in Figure 1.13.

The flexible cord on which the lampholder is suspended performs two functions. It carries the electric current to the lamp, and it supports the weight of the holders, lamp and shade. Its physical strength is, therefore, just as important as its current carrying capacity and it has to be selected with this in mind. At the ceiling itself, the wiring in (or on) the ceiling must be connected to the flexible cord. The connection is made by means of a ceiling rose, which is illustrated in Figure 1.14. It consists of a circular plastic housing with a terminal block inside and a bushed opening on the underside where the flexible cord to the lampholder can come out of the rose. In installations which have the main wiring inside the ceiling, this wiring enters the rose through the back or top of the rose; when the main wiring runs exposed on the surface of the ceiling, it enters the rose through a cut-out in the side of the rose.

Ceiling roses are made with three line terminals in addition to an earth terminal. The reason for the third line terminal is explained in Chapter 5 and it will be seen there that when this third terminal is used, it remains live even when the light attached to the ceiling rose is switched off. It must, therefore, be shrouded so that it cannot be touched by accident if ever the flexible cord is being replaced; complete circuit isolation for this task is strongly recommended. Ceiling roses are available which incorporate a plug and socket. The luminaire can then be quickly disconnected for maintenance or testing, without disruption to other parts of the same circuit.

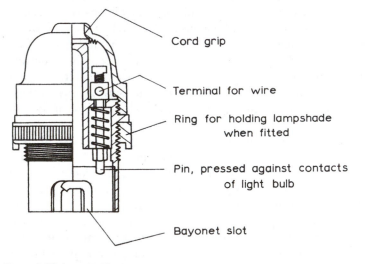

Cord grip

Terminal for wire

Ring for holding lampshade
when fitted

Pin, pressed against contacts
of light bulb

Bayonet slot

Figure 1.13 Lampholders

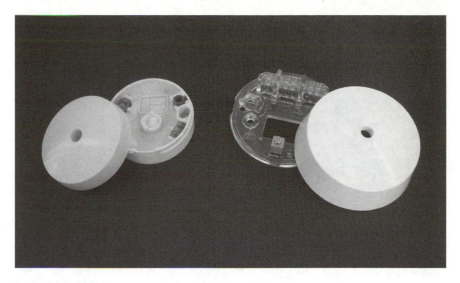

Figure 1.14 Ceiling roses

In some situations, it is undersirable to have the lampholder hanging on the end of a flexible cable while there is no objection to having the lamp at ceiling height. In such cases, one makes use of a batten lampholder, which is illustrated in Figure 1.15. It combines the terminal block of the ceiling rose with the lampholder in one fitting, and it can be screwed directly to a standard circular box on the ceiling. A batten lampholder could also be used to fix a light to a wall, but the lamp would project perpendicularly from the wall. The angled batten-lampholder shown in Figure 1.16 has the lampholder at an angle to the rose so that when the whole fiiting is put on the wall, the lamp is at a downward angle. Such angled battenholders can be obtained either with the lampholder at a fixed angle or with the angle adjustable.

Lampholders frequently have protective shields which are intended to prevent accidental contact with either metal parts or with the lampholder pins themselves. Lampholders with such shields are shown in Figures 1.13 and 1.15. These shields are often referred to as Home Office Skirts.

Pattresses

It can happen that an outlet, such as a socket outlet or ceiling rose, has to be placed a small distance in front of the structure available to support it. This can happen, for example, when a wiring system is installed on the surface of walls and ceilings and there is a step in the surface which the wiring cannot follow, so that it has to be supported off the surface. It is then necessary for some sort of distance piece to take up the gap between the fitting and the

Figure 1.15 Batten lampholders

Figure 1.16 Angled batten lampholder

surface behind it. Standard components are available for this and are known as pattresses. A box for use with a circular socket outlet is shown in Figure 1.17, which also gives a sketch showing the use of the box with surface conduit. The inclusion of the box makes it possible for the cables to enter the socket outlet from the back, whereas without it, there would be an untidy junction of the conduit with the bottom of the socket outlet. It is now fairly standard practice in commercial situations to install trunking which incorporates the socket outlets.

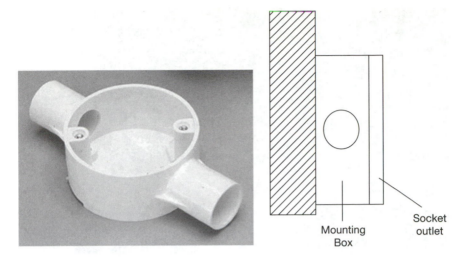

Figure 1.17 Mounting box

Figure 1.18 shows a pattress for use with batten lampholders. Figure 1.19 shows a different type of pattress. This is useful with some modern building methods in which the wiring is installed in a special skirting. The skirting is at floor level, but this is too low for socket outlets and the latter are, therefore, a little above the skirting so that at each outlet, cables have to rise a small vertical distance. The pattress shown provides a neat and convenient way of doing this. It has also been known to happen that in the course of erecting a new building, an electrical outlet is wrongly placed. For example, a heating pipe to a radiator may run right in front of the box left to take a socket outlet. The type of pattress shown in Figure 1.19 is a neat way of extending the wiring to an adjacent position, where the alternative might be to demolish large parts of a wall already built in order to give access to conduit buried in it, as the only means of extending that conduit.

Laboratories

Laboratories in schools, universities and industrial establishments often need special services which are not required in other areas. The most common electrical service of this kind is an extra low voltage supply. This is usually obtained from a stabilised supply unit which is plugged into the bench mains socket, the socket being installed on angled bench trunking. For higher current applications, a transformer from the mains, which can either provide a fixed secondary voltage or be of the tap-changing type to give a choice of voltages, or even a variable voltage transformer, may provide the supply. A

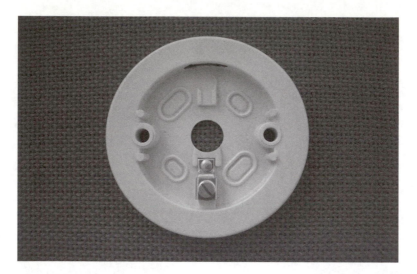

Figure 1.18 Pattress

Figure 1.19 Pattress

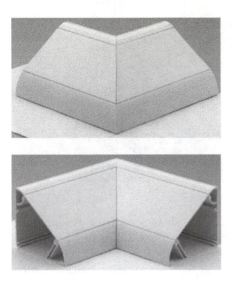

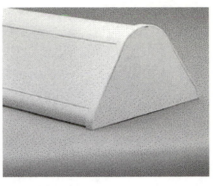

Figure 1.20 Bench trunking (courtesy of
M.K. Electric Ltd)

rectifier is often incorporated so that an extra low voltage d.c. supply is made available at the same time as an extra low voltage a.c. supply. Laboratory benches supplied through angled bench trunking, as shown in Figure 1.20, are provided with special terminals to connect equipment to the laboratory supplies which must be shrouded so that there are no live conductors exposed to touch as the laboratory equipment is being connected.

Connectors

It is often necessary to join cables together. In the wiring of buildings this is rarely done by soldering. Good soldered joints can be made in factory conditions, but the conditions existing on a building site, and the quality of work that can be done under such conditions, are such that joints may not be sufficiently reliable. Also, the time taken to make them would put up the cost of the electrical service considerably. Crimping the cables is a more cost-effective method of jointing cables; this is achieved by squeezing special lugs onto the cable conductor by means of a special tool. It is also common practice to join cables by means of connector blocks, which require only mechanical terminations to the cables. A connector block is illustrated in Figure 1.21. It consists of two screw-down-type terminals solidly connected to each other, mounted in an insulated casing. The end of each cable is pushed into one of the terminals, with the insulation taken up to the connector, with no bare conductor visible, and the screw is tightened on to it. The screw grips the conductor, holding it firmly in place and at the same time making a good electrical contact. As the two terminals are solidly connected within the insulated case, the result is that there is a good electrical path between

Figure 1.21 Connector block

the two cables. Joints and terminals made in this way must be available for inspection. In addition to this, all joints and terminations must be enclosed within a non-combustible material. Therefore, any accessory without an appropriate back plate must not be fixed to a combustible surface, such as a wooden partition, without the use of a pattress. A joint or termination made by welding, brazing, soldering, crimping, or encapsulating need not be available for inspection.

With such connector blocks, it is possible to join cables neatly within the boxes which have already been described. In general, joints should be avoided and single lengths of cable run from one piece of equipment to another, but when an occasion arises when this cannot be done, connector blocks may be used.

The author has tried in this chapter to give a survey of the more important accessories and to give an idea of the wide range available. It is not possible to describe every accessory made; a full knowledge can be obtained only by a study of many manufacturers' catalogues and, preferably, by the use of the accessories on actual sites.

Hazardous areas

There are industrial processes which involve a risk of fire or explosion. Generally, the risk arises because flammable vapours or dusts are present in the atmosphere. For example, in coal mines there is always the possibility of methane appearing in sufficient concentration to ignite or burn. In such cases any electrical equipment in the area subject to risk must be specially designed to reduce that risk.

The mere flow of electricity will not ignite a vapour unless the temperature becomes too high. The temperature can be kept low by adequate sizing of the cables so that this is not a problem as far as the installation is concerned. The surface temperature of motors, luminaires and other electrical equipment must, however, be considered. Vapour can also be ignited by a spark at a terminal or switch or as a result of mechanical damage causing a spark or local hot spot. There are various ways of designing equipment to reduce the risks in hazardous areas and these are now covered by British Standards which are harmonized with European standards if the national standards do not exactly match. If the national standards are identical, then they will be designated as a Euro-Norm EN.

Under the European ATEX directive 1999/92/EC, on the 'Minimum Requirements for Improving the Safety and Health Protection of Workers at Risk from Explosive Atmospheres', it is necessary to consider both the type and magnitude of the risk. The magnitude of the risk is the probability of a dangerous concentration of flammable vapour, and hazardous areas are classified into three zones according to the likelihood of such a concentration:

1   Zone 0 (ATEX category 1G {Gas}) A place in which an explosive atmosphere consisting of a mixture with air of flammable substances in the form of gas, vapour or mist is present continuously or for long periods or frequently.
2   Zone 1 (ATEX category 2G {Gas}) A place in which an explosive atmosphere consisting of a mixture with air of flammable substances in the form of a gas, vapour or mist is likely to occur in normal operation occasionally.
3   Zone 2 (ATEX category 3G {Gas}) A place in which an explosive atmosphere consisting of a mixture with air of flammable substances in the form of a gas, vapour or mist is *not* likely to occur in normal operation but, if it does occur, will persist for a short period only.

For dusty atmospheres the following definitions apply:

1   Zone 20 (ATEX category 1D {Dust}) A place in which an explosive atmosphere in the form of a cloud of combustible dust is present continuously or for long periods or frequently.
2   Zone 21 (ATEX category 2D {Dust}) A place in which an explosive atmosphere in the form of a cloud of combustible dust in air likely to occur in normal operation occasionally.
3   Zone 22 (ATEX category 3D {Dust}) A place in which an explosive atmosphere in the form of a cloud of combustible dust in air *not* likely to occur in normal operation but, if it does occur, will persist for a short period only.

If there is no likelihood at all of a flammable atmosphere the area is a safe one.

The magnitude of the risk which determines which zone an area is in depends on such things as the process producing the flammable gas or vapour or dust cloud, the rate of production in relation to room size, the risk of leakage and the distance of the area from the source of the hazardous material. These factors are assessed by a safety specialist who designates the zone classification of areas on a site and it is not usual for the electrical designer to have to do this him/herself.

The type of risk depends on the properties of the gas, vapour, or dust concerned. For gases, dangerous substances are, accordingly, classified into four groups, depending on the minimum ignition energy of the gas and on the ability of a flame emerging from a narrow joint to ignite it:

1   Group I, for which the typical or representative gas is methane, is reserved for mining applications only and is therefore of interest only to mining electrical engineers.
2   Group 11A is for gases with properties similar to propane and require more than 200 µjoules of energy to ignite.
3   Group IIB is for gases with properties similar to ethylene (> 60 µjoules to ignite).
4   Group IIC(>20 µjoules to ignite) is for the most hazardous gases, of which the typical one is hydrogen. These categories relate to the minimum ignition energy in µjoules required to cause ignition, at the most volatile gas air mixture.

It will be noted that the zones are numbered 0–2 in decreasing order of risk whereas the groups are numbered I–IIC in increasing order of risk. These classifications deal with the magnitude and type of risk.

Equipment designed for use in hazardous areas is itself classified according to the method used for achieving protection. Each type of protection is referred to by a letter.

Type d refers to equipment with a flameproof enclosure. The principle adopted with this type of protection is that a spark inside equipment should not cause fire outside it. It is not practicable to design equipment so that no air or vapour can get inside it. It is, however, possible to design it so that the air gaps between inside and outside are so narrow and so long that any flame starting inside will be extinguished before it has travelled to the outside. This is the method used for type d equipment.

Type e is a method of protection which applies only to non-sparking equipment. The design of the equipment is such as to keep temperatures low and give increased protection against mechanical damage which could cause an electrical fault. This is achieved by such features as non-sparking cable terminations, additional insulation, increased creepage and clearance distances, and, in the case of luminaires, special lampholders. The requirement of low internal temperature makes it inapplicable to heavily rated machines.

Type N is similar to type e but has a reduced level of protection. Consequently, whereas type e equipment can be used in zone 1, type N equipment can be used only in zone 2.

With type p protection, the enclosure of the equipment contains air or an inert gas at a pressure sufficient to prevent the surrounding vapour entering the enclosure. Since no enclosure is completely vapour-tight, there must be some leakage out of the enclosure. Equipment suitable for this method of operation must be capable of withstanding the necessary internal pressure, and must be connected to a network of compressed air or gas which contains a low-pressure switch to disconnect the electrical supply in the event of loss of pressure.

Intrinsically safe equipment limits the energy available for causing ignition. The maximum current which may flow depends on the voltage but, in general, most intrinsically safe equipment is designed for operation on extra low voltages. It is permissible to limit the current by means of a barrier diode. This type of protection is designated type i; it may be designated type ia or type ib according to the number of faults it can sustain during testing.

Table 1.1 is based on BS EN 60079–14:1997: Part 1, Electrical apparatus for explosive gas atmospheres. Electrical installations in hazardous areas (other than mines) show which type of equipment may be used in which zone. Within a zone in which it is permitted, type e, N, or p equipment may be used with gas of any group. Equipment with type d or i protection is further subdivided according to the group for which it is safe.

These provisions deal with the risks of ignition arising from operation of equipment under normal or fault conditions. It may also be necessary to limit surface temperatures. The safe temperature in an area does not necessarily depend on the magnitude or type of risk, and an additional classification is usual. Table 1.2 is based on BS 4683: Part 1/BS EN 50021 Electrical apparatus for potentially explosive atmospheres. Types of protection 'n', show the classes which are used to designate the maximum permitted surface temperature. It is possible for equipment having any type of protection to have any temperature classification, although one would not expect intrinsically safe equipment to have a lower class than T5 or T4 while it is difficult for other types of equipment to achieve classes T5 or T6. It should be noted that there is no real relationship between minimum ignition temperature and maximum surface temperature permitted. Hydrogen is a class IIC gas but its

Table 1.1 Equipment types

Zone	Type of protection
0	ia
1	ia,ib,d,e,p
2	i, ia, ib, d, e, p, N

Table 1.2 Temperature classification

Class	Maximum surface temperature °C
T1	450
T2	300
T3	200
T4	135
T5	100
T6	85

surface ignition temperature is T1. Each gas data must be checked thoroughly before specifying equipment.

Electrical equipment suitable for use in hazardous areas has to be marked with the protection it affords. The mark commences with the letters Ex, which have been internationally agreed to indicate explosion protection, continues with the type, and where relevant, the group for which the equipment has been certified, and concludes with the temperature classification. An example of marking would thus be Ex d IIB T5. Equipment will also be marked with atex markings CE 0000 II 2 G; CE suitable for use in the European Community, 0000 the certifying test house registration number, II explosion proof, 2 category, and G suitable for gas.

Nearly all the accessories described in this chapter, including switches, socket outlets and boxes, are available in versions with various classes of hazard protection. Distribution equipment and luminaires, which are discussed in Chapters 6 and 7, are also available in a variety of types of protection.

Enclosures

The enclosure of any equipment serves to keep out dirt, dust, moisture and prying fingers. This is a separate matter from protection against explosion; a piece of electrical equipment may have to be mounted outdoors and be protected against the weather where there is no risk of explosion, or it may be indoors in a particularly dusty but non-flammable atmosphere.

An internationally agreed system has been developed to designate the degree of protection afforded by an enclosure. It consists of the letters IP followed by two digits. The letters stand for International Protection and the digits indicate the degree of protection. The first digit, which may be from 0 to 6, describes the protection against ingress of solids. The second digit, which may be from 0 to 8, describes protection against ingress of liquids. In both cases, the higher the numeral the greater the degree of protection. The definitions of the levels of protection are given in Tables 1.3a and 1.3b which are based on BS EN 60529. Specification for degrees of protection provided by enclosures (IP code).

This method of classification can be applied to all the equipment described in this chapter and the distribution equipment and luminaires discussed in Chapters 6 and 7. Thus an enclosure which is rainproof might be designated 1P23 whereas one that is jetproof would be 1P55.

Table 1.3a Protection of persons against contact with live or moving parts inside the enclosure and protection of equipment against ingress of solid foreign bodies (protection against contact with moving parts inside the enclosure is limited to contact with moving parts inside the enclosure which might cause danger to persons)

First characteristic numeral	Degree of protection
0	No protection of persons against contact with live or moving parts inside the enclosure. No protection of equipment against ingress of solid foreign bodies.
1	Protection against accidental or inadvertent contact with live or moving parts inside the enclosure by a large surface of the human body, for example, a hand, but not protection against deliberate access to such parts. Protection against ingress of large solid foreign bodies.
2	Protection against contact with live or moving parts inside the enclosure by fingers. Protection against ingress of medium-size solid foreign bodies.
3	Protection against contact with live or moving parts inside the enclosure by tools, cables or such objects of thickness greater than 2.5 mm. Protection against ingress of small solid foreign bodies.
4	Protection against contact with live or moving parts inside the enclosure by tools, cables or such objects of thickness greater than 1 mm. Protection against ingress of small solid foreign bodies.
5	Complete protection against contact with live or moving parts inside the enclosure. Protection against harmful deposits of dust. The ingress of dust is not totally prevented, but dust cannot enter in an amount sufficient to interfere with satisfactory operation of the equipment enclosed.
6	Complete protection against contact with live or moving parts inside the enclosure. Protection against ingress of dust.

Table 1.3b Protection of equipment against ingress of liquid

Second characteristic numeral	Degree of protection
0	No protection.
1	Protection against drops of condensed water: drops of condensed water falling on the enclosure shall have no harmful effect.
2	Protection against drops of liquid: drops of falling liquid shall have no harmful effect when the enclosure is tilted at any angle up to 15° from the vertical.
3	Protection against rain: water falling in rain at an angle up to 60° with respect to the vertical shall have no harmful effect.
4	Protection against splashing: liquid splashed from any direction shall have no harmful effect.
5	Protection against water-jets: water projected by a nozzle from any direction under stated conditions shall have no harmful effect.
6	Protection against conditions on ships' decks (deck watertight equipment): water from heavy seas shall not enter the enclosure under prescribed conditions.
7	Protection against immersion in water: it must not be possible for water to enter the enclosure under stated conditions of pressure and time.
8	Protection against indefinite immersion in water under specified pressure: it must not be possible for water to enter the enclosure.

Standards relevant to this chapter are:

BS 67	Ceiling roses
BS 196	Protected-type non-reversible plugs, socket outlets, cable couplers and appliance couplers
BS 546	Two-pole and earthing pin plugs, socket outlets and adaptors
BS 1363	13 A plugs, socket outlets and boxes
BS 3535–2	Isolating transformers and safety isolating transformers. Specification for transformers for reduced system voltage
BS EN 60742	Isolating transformers, and safety isolating transformers

BS 3676/BS EN 60669–1	Switches for domestic and similar purposes
BS 4177	Cooker control units
BS EN 60309	Industrial plugs, socket outlets and couplers
BS 4573	Two-pin reversible plugs and shaver socket outlets
BS 4683	Electrical apparatus for explosive atmospheres
BS EN 50021	Electrical apparatus for potentially explosive atmospheres. Type of protection 'n'
BS 5125	50 A flameproof plugs and sockets
BS EN 60079–14	Electrical apparatus for explosive gas atmospheres. Electrical installations in hazardous areas (other than mines)
BS 5419	Air-break switches up to and including 1000 V a.c.
BS EN 60947–3	Specification for low-voltage switchgear and controlgear
BS EN 60529	Specification for degrees of protection provided by enclosures (IP code)
BS EN 50014	Electrical apparatus for potentially explosive atmospheres
BS 5733:1995	General requirements for electrical accessories
BS 6220:1983	Junction boxes
BS EN 50281–1–1,1–2	Protection of apparatus for use in presence of combustible dusts

IEE Wiring Regulations BS 7671 particularly applicable to this chapter are:

Regulations	412–03
Regulations	471–05
Section	476
Section	511
Section	512
Section	537
Section	553

Chapter 2

Cable

Introduction

Electricity is conveyed in metal conductors, which have to be insulated and which also have to be protected against mechanical damage. When the conductor is insulated to make a usable piece of equipment for carrying electricity, it becomes a cable. This nomenclature makes a convenient and logical distinction between a bare conductor and insulated cable, but in practice the terms 'conductor' and 'cable' are in fact used interchangeably and it is only the context which makes clarified what is being referred to. We shall try to avoid confusion and shall discuss conductors first and the insulation applied to them afterwards.

Conductors

The commonest conductor used in cables is copper. The only other conductor used is aluminium. Copper was the earlier one to be used, although aluminium has the disadvantage of being much weaker than copper. Consequently BS 7671 states that the minimum permissible cross-sectional area is $16\,mm^2$. Aluminium's greatest assets are that it is cheaper than copper, lighter, and that its price is less liable to fluctuations.

Conductors have usually been made except for the smallest sizes, by twisting together a number of small cables, called strands, to make one larger cable. A cable made in this way is more flexible than a single cable of the same size and is consequently easier to handle. Each layer is spiralled on the cable in the direction opposite to that of the previous layer; this reduces the possibility that the strands will open under the influence of bending forces when the cable is being installed. $1\,mm^2$ has a solid core, $1.5\,mm^2$ and $2.5\,mm^2$ is available as solid or stranded core; sizes above these are available as stranded core only.

Insulation

Every conductor must be insulated to keep them apart, keep the flow of current within the conductor and prevent its leaving or leaking from the conductor at random along its length. The following types of insulation are in use.

Thermoplastic PVC

Polyvinyl chloride is one of the commonest materials used by man today. It is a man-made thermo-plastic which is tough, incombustible and chemically unreactive. Its chief drawback is that it softens at temperatures above about 70 °C. It does not deteriorate with age and wiring carried out in PVC insulated cable should not need to be renewed in the way that wiring insulated with most of the older materials had to be. PVC insulated cable consists of cables of the types described above with a continuous layer or sleeve of PVC around them. The only restriction on this type of cable is that it should not be used in ambient temperatures higher than 70 °C.

Thermosetting insulation

There are plastics available as alternatives to PVC which have the advantage of being able to operate at higher temperatures. The most usual is XLPE, which is a cross linked polyethylene compound. Another alternative is hard ethylene propylene rubber compound, which is designated HEPR. These materials are normally used only in cables which have cable armouring over the insulation and an outer sheath over the armouring. The outer sheath is generally of PVC. The construction is then similar to that of the PVC wire armoured cable shown in Figure 2.3, the only difference being that the inner insulation is XLPE or HEPR instead of PVC.

Butyl rubber

This insulation is used for cables which are to be subjected to high temperatures. It is, for example, used for the final connections to immersion heaters, for the control wiring of gas-fired warm-air heaters and within airing cupboards. It can safely be used for ambient temperatures up to 85 °C. Butyl rubber also has greater resistance to moisture than natural rubber.

Silicone rubber

This is completely resistant to moisture and is suitable for temperatures from −60 °C to 150 °C. It is undamaged after repeated subjection to boiling water and low pressure steam, and is therefore used on hospital equipment which has to be sterilized.

Although it is destroyed by fire, the ash is non-conductive and will continue to serve as insulation if it can be held in place. A braid or tape of glass-silicone rubber will hold it, and cable made with this construction is very useful for fire alarms. Thermosetting rubber of 180 °C is used in hot-air saunas.

Glass

Glass fibre has good heat-resisting properties and is therefore used for cables which are employed in high-temperature surroundings. One example is the internal wiring of electric ovens. Another application which may not at first sight seem to require heat-resisting cable lies in flexible cords for luminaires. Although the object of an incandescent lamp is to convert electrical energy into light, most of the energy is in fact dissipated as heat. Many luminaires restrict the paths available for the removal of heat and in consequence produce high local temperatures. The high temperature is transmitted to the flexible cord both by direct conduction through the lamp socket to the conductors and by an increase in the local ambient temperature. If the flexible cord is to last any length of time, it must be capable of withstanding the temperature it is subjected to.

One type of flexible cord is made from tinned copper conductors insulated with two layers of glass fibre, which is impregnated with varnish. A glass fibre braid, also impregnated with varnish, is applied over the primary insulation. This type of cord can be used at temperatures up to 155 °C. If it is made with nickel-plated conductors and a silicone-based varnish, it then becomes suitable for temperatures up to 200 °C.

Paper

Paper-insulated cable was used for power distribution for nearly a century. It is too bulky to be used for the small cables of final circuits within buildings, or for most of the sub-mains. The smallest practicable rating is 100 A, and its chief use is for the Electricity Supply Company's underground low-voltage and medium-voltage distribution.

The conductor is either stranded copper or stranded aluminium, the latter becoming increasingly popular as its price advantage increases. Whichever is used, it is heavily stranded to give good flexibility, which is important in a cable of such comparatively large size. Paper specially made for the purpose is used as an insulator. It is essential that it should have good mechanical properties to be suitable for this application. Paper itself is a hygroscopic, fibrous material, and has to be impregnated with an oily compound to make it fit for use in cables. The compound used is a heavy mineral oil mixed with resin. On its own impregnated paper, insulation would be too fragile to be used unprotected, and a lead sheath is therefore applied over the insulation. Further strengthening and protection can be applied according to the intended use of the cable and the physical wear to which it may be exposed. A very good strong protection is afforded by steel cable or tape.

Figure 2.1 shows a single-core PVC-insulated steel wire armoured PVC-covered cable. This is conventionally referred to as a PVC/SWA/PVC cable. Figure 2.2 shows a three-core PVC-insulated steel wire armoured cable with a PVC covering. The abbreviation for this is PVC/S/SWA/PVC cable. A considerable number of variations on this basic design is possible and, for any given application, a cable can only be chosen with the help of a cable manufacturer's catalogue.

PVC is now used for the larger power and sub-main cables and has super-seded paper-insulated cables for these applications. The construction of such cables is similar to that of paper insulated cables, and another example is shown in Figure 2.3. This particular cable would be described as three-phase straight concentric, which would be abbreviated PCU/PVC/straight concentric/PVC cable. This type of cable is used to supply TN-C-S systems, where the armouring forms the CPC and the neutral conductor.

Figure 2.1 Single-core PVC/SWA/PVC cable

Figure 2.2 Three-core screened and armoured cable

Figure 2.3 Three-phase straight concentric cable

Air

Air itself is a good insulator. Whilst it cannot of course be wrapped around cables in the ordinary sense of wrapping insulation around, it does form the insulation when bare conductors are used.

Bare conductors are used principally on rising mains in high buildings. These are the mains distributing electric power from the main intake of a building to distribution boards at different levels. The scheme of distribution is discussed in Chapter 5 and here we are concerned only with the construction of the rising-main bars. Bare conductors used for rising mains must be correctly spaced from each other to give the necessary air gap for adequate insulation, be not subject to flexing under fault conditions, and should have a protective casing. They must be made inaccessible to unauthorized persons and must have freedom to expand and contract. There are several proprietary systems of bare rising mains, and a typical one is illustrated in Figure 2.4. It is frequently used for the vertical distribution in blocks of flats.

The conductors are held in porcelain or sometimes plastic cleats. Apart from supporting the conductors, the cleats keep them the correct distance away from each other for the air gap to have sufficient insulation for the working voltage of the system. The cleats are fixed to the back of a metal trunking which completely encloses the conductors. The dimensions are, of course, such that the air gap between the conductors and the trunking gives enough insulation. The front of the casing is hinged and can be opened for maintenance. It is possible to put a solid insulating plate across the inside of the casing at every floor level to form a barrier to air and smoke moving up and down the casing. In many places this has to be done to satisfy fire prevention regulations, and also BS 7671. Banks of fuses can be fixed within the casing to form a distribution board as part of the vertical distributor.

A similar system can be used for horizontal distribution. Here again there are several proprietary systems consisting of horizontal conductors supported on insulators inside metal trunking. They are used particularly in factories

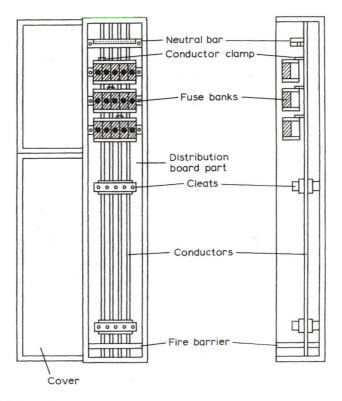

Neutral bar
Conductor clamp
Fuse banks
Distribution board part
Cleats
Conductors
Fire barrier
Cover

Figure 2.4 Rising mains

where they run horizontally at high level along the walls of workshops. Plain connectors can be fixed at short intervals and short cables run from each set of connectors to a switch fuse fixed on the wall immediately below or above the trunking. The switch fuse can then be connected to serve a machine near it on the floor of the workshop.

MICC

These letters stand for mineral insulated copper covered; this type of cable is also known as mineral insulated copper sheathed, which is abbreviated to MICS and as mineral insulated metal sheathed, abbreviated to MIMS. This last description may refer to aluminium sheathing, as well as to copper sheathing; aluminium was used as a sheathing some time ago. It may be encountered during refurbishments. All versions of this type of cable consist of single-strand cables embedded in tightly compressed magnesium oxide, which is enclosed in a seamless metal sheath. The construction is illustrated in Figure 2.5.

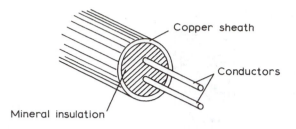

Figure 2.5 Mineral insulated copper sheathed cable

MIMS cable is extremely robust and, when properly installed, has an indefinite life. It can be used outdoors and for such use is usually supplied with an overall covering of PVC. It is then known as MIMS PVC sheathed. Since PVC is embrittled with ultraviolet light, this PVC covered cable should not be installed where it will be exposed to direct sunlight. This is not as drastic a restriction on its use as may appear since it is probably unwise to run any cable where it is so exposed that direct sunlight can reach it. In any such situation, it would also be too vulnerable to damage by vandalism and from animals.

Because of its robustness, MIMS requires no further protection, but will not withstand being struck by sharp objects. It is, therefore, more easily built into the structure of a building than other cables, nearly all of which must have some form of enclosure around them. Because it has an indefinite life, there is no need for facilities to make it possible to rewire the installation. For both these reasons, it can often be used where no other cable would be entirely satisfactory. MIMS cable can carry a higher current than other cables with the same size conductor because the insulation can withstand a higher conductor operating temperature. However, its current carrying capacity depends on whether it is bare, PVC-covered, exposed to touch, or in contact with a combustible material. It follows that for a given current the cable can be smaller if MIMS is used than if another type of cable is used. This is a very useful property which makes it possible to conceal MIMS cable in corners which are not large enough to hide the larger cable that would have to be used with another system.

The magnesium oxide insulation is hygroscopic and will lose its insulating properties if left unprotected against the ingress of moisture from the atmosphere. To prevent this happening, MIMS cable must be terminated in special seals and glands, which are supplied for the purpose by the cable manufacturers. If the cable is cut and the ends left unsealed for any length of time, as can happen in the course of work on building sites, moisture can penetrate the insulation and render the cable useless. In most cases, however, moisture will penetrate unsealed ends for only a short distance of not more than 50 mm. It is then sufficient to cut off the damaged end of the cable, after which the remainder can be used in the normal way. If the cable is carrying full rated current, it will operate at about 90 °C; care must be taken that the accessory or luminaire to which the cable is connected is designed to withstand 90 °C.

Sheathing

We have described how a cable is made from a conductor with insulation around it. Electrically, this is all that is needed to make a device to carry electricity from one place to another, but if the cable is to survive in use, it must also withstand mechanical damage, and the insulation, which is enough to achieve electrical protection, is seldom strong enough to give adequate mechanical protection. Something further, therefore, has to be provided over the insulation, and it can either be made an integral part of the cable or provided by entirely separate means.

For example, the steel armour of a Thermoplastic PVC cable, which has been described above, gives mechanical protection and is part of the structure of the cable. Similarly, the metal sheathing of MIMS cable gives the cable all the mechanical protection that is needed. Neither of these cables could be used without its built-in mechanical protection, and MIMS could certainly not even be made without it. In these cases, although one may try to draw a logical distinction between the function of insulation and that of sheathing, in practice the two must be done together. PVC insulated cable, on the other hand, is strong enough to be handled as it is during erection, but is too liable to mechanical damage to be left unprotected for long. There are two practicable ways of giving it additional protection. One way is to install it in either conduit or trunking and the other way is to put a sheath around the outside of the insulation. The first way gives protection by the use of a particular method of wiring and the second way does it by making the cable a sheathed cable. Methods of wiring are discussed in the next chapter and the rest of this one is devoted to types of sheathed cable.

PVC

Cable insulated with PVC often has a thicker PVC sheath over the insulation and is then described as PVC insulated PVC sheathed cable or, simply, PVC/PVC. More than one insulated conductor can be embedded in the same sheath, so that one can have single, twin, three or four-core PVC/PVC cables, If one of the conductors is intended as a circuit protective conductor, it requires no insulation, although it must be sleeved at terminals and connections, up to a cross-sectional area of 6 mm^2, and may be enclosed directly in the sheath. Figure 2.6 shows a cable known as twin and earth PVC/PVC. It has two PVC insulated conductors and one uninsulated conductor all embedded in the same PVC sheath.

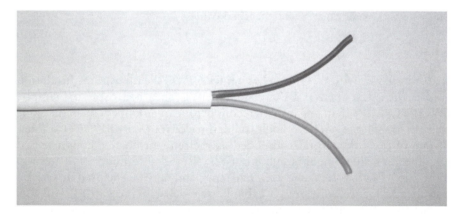

Figure 2.6 PVC insulated PVC sheathed cable (Courtesy of B.I.C.C.)

Rubber

Butyl rubber and silicone rubber cables are usually sheathed with thick butyl and silicone rubber respectively.

Flexible cord

Flexible cord is the name given to a particular type of cable. It is one which is flexible and in which the cross-sectional area of each conductor does not exceed 4 mm². Flexible cords are used for suspending luminaires and for connections to portable domestic appliances having low power consumption. They are, therefore, usually left exposed in rooms and, to be suitable for such use, are made with a variety of coverings.

Ordinary lighting flex consists of a stranded copper conductor with PVC insulation, covered with an outer layer of PVC. as shown in Figure 2.7. Circular flex is made for the connections to household appliances such as irons, kettles and so on, and consists of rubber-insulated cable inside an external cotton braiding. Either two or three rubber-insulated cables may be used and to obtain the circular cross-section, cotton padding is wound around them inside the outer braiding. This is illustrated in Figure 2.8.

Figure 2.7 Lighting flex

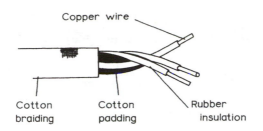

Figure 2.8 Circular flex

There are also flexible cords made with silicone rubber insulation with a covering of braided varnished glass fibre. Flexibles which have glass-fibre insulation and an outer glass-fibre braid have already been mentioned.

Lead

Cables insulated with paper and sheathed with lead have already been described.

Metal

The metal sheathing of MIMS cable is an integral part of the cable and has already been described.

Bare risers

These have already been described. They sometimes have a covering of thin PVC which is put over them for extra protection for maintenance personnel who may be working on a system with some of the conductors live. The covering does not perform the protective function of the other kinds of sheathing discussed.

Enhanced fire performance

The commonest insulation used today is PVC. Its ignition temperature is sufficiently high for it not to be regarded as a flammable material, that is to say, a fault in the cable is unlikely to ignite the insulation. But if a fire from some other cause engulfs the cable, PVC will burn and give off dense smoke and acid fumes which can create a hazard greater than the original fire. To avoid misunderstanding here, it should be added that a cable fault, particularly if the insulation is damaged, can ignite adjacent material such as loose paper or timber, even if it does not ignite its own insulation.

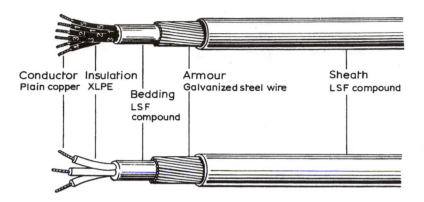

Conductor Insulation
Plain copper XLPE

Bedding
LSF
compound

Armour
Galvanized steel wire

Sheath
LSF compound

Figure 2.9 LSF cable (Courtesy of B.I.C.C.)

In order to give better performance in fires, alternative materials have been developed. One type of cable for enhanced fire performance has XLPE insulation with cable armouring bedded in a compound which has low smoke and fume properties and is sheathed in the same compound. From its low smoke and fume properties it is designated LSF; it consists of inorganic fillers in polymers such as ethyl vinyl acetate and ethylene propylene rubber. The construction is illustrated in Figure 2.9.

Other cables have EPR (ethylene propylene rubber) insulation with a sheath of elastomer which is heat and oil resistant and flame retardant, and is therefore designated HOFR. These cables are available with and without a cable armouring between the insulation and the sheath.

It will not come as a surprise that the better the performance of the cable, the more expensive it is. Consequently, it is important to consider carefully the application and precise requirements. It has only been possible here to give an indication of special-purpose cables available. In practice, final selection cannot be made without discussion with manufacturers and suppliers.

Co-axial cables

Radio and TV systems are now frequently built as part of the engineering services of new buildings. One aerial is made to serve a number of outlets at each of which a receiving set can be plugged in. The single aerial is usually at the highest point of the building or group of buildings in the system and is connected by cable to each outlet. The cable used for this does not carry large currents and is not subjected to large voltages but it does carry a weak signal at high frequencies. The signal must not be lost and to avoid loss of the signal, the cable must have a low impedance at the frequency being used. It must also be constructed so that it does not pick up unwanted high

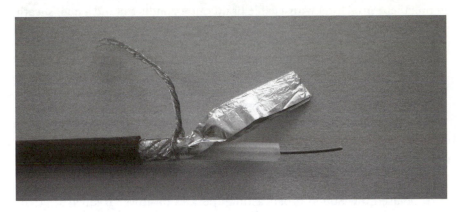

Figure 2.10 Coaxial cable

frequency signals, for example, by capacitance or inductance between itself and nearby mains cables.

To satisfy these requirements, radio and TV distribution systems are cabled with radio frequency cables. These normally have a single insulated conductor. A metal cover is placed over the insulation to screen the conductor from unwanted signals, and this cover is in its turn protected by an overall sheath of non-conducting material. Thus the single conductor is surrounded by a circular cover and a circular sheath which are concentric and have the conductor on their axis. Hence the cable comes to be known as coaxial cable. Such a cable is shown in Figure 2.10; it has its single inner conductor cased

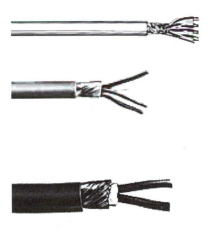

Figure 2.11 Audio-frequency cables

in polythene insulation with a cable braid outer conductor and a final sheath of PVC.

The inner conductor can be either solid or stranded, while the screen can take several forms. It can be a one-piece sheath in either aluminium or copper, or it can be of cable braid, which in turn can be either single or double, or it can be of steel tape or of lead. For the insulation, the commonest materials used are polythene, PTFE and polypropylene. The last part of the construction is the outer sheathing and this may be of metal tape, cable, metal braid, PTFE, lead alloy, PVC, nylon or polythene. Evidently, there is a large variety of coaxial cables and properties differ somewhat. The choice of what to use in any particular case is determined by the electrical characteristic required for that particular application and this depends on what equipment the cable is to be used for. Sound broadcasting operates on lower frequencies than television and cables for sound only do not need to meet quite such stringent conditions as those for television transmission. Audio-frequency cables suitable for microphone and loudspeaker connections for public address systems and for broadcast relay systems are similar to high-frequency cables but are not made to such exacting specifications. Examples of audio-frequency cables are shown in Figure 2.11.

Standards relevant to this chapter are:

BS 2316	Radio frequency cables
BS EN 13602	Copper wire for the manufacture of electric cables
BS 6004	Electric cables. PVC insulated, non-armoured cables for voltages up to and including 450/750 V, for electric power, lighting and internal wiring
BS 6007	Electric cables, single core unsheathed heat resisting
BS 6195	Insulated flexible cables
BS 6207–3	Mineral insulated cables
BS 6346	PVC insulated cables
BS 6480	Paper insulated cables
BS 6500	Electric cables, flexible cords
BS EN 50214	Flexible cables for lifts

IEE Wiring Regulations particularly applicable to this chapter are:

Regulation	412–2
Chapter	52

Chapter 3

Wiring

Introduction

To the average user the only important part of the electricity service is the outlets at which he received electricity. To the engineer concerned with designing or installing the service, the system of cables which links these outlets to each other and to the supply coming into the building is just as important and perhaps even more so. In practice, the electrical service is a complete interdependent system and the practical engineer thinks of it as a whole, but, as with the teaching of any subject, one has to break it down into parts in order to explain it in an orderly fashion which will make sense to a student with no previous knowledge of the subject.

In this chapter, we shall consider different ways in which cables can be installed in a building. The calculation of the size of particular cables we shall leave to Chapter 4 and the selection and grouping of outlets to be served by one cable we shall leave to Chapter 5. For this chapter, we assume that we know where cables are to run and discuss only how to get them into the building. This aspect of the electrical service can for convenience be called 'methods of installation'.

A method of installation consists of taking a suitable type of cable, giving it adequate protection and putting it into the building in some way. The subject can, therefore, be fairly logically considered by considering types of cable, methods of protection and methods of installation. The types of cable available and in general use have been described in Chapter 2. The protection against mechanical damage given to cable is sometimes part of the cable itself, as with PVC insulated PVC sheathed cables, and sometimes part of the method of installation, as with conduit systems. It can be more confusing than helpful to take a logical scheme of things too rigidly and, rather than deal with protection in a chapter of its own, we are dealing with it partly in the previous chapter and partly in this, according to whether it is associated with the cable or with the method of wiring.

It is probably true to say that one of the commonest methods of installing cables is still to push them into conduit and we shall devote most of our attention to this.

Conduit

In a conduit system the cables are drawn into tubing called conduit. The conduit can be steel or plastic. Steel conduit is made in both light gauge and heavy gauge, of which heavy gauge is much more frequently used. In both cases, it can be made either by extrusion or by rolling sheet and welding it along the longitudinal joint. The latter is specified as welded conduit and the former as seamless. Seamless conduit is generally regarded as the better quality. The different sizes of conduit are identified by their nominal bore and in the case of electrical conduit the nominal bore is always the same as the outside diameter of the tube. Thus 20 mm light and heavy gauge conduits both have the same outside diameter and consequently must have slightly different inside diameters. This is the opposite of the convention used for pipes for mechanical engineering in which the nominal bore usually corresponds more closely to the inside than the outside diameter. Electrical conduit is specially annealed so that it may be readily bent or set without breaking, splitting or kinking.

Heavy gauge conduit is normally joined together by screwed fittings; there is a standard electrical thread which is different from other threads of the same nominal diameter. A screwed connection between two lengths of conduit is shown in Figure 3.1. A male electrical thread is cut on the ends of both lengths of conduit to be joined and a standard coupler with a female electrical thread is screwed over them. A lock nut, which has been previously threaded well up out of the way on one of the male threads, is then wound down and tightened against the coupler. The screwed connection is relied on for continuity of the earth path and the lock nut is essential to prevent the socket working its way along the threads until it engages more on one conduit than on the other. The reason for wanting an earth path is discussed in Chapter 9. Methods of joining conduit to boxes of the kind described in Chapter 1 are shown in Figure 3.2. A bush of some sort must always be used to provide a smooth entry into the box, to avoid sharp corners which could damage the cable insulation, and in certain cases to maintain earth continuity.

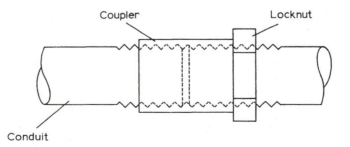

Figure 3.1 Conduit coupling

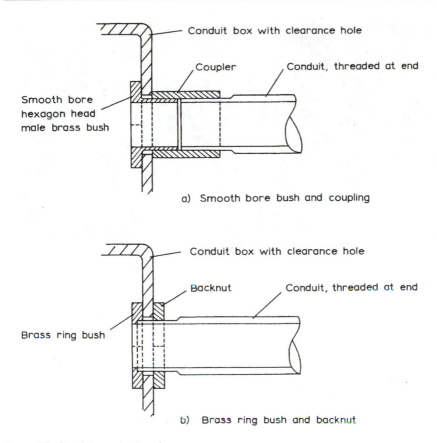

a) Smooth bore bush and coupling

b) Brass ring bush and backnut

Figure 3.2 Conduit entries into boxes

Connections to distribution boards and switchgear are made in a similar manner.

In addition to the boxes described in Chapter 1, other fittings are made for use with conduit. These include the sockets and bushes needed to make connections, and also bends and inspection covers, some of which are illustrated in Figure 3.3. The use of bends and inspection covers is not, however, regarded as good practice, because they provide inadequate room for drawing in cable and because they look unsightly when the installation is completed. For long lengths of run, inspection sleeves are available.

Conduit is thick enough for the cross-sectional area of the metal to provide a good earth continuity path. The conduit can, therefore, be used as the earth continuity conductor and no separate cable or wire need be used for this purpose. It is essential that the conduit, with all its fittings and screwed joints, should form a continuous conducting path of low impedance and the safety

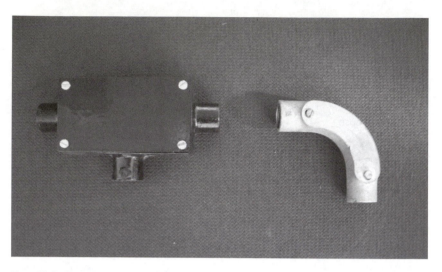

Figure 3.3 Conduit inspection fittings

of the installation depends on good electrical contact at all the joints. Even though it may be decided not to use the steel conduit as the circuit protective conductor, in preference for a separate protective conductor, usually copper, the conduit must be erected properly with tight joints. Since it is classed as an exposed conductive part of the installation, and therefore could become live in the event of a fault, it requires earthing properly.

Conduit is made in two standard finishes: black enamel and galvanized. It is almost universal practice to use galvanized conduit where it is exposed or where it may be subject to damp.

The final connection to machines and mechanical equipment such as pumps, boilers, fans, fan heaters, workshop equipment and so on is usually made in flexible conduit. The fixed wiring terminates in a box either in the wall near the equipment to be connected or on the surface of the wall, and from this box a short length of flexible conduit is taken to the equipment. Very often the machine is delivered to the site after the electrician has done the bulk of the work. At the time of installing the wiring, the position of the terminals on the machine is not known and so the outlet box can only be placed to within a foot or so of its exact position. Solid conduit from this to the machine could involve a large number of bends in a short distance which would be difficult to make and impossible to pull cable through. Flexible conduit can take up a gentle curve and also serves to isolate the fixed wiring from any mechanical vibrations on the connected machine, and allows for belt tension adjustment of the motor.

There are several types of flexible conduit. Metallic flexible conduit is shown in Figure 3.4. It is made from a stepped strip which is wound in a

Figure 3.4 Metallic flexible conduit

continuous spiral so as to produce a long cylinder with spiral corrugations. The material used is normally galvanized steel. Flexible conduit is also made in a number of plastic materials. In some of these the flexibility is conferred by a corrugated structure, as in the case of metallic flexible conduit, and in others by the flexible properties of the material itself.

Flexible conduit cannot be used as a protective conductor. This is obvious in the case of plastic flexible conduit which is made of non-conducting material, but it is so even in the case of metallic flexible conduit. The flexibility here is conferred by the corrugated structure, and as the conduit bends, the corrugations open out. They remain sufficiently overlapping to keep out dirt and moisture but are not in hard enough contact with each other to be relied upon to give an adequate electrical path. To make up for this, a separate circuit protective conductor must be run wherever flexible conduit is used. The circuit protective conductor is either put inside the conduit with the other cables or it can be placed outside the conduit. In either position, it must be bonded to the rigid conduit at both ends of its run. A clamp for connecting an external circuit protective conductor with solid conduit is shown in Figure 3.5

There are other applications for flexible conduit. It is required with certain systems of industrialized building in which sections of floors and walls are precast in factories away from the building site. In order that electrical wiring can be put into these slabs after they have been erected, conduit is cast in them and exposed ends are left at the edges where the slabs will be joined together on site. The slabs are lifted into position on the building and joined to each other by *in situ* concrete, grout or some other suitable structural method. At the same time as this is done, the exposed conduit ends, in adjacent slabs, are linked together by short lengths of flexible conduit. The flexible conduit can take up a gentle 'S' shape and thus make up for some lack of alignment between opposite ends of the fixed conduit. Small errors

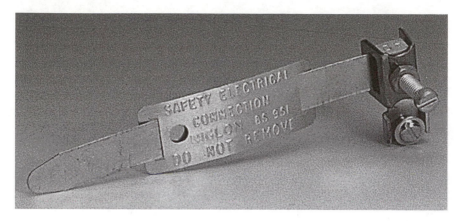

Figure 3.5 Earth clamp

in casting need not, therefore, cause a problem during assembly, although a very large misalignment will pull the flexible into such a sharp S that the site electrician will not be able to pull cables through it. Flexible conduit is also used to bridge electrical services from one to the other side of the expansion gap in structures.

A conduit system must be completely installed before any cables are pulled into it. It is, therefore, essential that it is set out so that an electrician can pull cables into it without difficulty. Conduit systems are intended to be rewirable; that is to say the intention is that 20 or 30 years after the building has been erected, it should still be possible to pull all the cables out of the conduit and pull new ones into it. If this is possible, then quite regardless of what happens when the building is first constructed, the layout of the conduit must be such that cables can be drawn into it when it is complete and finished.

The original reason for wanting to have electrical systems which could be recabled during the life of the building was that VRI cable deteriorates in about 20 years to the stage at which it should be removed. PVC cable appears to last indefinitely so that all modern installations which use this cable should not need rewiring. The use of electrical appliances has increased greatly in the last 50 years, and when old buildings which had VRI cable are rewired the opportunity is invariably taken of modernizing the installation by adding extra outlets and circuits. New cables then have to be run where there were no cables previously and the original conduit has at best to be added to and at worst abandoned altogether. Rewireability is then no help and in fact the need for a rewireable system is not as great as is often supposed.

On the other hand, there is always the possibility that a cable may become damaged during the construction of a building, and it is obviously an advantage if it can be replaced without difficulty after the building has been finished.

If the conduit is installed so that the system is rewireable, repairs will always be possible. The requirements for rewireability should, therefore, be kept to as far as possible, but the engineer in charge should have discretion to relax them if exceptionally difficult circumstances are encountered.

To achieve rewireability, draw-in boxes must be accessible from the surface, or in other words their covers must be flush with the finished surface. The covers can then be removed without any cutting away of plaster or brickwork. In addition, the length of conduit between successive draw-in boxes should not exceed about 10 m and there should not be more than two right-angle bends between successive boxes. A further requirement is that the bends themselves should be made with as large a radius as the position of the conduit within the building permits. This is the reason that specifications often insist that bends shall be formed in the conduit itself and prohibit the use of factory-made bends. The latter are necessarily of small radius and could damage insulation if cables have to be forced through them. Inspection bends do not provide adequate room for feeding cables through in a neat and workmanlike manner and the conduit should be so laid out that they are not necessary.

Care must be taken in the making of bends to avoid rippling or flattening of the conduit. The smallest sizes of conduit (16 mm and 20 mm) can in fact be bent over one's knee. This is not, however, to be recommended because it is unlikely that a neat bend without kinks or flattening the conduit will be produced. A bending block, as shown in Figure 3.6, is a better device. The bottom edge of each hole should be bevelled so that the conduit is not pulled against a sharp edge. The conduit to be bent is inserted in the hole and hand pressure is brought to bear to bend the conduit slightly. The conduit is then moved through the hole a short distance and the process repeated. Practice is necessary to make a good bend without kinks and not all electricians possess the necessary skill.

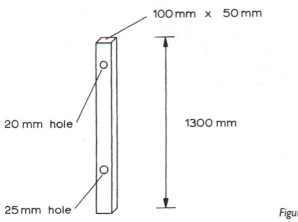

Figure 3.6 Bending block

For larger conduit, a bending machine is essential, and is to be recommended for all conduit. It is the only truly reliable way of making a good bend without reducing the internal cross sectional area. A bending machine is shown in Figure 3.7.

To allow ease of wiring and avoid damage as cables are drawn in, the number of cables in each conduit has to be limited. IEE Guidance Note 1 Selection and Erection or the IEE On-Site Guide gives guidance and methods of calculating required diameters of conduits for various numbers of cables. For cases not covered by these tables it is useful to employ the concept of space factor. This is defined as

$$\frac{\text{total cross sectional area of cables}}{\text{internal cross sectional area of conduit}} \times 100$$

Note that the space factor relates to the space taken up by the cable and not the unoccupied space.

It is harder to pull several small cables together than one large cable, and when a number of cables have to go in the same conduit, it is advisable to

Figure 3.7 Conduit bending machine

keep the space factor well below 40 per cent. Space factors of less than 20 per cent need not be considered at all extravagant. For the same reason, it is often better to use two size 25 mm conduits side by side than a single 32 mm or 50 mm even when in theory the latter is adequate.

Many types of insulation deteriorate if they become damp. It is, therefore, important that moisture should not collect in the conduit system. Moisture can occur through water entering during building operations and also later on through condensation of moisture in the atmosphere. A conduit system must be laid out so that it is well ventilated, which will prevent condensation, and so that water which does enter will drain to one or more low points at which it can be emptied.

It is good practice to swab through the conduit after it is erected and before cables are drawn in to remove any moisture and dirt which have collected. This is done simply by tying a suitable size of swab on the end of draw cable and pulling it through the conduit from one draw-in box to the next.

To avoid damage to cables as they are drawn in, burrs on cut ends of conduit must be removed with a reamer before the lengths of conduit are joined.

There are a number of positions in a building in which the conduit can be fixed. It can obviously be run on the surface of walls and ceilings, and when a building is constructed of fair-faced brick walls, surface conduit is usually the only practicable wiring system which can be adopted. If walls are plastered, the conduit can generally be concealed within the plaster. There must be at least 6 mm of plaster covering the conduit if the plaster is not to crack. Since plaster-depth conduit boxes are 16 mm deep, the total thickness of plaster must be at least 22 mm. If the architect or builder proposes to use a lesser thickness than this, it becomes necessary to chase the conduit into the wall so that some of the total distance of 22 mm between face of plaster and back of conduit is in the wall and some in the plaster. This is shown in Figure 3.8.

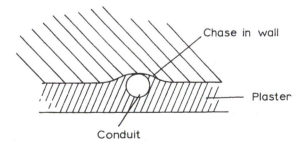

Figure 3.8 Conduit chased into walls

In many modern buildings, internal partitions which do not carry any of the structural load are made of breeze-blocks about 75 mm thick and in some cases as little as 50 mm thick. If these have to be chased to take 25 mm conduit, there is very little partition left. Using conduit with such partitions is a very real problem and the electrical engineer often has to abandon a conduit system in favour of one which is less robust but takes up less space.

Horizontal runs of conduit over floors can sometimes be arranged within the floor finish. Probably the most widely used floor finish is still the fine concrete screed. Provided the screed is sufficiently deep, the conduit is laid on top of the floor and just screeded over. If the screed is not deep enough to make this possible, it may be possible to cut chases in the floor itself so that the conduit is partly in the floor and partly in the screed. However, structural floors are nowadays designed to such close limits that the structural engineer may not permit the electrical engineer to have chases cut in the floor slabs. It is often necessary for conduits to cross each other in a floor and there are also other services, such as water and gas, which run in pipes laid in or over the floors. It is then almost inevitable that conduit has to cross one or other of these other services. It will be obvious that crossovers, whether of conduit and conduit, or of conduit and other services, are the places at which maximum depth is needed. It is these critical points which determine whether or not it is possible to accommodate the conduit within the floor finish. This must be discussed by the electrical engineer and the architect quite early in the design as the decision will affect the type of wiring which the engineer has to design.

Conduit can also be buried within concrete slabs. Many modern buildings have floors and even walls of concrete with very little or no finish on top of it; this is particularly true of industrialized methods of building. In such buildings, the only practicable alternative to putting wiring on the surface is to bury conduit within the structural concrete. This needs considerable care. The exact position of the conduit within the depth of the slab must be agreed with the structural engineer and close supervision is required of the work on site to ensure that the conduit is correctly placed. It has to be fixed in position immediately after the steel reinforcement has been laid in the shuttering and before the concrete is poured. If it is not well tied either to the reinforcement or to the shuttering, it may be dislodged as the concrete is poured and vibrated. Open ends of conduit which may have to be left at the end of the section of concrete being cast, ready for connection to the next piece of conduit, must be covered with metal or plastic caps to prevent cement or stones getting into the conduit. Every electrician of any experience can tell a horror story of a blocked conduit. The conduit boxes must also be filled with a material which will prevent cement and stones entering but can itself be easily removed once the concrete has set and the shuttering has been struck. The most commonly used material for this purpose is expanded polystyrene.

Once conduit has been cast inside a concrete slab, it is totally inaccessible for repair or replacement. The rules for installing it in such a way that the drawing in of cables is easy are, therefore, of exceptional importance. It is advisable for the conduit to have plenty of spare capacity for the number of cables to be drawn into it, for bends to be very easy and for there to be plenty of draw-in boxes.

When conduit is placed on top of a floor ready to be screeded over, workmen are liable to walk over it after it is laid and before the screed is poured. Light gauge conduit is not robust enough to stand up to this. The use of lightweight conduit is, therefore, usually confined to small domestic installations.

In wooden floors, conduit can be run under the floorboards. Where it has to run across joists, the latter must be slotted for the conduit to get through underneath the floorboards. The agreement of the structural designer must be obtained before joists are cut. This method is not, however, much used now; in wooden floors it is more usual to employ PVC sheathed cable run 50 mm from the top or the bottom of the joist, to prevent damage from the floor fixings. It does not need further protection.

Some thought has to be given to the relative position of conduit and boxes. The position of the conduit is determined by the route it takes through the structure. The outside of the box has to be flush with the finished surface, or in the case of a surface system the back of the box must be on the surface. The positions of the conduit and box being fixed independently of each other by different considerations, it may happen that the conduit is not in line with any of the outlet holes in the box, and some method has to be devised to overcome this mismatch.

Figure 3.9a shows surface conduit with a set in it to enter a surface box.

It is difficult to make this look neat and it is better to use a distance saddle and a special box which makes it unnecessary to set the conduit. Such a box is shown in Figure 3.9b. When the conduit is buried in the structure, it may have to be set as shown in Figure 3.9c. If the conduit is far enough inside the surface, a back-entry box can be used as in Figure 3.9d, but it must be remembered that this introduces a fairly sharp bend in the conduit which could make it harder to pull in the cable. Another possibility is to put the box in line with the conduit and fit an extension ring to the box to bring the cover forward to the surface. This is shown in Figure 3.9e.

When buried conduit has to feed surface distribution boards or switches, the conduit must be brought into a flush recessed box so that the cables enter the surface board or switch through the back. If necessary an extension ring has to be placed between the box and the surface. Figure 3.9f shows an example of buried conduit feeding a fuseboard on the surface.

Most buildings larger than a single dwelling have a three-phase supply, although nearly all the equipment in them is single phase. Although the regulations allow one to run television and telephone cables in the same conduit,

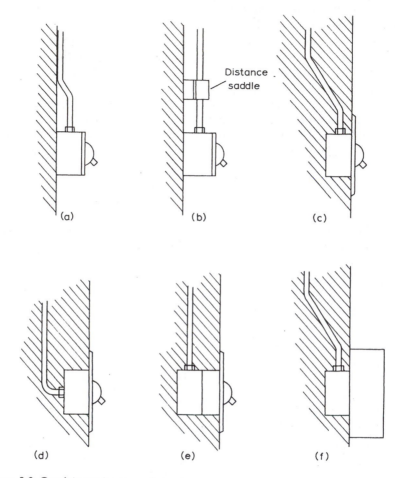

Figure 3.9 Conduit entries to equipment

provided that the lower voltage circuits are insulated for the highest voltage present, it is better not to do so. BS 6701:1994 recommends that there be a minimum distance between mains (Band II) and telecommunications circuits (Band I).

The next matter to receive our attention is how to fix conduit. Figure 3.10 shows various devices for fixing conduits. The pipehook or crampet, Figure 3.10a, is a satisfactory and simple fixing, but is too unsightly to be used on surface work. It can be driven into timber, brick or masonry, but is more likely to be dislodged than a screwed fixing; where the conduit is to be buried in plaster after it has been fixed, this does not matter because the plaster will hold the conduit in place, but where the conduit is to remain exposed a firmer fixing is desirable. The saddle hook shown in Figure 3.10b is by far the commonest fixing. It passes round the conduit and is secured to the wall by two screws. The only advantage of the clip shown in Figure 3.10c is that it saves one screw. It is not as secure as the saddle and the cost saving is not sufficient for a good engineer to use it.

Sockets and other conduit fittings necessarily have a larger outside diameter than the conduit itself. If these components are tight to a wall, the conduit must be slightly proud of the wall. Because of this, when an ordinary saddle is tightened, it will tend to distort the conduit. This can be prevented by the use of a spacer saddle, Figure 3.10d, which has the same thickness as the sockets. The spacer saddle has the further advantage that it prevents the conduit from touching damp plaster and cement which could corrode and discolour decoration.

When conduit is fixed to concrete, the time taken to drill and plug holes in the concrete is a very large proportion of the installation time. A spacer bar saddle has only one screw to be fixed to the wall and the saving in time can be greater than the extra cost of the material.

The distance saddle shown in Figure 3.10e holds the conduit about 10 mm from the wall. This spacing eliminates the ledge between the conduit and the

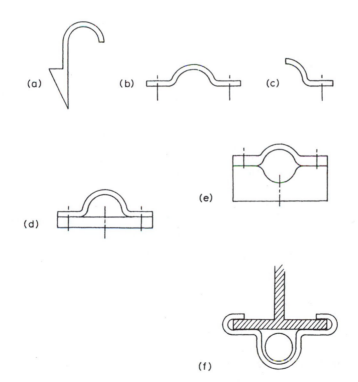

Figure 3.10 Conduit fixings

wall where dust can collect and makes it possible to decorate the wall behind the conduit. It also makes it impossible for minute drops of moisture to collect in the crack between conduit and wall and thus reduces the possibilities of corrosion. For these reasons, distance saddles are almost invariably specified by hospital boards and local authorities for surface conduit.

Conduit often runs across or along steel girders or joists, either exposed or within a false ceiling. It is not desirable to drill and tap structural steelwork and it is better to use girder clips of the type illustrated in Figure 3.10f. Whilst standard girder clips can be bought from conduit manufacturers, it is usually simpler to make special clips to suit individual conditions on each job. For multiple run and runs with other services, uni-strut is often used.

Electrical conduit is not thick enough to support its own weight over long distances without sagging. The supports must, therefore, be at quite close intervals, and the maximum distances which should be allowed between supports are as follows:

	Horizontal	Vertical
20 mm conduit	1.75 m	2.0
25 and 32 mm conduit	2.0 m	2.5
40 mm and over	2.25 m	2.5

The IEE Guidance Note 1 and the IEE On-Site Guide both give guidance on the maximum spacing of conduit fastenings.

The cables are drawn into the conduit with the help of a steel tape and a draw cable. The steel tape has a hemispherical brass cap on the end which prevents its sticking on irregularities at joints of the conduit and also helps guide it round bends. The tape also has a loop at its other end and a steel draw cable is attached to this. The cables themselves are then attached to the other end of the draw cable. The electrician attaches the cables by threading them through a series of loops in the draw cable. They should not all be attached to the same point otherwise there is a significant, sudden enlargement in the bunch of cables and this presents an edge which can catch in the bore of the conduit and which will be difficult to negotiate bends. When each cable is looped through the draw cable, it is folded back on itself and the end is taped. This gives a smooth surface to be pulled through the conduit and prevents sharp ends of small strands of cable from sticking out and catching the inside of the conduit. The method of connection is shown in Figure 3.11.

Pulling cable through conduit is a job for electrician and mate. One pushes the steel tape with the draw cable attached to it from one draw-in box to the next: as soon as the tape appears at the receiving box, the other takes it and pulls gently from that end. The latter then pulls the draw cable and finally the bunch of cables while the former feeds them into the conduit. The person feeding the cables in must do so carefully and must guide the cables so that they do not cross or twist over each other as they enter the conduit. If they

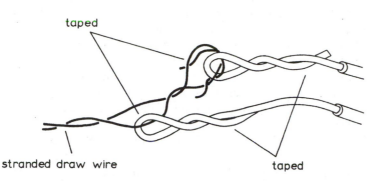

taping over loops and ends of wires not drawn

Figure 3.11 Connection of cable to draw cable

are allowed to twist, the whole bunch may stick and even if they can be forced in, it may be impossible to withdraw some of them later. The whole job requires great care and needs cooperation between the two people at opposite ends of the run. It is a help if they are within sight of each other and essential that they should be within earshot of each other. On the rare occasions when the run of conduit through the building from one draw-in box to the next makes it impossible for shouted directions to be heard from one end to the other, a third person will have to be called in to stand halfway and relay messages, or use an intercom.

In hot weather, the insulation of the cables is liable to become soft and tacky. Drawing it through the conduit may be made easier by rubbing French chalk on the cables. In other circumstances, when friction between the cables and the conduit is high and makes pulling in difficult, it may be advantageous to apply a thin coating of grease or tallow wax to the cables.

Plastic conduit

PVC conduit is being increasingly used in place of heavy gauge steel conduit. Its advantages are that it is cheaper and more easily installed than steel conduit and that it is non-corrosive and unreactive with nearly all chemicals. Although it is incombustible, it does soften and melt in fires and cannot be used at temperatures above 65 °C. At low temperatures, it becomes brittle and should not be used where it will be exposed to temperatures below 0 °C. Most specifications call for high-impact grade heavy-gauge PVC, which is tough enough to withstand the ill-treatment which all material receives on building sites. It will protect cables inside it just as well as steel conduit from nails accidentally driven into the conduit, but it is not quite as resistant as steel conduit to heavy blows and to crushing.

Heavy gauge PVC conduit is not resistant to blows, but has a slightly higher temperature range than the high impact grade, and is suitable for many types of industrial installation. Light-gauge conduit is cheaper but not so robust and may not always withstand the conditions existing on a building-site.

As the conduit is made of an insulating material, it does not provide a means of earth continuity. A separate circuit protective conductor must, therefore, be pulled into the conduit along with the other cables. A PVC insulated cable of adequate cross section may be used for this the circuit protective conductor as well as for the phase conductors. When a separate-circuit protective conductor is used, it may be necessary to connect lengths of it at wiring points. Therefore, PVC conduit fittings are supplied with an earth terminal.

As explained in the description of steel conduit, there are situations in which flexible conduit has to be used. In a steel conduit system, the flexibles do not provide earth continuity and a separate circuit protective conductor has to be run along each flexible length. If a large number of such connections occurs, one of the chief advantages of a steel conduit system, namely the way it gives earth continuity, is lost. In that case, it may be as well to use PVC conduit with a separate circuit protective conductor throughout.

Lengths of PVC conduit are joined by an unscrewed coupler which is cemented to the two pieces of conduit to be connected by means of a special solvent. The solvent used is made particularly for this application and is supplied by the makers of the conduit. PVC conduit boxes for use with PVC conduit have short sockets which make it possible to connect the conduit to the box with a coupler of the same type as is used for connecting lengths of conduit. The PVC can also be threaded, and push fit to threaded adaptors are made with the aid of which connections to boxes and equipment can be made in the same way as for steel conduit.

PVC has a high coefficient of expansion and provision must be made for thermal expansion wherever there is liable to be a temperature change of 25 °C or more and also wherever a run of more than 8 m occurs. The necessary allowance is made by means of expansion couplers. An expansion coupler is a coupling of extended length, one end of which is bored to a standard depth and the other end of which has a sliding fit over a longer distance than the standard coupling depth. Expansion is liable to make PVC conduit sag more readily than steel conduit and it needs fixing at closer intervals. Saddles should be fitted at a spacing of about 900 mm.

Bends can be made in PVC conduit as in steel conduit, but it is essential to use a bending spring inside the conduit to prevent the cross section becoming reduced in the bending process. The smaller sizes can generally be bent cold, but 32 mm conduit and larger must be gently heated for a distance of about 300 mm on either side of the intended bend.

One has to remember the susceptibility of PVC to high temperatures if one proposes to suspend luminaires from PVC conduit boxes. The heat from the lamp is conducted through the flexible cable and through the fixing screws, and it could happen that it softens the PVC box. To overcome this problem, it is possible to provide the boxes with metal inserts.

PVC conduit is made not only in the normal circular cross section but also with an oval section. The reduced depth of an oval section enables it to be accommodated within the thickness of plaster in places where the use of round conduit would make it necessary to chase the brickwork behind the plaster. This makes the oval conduit very useful for switch drops and for small domestic installations. In the latter case, it makes it very easy to add new wiring in an old house. The electrician can cut away and repair plaster whereas help might well be wanted from another tradesman if brickwork needed cutting.

The same PVC material is made as rectangular and semicircular channelling. This is intended primarily as a protection over PVC insulated PVC sheathed cable where the latter is installed on the surface of walls. It can also be used as a protection to PVC/PVC cable when the latter is buried in plaster, the justification for this use being that it saves depth and that the side of the cable next to the structural part of the wall does not need protection.

Flexible PVC conduit is available in two types. In the one, flexibility is conferred by a corrugated construction. In the other, the PVC itself is a plasticized grade so that the flexibility is a property of the material itself. Flexible PVC conduit can be used to negotiate awkward bends and in situations where rigid conduit would be difficult to install, and it is sometimes resorted to for the solution of unforeseen problems which so often seem to arise in the course of building work. There is, however, a danger to using it in this way. It is possible to take such advantage of the flexibility that the conduit curves so sharply that it is impossible to pull cables through it. If this happens the problem of installing the conduit has been solved only by the creation of a more difficult problem for the next stage of the erection process. Flexible conduit should, therefore, be used with caution.

PVC sheathed cable

There are many cases in which wiring can be installed in PVC/PVC without further protection. For example, this may be done in any voids in a building such as false ceilings and wooden floors. When the cable runs parallel to joists in a wooden floor, it can be clipped to the sides of the joists. When it has to run across them it is better to thread it through holes drilled in the neutral axis of the joists than to notch the top of the joists. Holes drilled on the neutral axis weaken the joist less than notches cut in the top, and because the cable is further from the floorboards on top of the joists, it is safer from nails driven into the floor. BS 7671 states that a cable passing through a timber joist must be 50 mm from the top or bottom of the joist, or be mechanically protected.

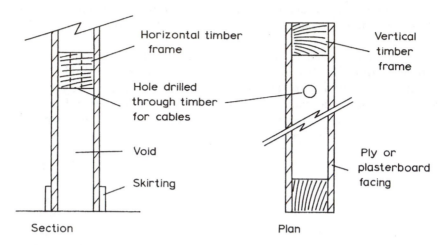

Figure 3.12 Dry partition

New buildings have internal partitions constructed of timber studding with light plasterboard facing, as illustrated in Figure 3.12, or preconstructed partitioning. This is particularly the case with proprietary industrialized systems of building. Such a partition has a void within it which is used for engineering services, and this is also a situation in which PVC sheathed cable without further protection is the most suitable system of wiring, provided that the cable is at least 50 mm from the surface. Voids of this sort, in which PVC sheathed cable is run, are usually sufficiently accessible to make rewiring, if not easy, at least possible. Fixing of accessories is made easy by the use of dry liner boxes as illustrated in Chapter 1 (Figure 1.1).

It may happen that the building structure is such that PVC sheathed cable on its own is the most suitable system to use, but that there are a few places where cable has to drop in plastered walls or run across floors. It is then desirable to give the cable additional protection at these places by running it inside conduit at these places only. This has the additional advantage of making rewiring easier. As the conduit is used only for short lengths for local protection, both light-gauge steel and PVC conduit are suitable.

PVC sheathed cable may be buried in plaster without damage. There is, however, the possibility that nails may be accidentally driven into the cables when pictures are being fixed to walls. Ideally, the cable should therefore be protected by conduit, but if there is not sufficient depth of plaster to make this possible it can still be given protection by shallow rigid PVC or galvanized metal channelling as shown in Figure 3.13. Many authorities feel that even this is not necessary. BS 7671 specifies areas within a wall in which cables are installed at a depth of less than 50 mm, where the cables do not need additional protection. Guidance is also given in the IEE Guidance Note

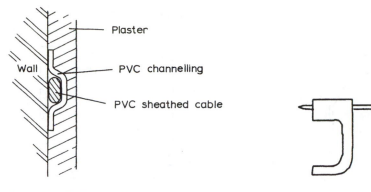

Figure 3.13 Cable buried in plaster   *Figure 3.14* Clip

1 and the IEE On-Site Guide. The basic rule is that cables can be run under plaster at a depth of less that 50 mm without protection, in straight lines between accessories, also within 150 mm of a change of direction of the wall.

There are situations where the appearance of an installation is of secondary importance, and where at the same time a surface system will not receive rough usage. Such a case might occur in an old building used for commercial purposes or in simple huts at a holiday camp. PVC sheathed cable may then be run on exposed surfaces without further protection. Since it is visible it will not be damaged accidentally by people trying to fix things to the walls.

PVC sheathed cable is fixed with moulded plastic clips. An example is illustrated in Figure 3.14. The clips should be spaced appropriate to the size of cables. IEE Guidance Note 1 Selection and Erection of Equipment and the IEE On-Site Guide give guidance on the spacing of cable clips.

Cable trunking

Where a large number of cables has to be run together, it is often convenient to put them in trunking. Trunking for electrical purposes is made of 18-gauge sheet steel, and is available in sizes ranging from 50 mm × 50 mm to 600 mm × 150 mm, common sizes being 50 mm × 50 mm, 75 mm × 100 mm, 150 mm × 75 mm and 150 mm × 150 mm although 50 mm × 100 mm and 100 mm × 100 mm are also available. It is usually supplied in 2 m lengths and one complete side is removable, as shown in Figure 3.15. The removable side, or lid, either screws on or clips on with a snap action. The latter arrangement is cheaper but a little more awkward to handle.

A variety of bends, tees and junctions is available from all manufacturers of such trunking. Some of these are shown in Figure 3.15. They enable the trunking to be taken round corners, to reduce in size as the number of cables is reduced and to allow a main run to serve a number of branches.

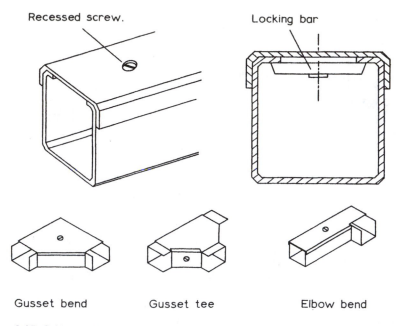

Recessed screw.

Locking bar

Gusset bend   Gusset tee   Elbow bend

Figure 3.15 Cable trunking

To put cables in such trunking one normally takes the lid off, lays the cables in and replaces the lid, but it is possible over short distances or straight length to pull the cables in as one does with conduit. Whichever method is adopted, the number of cables and size of trunking must be such that no damage is caused during installation. The same considerations apply as in the case of conduit.

Being so much larger than conduit, trunking can quite clearly not be buried in the walls of a building. It has to be run on a surface. There are occasions when there are many circuits running together inside a builder's work vertical duct which also contains other services such as heating pipes or gas. This is one situation in which cable trunking is an ideal way of installing the wiring. It can be similarly used in false ceilings. In both these cases, there must be sufficient doors or access traps to enable electricians to reach the trunking for rewiring.

Buildings such as assembly halls and gyms often have exposed steel lattice framework supporting the roof. It is then possible to run cable trunking neatly through the spaces of the lattice. Sometimes the architect will permit the cable trunking to be fixed under the beams and along them. Either method is simpler and neater than fixing several conduits parallel to each other on the surface of the ceiling, and has the further advantage that during the life of the building, the wiring can be altered very easily. Lighting trunking has additional folds in the cross section which makes it more rigid than conventional trunking and is able to span greater distances.

In workshops and laboratories there is usually a large number of machines and other equipment which have to be served with electricity. A conduit system can then become complex and, therefore, expensive. A simple and neat method of wiring these areas is to run trunking round the walls and to install all the circuits inside the trunking. In rooms of this class, this is quite acceptable and no one objects to the appearance of trunking visible on walls. Again there is the advantage that when machines are replaced or when new machines are installed, the consequent changes to the electrical service are easily made. The same consideration applies, but with added force, to factories.

When machines are placed in the centre of a room a good method of serving them is to run trunking at high level under the ceiling and drop to each machine with a length of conduit. It is, of course, possible to install conduit within the floor with an outlet near each machine, but there then has to be either rigid or flexible conduit at floor level, and if machines are moved or additional ones brought in the floor has to be dug up before the conduit can be extended to the new positions. For the initial installation the electrician would have to know the exact positions of the terminals of each machine before the floor is laid, and it is very seldom that either the builder or the final occupier of the factory can provide this information so early. The overhead system avoids the difficulty of locating exact positions of machines too early in the construction process and makes future changes more easy.

In some cases, particularly woodwork rooms in schools and colleges, long pieces of material such as timber have to be carried from stores across the room to various machines. It can then happen that vertical drops of conduit from the ceiling to the machines obstruct the material and cause difficulty in handling it. If this is likely to happen there may be no alternative to installing conduit within the floor, but the customer's attention should be drawn to the inflexibility of this arrangement.

It is also possible to install cable trunking neatly in the corner between a wall and ceiling. This is sometimes acceptable to an architect, and the author knows of at least one case where it has been done along the length of a public corridor in a block of flats. Similar situations could arise in offices and hospitals. It may be necessary to run many circuits the length of a corridor in such buildings and a conduit system would require many conduits cast into the ceiling slab of the corridor. If the slab is thin and heavily loaded structurally, as is apt to happen in modern building design, it becomes quite a serious problem to get the conduit into the slab within the restricted width of a corridor. The difficulty is avoided if the architect can be persuaded to accept a neat piece of surface trunking. There are now several proprietary systems of trunking specifically designed for such an application and giving a reasonably neat finished appearance.

The sides of cable trunking can be drilled to make holes at which conduit can enter the trunking. Joining conduit to trunking may be convenient where one circuit leaves a line followed by several circuits. All such holes must be fitted with smooth bore bushes to avoid sharp edges, which could damage insulation. If PVC sheathed cables run for part of their length in trunking, that is to say continue free without further protection, the edge of the hole in the trunking must be protected by a rubber grommet, or a suitable packing gland, sometimes referred to as a 'stuffing gland'. Should the metallic trunking not br required to serve as a circuit protective conductor, it must be erected so as to give good earth continuity, since it is an exposed conductive part.

Plastic trunking

Cable trunking is also made out of rigid high-impact PVC. In this case, the lid clips on, as will be clear from the cross section in Figure 3.16. Bends and fittings similar to those for steel trunking are made, and the plastic trunking is used in exactly the same way as steel trunking. Since the trunking is non-conductive, an additional circuit protective conductor(s) must be provided for earth protection to the circuit(s) served by the trunking.

Proprietary systems

A number of proprietary systems of wiring have been introduced in the last few years. Some of these are intended specifically for use with particular methods of industrialized building, while others are intended to industrialize the wiring operation independently of the building method so that they should be equally useful for all methods of building. One of the latter is the Simplex PVC System.

This consists of ordinary PVC insulated cables drawn into a PVC conduit of oval section. The circuit protective conductor is moulded in with the conduit, as can be seen from Figure 3.17. Each of the other cables has its own passageway within the conduit. The conduit itself is made from a flexible

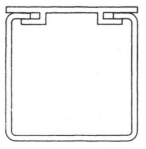

Figure 3.16 PVC trunking

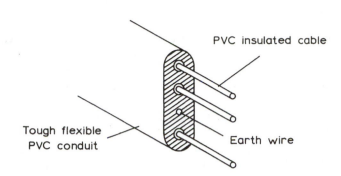

PVC insulated cable

Tough flexible
PVC conduit

Earth wire

Figure 3.17 Simplex system

grade of PVC and the entire assembly of insulated cable within conduit is flexible. From the installer's drawings, the manufacturers make a kit consisting of cable already within the conduit, cut and formed to the lengths needed on the building. The kit is delivered to site and simply laid in position, a process which eliminates most of the ordinary site work required for a conduit system. Although it is supplied with the cable already in the conduit, the system is rewirable because each cable is loose in its own passage. Suitable conduit boxes for junctions and accessories are supplied as part of the system.

There are problems which can arise with such a system. The conduit and cable are cut to size at the factory from drawings. A slight error in setting out of the building can result in the kits not fitting at site, with many unpleasant recriminations between designer, supplier and installer. Discrepancies can occur even if dimensions are taken on site; usually a typical house or room is measured and all of that type are made the same. If the building setting out varies from one to another, some of the kits may not fit exactly and the site electrician may have some adjustments to do. If every room has to be individually measured, a great deal of the time-saving of the system is lost.

Another system takes the form of trunking in the shape of skirting, which is placed around the bottom of walls in place of ordinary skirting. The system includes suitable corner pieces and boxes to hold socket outlets and other accessories. This particular system is very useful for buildings constructed from concrete slabs precast in moulds, but it is still necessary to find some way of running switch drops in the wall and of taking cables from one room to another without blocking door openings.

There are several other proprietary systems, which generally tend to be variations on these themes, and which all have their individual advantages and disadvantages.

MICC

Mineral insulated cable has been described in Chapter 2. It was there explained that its chief advantage is that it needs no protection and can be put into places where it would be difficult to install other cabling systems. The fact that it needs no protection and is so robust makes it very easy to install.

It can be clipped to walls and ceilings in a similar way to PVC sheathed cable. Sharp bends should, however, be avoided, and a safe rule is to keep the radius of each bend to more than six times the cable outside diameter. Clips or saddles should be fixed at a spacing equal to 75 times the cable outside diameter. If the cable is to be buried within the structure, it should be fixed down firmly before concrete or cement is poured over it.

Accessories are contained in standard boxes and the MICC cable is brought into the boxes. Where it enters a conduit box or the terminal box of a machine, it ends in a seal and a gland. The seal forms the end of the cable and prevents moisture getting into the mineral insulation; it seals the cable. The gland joins the cable to the cable entry on the box, switch or other equipment and provides earth continuity between the cable sheath and the box or equipment case. An assembled seal is shown in Figure 3.18 and the procedure for making it is as follows.

The end of the cable is cut to length and a notch is made round the sheath with a ringing tool. The sheath is then stripped off the cable, from the cable end to the notch, and the mineral insulation is broken away to expose the conductors. Alternatively a proprietary stripping/ringing tool may be used. At this stage, the gland should be slipped over the cable and pushed up out of the way while the seal is being finished. The gland will then be in place to be brought forward over the seal after the latter is completed.

The insulating sleeves are now assembled. The sleeves are cut to the length required, which may need extension sleeving for very long tails. When the sleeve is pushed through the hole in the cap, the wedge prevents it from being pulled right through and keeps it in place after the seal is assembled.

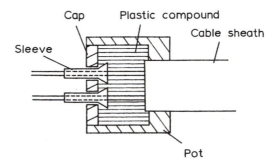

Figure 3.18 MICC cable seal

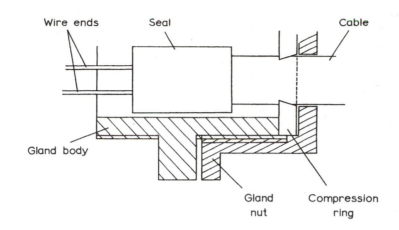

Figure 3.19 MICC gland

The next step is to push the pot over the end of the cable. It is made to suit the cable and is a fairly tight fit, so that it has to be screwed on. It is screwed on until the cable sheath is level with the shoulder at the base of the pot. The pot is then packed with a plastic compound, which is pressed firmly in to fill the whole of the pot. The cap and sleeve sub-assembly is now pushed over the ends of the cables and forced into the end of the pot, which is crimped over the cap. This final operation can conveniently be done with a combined compression and crimping tool specially made for this particular job. It is good practice to test each end for insulation resistance after the end has been made off; if the test is left until both ends are complete, there is no way of knowing which end is faulty should one of the ends be made off incorrectly.

The gland is shown in Figure 3.19. It consists of a gland body, a compression ring and a gland nut. The compression ring is comparatively soft and as the nut is tightened onto the body the ring is compressed between them and deforms. As it does so, the weakened ridge on its inside diameter bites into the outside of the cable sheath and makes a firm electrical and mechanical bond between the sheath and the gland. The gland is thus fixed to the cable over the seal and has a projecting male thread which can be inserted into a luminaire or conduit box and secured by a ring bush and back nut. For hazardous areas a special gland is required

External wiring

It is sometimes necessary to run cables from one building to another. This can be done either with cables running under the ground or with overhead cables. Cables that are to be run underground can be armoured paper, armoured PVC or MICC cables. All these are strong enough to be laid directly in the ground and buried, but in order that they should have reasonable protection against damage they should be laid at least 600 mm below the ground level. Since they all have metal armouring or sheathing, no protection in the ground is really necessary, but it is very usual to provide a bed of sand, and cover the cable loosely with tiles before the trench in which it has been laid is backfilled. If someone later has occasion to dig the ground near the cable they will hit the tiles first and be warned that there is something underneath them. Tiles are available for this use which have lettering on them saying 'Danger – Electric Cables'; they are known as electrical tiles. A cheaper alternative is plastic tape with the same lettering. This has almost universally superseded tiles although it may be questioned whether it will be noticed before the digging tool has gone through it and the cable. Another method is to install over ground markers showing the line of the run of the underground cable

It is also possible to bury conduit in the ground and pull cables through it in the ordinary way. Because of the danger of corrosion in the soil this is not however a good practice. It is better to use builder's polythene pipe as ducts instead of conduit, and in fact this is very often done. It is harder to provide frequent access to underground ducts than to conduit in a building, and the lengths between draw-in points can become rather large. At the same time there is plenty of room in the ground for large-diameter pipes, and it is a sound precaution never to use anything smaller than a 100 mm polythene or earthenware duct.

In certain cases it is common practice to use polythene conduit underground. This happens for example when the cable from a communal TV aerial has to cross from one building to another on the same site. It is also the standard method of bringing telephone cables into a building in urban areas where the main telephone cables are in the road outside the new building. Telephone cables are quite small and can be easily pulled into 20 mm conduit over considerable distances.

Buried cables rely on conduction of heat through the soil to dissipate the heat generated by the current in the resistance of the cables. If there are other services which heat the soil locally then the rate of dissipation of heat could be reduced, and the current carrying capacity of the cables would then also be reduced. The obvious example of a service which would have this effect is a district heating main. But in addition to this consideration some thought must be given to what happens when maintenance work is done on underground services. It is undesirable that workmen who may have to expose a length of buried gas or water main should have to dig near a live electric cable. There are thus two reasons why underground cables should be kept well away from other buried services. A good practical rule is to have a minimum distance apart of 2 m.

There may be cases where cables have to cross from one building to another overhead. This situation will normally arise where cost is the overriding factor and neither restrictions on headroom nor appearance are of great concern. For very short distances, as for example from a house to a shed, a piece of conduit can support its own weight over the gap to be spanned and an ordinary conduit system can be used. This method is not suitable for distances of more than about 3 m. For larger distances special overhead cables must be used. Cables made for this purpose consist of solid drawn copper or aluminium conductors covered with a PVC sheath and are suitable for spans of up to 30 m. They can traverse greater distances provided they are supported every 30 m. If supports cannot be found on walls or roofs then wooden or metal poles must be erected to carry cleats on which the cable can be supported.

The limitation on span can be overcome by the use of a catenary cable, which can be used in one of two ways. A separate catenary cable of adequate strength can be strung between the two end supports and a sheathed cable can be suspended from the catenary at regular intervals of about 2 or 3 m.

Alternatively it is possible to obtain cable which incorporates a catenary cable within the sheath. Such cable is specially made for overhead use, and the manufacturer's recommendations on spacing should be noted and adhered to.

Since air is a good insulator, overhead cables which are out of reach of people or animals do not need further insulation. The cables we have just described are sheathed, but overhead line cable is also made consisting of bare copper or aluminium conductors of a size to have enough mechanical strength to support themselves. These cables can span long distances and are used by electricity companies for their distribution systems outside towns. They are used much more in public supply systems than in building services. Whatever method of running overhead cables is used, at the end of the overhead section the cables must be connected to the cables within the building in a terminal block and in such a way that there is no mechanical strain on them.

Cable entries

The entry of cables from the outside to the inside of a building sometimes causes difficulty. There must obviously be a hole in the wall which has to be tight round the cable and which has to be sealed to prevent dirt, vermin and moisture entering. Whether the cable is an armoured type laid directly in the ground or whether it is drawn into a duct, the most practicable way of making the entry into the building is by means of an earthenware duct built through the wall below ground level. When the cable has to bend up to rise on the inside face of the external wall, a duct bend can be built into the wall.

After the cable has been pulled through the polythene or earthenware duct, a seal is made round it within the duct with a bituminous mastic compound. Normally this is inserted from the inside of the building. The essential requirement is to make the seal watertight; it will be readily understood that a seal which prevents water coming through will also stop dirt and small animals. In difficult cases one can make a metal plate to overlap the earthenware duct with a hole in it of a diameter to be a push fit on the cable. The duct is filled with mastic, the metal plate is pushed over the cable to cover the end of the duct and is screwed back to the wall, and the edges of the plate are then pointed with mastic. This construction gives an effective water seal.

Temporary installations

Temporary installations must be just as safe as permanent ones. There is therefore no reason for departing from any of the principles of design and installation which are used for permanent systems. The methods of cable sizing and schemes of distribution which are described in the following chapters apply to temporary installations as well as to permanent ones. The methods of installing cables which we have discussed in this chapter are all designed to give adequate safety and can be used on any temporary installation.

This book deals with design rather than installation, and methods of wiring have been described from this point of view. Standards relevant to this chapter are:

BS 31	Steel conduit and fittings
BS 731	Flexible steel conduit
BS 951	Earthing clamps
BS 4568	Steel conduit and fittings with metric threads
BS 4607	Non-metallic conduit and fittings
BS 4678	Cable trunking
BS EN 60423	Outside diameters of conduits
BS EN 50086–1	Conduits for electrical installations

IEE Wiring Regulations particularly applicable to this chapter are:

Chapter 52
IEE Guidance Note 1
IEE On-Site Guide

Chapter 4

Cable rating

An important part of any electrical design is the determination of the size of cables. The size of cable to be used in a given circuit is governed by the current which the circuit has to carry, so the design problem is to decide the size of cable needed to carry a known current. Two separate factors have to be taken into account in assessing this, and the size of cable chosen will depend on which factor yields the most suitable value in each particular case.

A conductor carrying a current is bound to have some losses due to its own resistance. These losses appear as heat and will raise the temperature of the insulation. The current the cable can carry is limited by the temperature to which it is safe to raise the insulation. Now the temperature reached under continuous steady state conditions is that at which the heat generated in the conductor is equal to the heat lost from the outside of the insulation. Heat loss from the surface is by radiation and conduction and depends on the closeness of other cables and on how much covering or shielding there is between the cable and the open atmosphere. Thus the heat loss and, therefore, the equilibrium temperature reached depends on how the cable is installed; that is to say whether it is in trunking, or conduit, on an exposed surface, how close to other cables, and so on. To avoid tedious calculations, tables have been prepared and published (appendix to BS 7671) which list the maximum allowable current for each type and size of cable.

The tables give a current rating for each type and size of cable for a particular method of installation and at a particular ambient temperature. For these basic conditions a cable must be chosen the rated current of which is at least equal to the working current. For other methods of installation and ambient temperatures the tables give various correction factors. The fuse or circuit breaker rating has to be divided by these to give a rated current and a cable then selected such that its tabulated current is at least equal to this nominal current.

Particular care has to be taken where cable is run in a thermally insulated space. With increasing attention to thermal insulation of walls this is likely to become a more frequently occurring situation, and BS 7671 now require a cable to be de-rated when it is used in such a situation.

As is explained in Chapter 9, every cable, which may be subject to over-load, short circuit, or earth fault, must be protected against overload and/or short circuit. A generic term is overcurrent, which is any current that exceeds the rated value of current-carrying capacity of the cable. The overcurrent may be caused by (a) an overload, which is an overcurrent occurring in a circuit that is electrically sound; (b) a short circuit, which is an overcurrent between live conductors having a potential between them in normal circumstances, due to a fault of negligible impedance between them, or (c) an earth fault. The working current must be such that if it is exceeded, the resulting rise in temperature will not become dangerous before the protective device cuts off the current.

When a short circuit occurs, the cable is carrying the fault current during the time it takes the protective device, whether a fuse or a circuit breaker, to operate and disconnect the circuit. Because this time is very short, the cable is heated adiabatically and the temperature rise depends on the fault current and the specific heat capacity of the cable. The short circuit current depends upon the impedance of the source and the cables in the short circuit. The earth fault current depends on the earth fault loop impedance, which is explained in Chapter 9. This impedance is the sum of the impedance of the phase conductor R_1 and the impedance of the protective conductor R_2 and the impedance of the source. BS 7671 requires that both the earth-fault loop impedance, the short-circuit impedance, and the time for the device to operate are such that its protective device will operate before a dangerous temperature is reached.

In most cases the protective device will have a breaking capacity greater than the prospective short-circuit current, and this allows one to assume that the current will be disconnected sufficiently quickly to prevent overheating during a short circuit. The cable size selected from the rating tables for the working current is then adequate.

If the protective device is selected for short-circuit protection only, then a check must be made by means of the formula

$$t = \frac{k^2 S^2}{I^2}$$

where t = time in seconds in which protective device opens at a current of I A
   k = a constant, given in the Regulations for different cables
   S = minimum cross-sectional area of conductor in the cable, mm^2
   I = short circuit current, A.

If necessary the cable size must be increased above that provisionally selected from the tables in order to satisfy this condition.

Alternatively, the cable size can be retained and a fuse or circuit breaker with a faster operating time used.

The protection must also operate if the overcurrent is not a short circuit but a comparatively small multiple of the working current, an overload. HRC fuses and circuit breakers can take up to four hours to operate at a current 1.5 times their rated current. The cable temperature will rise during this time and the working current must allow a safety margin to take account of this. The rating tables in BS 7671 include the necessary margin for HRC fuses and circuit breakers.

However, rewireable fuses (BS 3036) take longer to operate and a larger margin is therefore necessary. The rating tables therefore include a factor by which cables must be de-rated if rewireable fuses are going to be used to protect the cables.

The resistance of the conductor also results in a drop of voltage along its length. Because of this drop, the voltage at the receiving end is less than that at the sending end. Since all electrical equipment used in a building is designed to work on the nominal voltage of the supply in the building, it is necessary to limit the amount by which the voltage drops between the point of entry into the building and the outlet serving an appliance. In other words, the voltage drop in the wiring must be kept reasonably low. BS 7671 require that the voltage drop in the wiring should not exceed a value appropriate to the safe functioning of the equipment. BS 7671 limits the volts drop to 4 per cent of the nominal voltage.

The drop in volts is obtained by Ohm's law as the product of the actual current flowing and the total resistance of the actual length of cable. One therefore wants to know the resistance per unit length of cable. The cable-rating tables already mentioned give this, but for convenience of use, instead of giving it as ohms per metre, they quote it as voltage drop per amp per metre length of cable. This makes it a very simple and quick matter to calculate the actual drop over the actual length for the actual current. If this is more than the acceptable drop the larger size of cable must be chosen and the calculation repeated.

Referring to BS 7671, Table 4A1 shows various accepted methods of installing wiring systems; these are termed 'reference methods'. Reference methods vary; reference method 1 is sheathed cables clipped direct or lying on a non-metallic surface; reference method 3 refers to cables installed in conduit or trunking; method 4 refers to single-core cables enclosed in conduit installed in a thermally insulating wall or ceiling, the conduit being in contact with the thermal insulation on one side.

From Table 4D2A, which is at slight variance from Table 4D5A, with the tabulated rating of a 2.5 mm^2 single-phase multicore thermoplastic non-armoured 70 °C PVC cable (typically twin and earth) is, reference method 1 given 27 A, reference method 3, 24 A, and reference method 4, 19.5 A. Table 4D5A refers to installation method 15 and reference method 1. Note the differences between installation and reference methods. Note how the current rating of the cable increases as the installation method allows more heat to be dissipated.

The assumed ambient temperature is 30 °C. The maximum conductor operating temperature is 70 °C. Therefore it can be assumed that the above currents will raise the temperature of the cable by 40 °C.

The tables assume that the circuits are run individually. It is normal practice to run more than one circuit in an enclosure or to bunch multicore (more than one core) together. If the circuits were grouped with other circuits, or if multicore cables were bunched with other multicores, the heat dissipation properties of the circuits or cables would be reduced; the more cables there are in the group the dissipation properties of the cable are reduced. Then if the cables were loaded to their ungrouped level when they are grouped they would overheat. The number of grouped circuits must therefore be taken into account. Table 4B1 gives correction factors to apply for grouping Cg. If an enclosed circuit as in method 3 or 4 is taken, or it is bunched and clipped direct to a non-metallic surface multicore (method 1) for two circuits or two multicore cables, the correction factor is 0.80. This means that for two circuits, only allowed 80 per cent of the single circuit current is allowed. For three circuits, the factor is 0.70 This means that for three circuits, only 70 per cent of the single circuit or multicore current is allowed.

How is the factor applied?

Figure 4.1 represents one single-phase thermoplastic 70 °C circuit enclosed in conduit installed as reference method 3; the minimum fuse size is chosen from the range of fuses from BS88, the minimum rating of fuse is 50 A. For the fuse to protect the cable against overload, the minimum cable rating, Iz, is 50 A. Also, the minimum tabulated rating, It, for the cable is also 50 A. The methods of calculation in BS 7671 make 'It' the subject of the formulae used.

If the cable is grouped with three other circuits (four in total), the correction factor is 0.65. The correction factor is applied as a divisor to the protective device rating. Therefore the minimum rating Iz, or the minimum tabulated rating It of the cable will be

$$It = In/Cg = 50/0.65 = 76.92\,A$$

BS 88 Fuse

Design current Ib = 45A

Figure 4.1 Device rating related to design current

Figure 4.2 Effect of grouping cables

In other words a cable which will carry 76.92 A is acceptable, but the cable must be de-rated to a factor of 0.65:

$$76.92 \times 0.65 = 50$$

Therefore, in these conditions, the cable is rated at 50 A. We are selecting a larger size of cable because of the reduction in current carrying capacity due to grouping.

If the cable is installed in an ambient temperature of 30 °C and loaded with the maximum rated current, the final temperature will be 70 °C. Then, if the cable is installed at a temperature above 30 °C, the starting temperature of the cable will be higher, and the running temperature will also be higher. Therefore, to prevent the cable from overheating, we must make adjustments to the current carrying capacity of the cable, if it is installed in an ambient temperature above 30 °C. Table 4C1 relates to correction factors (Cg) for ambient temperature. For general purpose PVC at 35 °C the correction factor is 0.94. This means that the cable may only be loaded to 94 per cent of its 30 °C capacity.

Table 4C1 is for all protective devices other than rewireable fuses. For rewireable fuses, Table 4C2 is applicable.

If the above circuit is run with three other circuits (four in total), there are two correction factors to apply, one for grouping and one for ambient temperature above 30 °C. The minimum rating of the cable will be

$$Iz = In/Cg \times Ca = 50/(0.94 \times 0.65) = 81.83 \, A$$

One must also consider if the cable is run in heat-insulating material, whether its ability to dissipate heat will be impaired. To take this into consideration Table 52A gives the correction factor to apply when a cable is enclosed in thermal insulation.

The correction factor Ci is applied to the length of the cable. The formula is now amended to

$$Iz, \text{ or minimum } It = In/Cg \times Ca \times Ci$$

When considering overload protection earlier, it was mentioned that when a rewireable fuse was used, a factor of 0.725 is used. The formula is now amended to

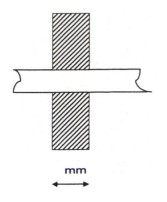

mm

Figure 4.3 Cables enclosed in thermal insulation

minimum It = In/Cg × Ca × Ci × 0.725

If any of the factors are not applicable, ignore them or replace with a 1.

Example 3 single-phase 240 V 36 A loads are to be supplied by means of 70 °C thermoplastic PVC twin and earth cables having copper conductors, 25 m in length, in an area having an ambient temperature of 35 °C (Ca = 0.94). The cables are touching and single-layer clipped to a non-metallic surface (for 3 circuits Cg = 0.79). The overcurrent device at the origin of the installation is a type-B MCB to BS EN 60898. Calculate the minimum permissible cable size.

Reference method = 1
Design current Ib = 36 A. Nominal rating of the device In = 40 A
Cg = 0.79, Ca = 0.94 Ca × Cg = C , where C = combined factor to apply
C = 0.79 × 0.94 = 0.7426
minimum tabulated rating It = In/C 40/0.7426 = 53.86 A

Consulting manufacturer's appropriate table, or at the BS 7671 Table 4D5A, column 4, It = 64 A. Therefore, the minimum size with respect to current carrying capacity is 10 mm².

Regulation group 525–01, states that the voltage at the terminals of a piece of equipment should be appropriate for the standard to which the equipment was manufactured. If no value is stated, the voltage should be such that the equipment operates safely. The safety aspect is satisfied if the volt drop between the terminals of the incoming supply and the terminals of the equipment, if directly connected to the mains, or the socket outlet, does not exceed 4 per cent of the nominal voltage of the mains.

$$230 \times \frac{4}{100} = 9.2\,V$$

We now need to check that the voltage drop in the $10\,mm^2$ cable is within these limits.

Table 4D2B gives voltage drop in millivolts per ampere per metre. To calculate the voltage drop, multiply

$$\frac{mV/amp/metre \otimes Ib \otimes Metres}{1000}$$

$$= \frac{4.4 \times 36 \times 25}{1000} = 3.96\,V$$

Therefore, the minimum permissible size is $10\,mm^2$.

If the circuit was protected by a rewireable fuse to BS 3036, the design of the circuit would be slightly different.

Reference method 1
Design current Ib = 36 A. Nominal rating of the device In = 45A
Cg = 0.79, Ca = 0.97,Ca × Cg × 0.725 = C , where C = combined factor to
    apply
C = 0.79 × 0.97 × 0.725 = 0.555
minimum tabulated rating It = In/C 45/0.555 = 81 A

Now look at Table 4D5A, column 4, It = 85. Therefore, the minimum size with respect to current carrying capacity is $16\,mm^2$.

$$\frac{mV/amp/metre \times Ib \times Metres}{1000}$$

$$= \frac{2.8 \times 36 \times 25}{1000} = 2.252\,V$$

Therefore, the minimum permissible size is $16\,mm^2$ ($10\,mm^2$ with type-B MCB to BS EN 60898). Note that semi-enclosed fuses should be rigorously avoided these days. BS 7671 expresses a preference for cartridge-type fuses.

In most cases, there will be a number of sub-mains from the electrical intake of the building to distribution fuse boards, and from each of these there will be a number of final circuits. The allowable voltage drop is the sum of the drops in the sub-mains and in the final circuits, and there is no restriction on how it is shared between the two. The position of each distribution board will affect the lengths both of sub-mains and of final circuits and thus of the voltage drop in each of them. There is no single correct way in which these parameters must be combined, and the design can only be done by a process of trial and error tempered by the designer's own experience and judgement. There is plenty of scope for a designer to exercise his personal initiative and intuition in positioning distribution boards and selecting cable sizes to arrive at an economical design. In general, it is a better all-round solution to take the final distribution board as near to the current, using equipment as possible, thus reducing the length of the final circuits to a minimum.

If the overcurrent protection device at the origin of the circuit is for short-circuit protection only, as would be the case for a motor circuit, then the formula stated in BS 7671 section 434–03 is employed:

$$t = \frac{k^2 \times S^2}{I^2}$$

where t = time taken to reach the limit temperature
K = is a factor taken from table 43A BS 7671
S = cross sectional area in mm2
I = fault current.

For example: a motor circuit is supplied by means of $4\,mm^2$ thermoplastic 70 °C PVC copper cables. The protection device at the origin of the circuit is a 50 A BS 88–2.1 fuse. The prospective short circuit current is 300 A. The K value for thermoplastic 70 °C PVC copper cables is 115. The time for the cable to reach its limit temperature is

$$t = \frac{115^2 \times 4^2}{300^2}$$
$$= 2.35 \text{ s}$$

To take a typical BS 88 fuse, 300 A, flowing through a 50 A fuse would disconnect in about 1.2. Therefore, the fuse would operate before the cable reached its limit temperature, the cable being protected against short circuit.

Because of the cable resistance, 10 m along the run the short-circuit current will be attenuated to 263 A, giving a time to reach the limit temperature of above 3 s. The disconnection time would, however, increase to about 2.5 s. The cable is still protected.

Mention should also be made of the circuit protective conductor. The function of this is described in Chapter 9. Under normal conditions it carries no current and it conducts electricity only when an earth fault occurs and, then, only for the short time before the protective device operates. BS 7671 gives two alternative ways of determining its size. The first is by the use of the same formula as above, transposed to make S the subject of the formula, as has been quoted above, for checking the short circuit rating of the live conductor. Alternatively, the regulations give a table which relates the size of the protective conductor to the size of the phase conductor. The effect is that for circuits up to 16 mm^2, the protective conductor minimum size must be equal to the line or phase conductor, for 25 mm^2 and 35 mm^2 phase conductors, the protective conductor must be at least 16 mm^2, and for phase conductors over 35 mm^2 the cross section of the protective conductor must be at least half the cross section of the phase conductor.

BS 7671 IEE Wiring Regulations particularly applicable to this chapter are:

Section   521–7
Section   522
Section   523
Section   524
Section   525
Section   543
Appendix   3
Appendix   4

Chapter 5

Circuits

The final outlets of the electrical system in a building are lighting points, socket outlets and fixed equipment. The wiring to each of these comes from an excess current protection device (fuse or circuit breaker) in a distribution board, but one fuse or CB can serve several outlets. If the circuit supplies current using equipment, wiring from one fuse or CB is known as the final circuit, and all the outlets fed from the same fuse or CB are on the same final circuit. The fuse or CB must be large enough to carry the largest steady current ever taken at any one instant by the whole of the equipment on that final circuit. Since the fuse or CB protects the cables, no cable forming part of the circuit may have a current carrying capacity less than that of the fuse, unless the characteristics of the load or supply are such that an overcurrent cannot occur. The size of both the fuse or CB and cable is, therefore, governed by the number and type of outlets on the circuit.

It is unusual to have a fuse of more than 45 A in a final distribution board in domestic premises, and the cables normally used for final circuits are 1.5 mm^2, 2.5 mm^2 and 6.0 mm^2, according to the nature of the circuit. Lighting is almost invariably carried out in 1.5 mm^2 cable and power circuits to socket outlets in 2.5 mm^2. 6.0 mm^2 and 10 mm^2 cable is used for circuits to cookers, instantaneous water heaters, showers, and other large current-using equipment, such as machine tools in workshops. These sizes are so usual that it is better for the designer to restrict the number of outlets on each final circuit to keep within the capacity of these cables than to specify larger cables. If he does choose the latter course there is a real danger that the site electrician will install the cables he is used to, instead of complying with the designer's specification. These considerations will not, of course, apply in a factory in which individual machines can take very heavy currents.

It is worth noting here that a single phase 1 hp motor takes a running current of about 6 A and a starting current of something under 30 A. These currents would also be taken by each phase of a three-phase 3 hp machine. Therefore, quite large machine tools impose no bigger a load than a cooker, and can be served from a fuseway on a standard distribution board. The distribution in a workshop or medium sized factory can follow the same principles as that in a domestic or commercial building. Indeed, in a technical college, the electrical load in the metal workshops can well be lower and impose fewer problems than that in the domestic science rooms with their many cookers.

For factories with heavier machinery, distribution boards with 60 A or 100 A fuses or CBs can be used, with correspondingly larger cables. For factories with very large loads, the normal type of distribution board ceases to be practicable and other means of arranging the connections to the machinery are adopted.

We have said that the fuse or CB must be rated for the largest current taken at any one instant by all the equipment on the circuit. This is not necessarily the sum of the maximum currents taken by all the equipment on the circuit, since it may not happen that all the equipment is on at the same time. One can apply a diversity factor to the total installed load to arrive at the maximum simultaneous load. To do this, one needs an accurate knowledge of how the premises are going to be used, which one can get by a combination of factual knowledge and intuition. IEE Guidance Note 1 and the IEE On-Site Guide include a scheme for applying the diversity factor, and circuits designed in accordance with this should comply with the regulations; nevertheless the author of this book thinks that a capable designer will not rely on such a rigid guide to the total exclusion of his own judgement. A general knowledge of life and how different buildings are used may be of more help than theoretical principles.

It will be easier to understand the ideas underlying the use of circuits intended for fused plugs if we first consider the limitations of other circuits.

The fuse or CB in a final circuit may not have a rating greater than that of the cables in the circuit. If it did, it would not protect the cables against overloads falling between the capacity of the cables and the normal current of the fuse. However, neither the designer of the building wiring nor the installer has any control over the sizes of flexible cables attached to portable appliances which will be plugged in at socket outlets, although BS 7671 is directed to fixed installations only. When electricity was first introduced for domestic use, the system adopted for house wiring in the UK was that 2 A socket outlets were provided to serve radios and portable lamps which would have small flexible cable, 5 A outlets were provided for larger equipment and 15 A sockets for the heaviest domestic appliances such as 3 kW fires, which would be supplied with substantial flexible cables. If carefully designed and properly used, such a system would give reasonable protection, not only to the permanent wiring of the building, but also to the flexibles and the portable appliances plugged in at the socket outlets. Unfortunately, the multiplicity of plugs and sockets made life difficult for the householder and tempted him to use multi-way adapters, which totally defeated the object of having different sized outlets. Also, the use of electricity has greatly increased since its first introduction to domestic and commercial premises, so that it has become necessary to have a large number of socket outlets in each dwelling and in every office. With the original system of wiring, it would have been necessary to have many more fuses, the fuseboards would have become larger, more numerous, or both, and the cost of the installation would have increased rapidly.

It was to overcome these difficulties that 13 A socket outlets with fused plugs were introduced a few years after the Second World War. The socket outlets are made to BS 1363 and the fuses that go in the plugs to BS 1362. The fuse in the plug protects the flexible cable. Any fault in the appliance or any damage to the flexible cable will blow the fuse in the plug; provided this fuse is correctly rated to protect the appliance, it does not matter if the fuse in the permanent wiring has a higher rating. This latter fuse now has to protect only the permanent wiring up to the socket outlet. The permanent wiring can, therefore, be designed without consideration for protection of appliances, which have been given their own protection. There is no longer any need to have different outlets for different classes of appliance, and it is possible to standardize on one type of socket and one type of plug.

This system depends on matching the fuse in the plug to the appliance. Fuses for these plugs are made to BS 1362 in ratings of 3 A, 5 A, 10 A and 13 A. Modern appliances are usually supplied with a moulded plug, and are properly fused by the manufacturer.

Fused plugs bring a further advantage. Whereas a 15 A socket had to be assumed to be feeding something taking 15 A, a 13 A socket with a fused plug may well be feeding equipment taking 2 A or less. Therefore, where there are several 13 A outlets, it becomes permissible to make use of a diversity factor in deciding on the circuit loading.

This is taken into account in the standard circuit arrangements given in the IEE Guidance Note 1 or the IEE On-Site Guide, which should be used wherever possible.

A ring circuit with socket outlets for 13 A fused plugs cabled in 2.5 mm^2 PVC cable and protected by a fuse or circuit breaker rated at 30 A or 32 A can serve any number of outlets but the floor area covered must not be more than 100 m^2. A radial circuit for this type of outlet can serve a floor area of 50 m^2 if it is cabled in 4 mm^2 cable and protected by a 30/32 A HRC fuse or circuit breaker. If it is cabled in 2.5 mm^2 cable and protected by any type of fuse or circuit breaker rated at 20 A, it is restricted to a floor area of 20 m^2. In either case there can be any number of outlets within this area.

Any number of fused spurs may be taken from any of these three circuits, but the number of unfused spurs is limited to the number of socket outlets on the circuit. Water heaters having a capacity of over 15 l, and comprehensive space heating schemes must be provided with their own circuit.

The cable sizes quoted are for copper conductors with PVC insulation. IEE Guidance Note 1 and the On-Site-Guide give different sizes for MICC cables.

Socket outlets of 15 A and 5 A must be assumed to supply appliances taking 15 A and 5 A respectively, and no diversity may be applied to circuits containing such outlets. The circuit may, however, contain any number of such outlets provided the rating of the protective device is equal to the sum of the ratings of the outlets on the circuit. Thus a circuit with a 15 A fuse may feed one 15 A socket or three 5 A sockets. The framers of these regulations had chiefly in mind domestic installations, and the arrangement may be departed from in non-domestic installations if the exact usage is known. To illustrate this we can take as an example a hospital ward in which a socket outlet next to each bed is needed for portable cardiographs or X-ray equipment. It is also desirable to ensure that only certain equipment can be connected to these sockets. This may be done by installing 15 A outlets and providing 15 A plugs only for the equipment which is to use these special outlets. It may be known that although there is to be one of these outlets next to each bed, only one patient in a ward will be treated at one time. In such a situation it is clear that twenty socket outlets could be put on one circuit and yet that circuit would never carry as much as 15 A, and an exception from the standard circuit could therefore be made or, alternatively, sockets which are similar to the BS 1363 pattern but with the earth pin turned through 90°. The fuse advantage of the plug is, therefore, maintained, but only dedicated equipment may be plugged in.

A cooker, whether served through a control switch or through a cooker control unit, should be on a circuit of its own. The cooker control unit may incorporate a socket outlet, which will be on the same circuit. The circuit rating should be that of the cooker. Two cookers in the same room may be on a single circuit provided its rating does not exceed 50 A. For domestic cooker circuits, IEE Guidance Note 1 and the IEE On-Site Guide give the diversity to be applied.

We have referred to a ring circuit and we must now consider what this is. As its name implies, a ring circuit is one which forms a closed ring; it starts at one of the ways of a distribution board, runs to a number of outlets one after another, and returns to the distribution board it started from. This is illustrated in Figure 5.1. The advantage of this arrangement is that current can flow from the fuseway to the outlets along both halves of the ring, so that at any one point the cable carries only part of the total current being taken by the whole circuit. It is this feature which makes it possible for the fuse rating to be greater than the cable current rating. The fuse carries the sum of the currents in the two halves of the ring and will blow when the current in one part of the ring is about half the fusing current of the fuse. For 2.5 mm^2 PVC thermoplastic cable to be used for a 30/32 A ring, its current carrying capacity after applying rating factors must not be less than 20 A.

A circuit which runs only from the fuseway to the outlets it serves without returning to the fuse, is called a radial circuit, to distinguish it from the ring

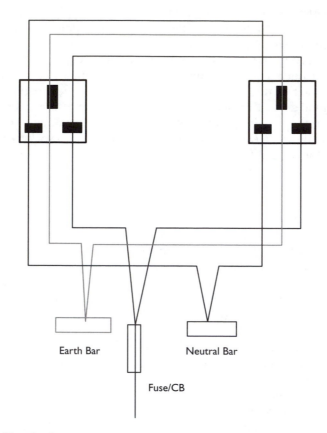

Figure 5.1 Ring circuit

circuit which we have just described. Every circuit is necessarily either radial or ring.

In explaining the rules for the number of outlets on a ring circuit, we have spoke of spurs, and we should pause to explain what is meant by this. Ideally the outlets on a ring are placed so that the cable can run from the first to the second and from the second to the third without doubling back on itself. If one outlet is a long way from the others, this doubling back may be expensive in cable and it may be cheaper to serve the odd outlet by a radial branch or spur from the ring. The reasoning which applies to the choice of cable and fuse size for the ring does not apply to the cable in the spur. This length of cable must be protected against overload and short circuit. The maximum load which can be connected to a non-fused spur is a twin 23 A socket, the maximum load is therefore 26 A. The cable must be rated accordingly. Alternatively, a fused connection unit is a convenient device for providing fusing. The maximum fuse in this case is a 13 A fuse. It will be seen from the rules given above that a considerable number of spurs may be taken from one ring, but in practice this is very seldom done.

Fused connection units are also used for connecting fixed appliances to ring circuits even when they are close to the line of the ring. The fuse in the connection unit performs the same function as the fuse in the plug of a portable appliance and protects the short length of cable between the outlet and the appliance.

Although the ring circuit was developed for domestic premises, it is equally useful for commercial premises and is frequently used for the power wiring of offices and shops. In housing, it is standard practice to put all the socket outlets on one floor of a house on one circuit. Consideration should be given to a separate circuit for a domestic kitchen. A little more thought is clearly needed in the layout of the circuits in commercial premises. The number of outlets on a ring is ultimately limited by the rating of the fuse. For premises other than factories, it is almost universal to run ring circuits in $2.5\,mm^2$ PVC cable and to fuse them at 30/32 A. The designer must assess the maximum current likely to be taken at any one time and plan such a number of separate circuits that none of them will be required to supply more than 30/32 A at a time. When doing this, it should be remembered that the use of electricity has increased enormously in the past few decades and is likely to go on increasing. It is, therefore, possible that within the lifetime of an installation more appliances will be plugged in simultaneously than is usual today, and also that individual appliances may be heavier users of current than the appliances in common use today. Some allowance must be made for a future increase of use, and in the absence of any other way of doing it, the author feels that it is prudent to restrict the present maximum current to say 15–20 A per ring circuit.

In a school or college workshop, it is often desirable for an emergency stop button to switch off all machines. The usual arrangement is that prominent stop buttons are fixed at two or three easily accessible places in the workshop so that in the event of any pupil having an accident, the machine may be stopped quickly wherever the person in charge happens to be at the time. All machines have to be controlled together so that if an emergency button is pushed, they all stop. A further requirement for safety is that the circuit must be such that the machines will not start again until the emergency stop has been reset. There are basically two ways in which an emergency stop circuit to meet these requirements can be carried out.

If the machine tools are large and each takes a large current, it will be better to feed each one on a separate radial circuit on its own final circuit. There will then have to be a distribution board with a number of fuseways/CBs serving a number of machines. The incoming supply to this board can conveniently be taken through a contactor which is normally open but is held shut when the operating coil is energized. The circuit of the operating coil is taken around the workshop and goes through as many emergency stop buttons as are needed. The result is that when any one of these buttons is struck, the operating coil is de-energized, the contactor opens, and the entire fuseboard is de-energized. Everything fed from that board then stops.

A large workshop may have so many machines that it requires two or three distribution boards to supply them all. The emergency circuit must then shut off the supply to all of these boards. It would be possible to take the sub-mains to several distribution boards through a multipole contactor with one pole for each phase and each neutral, but such contactors are not readily available, and it is better for each distribution board to be fed through its own contactor. The emergency stop circuit can contain a relay with one pole for each contactor, and the operating coil circuit of each contactor is then broken by the relay when the relay itself is de-energized on the interruption of the emergency circuit. This is a simple arrangement, but needs an extra circuit for the relay, and this circuit cannot come from any of the distribution boards which the relay controls. One way of avoiding the extra circuit and the relay would be to cable the operating coils of the contactors in parallel so that they were all part of a single circuit. This would have the disadvantage that at least one of the contactors must have its coil and main contacts fed from two different sources, so that it would be possible for the coil to be live when the main feed to the contactor had been disconnected. Such an arrangement can cause damage to unwary maintenance electricians and is not recommended. It is safer to pay for the relay.

Similar circuits can be adopted whenever it is necessary to control a large number of points together or from a remote place. The external lights of a hotel or public building may, for example, be sufficiently extensive to require several ways of a six or eight-way distribution board. If the distribution board is controlled by a contactor, all the lights can be switched together on one switch, which is in the operating coil circuit of the contactor.

The second method of providing an emergency stop circuit is appropriate for smaller workshops in which it may be cheaper and quite satisfactory to serve all machines from a single-ring circuit. The outlets on the ring main take the form of fused isolators, and each machine is connected locally to its own fused isolator. The emergency circuit still works a contactor, but in this case, the contactor is on the load side of the fuseboard. The supply is taken from the fuse to the contactor, and the ring starts from and comes back to the contactor. The operation of the emergency stop cuts out everything fed from this one fuseway but leaves in operation circuits from all the other ways of the distribution board. For a small workshop, this saves the expense of a separate distribution board for the machines only.

We have so far discussed mainly power circuits and must now say something about lighting circuits. It is usually necessary to have several lights on one circuit with each light controlled by its own switch. Figure 5.2 shows the wiring arrangement used to achieve this. It also shows circuits for two-way and for two-way and intermediate switching.

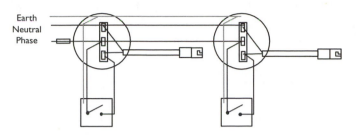

(a) Two one-way lights on a loop-in system

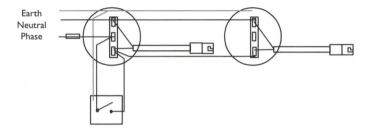

(b) Two lights controlled by one switch

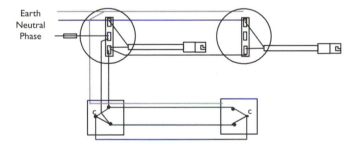

(c) Two-way circuit controlling two lights

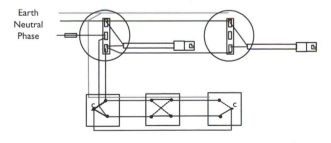

(d) Two-way and intermediate

Figure 5.2 Lighting circuits

Examination of these diagrams will reveal that the flexible cord to the lampholder is protected by the fuse in the whole lighting circuit. It is usual that this fuse does not have higher rating than the smallest flexible cord used on that circuit, although, strictly speaking it does not need overload protection since the maximum lamp size that can be connected to the bayonet lampholder is 200 W. The flexible cord does need short circuit protection. In domestic premises flexible cords will almost inevitably be 0.75 mm² rated at 6 A and so domestic lighting circuits should not be fused at more than 6 A. Now a 150 W tungsten bulb takes 0.65 A and consequently a 6 A circuit can have nine of these on simultaneously. In an average house, the 6 A limit will not be exceeded if there is one lighting circuit for upstairs and one for downstairs, but in a large house it may be necessary to have more lighting circuits than this.

In commercial and industrial premises far too many circuits would be needed if they were all restricted to 5 A. There is no objection to lighting circuits being rated at 10 or even 15 A, but the designer and installer must make sure that all pendant cords to lights are of the same rating as the rest of the circuit.

It has been explained in Chapter 1 that in the wiring of buildings, cable joints are not made by soldering but by mechanical connectors, or crimping. It is a help to maintenance if loose connector blocks can be avoided and cables joined together only at the various outlets. Furthermore, each connector adds a small joint resistance and it is advantageous to keep the number of these down to a minimum. Mechanical connections cannot be avoided at the outlets, but the number of joints can be reduced if no connections are made except at the outlets. This method of joining cables only at outlets is known as the 'looping in' system, and the diagrams in Figures 5.1 and 5.2 show how it is achieved. One piece of cable or three single cables for cables in conduit or trunking run from the distribution board to the first outlet (socket outlet or ceiling rose as the case may be) to the second outlet. If the wiring is properly planned and carried out there need be no joint in this length. A second run of cable runs from the second outlet to the third, and so on. Both these cables connect to the same terminal at the second outlet and thus the circuit becomes continuous. No joints are needed except at the outlets. This means that the joints are easily accessible.

The looping in system is the reason for having the third terminal on a ceiling rose, which we described in Chapter 1. It can be seen from Figure 5.2 that the third terminal (excluding the earth terminal) is needed to join the incoming and outgoing phase cables. It remains live when the light attached to the rose is switched off, and can give an unpleasant surprise to the home handyman replacing a luminaire. All circuits should be effectively isolated before work is carried out. All good ceiling roses have this terminal shrouded to prevent accidental contact, but nevertheless, some specifications insist that only two terminal roses be used. The looping could be done at the switch, as

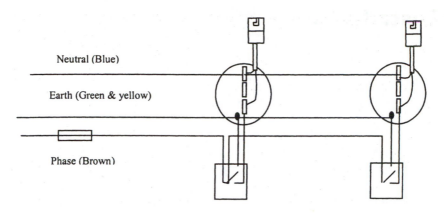

Neutral (Blue)

Earth (Green & yellow)

Phase (Brown)

Figure 5.3 Looping at switch

shown in Figure 5.3, but it is difficult to visualize a building in which this scheme would not require very much more cable than that of Figure 5.2.

We have described the way in which outlets are conventionally grouped and arranged in final circuits. Each of these sub-circuits is fed from a fuse on a distribution or fuseboard and the next step in describing a complete electrical system is to show from where the distribution board obtains its supply. This we shall do in the next chapter.

IEE Wiring Regulations particularly applicable to this chapter are:

Section   314
Section   463
Appendix 4

Chapter 6

Distribution

Electricity is supplied to a building by a supply authority; in the UK this is an area electricity company, while in other countries it may be an electricity supply company or public body. The supply is provided by a cable brought from outside into a suitable point in the building which is referred to as the main intake, and from this the electricity has to be distributed to all outlets which use it. The incoming cable may be a 120 or 150 mm² PVC insulated cable and the current flowing along it must be divided between a number of smaller cables to be taken to the various final destinations throughout the building. This division is the function of the distributing system.

In Chapter 5, we described the final circuits which serve the final outlets. Each final outlet takes a comparatively small current, and it would be impracticable to serve it with a large cable. As we have seen, the final circuits are most commonly cabled in 1.5 mm², 2.5 mm², 4 mm² and 6 mm² cables. The cable size in turn limits the number of outlets on each circuit, and in a building of any size a large number of circuits is needed. It would be very expensive to run all the final circuits from the main intake point. Also, voltage drop in cables of this size over a long distance would be excessive. It is more economic and more practical to divide the supply first over a few large cables and then into the final small cables in a second step. The normal method is to distribute current from the main intake to a number of distribution or fuseboards, each of which splits it further among a number of final circuits. A typical scheme is shown diagrammatically in Figure 6.1.

The cable from the main intake to a distribution board is known as a sub-main, and it must be rated to carry the maximum simultaneous current (after diversity has been taken into account) taken by all the final circuits on that board. Once this current is known, the size of the cable can be determined by current-carrying capacity and voltage drop, as explained in Chapter 4.

The protection devices in the distribution board protect the final circuits, but the sub-main cable also needs protection against short circuits and overloads, and there must be a fuse or other protective device at the main intake. We can note the principle that every cable must be protected for short

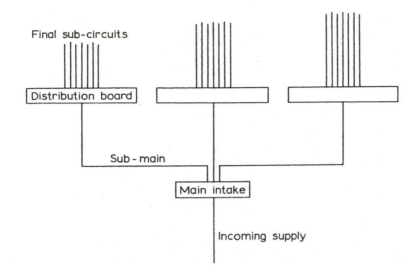

Final sub-circuits

Distribution board

Sub - main

Main intake

Incoming supply

Figure 6.1 Distribution

Figure 6.2 Switch fuse (Courtesy of Eaton Electric Ltd)

circuit at its feeding end, for overload protection it is permissible to protect the cable along its run. A convenient device for protecting a sub-main cable is a switch fuse. A switch fuse is illustrated in Figure 6.2, and it can be seen that it consists simply of an isolating switch and a fuse carrier housed together in a substantial casing. The one illustrated is a three-phase switch fuse and, therefore, has three poles on the switch and three fuses. The fuse protects the cable leaving the switch fuse and the switch is useful for isolating the sub-main from the rest of the electrical system when this is required for maintenance or alteration work. The switch is designed to make and break the rated current of the switch fuse, and units are made in a series of standard ratings. A typical model, for example, is manufactured in increasing sizes rated at 30, 60, 100, 160, 200, 400, 600 and 800 A.

A switch fuse also includes terminals which enable the earth cables on the incoming and outgoing sides to be connected together. Under no circumstances must there be a break in this circuit as it would destroy the safety of the system. The neutral cable on the other hand can be taken through the switch fuse in one of two ways.

The more usual way is for the switch to include terminals for connecting the incoming and outgoing neutrals in the same way as the earth cables. The alternative is for it to have a switch blade in the neutral line as well as in the phase lines, thus making it a 4-pole device. In this case there is a solid link instead of a fuse in the neutral line.

A fuse switch, illustrated in Figure 6.3, is similar to a switch fuse, but in this case the fuse carriers are mounted on the moving blades of the switch.

The whole of the current going into the sub-main passes through the switch fuse which carries no current for any other part of the system.

The total incoming current must be divided to go to several switch fuses, and the simplest device for distributing current from one incoming cable to a number of outgoing ones is a busbar chamber. This consists of a number of copper bars held on insulating spacers inside a steel case. It is shown in Figure 6.4. Cables can be connected to the bars anywhere by means of cable clamps which are usually bolted to the bars. The incoming cable can be connected to the bars at one end or at some convenient point along them. Connecting the incoming cable to the centre of the busbar enables 300 A

Figure 6.3 Fuse switch (Courtesy of Eaton Electric Ltd)

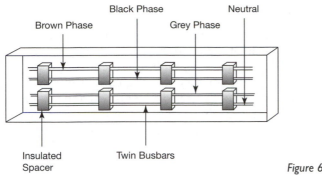

Figure 6.4 Busbars

busbars to supply a total load of 600 A with 300 A flowing each way from the connection. Care must be taken that the loads are distributed properly. Therefore outgoing cables are connected at suitable intervals along them. The switch fuses are usually mounted immediately above and below the busbar chamber so that the connections, or tails, from the busbars to the fuses are kept as short as is reasonably possible. These tails are of the same size as the cables leaving the switch fuse but are protected only by the fuse on the main intake. It is not normally permissible to protect a cable with a fuse rated at more than the maximum current carrying capacity of the cable. It may, however, be done for short tails between busbars and switch fuses. Provided that its length is no greater than 3 m, the cable is installed such that short circuits are unlikely to occur, and installed to reduce the risk of fire or danger to persons. A short circuit or overload on the load side of the switch fuse will blow the switch fuse and thus stop current through the tail, and a short circuit on the tail will produce such a heavy overcurrent that the main intake fuse will blow. For the fuse protecting the mains cable to protect the tails, the formula as explained in Chapter 4 is employed, $t = K^2 S^2 / I^2$ where t is the time in seconds for the cable to reach its limit temperature under fault conditions, K is the constant for the cable, S is the cross-sectional area of the cable, and I is the prospective short-circuit current.

Another matter which requires attention in the intake room is metering. The supply authority will want to meter the supply afforded and will want to install a meter at the intake position. If it is a small enough supply, the whole of it can be taken through the meter. The arrangement then is that the incoming cable goes first to a fuse which is supplied, fixed and sealed by the electricity company, and from there to the meter, which is also supplied and fixed by the electricity company. The fuse is the electricity company's service cut out and it is sealed so that only they have access to it. From the meter, the cable is connected to the busbar chamber. It is normal for the installer to provide the last piece of cable from the meter to the busbars but to leave the meter end of it loose for the electricity company to connect to the meter.

If the building takes a very large current, a different arrangement is used. It is not practicable to take a large current directly through a meter and large supplies are metered with the help of current transformers. The arrangement is similar to that described in the last paragraph, but the place previously occupied by a meter is taken by the primary coil of a current transformer. The output from the secondary coil of the transformer is taken to the meter, which can be made to give a direct reading of the current in the primary coil by suitable calibration. Some current transformers are made to slip over the busbars, or the mains cable cores if the busbar is not supplied from one end, and use the bars, or cable conductors as a primary coil. The method to be used should be agreed with the electricity company before installation commences even if this is one or two years before the building is to be finished and a supply of electricity will be needed. It is very embarrassing if, when the electricity company come to connect the supply, they find that there is not enough space for their equipment and it is much better to agree everything well in advance.

The size of busbars is determined by the current they are to carry which is normally the whole current of the building if the busbar is supplied from one end. The current carrying capacity is governed by temperature rise and has been tabulated in published data in the same way as the current carrying capacity of cables. The spacing between the bars is determined by the voltage at which they are to operate, since the air gap between adjacent bars and between bars and case is the only insulation provided. Busbars must also be capable of taking short-circuit currents for the time it takes for fuses or circuit breakers to operate. In a short time, the bars will not overheat and the short-circuit capacity is a measure of the mechanical forces which the bars will withstand. A heavy current gives rise to large electro-mechanical forces and the bar supports have to be capable of withstanding these. Busbars are obtained from specialist manufacturers and the electrical services engineer does not usually design his own. Further details on the methods of calculation would, therefore, be beyond the scope of this book.

A busbar chamber with a large number of switch fuses takes up a lot of wall space. It can also look untidy. Both these disadvantages can be overcome by the use of a cubicle switchboard. Such a board contains the busbars and the switch fuses all housed together in one large panel, a typical example being shown in Figure 6.5. It works in exactly the same way as the busbar chamber with separate switch fuses, but is made in the manufacturer's factory instead of being assembled on site, and all the interconnecting wiring is inside the casing of the switchboard. This makes it possible to arrange the switch fuses in a more compact way and to fit all the equipment into a much smaller space.

The meters can also be included within the composite switchboard. It is usual to have an incoming isolator or switch fuse which both protects the

Figure 6.5 Cubicle switchboard (Courtesy of Eaton Electric Ltd)

board against short circuits and makes it possible to isolate the board for maintenance.

Such a switchboard does, however, have disadvantages. First, although it requires less space than a site assembly of individual pieces of equipment, it is likely to cost more. Second, it is not easy to add further switch fuses to it once it has been made. A main intake consisting of separate pieces of equipment can very easily be extended; it is a simple matter to make an extra connection to the busbars and to take another pair of cables out through a short length of conduit to a new switch fuse fixed to any free wall space in the intake room. This is often necessary during the life of a building, and sometimes even before a new building is completed, since building owners are apt to change their minds and want equipment installed which they had not thought of when building operations started. Unless blank spaces have been left in a cubicle switchboard it cannot be extended to take more switch fuses, and even if spaces have been left they often turn out to be not quite large enough for an unforeseen and unexpected extension.

In general each sub-main goes from the main intake to a distribution board. This consists of a case inside which is a frame holding a number of fuse carriers. Behind the frame, or sometimes alongside it or above it, is a busbar to which the incoming sub-main is connected. From the bar, there is a connection to one side of each fuseway or circuit breaker provided. Each final circuit is then connected by the installer to the outgoing terminal of one of the fuses/CBs. The circuit is completed when a fuse carrier with a fuse is pushed into the fuseholder, or the CB is closed. A second busbar is provided to which the incoming neutral and the neutrals of all outgoing circuits are connected. A typical distribution board is shown in Figure 6.6. The only difference between a distribution board and a fuseboard is the name.

Standard distribution boards usually have either 4, 6, 8, 12, 16, 18 or 24 fuseways/CBs. Both single and three-phase boards are available, the latter having three fuseways/CBs for each outgoing circuit. It is not necessary to utilize all the available fuseways/CBs on a board, and in fact it is very desirable to leave several spare ways on each board for future extensions, although the sizing of the cable supplying the board must be capable of supplying the additional load. Trunkings and conduits will also need to be sized with future extensions in mind. These are often required before a building is even finished, and are almost certain to be wanted during the life of an installation which may last 40–60 years. A label must be provided inside the cover of every distribution board stating which fuse serves which outlets.

The position of distribution boards within a building must obviously depend on the plan of the building. Apart from architectural considerations, it is a matter of balancing the lengths of sub-mains and the lengths of final circuits to find the most economic way of keeping the total voltage drop between intake and final outlet to a minimum. It is possibly better to keep sub-mains long and final circuits short, but it is also desirable to keep the number of distribution boards down by having a reasonably high number of final circuits on each board. To achieve this without excessively long final circuits, one must have the board fairly central for all the circuits it is serving.

In some cases, it is convenient to have a subsidiary control centre between the main intake and the distribution boards. When this is done a main cable runs from the main intake to the subsidiary control centre, sometimes referred to as a load centre, which is itself similar in construction to the main intake. The main cable is supplied through a switch fuse, fuse switch, or circuit

Figure 6.6 Distribution board (Courtesy of Eaton Electric Ltd)

breaker at the main intake end and leads to busbars at the subsidiary centre. The arrangement is shown schematically in Figure 6.7. Such a scheme would be adopted only in a large building, but is very useful when several distribution boards have to be placed a long way from the main intake. It is more economical to keep the voltage drop down with one large main cable for the greater part of the distance to be covered than with several sub-mains running next to each other along the same route. It also requires less space for the cables. It is particularly useful when the premises being served consist of several different buildings. Normally, the electricity company will provide only one incoming service to one set of premises and if there are several buildings, the distribution to them must take place on the consumer's side of the meters. It is very convenient to run one main from the intake to a centre in each building and then distribute in each building from its own centre. Colleges and hostels are examples of consumers who may have several buildings on one site all forming part of the same premises.

The subsidiary control centre is also a good solution to the problem of extending existing buildings. A great deal of new building in fact consists of extensions to existing premises, sometimes by actual enlargement of an existing building or erection of a new building on spare ground within the site of the existing one. It is comparatively easy and does not need much room to add one switch fuse at the main intake. From this, it is again a comparatively simple matter to run one new cable to the new building. Here it is possible to plan a subsidiary distribution centre with as many switch fuses and sub-mains to as many distribution boards as are necessary. In this way, the amount of alterations in the existing building is kept to a minimum and the new building is treated as an entity in itself.

When an extension is made it may be necessary for the electricity company to increase their service cable. This will depend on the existing load, the new load and the margin by which the capacity of the existing service cable exceeds the existing load. Whenever extensions are planned the capacity of the service cable must be checked with the supply authority, but replacing an incoming service with a larger one is not a difficult operation and does not add greatly to the work which has to be done in the existing part of the building.

In the UK, the electricity company's final distribution network to their customers is at 400 V three-phase four-wire, but all domestic and nearly all commercial equipment requires a single-phase 230 V supply. Motors above 2.5 kW are now very often three phase and they can be found in boiler-rooms, kitchen ventilation plants, air conditioning plant rooms, lift motor rooms and similar places in buildings such as office blocks, schools and colleges, hospitals and blocks of flats. Any equipment of this nature will usually need a three-phase supply, but distribution to lights and to ordinary socket outlets for power purposes must be at 230 V single phase. Whenever there is three-phase equipment in a building the supply authority must obviously be asked

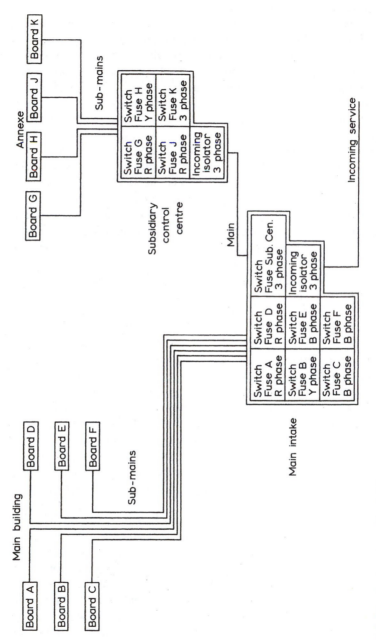

Figure 6.7 Distribution through subsidiary centres

to bring in a three-phase supply. Where there is no three-phase equipment in a building single-phase supply would be enough, but there is another consideration which has to be taken into account. The supply authority wants its load to be evenly spread over the three phases of its network and this may need the cooperation of the consumers. For individual dwellings, whether flats, maisonettes or houses, the supply authority will bring in only a single-phase cable, but it will arrange the supplies to adjacent or nearby dwellings so that the total supply is balanced over the three phases. Thus in a new development either each dwelling will be on a different phase from its immediate neighbour or small groups of dwellings will be on different phases from adjacent groups. For larger buildings, the electricity company will demand the cooperation of the consumer, or more properly of the engineer who plans the installation. The company will insist that the consumer accepts a three-phase supply even if there is no three-phase equipment to be connected, and it will further insist that the demand is as nearly as possible balanced over the three phases. The designer must take some care about how he achieves this balance and he has to fulfil other requirements at the same time.

Most people are used to an electric supply at 230 V in their homes and expect the same in offices and public buildings. This is quite high enough to be dangerous, and it is largely for reasons of safety that the USA and some other countries have standardized domestic supplies at 110 V. It would be most undesirable to expose people to even accidental contact with 400 V and it is preferable to keep the three phases away from each other. In other words, the three-phase supply comes into the main intake and if necessary to subsidiary control centres but sub-mains and distribution boards are all single phase. An exception must, of course, be made for any sub-mains and distribution boards serving three-phase machinery. Single-phase outlets near each other should be on the same phase, and distribution boards close to each other should also be on the same phase.

The IEE Regulations, which are almost invariably made to apply to installations in this country, stipulate that where fixed live parts between which there is more than 250 V are inside enclosures which although separate from each other are within reach of each other, a notice must be displayed giving warning of the maximum voltage between the live parts. Within reach is usually taken to mean 6 ft or 2 m. It is clearly not pleasant to have a lot of notices in a building saying 'Danger – 400 volts' and one therefore plans the distribution within a building so that circuits on different phases are kept more than 2 m away from each other.

A very convenient way of doing this is to divide the building into three zones each of which is served by one phase. These zones must be of such sizes that each takes approximately the same load, in order that the total load is spread as nearly as possible equally over all three phases. The zones are not necessarily of the same area; for example a three-storey school may have classrooms on two floors and laboratories on the third and the laboratories may account for more than a third of the total load. In such a case, a convenient division could be half the laboratories plus a third of the first floor on the red (brown) phase, the other half of the laboratories plus a further third of the first floor on the yellow (black) phase, and the remaining third of the first floor plus the whole of the ground floor on the blue (grey) phase, but obviously the division must depend on the building and no general rules can be laid down. The designer must have enough personal judgement to settle each case on its merits. An advantage of having mixed phases is that if one phase goes down, there is lighting supplied on other phases.

It is helpful to label the three zones on a plan of the building. This will avoid confusion and draw attention to anomalies. It has the added and very important advantage of making the designer's intentions clear to the workmen on site and so reducing the risk of mistakes.

When a building is zoned it is worth checking all two-way light switches. Suppose, for example, that ground and first floors are on different phases, and that the light on the stairs is cabled on one of the first-floor circuits. If it has two-way switching, the downstairs switch may be next to a corridor light switch which is on a ground-floor circuit and, therefore, on a different phase. This should be avoided and is best prevented by careful labelling of circuits and phases on the drawings during design.

Even where three-phase equipment has to be connected, the rules for separation of phases should still be applied to all single-phase outlets near the three-phase equipment. Operators and maintenance workers will be expecting a high voltage on the three-phase equipment, but will not be expecting a high voltage to appear between a pair of single-phase outlets near it.

Another point which has to be considered when the distribution through a building is being planned is the position of other services. If a fault develops on an electric cable its sheath or protective metal casing, an exposed conductive part, could become live. The various methods of giving protection against the consequences of such faults are described in Chapter 9, but the dangers arising from cable faults should also be guarded against when the cable routes are selected. If a live conductor breaks and touches the outer sheath or conduit the exposed parts become live. It must automatically disconnect quickly.

For this reason good practice requires electrical wiring to be separated from other services. There should be at least 150 mm between them. The earth metalwork of the other services should be bonded to the main earthing terminal of the electrical supply. This ensures that whatever happens the other service is at the same potential as the main earthing terminal.

The tariff which the electricity company will apply should be discussed with them when the installation is being planned. There are many tariffs available, and they differ from company to company. The consumer may find that electricity can be obtained more cheaply on a tariff which employs different rates for current used for power and for light. If this is so, the power and the light must be metered separately, and the designer must keep power and light circuits separate. Clearly a decision on this must be made before the design is drawn up, and this can only be achieved after negotiations with the electricity company; these should, therefore, be the first part of a designer's job.

If separate metering is decided on, it will be necessary to use split busbars at the intake. These are simply two lengths of busbars separated by a short distance from each other, but contained within the same casing. Externally, the appearance is the same as that of a single metered system, but internally the connections to the light and power systems are kept separate. The electricity company, of course, supplies two meters. Cubicle-type main panels can be similarly arranged to keep the two services separate.

Each distribution board must be either for power only or for light only and must be fed by a sub-main from the appropriate set of busbars. In a large building with many outlets and, therefore, a considerable number of final circuits, it is normally quite easy to have separate boards for light and power. For example, a technical college may need perhaps two lighting circuits and two power circuits in each laboratory, and a group of four laboratories may be so arranged that they can be conveniently served from one place. A pair of twelve-way distribution boards in this place will provide the additional circuits needed for corridors and leave reasonable spare capacity. As two boards would be needed in any case and there are almost equal numbers of lighting and power circuits to be accommodated, it is quite convenient to have one board for power only and one board for lighting only. In small buildings, on the other hand, separation of light and power may make it necessary to use more distribution boards than would otherwise be required. Thus a sports hall may have four lighting circuits and only two socket outlets which can go on one power circuit. A six or eight-way board would conveniently serve them all, leaving some spare capacity for future extensions. If the power is metered separately, a separate board will be needed for the single-power circuit and it will probably have to be a three-way board because this is the smallest size commercially available. A second sub-main will also be required and consequently an additional switch fuse at the intake. The result is a substantial increase in the cost of the installation, and the design engineer should keep this in mind when assessing the relative merits of different tariffs.

We have so far been talking in terms of distribution within a single large building. The same principles apply to distribution to dwellings but are modified by the fact that each occupier is a separate customer of the supply authority and must have a separately metered supply. In a suburban development of detached and semi-detached houses, the supply authority will bring a single-phase service cable into each house. The number of circuits in a house is small enough to be accommodated on a single distribution board

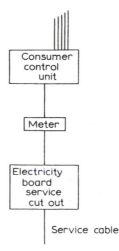

Service cable

Figure 6.8 Domestic service

so that there is no need for sub-main distribution. The scheme thus becomes as shown diagrammatically in Figure 6.8. The incoming cable goes to a service cut out which is supplied, fixed and sealed by the electricity company. As a domestic supply does not normally exceed 100 A the whole can go through the meter and there is no occasion for the use of transformers. From the meter the cable goes directly to the distribution board. This must be supplied and fixed by the installer, who also provides the short tail to connect it to the meter. The tail is left loose at the meter for the electricity company to make the connection into the meter. In the case of a serious fault the service cut out will disconnect the consumer from the service cable and thus prevent the fault affecting the rest of the board's distribution network. It is obviously convenient to have all these pieces of equipment close together.

There are distribution boards made specially for domestic use, and these are known as consumer control units (CCU). They are very similar to ordinary fuseboards but are single-phase only and incorporate a double-pole isolating switch on the incoming side, a residual current device may also be used as the main isolator. Manufacturers also supply CCUs with split busbars, one busbar supplied through an isolator, the other busbar supplied through a residual current device. Whichever method is employed, this makes it possible to cut off the supply from fuses or circuit breakers before changing or withdrawing them. On a larger building, it is not so necessary to have an isolator on each board because the sub-main and board can be cut off together at the intake end. CCUs are available with 60 A or 100 A isolators and are made with up to 12 fuseways/CBs. A fairly typical arrangement of circuits for a semi-detached house is given in Table 6.1a and for a flat in a block with central heating in Table 6.1b. If a house requires a bigger supply than 100 A, it cannot be cabled through a domestic CCU and it must be

Circuits	Serving	Rating amps
1	Upstairs lights	6
2	Downstairs lights	6
3	Garage and outside lights	6
4	Upstairs ring main	32
5	Downstairs ring main	32
6	Immersion heater	15
7	Shower unit	45
8	Cooker	45
8	Spare	–

(a)

Circuits	Serving	Rating amps
1	Lights	6
2	Ring main	32
3	Cooker	32
4	Bathroom ventilation fan	10
5	Clothes dryer	10
6	Motorized valve on heating	10
7	Spare	–
8	Spare	–

(b)

Table 6.1 Domestic circuits

treated as a small commercial building with an intake put together from standard commercial fuse and distribution gear.

In a block of flats the arrangement within each flat is the same as that within a house, as just described, but some means must be found to take the supply authority's cable through the block to each flat. In a small block, it may be practicable to bring into the block as many cables as there are flats and run them within the block to the individual flats. In this case, they will probably be PVC/SWA/PVC cables, but in a block of any size this would be a cumbersome solution, and the distribution on the board's side of the meter is similar to that which is used on the consumer's side of the meter in commercial buildings. The supply authority brings in one service cable to a service head which contains a fuse. From this, it takes a main cable feeding a series of distribution boards, and from each way on a distribution board it takes a sub-main into one flat. The protection device on the distribution board protects the flat supply cable and, therefore a service cut-out is not needed in the flat itself.

Usually there are only a small number of flats on each floor and they can be served individually from a single distribution board. Successive floors in a block of flats are either identical or very similar, so that the various distribution boards are vertically above each other, and the main to them rises vertically. A convenient and very common way of carrying out the vertical distribution is by means of bare rising mains of the type illustrated in Figure 2.4 (Chapter 2). A distribution scheme of this type is shown diagrammatically in Figure 6.9, and a typical floor plan is shown in Figure 6.10. It will be seen from Figure 6.9 that the rising main carries all three phases, but that each distribution board is connected to only one phase. In this way, the flats are allocated between the phases so as to make the total load as nearly balanced as possible. It has to be assumed that all flats impose the same load.

In this example, the electricity company service cable enters the building through an earthenware duct through the foundations, and terminates in a service head in a cubical recessed in a wall at ground-floor level. From this, the bare rising mains, enclosed in a sheet steel case, rises through the building. The architect has chosen to have the enclosing case semi-recessed in the corridor wall, but it could equally well be fully recessed, completely hidden inside a builder's work duct or completely exposed. On each alternate floor a six-way distribution board is attached to the rising main bars. The system used enables the board to form part of the enclosing case. From each distribution board three 25 mm conduits rise to the floor slab above and three drop to the slab below, and within the slabs these conduits continue to a position just inside each flat. They terminate where the meter will be fixed and the CCU is fixed next to the meter. A three-core 25 mm^2 PVC insulated cable is pulled through this conduit from the distribution board to each meter position. Alternatively PVC/SWA/PVC cables may be used instead of cables in conduit.

It will be noticed from the first-floor plan that there are actually two identical distribution systems within the building, each serving half the flats on each floor. This was done to avoid long and difficult horizontal runs at each level and also to keep the load on each rising main to below 400 A per phase. The whole of this distribution system is the property of the electricity company, who remain responsible for its maintenance. It may be installed during construction of the block by the company's own staff or by contractors employed by the developer, in which case the contractors must work to the company's specification. Which method is to be employed must be agreed beforehand by the developer and the company; the plan of the installation must also be agreed between them when the building and its electrical system is being designed.

People do not stay at home all day and it is often difficult for meter readers to enter to read the meter. It is an advantage if the meter can be read from outside the dwelling, and on many new developments the supply is arranged to make this possible. One method is to have the meter in a purpose-made cupboard in the outside wall of the dwelling. The CCU can be in an adjacent cupboard on the inside of the dwelling. Alternatively the CCU can

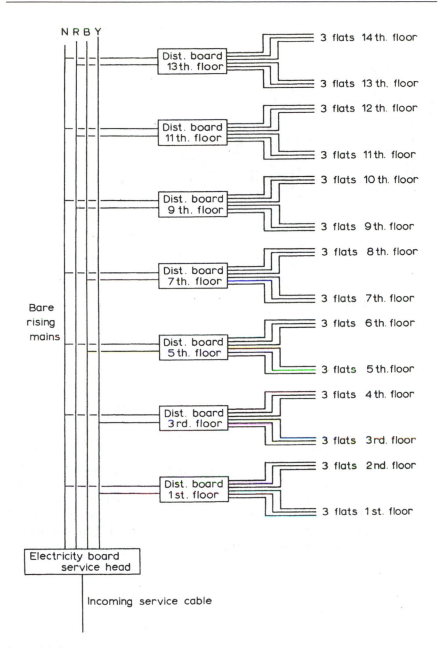

Figure 6.9 Distribution to flats

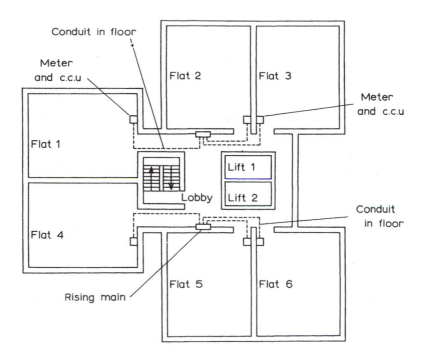

Figure 6.10 Distribution to flats

be in any other convenient position inside the dwelling and instead of a short tail from meter to CCU there is a fairly long piece of cable. As this is likely to be at least a 25 mm² cable which cannot be bent too sharply the route it is to take should be planned beforehand to make sure the cable can be drawn in. In the case of a block of flats, instead of having the meter outside each flat, all the meters can be grouped together in some convenient central point. Figure 6.11 is a modification of Figure 6.10 with external meters. The six meters served by each distribution board are housed in a meter cupboard next to the distribution board, each meter being connected by a short tail to the corresponding fuse in the distribution board. The conduit to each flat runs from the meter cupboard instead of from the distribution board, and goes straight to the CCU in the flat.

The second way of reading meters from outside is to use repeaters or slave indicators. A repeater, sometimes known as a slave indicator, is an indicating dial, identical to that in the meter itself, driven remotely from the meter. If this method were adopted in the example already discussed, the meters would be within the flats as shown in Figure 6.10, Next to the distribution board would be a cupboard containing six repeaters, which would take the place of the meter cupboard shown in Figure 6.11. 25 mm² cable would be taken through the conduit from the distribution board to each meter. An additional

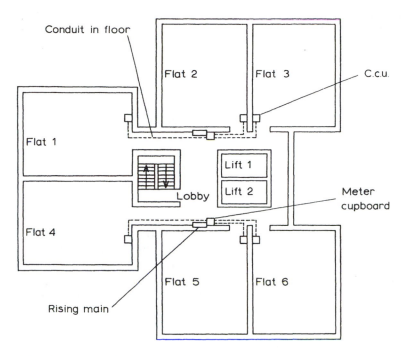

Figure 6.11 Plan with external meter cupboards

1.5 mm² cable would run in the same conduit back from the meter into the distribution board and through the side of the board into the repeater cupboard. Here it would be connected to the repeater belonging to the flat in question, and the repeater would reproduce the reading on the meter.

Standards relevant to this chapter are:

BS EN 60947–2 Specification for low voltage switchgear and controlgear
BS EN 60947–3 Specification for low-voltage switchgear and controlgear
BS 5486 Low voltage switchgear and controlgear
BS 6121 Mechanical cable glands for elastomer and plastics insulated cables
BS EN 50262 Metric cable glands for electrical installations
BS 6480 Impregnated paper insulated cables for voltages up to 33000 V

IEE Wiring Regulations particularly applicable to this chapter are:

Section 537

Chapter 7

Lighting

Introduction

Illumination and the design of lighting layouts is a subject on its own. There are books dealing comprehensively with it and it is not proposed to condense the matter into a single chapter here, but once a lighting layout has been arrived at, it is necessary to design the circuits, wiring and protection for it; this is an aspect of lighting design which tends to be overlooked in books on illumination and which we propose to discuss in this chapter. The electrical requirements of a lighting system depend to a considerable extent on the kind of lamps used and we shall describe the different available types in turn.

Incandescent lamps

These are also known as tungsten lamps, or GLS general lighting service, and are in fact the ordinary bulbs still most commonly used in homes. They consist of a thin filament of tungsten inside a glass bulb. When a current is passed through the filament, heat is produced and the temperature of the filament rises. The filament is designed so that it reaches a temperature at which it generates light energy as well as heat, which means that the filament glows or is incandescent and hence the lamp is called an incandescent one. The higher the temperature of the filament, the more efficient is the conversion of electrical energy into light energy, but if the temperature becomes too high the filament melts and breaks. Tungsten has a melting point of 3382 °C, and most modern lamps have filaments running at about 2800 °C, although some special lamps may run at 3220 °C.

The colour of the light produced depends on the temperature, becoming whiter as the temperature rises. At 2800 °C, it is rather yellow, but as no material is known which can be operated at a higher temperature than tungsten, lamps of this type cannot be made to give a daylight colour.

To prevent the filament from oxidizing, all the air must be evacuated from the bulb, and the early lamps were of the vacuum type. It was found that in a vacuum tungsten evaporated and blackened the inside of the bulb. This problem has been solved by filling the bulb with an inert gas at a pressure such that when the bulb is hot the pressure rises to about atmospheric pressure. The gas used is generally a mixture consisting of 93 per cent argon and 7 per cent nitrogen. Unfortunately, the gas conducts heat from the filament to the bulb, thus lowering the temperature of the filament and reducing the efficiency and the light output of the lamp. To overcome this effect as much as possible, the filament must be wound to take up as little space as possible. It is for this reason that gas filled lamps have the filament either single coiled or coiled coil.

The connections of the filament are brought out to the lamp cap. This is the end of the lamp which fits into the lampholder when the lamp is put into a luminaires. Lamp caps are shown in Figure 7.1. The commonest is the two-pin bayonet cap (Figure 7.1a) which is standard in the UK for all sizes up to and including 150 W. It can be inserted into the lampholder either way around and for applications where the lamp must be fixed in one position only a three-pin bayonet cap is available. Clearly a special lampholder is needed for it. Figure 7.1c shows the Edison screw cap, in which the screw, thread forms one of the terminals. The Edison screw cap is made in five sizes covering all types of lamps from street lamps to flash bulb lamps, but the only common sizes used in this country are the Goliath (usually abbreviated to GES), small (SES) and miniature (MES). Bulbs of 200 W and over use the GES cap.

It will be noticed that the traditional Edison screw affords slightly greater risk of accidental contact with the terminal when one is putting a bulb into

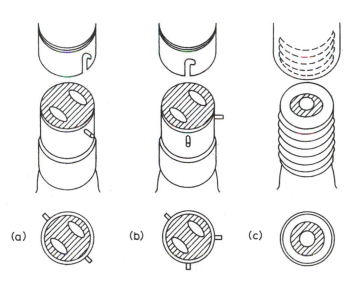

Figure 7.1 Lamp caps

a lampholder. The screw thread is the neutral which should never be at line voltage, and it is possible to hold the bulb without touching the thread, so that there are two reasons why there should not be any danger. Nevertheless, if the circuit wiring is of the wrong polarity, which is not an entirely unknown fault to occur, and at the same time an inexperienced person is clumsy with the bulb, there is a risk of shock. However, lamps inserted into E14 and E25 lampholders to BS EN 60238 do not make contact with the outer terminal until the last twist if the lamp. Therefore in this case, BS 7671 IEE Wiring Regulations states that it is not necessary to connect the phase conductor to the centre contact, although for conformity it is advisable that the centre contact is always connected to the phase conductor. The bayonet cap is used as the standard in the UK up to 150 W, which is the largest bulb likely to be used in domestic premises, although 200 W lamps are available. Some continental countries use the Edison screw for all sizes.

The characteristics of incandescent lamps are shown in Figure 7.2. The graph shows how very sensitive the life is to change of voltage. For example an increase of 2½ per cent above normal voltage increases the efficiency by 2½ per cent and the light output by 7 per cent but reduces the life by 20 per cent. The graph also shows that for voltages below normal the light output falls more rapidly than the voltage, which is something to be borne in mind when one considers the voltage drop that can be accepted in the circuit wiring to the lamps.

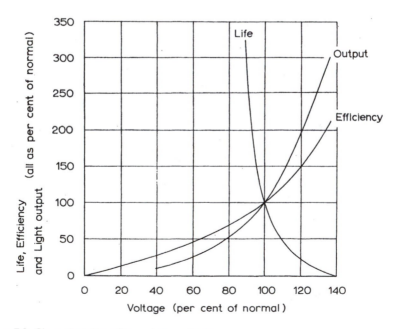

Figure 7.2 Characteristics of incandescent lamps

The current taken by an incandescent lamp is purely resistive. Because of this, there is no adverse effect on the circuit power factor and no special consideration has to be given to the switches used. The situation is different for most of the other types of lamp.

The heat given off by incandescent lamps, especially the larger sizes, must be taken into account in both the design of luminaires for incandescent lamps and in the selection of luminaires for a lighting scheme. The luminaires must allow enough natural ventilation to keep the normal working temperature of the luminaires and wiring reasonably low. This is particularly important where luminaires are made of plastics with softening temperatures in the region of 60 °C. In such cases, the maximum size of bulb which may be used in a luminaire is limited not by the physical dimensions of the luminaire but by the heat generated.

When incandescent lamps are used for stage lighting or for special effects they can be dimmed by the insertion of a thyristor control circuit. This affords an efficient way of gradual and continuous dimming.

Voltage control units with thyristor circuits can be made sufficiently compact to be incorporated in a light switch. Combined switch and dimmer units of this type are used where variable light effects are required in places like hotels and housing.

Tungsten halogen lamps

In a conventional incandescent lamp the filament loses material by evaporation. The inert gas inside the bulb reduces the rate of evaporation but cannot prevent it completely. A further improvement can be obtained by adding a halogen to the gas, which gives rise to a reversible chemical reaction. Tungsten evaporates from the filament and diffuses towards the bulb wall. Provided the temperature is favourable the tungsten combines with halogen at the walls and the resulting tungsten halide diffuses back to the filament. At the temperature prevailing at the filament the tungsten halide dissociates into tungsten and halogen and the tungsten is deposited back on the filament.

Successful operation of such a lamp depends on the achievement of suitable temperatures at both the filament and the bulb wall. This makes it necessary for the filament to be at a higher temperature than in an ordinary tungsten lamp and for the bulb to be smaller. The bulb has to be at a temperature of about 250 °C, and in order to withstand this it has to be made of fused silica or high melting-point glass.

For a given power a tungsten halogen lamp has a longer life and a higher light output than an ordinary tungsten lamp. The high temperature makes it of limited use in domestic or commercial lighting but it finds application in floodlighting and the lighting of film and television studios. It is probably most widely known for its use in automobile headlamps, but that is an application entirely outside the scope of this book.

Fluorescent lamps

The action of a fluorescent lamp depends on the discharge of a current through a gas or a vapour at a low pressure. If a tube containing a vapour has an electrode at each end, a current will flow through the vapour provided electrons are emitted by one electrode (the cathode) and collected by the other (the anode). Electrons will be emitted if the potential gradient from anode to cathode is great enough; the potential difference required to cause emission decreases as the temperature of the cathode increases, and therefore lamps designed to operate at normal mains voltage have cathodes which are heated to a dull red heat. They are known as 'hot cathode' lamps.

Even when the cathode is heated, a voltage has to be applied between the electrodes to start the discharge, and the minimum voltage needed is known as the striking voltage. After the discharge has started a voltage is still needed between the electrodes to maintain the discharge, but the maintaining voltage is less than the striking voltage.

A current flowing through a gas or vapour at low pressure causes the gas or vapour to emit radiation at wavelengths which depend both on the nature of the vapour and on its pressure. An incandescent lamp gives out light energy at all wavelengths in the spectral range, whereas a fluorescent lamp gives it out at certain discrete wavelengths only. The wavelength of the radiation emitted may be in the visible spectrum or above it or below it, and one of the functions of the lamp is to convert all the primary radiation into useful visible radiation.

A fluorescent lamp consists of a long glass tube containing a mixture of mercury vapour and argon gas at a pressure of 2 to 5 mm mercury. When the lamp is cold, the mercury is in the form of small globules on the tube surface, and the argon is needed to start the discharge. As soon as the discharge starts the temperature rises sufficiently to vaporise the mercury which then takes over the conduction of practically the whole current. At either end of the tube, there is an electrode made of a tungsten filament coated with an alkaline earth metal having suitable electron emission properties. Each electrode acts as cathode and anode on alternate half cycles of the a.c. supply. Anode plates in the form of metal fins are provided round each electrode to assist it in collecting electrons during the half cycle in which it acts as anode. The inside of the tube is coated with a fluorescent powder. A fluorescent material is one which has the property of absorbing radiation at one wavelength and emitting radiation over a band of wavelengths in another region of the spectrum. It emits radiation only while receiving it; a material which continues to emit after the incident radiation has ceased is called phosphorescent and it is an unfortunate confusion that the fluorescent materials used in commercial lamp manufacture are commonly called phosphors.

Thus in the fluorescent lamp the radiation emitted by the current discharge through the mercury vapour is absorbed by the fluorescent coating which

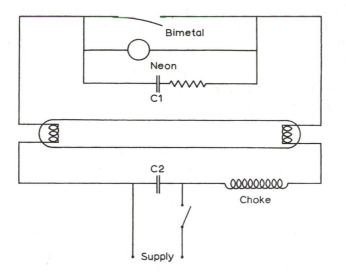

Figure 7.3 Fluorescent lamp circuit

then emits a different radiation. The fluorescent coating is most susceptible to excitation by ultraviolet radiation, and it is the need to have the radiation from the mercury in this region that determines the operating pressure. The secondary radiation emitted by the coating is in the visible spectrum and its colour depends on the material used for the coating. So many fluorescent materials are now known that it is possible to obtain almost any colour, including an almost exact reproduction of daylight.

The circuit needed to operate such a lamp is shown in Figure 7.3. As we have explained, the voltage required to maintain the discharge is less than that required to start it, and therefore once the discharge has started the voltage across the lamp must be reduced. If it were not reduced the current through the lamp would go on increasing until the lamp was destroyed. The necessary reduction is achieved by a series ballast which takes the form of an inductance or choke. Initially, when there is no discharge through the lamp, the entire voltage of the mains is applied across the electrodes. As soon as the discharge is established, current flows through the lamp and choke in series, a potential difference is developed across the choke, and the voltage across the electrodes is reduced by the voltage across the choke.

The circuit also includes a starter switch which consists of a small neon glow lamp and a bi-metal strip. When the lamp is cold, the bi-metal switch is open so that the whole of the mains voltage appears across the neon glow lamp which discharges. The heat of the discharge heats the bi-metal until the contacts on the end of the bi-metal close. There is now a circuit formed by both electrodes of the main lamp, the bi-metal and the choke. A small current flows through this circuit and heats the electrodes. However, the bi-metal short circuits the neon, which ceases to glow and, therefore, to heat the bi-metal. In consequence, the bi-metal cools and after a time it opens again. This interrupts the circuit which, being highly inductive, responds with a sharp voltage rise across the switch. Since the switch is in parallel with the lamp the voltage rise is also applied across the lamp and is sufficient to start the discharge. The choke now takes the normal current and reduces the voltage across both lamp and switch. This reduced voltage is not enough to start another glow at the switch, but if for any reason the main discharge fails to start, then mains voltage again appears at the glow lamp and the sequence starts again. This happens if the choke is faulty and reduces the voltage across the lamp below that required to maintain the discharge. When the lamp has started the electrodes are kept hot by the current through the lamp which also flows through the electrodes.

The starting sequence described takes a few seconds. This delay can be avoided with the instant start circuit shown in Figure 7.4. The electrodes are supplied from low-voltage secondaries of a transformer, and carry the full heating current continuously. A metallic strip runs the whole length of the tube and close to it, and is connected to earth. When the lamp is switched on a capacitive current flows from the electrodes to the earthed strip and is just sufficient to ionize the gas in the tube and thus enables an arc to strike

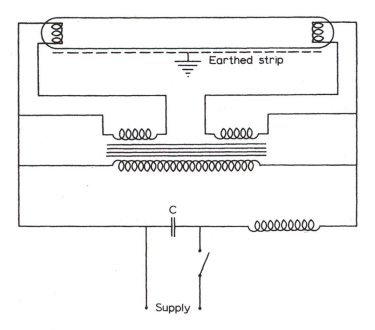

Figure 7.4 Quick-start circuit

from end to end. As soon as the arc has struck, the choke reduces the voltage across the lamp to its normal operating value and the current in the heaters also reduces as a result of this. Although it is possible to use ordinary lamps with quick-start circuits, it is not wise to do so because the heaters carry a higher current than when they are used with switch start circuits. For this reason, only tubes designed for quick-start should be used in fittings having quick start circuits.

Figure 7.3 shows a small capacitor across the switch contacts. The capacitor is inserted to suppress radio interference. Figures 7.3 and 7.4 both show a larger capacitor across the entire circuit. This one is included to correct the power factor, which would otherwise be unacceptably low because of the inductive choke.

The capacitors, switch and choke are usually housed within the luminaire which holds the lamp. It is important that the luminaires used are suitable for the lamps they are intended to employ. The current taken by a luminaire with fluorescent lamps is inductive with a power factor of about 0.8. The switches controlling fluorescent lights, therefore, have to break inductive circuits and must be capable of withstanding the voltage rise which occurs when an inductive circuit is broken. The voltage rise can cause arcing across the switch contacts, and if this is serious enough and occurs often enough it will destroy the switch. Most modern switches are capable of breaking an inductive current of the value at which the switch is rated, but the older switches designed only for incandescent lights had to be de-rated when they were used on circuits serving fluorescent lights.

There are some occasions when the switchgear for the luminaire, that is to say the capacitors, switch and choke, is mounted remotely from the luminaire. One case in the author's experience was in a swimming pool where the lamps were mounted behind a pelmet around the perimeter of the hall. The architectural design was such that there was no room for ordinary luminaires containing the gear, and the lamps were simply clipped to the pelmet. Each end of each lamp was plugged into a two-pin socket from which cables ran to a remote cupboard. Inside the cupboard there was a series of trays each of which contained the control gear for one lamp. Another case was in an air-conditioned computer room. Much of the heat lost from a fluorescent light is generated in the control gear rather than in the lamp, and in order to keep the heat load on the air-conditioning plant as low as possible, it was decided to keep the control gear out of the air-conditioned room. The method used for doing this was similar to that in the previous example.

Fluorescent lamps have a lower surface brightness than incandescent ones and have a higher efficiency in terms of light energy given out per unit of electrical energy consumed.

Fluorescent tubes can be made in the shape of a U or an annulus. The production process is more difficult and therefore these tubes are more expensive than the commoner linear ones. However, advances in production techniques have made it possible to produce tubes so compact that a complete lamp can be little bigger than a large incandescent lamp. Small diameter tubes formed into an annulus have found application in domestic and commercial lighting and can be used in bulkhead luminaires not much larger than the corresponding incandescent ones. A further development is a U tube bent again and enclosed in an outer bulb which looks like an incandescent lamp. It has also proved possible to make the control gear so small that it can fit inside the outer bulb which can then have an end cap suitable for plugging into a standard incandescent type lampholder. The Philips SL and Thorn 2D lamps are of this type and can be used to replace incandescent lamps without any change to the fittings.

Fluorescent lamps cannot be dimmed simply by the insertion of a resistance to reduce the current through the lamp. If a reduced current flows through the tube, it does not heat the cathode enough to bring about emission of electrons. Successful dimming requires that the electrodes be permanently heated while the tube current is varied, and this can be done by supplying the electrodes with a separate heating current from a low-voltage transformer. A suitable circuit is shown in Figure 7.5 and the similarity with the quick-start circuit of Figure 7.4 can be noted. The transformer provides a permanent heating current which is independent of the current through the tube and the latter current is varied by the resistor. In this way, variation of the tube current does not cut off electron emission from the cathode.

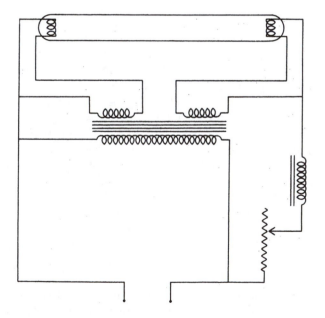

Figure 7.5 Fluorescent dimming circuit

The tube current can also be varied by a thyristor. The arrangement is similar to Figure 7.5, but a thyristor circuit takes the place of the resistor. While permanent heating current is circulated to the electrodes, the thyristor controls the proportion of each cycle of the alternating supply during which striking voltage is applied to the tube. This determines the length of time in each cycle during which current flows through the tube, and hence the light output. Tri-phosphor tubes save 20 per cent energy consumption when compared to conventional tubes. This saving is further increased to up to 40 per cent if electronic ballasts are used.

Mercury lamps

Mercury lamps are discharge lamps which operate on the same principle as fluorescent lamps. At sufficiently high pressure the radiation emitted by the mercury is in the visible spectrum so that such a lamp can be used without a fluorescent coating. The original mercury lamps had no coating, but modern lamps are provided with one in order to improve the colour rendering. It also increases the lamp efficiency.

The basic mercury lamp consists of an arc tube with an electrode at each end and a starting electrode near one of the main electrodes, the electrodes themselves being similar to those in the fluorescent lamp. The starting electrode is connected to the opposite main electrode through a high resistance. The arc tube is fitted inside an outer glass envelope. In the UK the main types are designated MBF. The construction of an ordinary MBF lamp is shown in Figure 7.6. The two main electrodes are sealed inside the arc tube with a starting electrode near the lower one connected to the upper one through a high resistance outside the tube. The arc tube is made of fused silica and the operating pressure inside it is between two and ten atmospheres. It is held inside an outer envelope of heat-resisting glass, and the resistance between the starting and main electrode is also within this envelope. The connections are brought out to an end cap at the base of the outer envelope.

The radiation from the arc tube is greenish-white in the visible spectrum with some ultraviolet. The latter is converted into a visible red by a fluorescent coating on the inside of the outer envelope and the combined light from the are tube and the coating has a colour which is considered acceptable for street lighting and for some factory and warehouse applications. In order to prevent oxidation and internal arcing the outer envelope is filled with an inert gas at a pressure between 0.04 and 0.9 atmosphere.

When the lamp is switched on the voltage is sufficient only to start a small discharge between the starting electrode and the nearby main electrode. The small discharge makes the argon in the tube conductive and this enables a discharge to start between the main electrodes. This discharge bypasses the starting electrode, warms the tube and evaporates the mercury. As it evaporates the mercury takes over the conduction of the main discharge.

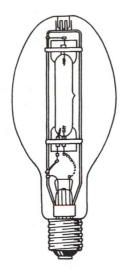

Figure 7.6 MBF lamp

After two or three minutes, steady conditions are reached and the mercury emits its radiation. The current through the discharge is limited by a choke.

A capacitor is also included in the circuit for power factor correction, and the capacitor and choke must be contained either in the luminaire or in a casing conveniently near it. When these lamps are used for street lighting the control gear can be accommodated inside the column on which the lantern is supported. If it is intended to do this, the column manufacturer's specification must be checked to make sure that the column is large enough to hold the gear.

When the lamp is switched off, it will not restart until it has cooled and the pressure has dropped again. This takes two to three minutes, but the lamp will not come to any harm if it is left switched on while cooling down. In other words, if the lamp is switched off and switched on again immediately, it will not re-light immediately but will not be damaged.

Both the light output and the power consumed increase linearly with an increase of supply voltage. The relationship is shown in Figure 7.7.

A variation on this lamp is the MBTF which has an additional tungsten filament inside the outer envelope. The tungsten filament is connected in series with the discharge tube and acts as a ballast. Consequently there is no need for a choke and, because the filament is not inductive, no power factor correction capacitor is required either. The filament has to be specially designed to fulfil its primary function of controlling the lamp current whilst also having as long a life as the arc tube and being capable of withstanding the starting conditions; at starting the voltage drop across the are tube is low with the result that the voltage across the tungsten filament is higher than during operation. The light from the filament provides additional colour

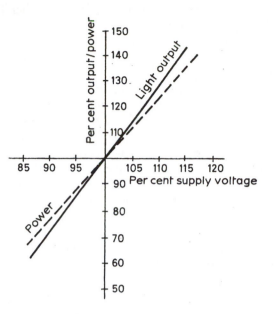

Figure 7.7 Characteristics of MBF lamps

correction. This and the absence of control gear are advantages, but the lamp has a lower efficiency than the MBF.

Another version is the MBFR. This has an outer envelope with a parabolic reflector shape. It has an internal coating of fine titanium dioxide powder which has a high reflectance in the visible region. The fluorescent coating is applied on top of this, but the front surface of the bulb is left clear.

The ME is a lamp which operates at a working pressure above 30 atmospheres and a correspondingly high temperature. This necessitates a special construction of the electrodes and the use of quartz instead of glass for the outer envelope. At powers above 1000 W, a.c. operation leads to pitting of the electrode surfaces and d.c. operation is preferable. ME lamps are used for optical projection, for which they are suitable because of the small physical dimensions in relation to the amount of light produced.

The MD lamp operates at pressures of 50 to 200 atmospheres. This makes it so hot that it has to be water cooled. Consequently it can only be used in optical equipment which incorporates a water pumping system; even then it has a very short life.

Sodium discharge lamps

Sodium discharge lamps have a similar action to mercury lamps, but the filling used is sodium instead of mercury. Lamps designated SOX and SLI work at low pressure and their luminance is low. They therefore have to be very long to give a good light output; in order to reduce the overall length the tube of an SOX lamp is bent into the shape of a U and the resulting construction is shown in Figure 7.8. The SLI lamp has a straight tube and is therefore double ended.

To withstand the sodium vapour the inner tube is made of ordinary glass with a thin coating of special glass fused onto its inner surface. The inner tube is enclosed in a double-walled vacuum flask. Each electrode consists of a coated spiral whose ends are twisted together; there is no flow of heating current through the electrode as there is in a mercury lamp. Neon is contained within the inner tube with the sodium and starts the discharge. When the lamp is cold the sodium condenses and exists as small globules along the length of the tube. It is important that they should be fairly evenly distributed along the tube, and, therefore, the lamp must be kept nearly horizontal. At the same time, the sodium must not be allowed to condense on the electrodes. To satisfy this requirement luminaires for sodium lamps are arranged to hold the lamp tilted slightly above the horizontal.

The operating pressure is very low, being in the region of 1 mm mercury, although the vapour pressure of the sodium alone is of the order of 0.001 mm mercury, the rest being due to the neon. To start an arc through the neon when the lamp is cold requires a voltage higher than normal mains voltage (about 450 V). The necessary striking voltage is obtained from an auto-transformer which is specially designed to have poor regulation, that is to say the voltage when current flows drops greatly below the no-load voltage.

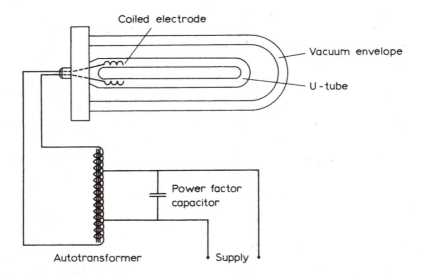

Figure 7.8 Sodium discharge lamp

Consequently, as soon as the discharge starts the voltage drops to that required to keep the discharge going. The transformer thus performs the functions of the ballast and no separate choke is required. A capacitor for power factor correction is, however, needed.

The discharge which starts in the neon is of a red colour. This warms the tube and gradually vaporizes the sodium. After about twenty minutes, the sodium is fully vaporized and gives its characteristic yellow colour. The sodium discharge lamp is the most efficient means so far known of converting electrical into light energy, but because of its peculiar colour the low pressure sodium lamp is limited to street lighting and similar applications. The control gear, consisting of autotransformer and power factor capacitor, is usually accommodated within the column which supports the luminaire. Alternatively, it can be housed within the luminaire and this is done in floodlights and other luminaires intended for mounting at low level.

High-pressure sodium lamps give a rather sunny yellow light. For this reason when first introduced they were called solarcolour lamps, but they are now more generally referred to by the designation SON. They are suitable for factories and warehouses and are now also widely used for street lighting and floodlighting. The pressure within the arc tube when the lamp is fully warmed up is between 30 and 60 kPa. The lamp runs at a temperature of 1300 °C and to withstand the corrosive properties of sodium at this temperature alumina ceramic is used in the manufacture of the tube.

As with the low-pressure sodium lamp, the SON lamp does not have heated cathodes or auxiliary electrodes, but starts cold with a high voltage pulse. A typical circuit is shown in Figure 7.9. The circuit comprises a

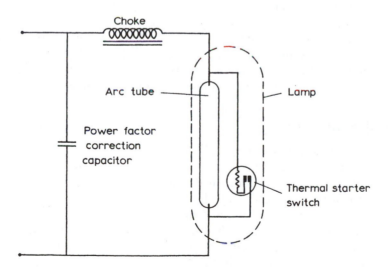

Figure 7.9 Typical solarcolour lamp circuit

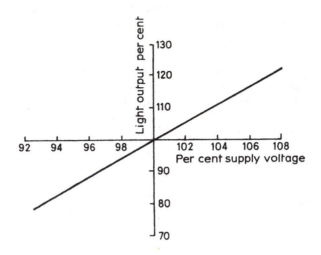

Figure 7.10 Performance of SON lamp

thyristor starting circuit, which pulses a high voltage across the lamp, once the lamp strikes the pulse generator is shut down and the current through the lamp is restricted by the ballast.

High pressure sodium lamps can work either vertically or horizontally. They may be mounted at any angle below 20° above the horizontal. The tube does not have to be as long as the low-pressure sodium tube and the construction and shape are similar to those of the mercury discharge lamp.

High pressure sodium lamps have a very high efficiency and a long life. Most high-pressure sodium lamps have rated lives of more than 24,000 hours. Both light output and the power consumed increase very rapidly with an increase in the supply voltage and the design of the ballast has to be such as to limit variation in the applied voltage in order to preserve lamp life. Figure 7.10 shows the variation of light output with voltage.

Metal halide lamps

The colour rendering of a mercury lamp can be improved by the addition of another metal. It is, however, necessary that the metal used should have a sufficiently low vapour pressure at the operating temperature of the lamp, and that it should not react with the material of the arc tube. This can be achieved by using the metal in the form of its halide salt.

The general design of metal halide lamps is similar to that of mercury lamps. When one of these lamps is first ignited the output is due to the mercury. As the temperature rises the metal halide, which is initially solid, melts and vaporizes. The high temperature causes it to dissociate into metal and halogen, and emission of light commences. The tube walls are cooler than the interior of the tube and the metal and halogen recombine on the surface of the walls; this has an important effect in preventing chemical attack on the silica walls.

The metal halide lamp with a clear glass outer envelope is designated MBI. When the outer envelope has a fluorescent coating the designation becomes MBIF. A linear version for use in floodlighting and in television studios is designated MBIL.

These lamps have a better colour rendering than MBF or incandescent lamps. They also have better colour rendering than SON lamps but are not so efficient and therefore SON lamps are still preferred where colour rendering is not so important. Metal halide lamps are finding use in offices, supermarkets and large stores. They can also be used for high bay warehouse lighting and floodlighting, but it is in these applications that the higher efficiency of the high-pressure sodium lamp is generally thought to be more important than the colour rendering.

Cold cathode lamps

These include both neon advertising lights and lamps for illumination used in large stores, cinemas and similar areas.

If a sufficiently large potential difference is applied between the electrodes of a discharge tube, the arc can be struck and maintained without any heating of the cathode. With a hot cathode, the volt drop across the electrode is small, but with a cold cathode, it is higher. A long tube helps to keep a larger part of the total applied voltage drop across the arc and a smaller part across the electrode, and cold cathode lamps are, therefore, made longer than the hot cathode lamps described previously. The greater length, in fact, increases the efficiency and hence also the light output. It is because of this that they are used in stores and cinemas and under the projecting canopies which are now so popular at the entrances to commercial buildings, including hotels.

The high voltage required is provided by transformers, and in order to keep the amount of high voltage wiring to a minimum the lights are supplied with transformers in self-contained units suitable for direct connection to the mains. A common arrangement has three 2.75 m-long tubes physically parallel to each other, but electrically connected in series. The circuit diagram of such a luminaire is shown in Figure 7.11. The two transformers and all the high voltage wiring are sealed within the luminaire and are not accessible.

The two primaries are in parallel across the mains supply, and each has a power factor correcting capacitor. The high-voltage windings each have one end connected to earth and are so arranged that the voltage between their two other ends is double the maximum voltage to earth. The transformers give a voltage high enough to strike the arc. As in the case of the transformers used with the hot cathode sodium lamps, they are designed to

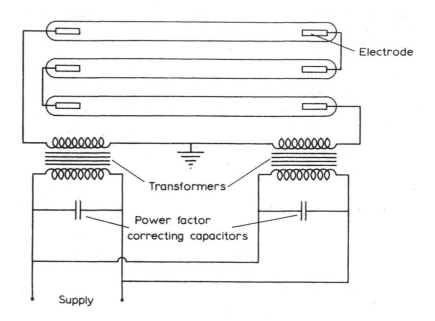

Figure 7.11 Cold cathode lamps

have poor regulation so that once the arc has been struck, the voltage drops to that required to maintain the arc. For a typical three-tube luminaire the striking voltage is 3600 V and the running voltage 2000 V.

The great advantage of the cold cathode tube is its very long life, which is in the region of 15 000 hours as against about 5000 hours for an ordinary fluorescent tube. It also maintains its output better throughout its life, and starts instantly. Its life is not reduced by frequent switching. When the tube is used for lighting it is filled with mercury vapour and has a suitable fluorescent coating on its inside surface. As with ordinary fluorescent tubes a variety of colours is available.

The length of cold cathode tubes makes them suitable for bending into special shapes. This makes them useful where special decorative effects are wanted and also, of course, for advertising purposes. For advertising use many different colours can be obtained by the use of different types of glass, which may be coloured or have fluorescent coatings. The earliest gas used was neon, and 'neon light' has stuck as the popular generic name for all advertising lights of this type.

The tubes can be bent into the shape of letters or other symbols and successive tubes can be connected in series, an example of such an arrangement being shown in Figure 7.12. For letters like H or T the tube must be bent back on itself.

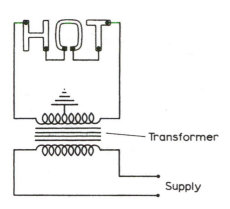

Figure 7.12 Decorative cold cathode lamps

The voltage required to start the tubes depends on their length, the type of gas and its pressure and on the design of the electrodes. The manufacturers normally quote the running voltage per metre of tube and the voltage drop at each pair of electrodes, from which the designer can calculate the voltage which has to be provided from the secondary of the transformer. A magnetic shunt is provided inside the transformer to enable the tube current to be adjusted when the sign is commissioned. This is not a task to be undertaken lightly, because of the very high voltages involved.

Stringent safety regulations for high-voltage advertising signs have been drawn up by the Institution of Electrical Engineers, and recommendations are also given in BS 559:1998. No part of the installations may have a voltage to earth greater than 5000 V. and if the centre point of the secondary side is earthed the voltage available between the opposite ends of the series of tubes is 10 000 V. This limits the length of tubes which can be served from one transformer. If greater lengths are required, the sign must be split into several lengths each having its own transformer. The transformers are normally housed inside weatherproof steel containers which are fitted on the outside of the building. A transformer rated at more than 250 VA must be supplied on a separate final circuit not serving any other equipment or any other transformer. If the transformers are smaller than this, up to four of them may be put on a common sub-circuit, but the total rating of one circuit may not exceed 1000 VA. Particular care must be taken with the high-voltage wiring which should be lead-covered armoured cable. It must be restrained from swaying in the wind because this would strain both the conductor and the insulation.

A typical circuit is shown in Figure 7.13. A lockable switch is provided so that anyone doing maintenance on the installation can be sure that no other person can inadvertently turn the supply on. The fireman's switch is mounted outside the building in a prominent position but out of reach of the public. It is for the use of the fire brigade, who want to turn off all high-voltage

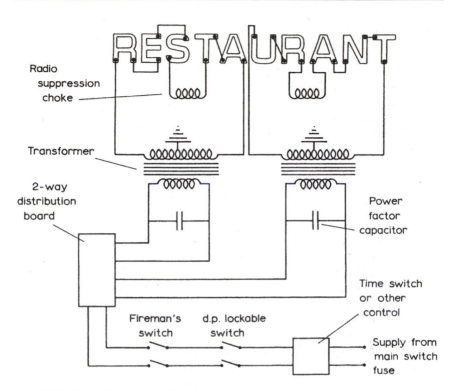

Figure 7.13 Circuit for display lighting

sources before spraying water anywhere near them. A choke is connected in each high-voltage circuit to suppress radio interference.

Flicker

With the exception of the incandescent ones, all the lamps we have described go on and off 100 times a second when working on a 50 Hz supply. This is too rapid a flicker to be noticeable to the eye, but it could with older types of fluorescent tube produce a stroboscopic effect on rotating machinery, which may appear either to be stationary or to be moving at a much slower speed than it really is. Such an illusion can obviously be a source of danger and should be avoided. If adjacent lamps go on and off at different times, that is to say if they are out of step with each other, the effect is reduced, and it is possible to obtain this breaking of step with twin lamp luminaires. The luminaire is made with one choke for each lamp but only one capacitor. The capacitor is arranged in series with only one of the lamps, and the chokes and capacitor are so sized that although the combined current through both lamps has the usual power factor of about 0.8, the current through one lamp leads the voltage while the current through the other lags. The two lamp currents are neither in step nor 180° out of phase and, therefore, extinguish and re-light at different instants. Luminaires of this kind are known as lead/lag luminaires and are often specified for workshops and factories. Tri-phosphor fluorescent with electronic ballast operates at 20 kHz.

Circuits and controls

The way in which luminaires are connected in circuits has been described in Chapter 5. We showed in that chapter how a switch could control each light or each group of lights. The switch would be one of the types described in Chapter 1. There are, however, other methods of control possible and they are particularly important for street-lighting and other external lights for which some form of automatic control is almost essential.

The first method and one still widely used is by means of a time switch. Time switches are made with an enormous variety of dials, or digital displays, for almost any conceivable application can be found from some manufacturer's standard range of products, but in exceptional cases special dials or digital display can be made to order. For street or external lights, the usual requirement is for the lamps to be turned on at sunset and off either at midnight or at sunrise. The times of sunset and sunrise vary throughout the year, and solar compensating dials are made for time switches to follow the annual variation in sunset and sunrise. As the variation depends on latitude, different dials/displays are made for different zones of latitude.

In the UK street-lighting is the responsibility of the local authority. The usual arrangement is for the electricity company to supply each column directly off its main running through the street, or if necessary off a main laid specially for the lights. A time switch is fixed inside each column, and switches the current to the luminaire at the top of the column. The supply is not metered because one knows the total hours in a year during which a solar dial switch is on and also the rating of the lamp, and can thus calculate the number of units of electricity consumed in a year. The column also contains a service head fuse, on the supply side of the time switch.

A new housing development may often include estate roads which are constructed by the developer, but which will ultimately be taken over by the local authority. The same system of road-lighting can be adopted, but it is advisable to agree the details with the street-lighting department of the local authority beforehand. The system can also be used where the roads are to remain private, but the agreement of the electricity company must be obtained in advance because the method of supply may affect the tariff they will want to apply.

The design engineer should make sure to select and specify columns which have a space inside them large enough to contain the time switch and fuse; there are light duty columns which do not have a wide enough base.

If the external lights are not too far from buildings, final circuits can serve them from distribution boards within the buildings. The cable sizes should be checked for voltage drop, and may need to be greater than ordinary lighting circuits. For running underground PVCSWAPVC or MICC, cable is probably the most suitable. A circuit to several lights is taken through a time switch and the time switch can be conveniently mounted next to the distribution board. It is also possible to obtain a modular-type distribution board which has a time switch to be mounted on the DIN rail inside the board. Internal lights may also be controlled by a time switch, and this may be a convenient way of switching, say, corridor lights in an office block.

When lights, whether internal or external, are supplied through a time switch served from a distribution board, the supply is of course part of the metered supply to the building. Whether this is more or less desirable than an unmetered but timed supply depends on the agreement between the consumer and the supply authority.

The other method of automatic control of lights is the use of photoelectric cells. In this method, a photoelectric cell is arranged to make a circuit when the illumination falls below a set value and to break the circuit when the illumination rises. The advantage over a time switch is that the control takes account of weather conditions. There are summer evenings which, because of storm clouds, are almost as dark as winter evenings, but a time switch cannot distinguish between a cloudy day and a clear one. Furthermore, in the UK at least, a time switch must usually be reset twice a year because of British Summer Time, whereas a photoelectric cell needs no alteration.

When photoelectric cells are used, the lighting circuits can be arranged in the same way as when time switches are used. There can be one cell to each light, or there may be one cell for a circuit on which there are several lights. In the latter case, if the circuit is switched directly by the cell, the number of lights on the circuit is limited by the current which the cell can switch. The maximum current which a given cell can switch may be lower if the current is inductive than if it is resistive, so that a cell may be able to switch fewer fluorescent lights than incandescent ones. Nevertheless, a small cell can be used to control many lights, or even several different circuits, if it is used with a relay. The cell is placed in the operating coil circuit of the relay and the relay main contacts switch the lights. A multipole relay makes it possible for one photoelectric cell to control several lighting circuits.

The position of the photoelectric cell requires a little thought. It must be close to the area illuminated by the lights it controls, in order to react to the daylight in that area. At the same time, it must not receive direct light from any of the lamps it controls; if it did, as soon as they came on, it would switch them off again, so that they would flicker on and off continuously. Nor must it receive direct light from any other lamps which may be turned on at night, otherwise switching on one set of lights will immediately switch off the other set. In general, the illumination on the photocell during the hours of darkness when the lights are on must be less than the level at which the cell switches the lights. Most outdoor artificial lighting produces illumination levels much lower than daylight and a photocell set at the minimum acceptable daylight level will not turn the lights off until daylight is again adequate, but there are areas, such as the forecourts of garages, supermarkets and cinemas, where the artificial lighting approaches full daylight level, and in these cases it is certainly difficult, and may even be impossible, to design a photoelectric scheme of control. For ordinary street lighting, a cell placed in the top of a column above the lantern will respond adequately to natural light falling on the road and can be shielded from the light of the lamp.

The number of hours in a year during which a photoelectric cell will be in the 'on' position cannot be known exactly. The supply authority may, therefore, be unwilling to agree to the use of an unmetered supply. Nevertheless, several local authorities are using photoelectric cells to control street lighting and have negotiated a suitable method of payment with the area electricity company.

Emergency lights

Many buildings must have some form of emergency lighting to come on if the electric supply to the ordinary lights fails. BS 5266: Emergency lighting, BS EN 1838, BS 5266–7: Lighting applications. Emergency lighting are the codes of practice to which to refer. One of the possible causes of failure is a breakdown in the supply authority's service to the building and, therefore, the emergency supply must be independent of the service into the building.

Electric lighting for emergency use can be provided if the building has a standby generator. A generator can be installed to take over the entire supply to a building, so that the only special provision for emergency lights need made is to cover the time between the mains supply fails and the standby generator is up to speed , but for economy the standby generator is often rated at less than the ordinary mains service to the building. The distribution then has to be arranged so that only a part of the service within the building is fed by the generator, and only a few of the lights should be included in this part. There is no need for full lighting under emergency conditions, and lighting in the main corridors and staircases is usually enough. High risk task areas need special consideration.

Emergency supplies are of particular importance in hospitals and no new hospital should be built without a standby generator, but buildings like schools, offices, theatres and blocks of flats seldom justify the expense. For these buildings emergency lighting is almost invariably provided, by self-contained battery luminaires.

Emergency lights are fitted throughout the building. They come on only when the mains fail (a non-maintained system) and cannot be used while the mains are healthy. They are not intended to give full illumination, but only

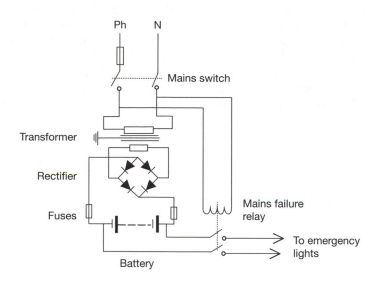

Figure 7.14 Central emergency system

to provide sufficient light for people to make their way out of the building safely. A minimum of 1 lux should be achieved, and 5 lux near fire-fighting equipment. Emergency lighting in high-risk task areas such as near hot vats should have an illumination of 10 lux. Manufacturers' data will give luminaire spacings at given heights to achieve these lighting levels. One light on each landing and perhaps one in the centre of any particular corridor should be perfectly adequate. A number of low-power luminaires is generally better than one large luminaire. These lights work on low voltage d.c. and are fed from a battery. A trickle charger permanently connected to the mains ensures that the battery is always fully charged. The lights are cabled from the battery through a relay, the contacts of which are closed when the coil is de-energized. The coil is fed from the mains and as long as the mains are on, the contacts are held open. Thus as long as the main supply is healthy, the battery lighting circuit is kept open, but immediately the mains fail the relay contacts close and the emergency lights come on. The circuit diagram is given in Figure 7.14.

There are battery chargers and relays purpose-made for this kind of application. The charger must be left permanently switched on, and contains the relays necessary to stop the charging current when the battery is at full charge. It can be supplied by a final circuit from any convenient distribution board, but there should be no other outlets on the same final circuit. Alternatively, it can be fed directly from a switch fuse at the main intake.

Because the emergency lights work at a low voltage, the voltage drop in the cable to them can become considerable and may present something of a problem. Whereas a 60 W bulb on a 230 V supply takes 0.26 A, a 24 W bulb on a 24 V supply takes 1.0 A and the voltage drop in a cable of a given size is about four times as great. At the same time, a drop in a cable of 2.4 V in 230 may reduce the light output by perhaps 2 per cent but the same drop of 2.4 V in a 24 V system is proportionately ten times as great and could reduce the light output by a fifth or a quarter. Low-voltage cables must, therefore, be adequately sized. It is in any case inadvisable to design an emergency system for less than 48 V d.c., which is a convenient standard battery-output voltage. Even with a 48 V system and ample cable sizes, there must obviously be a limit to the number of lights which can be served from one battery and to the distance the furthest light can be from the battery. A large building may, therefore, need several separate battery systems. Legislation has made it more essential to provide lights to mark fire-escape routes from buildings. The lights used for this are of very low wattage and, consequently, the voltage-drop problems are somewhat eased.

The emergency lights themselves are ordinary luminaires which take a low-voltage d.c. bulb. These are very energy expensive, and using a fluorescent through an inverter will reduce the current required by the circuit. There is a more common method of emergency lighting which makes use of special luminaires, each of which contains its own battery, charger and relay. The luminaire effectively houses a complete low-voltage system just large enough to operate one light. The use of such luminaires makes it unnecessary to run a low-voltage circuit throughout the building. With this system, the emergency luminaires are put in the most suitable places for emergency illumination and are fed from any convenient lighting circuit. In some cases, it may be convenient to have two or three emergency lights on a circuit of their own and in other cases, it may be convenient to have an emergency light included in one of the normal lighting circuits.

Such self-contained emergency luminaires are made in a variety of shapes and with a variety of light sources. They may be incandescent, fluorescent light, or LEDs and can take the form of illuminated signs. An emergency light with the word 'EXIT' supplemented with pictograms has an obvious application, although pictograms without the use of text are now preferred. They are usually on at all times that the building is occupied (maintained system). It has been known that the maintained lights are supplied through a relay which is controlled from the burglar alarm system, so that the lights are off when the building is unoccupied. Examples of emergency lights are illustrated in Figure 7.15. An important advantage of these self-contained luminaires is that they require little maintenance although the battery lifespan is limited and the standard on emergency lighting BS 5266–1 gives requirements for testing the system, and requires that the three yearly test be carried out annually for batteries over three years old. It also stipulates minimum lighting levels for the emergency lighting. Modern luminaires of this type may include a self-monitoring facility. Another advantage is that locally supplied

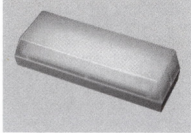

Figure 7.15 Emergency lights
(Courtesy of Gent & Co. Ltd)

emergency luminaires will respond to a local outage of supply, whereas a central system will only respond to a mains supply failure.

Hazardous area luminaires

The principles on which hazardous area accessories are designed are explained in Chapter 1. Most types of luminaire are also available in hazardous area versions. When these are specified, it is important to make sure that the ones selected are suitable for the zone and group appropriate to the area in which they are to be fitted.

Standards relevant to this chapter are:

BS 559	Electric signs and high voltage luminous discharge tube installations
BS EN 60400	Lamp holders for tubular fluorescent lamps and starter holders
BS 5266	Emergency lighting
BS EN 1838, BS 5266–7	Lighting applications; emergency lighting
BS 5499	Exit signs
BS EN 60598–1	Luminaires
BS EN 61184	Bayonet lampholders

Chapter 8

Power

The majority of outlets to be used for power services are socket outlets of the types described in Chapter 1. The various ways in which power circuits can be arranged have been described in Chapter 5. It is usually found that as soon as more than two or three socket outlets are to be supplied, it is more economical to serve them from ring circuits than from radial ones. On ring circuits, only 13 A BS 1363 socket outlets should be used in order to ensure that the plug must be of the fused type and that the appliance and flexible cable to it do not rely on the ring-circuit fuse for protection. There is little more one can add about socket outlets and it remains in this chapter to say something about connecting fixed appliances and larger equipment.

Fixed appliances of small ratings, by which we mean up to 3 kW, can be served through fused connection units from the ring mains serving the socket outlets in the same area as the fixed appliance. A 3 kW electric fire is one example of a fixed appliance which might be supplied in this way. If the socket outlets in the area are on radial rather than ring circuits then each fixed appliance must have a separate radial circuit of its own. It is often convenient to supply equipment such as motorized valves on hot-water heating systems, roof-mounted extractor fans in kitchens, tubular heaters in tank rooms and so on by a separate circuit for each item or group of items. There is nothing wrong technically with supplying them by a fused connection unit from an adjacent general-purpose ring main provided the permanent load they put on the ring is taken into account in assessing the number of socket outlets that can be permitted, but these items have a different function from the general-purpose socket outlets and it is logical to serve them separately. Separation by function can be an asset to maintenance; there should be no need to isolate all the socket outlets in part of a building when work has to be done to a toilet extractor fan. On the other hand, a separate circuit to one small piece of equipment may seem an extravagance. No general rule can be made, and the designer must decide each application on its particular circumstances.

Equipment larger than 3 or 4 kW must in any case have a circuit for every individual item. This applies to cookers, each of which must be connected through a cooker control unit. One cooker control unit may control more than one appliance if they are in the same room. This would apply to a hob and separate oven. A cooker with four hot-plates, a grill and an oven can take 35 A when everything in it is switched on, but rarely is it used in this way. Consequently the IEE Guidance Note 1 and the IEE On-Site Guide suggest a diversity factor to apply to domestic cooker circuits. In restaurant and school kitchens the cookers are likely to be in full use for the greater part of the time. Cooker control units are generally rated at 45 A and if they and the cookers are to be properly protected, the circuit fuse must not be greater than 45 A. It follows that the circuit cannot serve anything in addition to the cooker control unit without being overloaded.

Other large equipment is likely to consist of motors driving pumps and fans in plant rooms and machine tools in workshops and factories. In the case of plant rooms each machine is almost invariably on a circuit of its own. Having more than one motor on a circuit would make it necessary to use very heavy cable and would in general be less economic than using a larger amount of smaller cable. It would also be extremely inconvenient to have several machines put out of action if one of them blows it fuse. This is particularly the case when one machine is intended as a standby for another. Similarly in factories it is usual to have each machine on a circuit of its own. In small and medium-sized factories the most convenient wiring method is probably one using conduit and trunking. In such places there is seldom any objection to installing conduit and trunking on the surface of walls, and this is cheaper than burying it in the fabric of the building. It also makes it quite easy to alter the wiring when new machines are installed or the factory is rearranged. For the same reason, it is also better to run the wiring at high level under the ceiling and drop to the machines than to run it within the floor.

In large factories, a busbar system is often used. Bare conductors enclosed in a casing are run round the factory, preferably at high level, either on the walls or under the ceiling. A switch fuse is connected to these conductors as close as possible to each machine, and the connection from the switch fuse is taken through conduit or trunking to the machine. Each machine is thus on its own circuit, but no sub-mains other than the busbars are needed. The busbars must be protected by an adequate switch fuse at the intake. It is easy to connect a new switch fuse at any point of the busbars and the electrical installation is thus both convenient and flexible.

In small workshops, for example, metalwork and engineering rooms in secondary schools, the machines used may be small enough to make it practicable to serve a number of them from one ring circuit. Each machine is connected to the ring through a fused isolator or through a switch fuse. The fuse is necessary to protect the final connection to the machine, which is necessarily of a lower rating than the ring main, and to protect the internal wiring of the machine that will also be of smaller cable than the ring main.

The cables of the ring main should be capable of carrying at least 70 per cent of the total current taken by all the machines, and it will be found that this very soon restricts the size of workshop that can be treated in this way.

It should be appreciated that everything that has been said about power circuits applies equally to three-phase and single-phase circuits. Where three-phase machines are used three or four cables, according to the system, plus an earth connection, are installed, and distribution boards, isolators and circuit breakers are of the three phase-pattern, but the general circuit arrangements are the same as for single-phase circuits.

All mechanical equipment requires maintenance, and all machines and equipment must, therefore, be installed in such a way that maintenance is possible. One of the things that has to be done before maintenance work is started is the turning off of the electricity supply, and it must be possible to isolate each machine or group of machines. It has been known to happen that an electrician has turned off an isolator in a switch room and gone to work on a machine some way from that room, that someone else has come along later, not realized that anyone was working on the machine and has turned the isolator on again. Not only has this happened, it has caused deaths. Consequently, most safety regulations, especially *The Electricity At Work Regulations*, now require that there should be an isolator within reach of the machine, or is lockable – in any case the isolation must be secure. The intention is that no one can attempt to turn the supply on without the person on the machine becoming aware of what is happening. For small machines, such as roof extractor fans, connecting the machine to the wiring through a socket and plug near the machine is a convenient and satisfactory way of providing local isolation. For larger machines, a switch or isolator or disconnector as it is now known has to be installed.

Chapter 9

Protection

Introduction

It is a truism that electricity is dangerous and can cause accidents, if not treated with respect. A large part of any system design is concerned with ensuring that accidents will not happen, or that if they do, their effects will be limited. It might be reasonably argued that these considerations are the most important part of a design engineer's task. In the previous chapters, we have spoken about choice of accessories, selection of cables and their correct sizing, the arrangement of outlets on a number of separate circuits and the proper ways of installing cables and we have pointed out the need for protecting cables against mechanical damage. If these matters are given the care they deserve, the likelihood of faults on the electrical installation will be small. Nevertheless, it is still necessary to provide protection against such faults as may happen.

The general principle of protection is that a faulty circuit should be cut off from the supply and isolated until the fault can be found and repaired. The protective device must detect that there is a fault and must then isolate the part of the installation in which it has detected the fault. One could perhaps suggest many theoretical ways of doing this, but it is also necessary that the method adopted should bear a reasonable proportion to the cost of the whole installation. Historically, the methods, which could be adopted at any time, depended on what devices could be economically manufactured at that time, but once a method has been adopted it tends to remain in use and newer products do not completely supersede it. Enthusiasts sometimes stress the advantages of a new idea while forgetting that the older method had some favourable features which the new one does not match. The result of developments is that at present there are several protective devices available and except for BS 3036 Fuses (rewireable) there appear to be no overriding grounds for preferring any one to the others.

The devices available restrict the type of protection that can be given. A logically ideal system of protection against all possible faults cannot be made economically, and the protection designed must make use of the equipment commercially available. This can lead people to argue from the available techniques to the faults to be guarded against, and in the process become so obsessed with the ease of guarding against an improbable fault that they forget the importance of protection against a more likely one. It seems more satisfactory to start by considering the faults that may happen.

Two dangers to be prevented are fire and shock to people and livestock. In turn these dangers can arise from three kinds of fault, namely a short circuit, an overload and a fault to earth.

If through a fault in the wiring or in an appliance the line or phase and neutral conductors become connected, the current that flows is limited only by the sum of the resistance of the cables of the permanent wiring and the impedance of the accidental contact between the two cables the latter generally being regarded as negligible. If the fault connecting the line and neutral has a negligible impedance the two conductors are effectively short circuited. The current that flows through the conductors is a short-circuit current, and is very high and if allowed to continue would burn the insulation. The high conductor temperature resulting from the excessive current could start a fire. If the excess current continues to flow further after the insulation has been damaged, there is also a possibility that the conductor might touch exposed metal and give a shock to anyone touching the metal.

If the fault that connects the line and neutral has some impedance the current flowing through the fault and conductors is less than the current in a short circuit of negligible impedance. It is still likely to be higher than the maximum current the circuit can safely carry and if it persists over a period of time, it can cause serious damage. When an overcurrent is flowing in a circuit, which is electrically sound, it is described as an overload. An overload can be caused by an electric motor stalling.

When an excessive mechanical load is imposed on an electric motor it continues to run but draws a higher than normal current from the supply. The circuit supplying the motor, therefore, carries a higher current than it has been designed for, and although it is not as high as a short circuit current, it can still be high enough to be dangerous. A fault in the internal wiring of a motor can also cause an electrical overload, although if it is serious enough it is likely to amount to a short circuit.

A fault to earth occurs if through some defect the line conductor becomes connected to earthed metalwork. The effect is similar to a short circuit, but whereas a short circuit will not raise exposed metalwork, termed exposed conductive parts, above zero potential, an earth fault will. We can see this by looking at Figure 9.1 which shows diagrammatically an electric fire with an earthed metal case. Suppose the fire becomes damaged and the phase cable touches the case at point A. A current will flow through the case and circuit protective conductor to earth at point B, which would normally be the earth at the electricity distribution company's transformer.

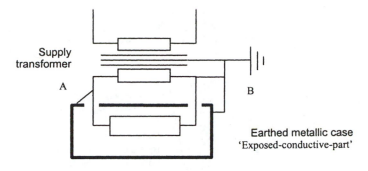

Figure 9.1 Earth fault

Now let

Uoc = Open circuit supply transformer voltage
I = Fault current flowing
Z_L = total impedance from line connection of supply transformer through line conductor, fault and the circuit protective conductor to earth connection at supply transformer
Z_c = impedance of earth path from fault back to earth connection
Z_s = Total impedance of the fault circuit.

Then the current flowing will be Uoc/Z_s, and the voltage drop between A and B will be $IZ_c = UocZ_c/Z_s$. Now Z_c/Z_s is likely to be of the order of 0.4 to 0.5, so that on a Uoc of 240 V the metal case at A will be raised to about 100 V.

We cannot explain how electrical circuits in buildings are protected against short circuits, overloads and earth faults without referring to the various protective devices which can be used. To make our account intelligible we propose first of all to describe the devices available and then go on to discuss how they are applied in practice.

Rewirable fuses

The earliest protective device consisted of a thin fuse cable held between terminals in a porcelain or bakelite holder. It is illustrated in Figure 9.2. It is inserted in the circuit being protected and the size of fuse cable is matched to the rating of the circuit. The fuse is designed so that if the current exceeds the rated current of the circuit the fuse cable melts and interrupts the circuit. Although commonly called rewirable fuses, their correct name is semi-enclosed fuses, and it is by this name that they are referred to in *British Standard* 3036 and in the *IEE Regulations* BS 7671.

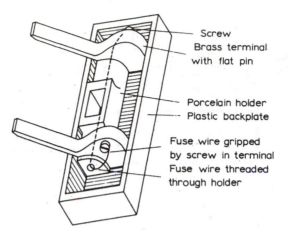

Figure 9.2 Rewirable fuse

HRC fuses

The rewirable fuse has limited breaking capacity. If a very large current flows the fuse cable melts very rapidly and a large amount of energy is released. It can be large enough to cause serious damage to the fuse carrier. It was found that some of this energy can be absorbed by a packing of inert fibrous or granular material wound with cable, and this led to the development of the cartridge fuse, illustrated in Figure 9.3.

The fuse element is mounted between two end caps which form the terminals of the complete fuse link. The fuse element is surrounded by a closely packed silica filler and the whole is contained in a ceramic casing. When the fuse element melts, or blows, the silica filler absorbs the energy. Fuses of this type are known variously as high rupturing capacity (HRC) or high breaking capacity (HBC) fuses or, less technically, as cartridge fuses.

Operation of fuses

Both rewirable and cartridge fuses work in a similar way. The current heats the fuse element until the latter melts, after which there is an arc between the

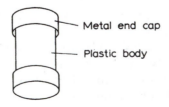

Figure 9.3 Cartridge fuse

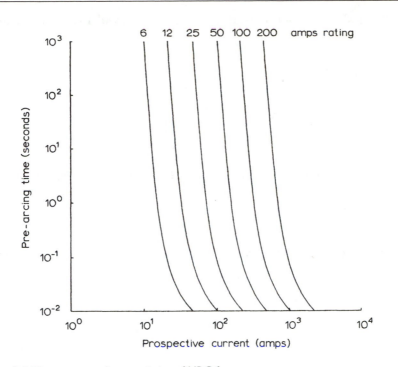

Figure 9.4 Time-current characteristics of HRC fuses

ends of the broken element, and finally the arc extinguishes and the circuit is completely interrupted.

The time taken for the fuse to melt depends on the magnitude of the current, and a fuse will have a characteristic curve of time against current. A set of such characteristic curves is shown in Figure 9.4. The total operating time is the sum of the melting, or pre-arcing, time and the time during which there is an arc, known as the arcing time. The arcing time varies with the power factor and transient characteristics of the circuit, the voltage, the point in the alternating cycle of supply at which the arcing commences and on some other factors. It is not, however, of significant length except for very large overcurrents when the total operating time is very short.

The *minimum fusing current* is the minimum current at which a fuse will melt, that is to say the asymptotic value of the current shown on the time-current characteristics. The *current rating* is the normal current. It is the current stated by the manufacturer as the current which the fuse will carry continuously without deterioration. It is also referred to as current carrying capacity and other similar terms. The *fusing factor* is the ratio

$$\frac{\text{minimum fusing current}}{\text{current rating}}$$

When a short circuit occurs, the melting process is adiabatic and the melting energy is given by

$$W = \int_0^{t_m} i^2 \, R \, dt$$

where

W = melting energy
i = instantaneous current
R = instantaneous resistance of that part of element which melts on short circuit
t = time
tm = melting time.

R is assumed to vary in the same manner with i and t for all short circuits and the quantity

$$\int_0^{t_m} i^2 \, dt$$

$$\int_0^{t_m} t^2 \, dt$$

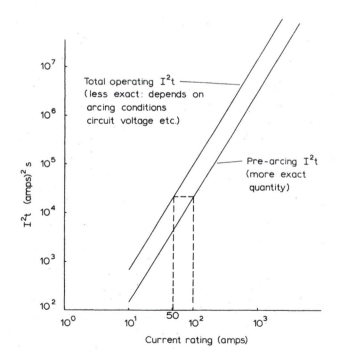

Figure 9.5 Short circuit I^2t characteristics

is approximately constant for the pre-arcing time of a fuse. It is often called the pre-arcing I^2t. It is this quantity which determines the amount of excess energy passing through the circuit before the circuit is broken and it is particularly important in the protection of semiconductor circuits and the reduction of overheating in power circuits. Typical I^2t characteristics are shown in Figure 9.5.

Oscillograms of the operation of a fuse are shown in Figure 9.6.

CB

An alternative to a fuse element which melts when overheated is a circuit breaker. A circuit breaker (CB) is one which has a rating similar to that of a fuse and is about the same physical size as a fuse carrier of the same rating. A typical circuit breaker is shown in Figure 9.7.

It has a magnetic hydraulic time delay, and the essential component is a sealed tube filled with silicone fluid which contains a closely fitted iron slug. Under normal operating conditions the time delay spring keeps the slug at one end of the tube (a).

When an overload occurs, the magnetic pull of the coil surrounding the tube increases, and the slug moves through the tube, the speed of travel depending on the magnetic force and, therefore, on the size of the current, (b). As the slug approaches the other end of the tube the air gaps in the magnetic circuit are reduced and the magnetic force is increased until it is great enough to trip the circuit breaker, (c). With this mechanism the time taken to trip is inversely proportional to the magnitude of the overload.

When a heavy overload or a complete short circuit occurs, the magnetic force is sufficient to trip the circuit breaker instantaneously in spite of the large air gaps in the magnetic circuit, (d). In this way, time delay tripping is achieved up to about seven times rated current, and instantaneous tripping above that level.

An alternative design has a bi-metal element which is heated by the circuit current and operates the trip catch when it deflects. A simple magnetic coil is included to trip the catch on short circuit, so that the resulting characteristic is similar to that of the magnetic-hydraulic type. The thermal-magnetic type is liable to be affected by the ambient temperature. If several CBs are mounted inside a closed distribution board, the heat from the currents passing through all the circuits in the board will raise the temperature inside the enclosure. Thermally operated CBs used in this way may have to be de-rated to prevent their tripping before an overload occurs. The effect of ambient temperature can, however, be reduced and the need for de-rating obviated by designing the bi-metal to run at a relatively high temperature. Typical time-current characteristics of CBs are given in Figure 9.8.

The CB has a toggle switch by which it can be operated manually. This switch is thrown into the off position when the overload device trips the

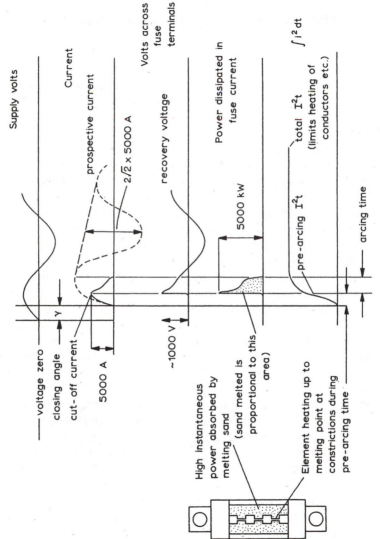

Supply volts

Current

prospective current

$2\sqrt{2} \times 5000$ A

Volts across
fuse
terminals

recovery voltage

Power dissipated in
fuse current

$\int i^2 dt$

5000 kW

total I^2t
(limits heating of
conductors etc.)

pre-arcing I^2t

arcing time

voltage zero

closing angle γ

cut-off current

5000 A

~1000 V

High instantaneous
power absorbed by
melting sand
(sand melted is
proportional to this
area)

Element heating up to
melting point at
constrictions during
pre-arcing time

Figure 9.6 Oscillograms of fuse operation

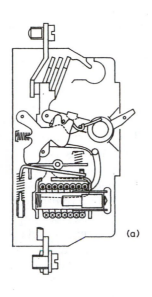

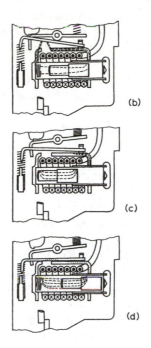

Figure 9.7 Circuit breaker

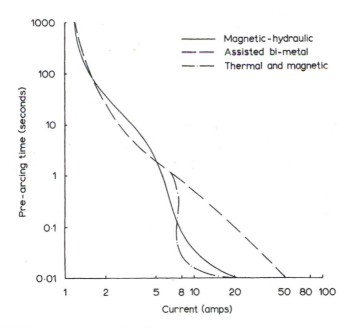

Figure 9.8 Time-current curves for CBs

breaker, and the CB is reset by the same switch. CBs can, therefore, combine the functions of switch and fuse, and in some cases this is a very useful and economic procedure. In a factory or store, for example, one may want to control the lights for a large area from a bank of switches at a single point. If a distribution board with CBs is placed at this point, it is possible to dispense with a separate bank of switches.

RCD

Another device frequently used is the residual current device (RCD). This is a circuit breaker which detects a current leaking to earth and uses this leakage current to operate the tripping mechanism. The leakage current is a residual current and gives the device its name. It should be noted here that this device will not protect against short circuit and overload. Residual current devices which do incorporate overcurrent protection are referred to as RCBOs.

The principle of the RCD is shown in Figure 9.9. The load current through the circuit is fed through two equal and opposing coils wound on a common transformer core. On a healthy circuit, the line and neutral currents are the same and produce equal and opposing fluxes in the transformer core. However, if there is an earth fault, more current flows in the line than returns in the neutral, and the line coil produces a bigger flux than the neutral coil. There is thus a resultant or residual flux which induces a current in the search coil, and this in turn operates the relay and trips the breaker. Some RCDs are manufactured with electronic circuitry which simulates the above operation.

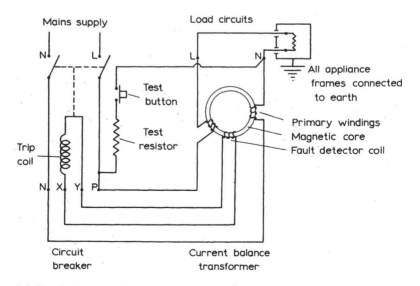

Figure 9.9 Residual current device

The value adopted for the rated tripping current, which is defined as the out-of-balance current at which the circuit breaker will trip in less than 0.1 s, is a maximum of 30 mA for protection against electric shock. The unit always includes a test button which simulates an out-of-balance condition by injecting a test current bypassing one of the principal coils. A resistor limits the magnitude of the test current so that the test also checks the sensitivity of the breaker. It should be noted that the test switch checks the operation of the residual current circuit breaker, but does not check the soundness of the earth continuity conductor. It is a requirement of BS 7671 that if an installation incorporates one of these devices a notice shall be fixed near the origin of the supply stating that the device shall be tested quarterly, by the operation of the test button. This is to ensure that the mechanical parts are kept operational. The author recommends that a notice be also fixed near to the RCD itself. The origin of the supply may be in a seldom-accessed place.

Isolating transformers

In some applications a double-wound transformer can achieve adequate protection for the system on its secondary side. The secondary is not earthed and the construction of the transformer is carefully designed to prevent any possibility of contact between the secondary and primary windings. The voltage between the line and return connections of the secondary is fixed, but because no part of it is earthed or connected to any other fixed point, the voltage relative to earth is quite undetermined. In other words the line can be at 230 V above earth and the return at earth, or the one can be at 120 V above earth and the other at 120 V below earth, or the line can be at earth and the return at 230 V below earth, or any other combination.

Thus, if anyone in contact with earthed metal touches the line conductor, the line is brought immediately to earth potential and the return drops to 240 V below earth. The same thing happens if through a fault in an appliance a conductor touches earthed metal. This prevents danger of shock. It is important to note that the system will not ensure safety if more than one appliance is fed from the transformer. Figure 9.11 shows two appliances near some earthed metalwork. Suppose a fault develops at A. The line conductor will be held at earth potential and the return conductor will be at mains voltage below earth. The circuit continues in operation and there is now no protection against a second fault occurring at another point such as B.

The chief use of isolating transformers is in shaver units fixed in bathrooms to supply electric razors. There is practically no possibility of two independent faults occurring in such an application. For other applications the system must be erected so as to prevent faults, or protect against faults.

We have now reviewed the equipment that is available to protect electrical installations in buildings and can go on to consider the nature of the protection that is needed.

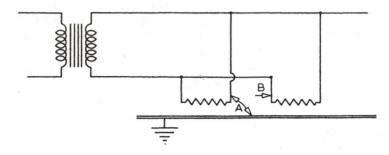

Figure 9.11 Wrong use of isolating transformer

Capacity of circuit

The methods by which a cable is sized for the duty it has to perform have been explained in Chapter 4. There is no need to be worried about the effects of a fault on the voltage drop; it is the high current that has to be guarded against. The protection has to safeguard the circuit against overcurrent, and an overcurrent is any current higher than the rating of the cable. Now the cable rating (Iz) must be rated equal to or greater than the nominal current rating of the protective device (In). Also the nominal current rating of the protective device must be rating equal to or greater than the normal current of the circuit concerned (Ib), therefore the following expression must be satisfied

$$Iz \geq In \geq Ib$$

The guiding principle to be followed is that every cable in a permanent installation in a building must be protected if it is liable to be subjected to overload or short circuit. The protective device must not have a current rating greater than that of the cable, and in most cases it will have a rating either equal to or only just less than that of the cable. It follows that at every point at which a smaller cable branches from a larger one there must be a protective device to safeguard the smaller cable. In conventional systems, this is provided by the use of switchgear and distribution boards where a main divides into two or more sub-mains and where a sub-main divides into a number of final circuits. It is also because every branch has to be protected, that a fused connection unit is installed whenever a single branch is taken off a ring main, and the fuse at the origin does not protect the spur.

Fault currents

The current normally plotted on the time-current characteristics of fuses and circuit breakers is that known as the *prospective fault current*. This is the current, which would flow in the circuit if the fuse were not there, and a short circuit or earth fault current occurred. It is indicated as a dotted line in Figure 9.6. In practice, the fuse will open the circuit before this prospective current is reached; the fuse is said to cut off and the instantaneous current attained is called the cut off current.

The wave form of the prospective fault current depends on the position of the fault within the whole of the supply network, the relative loading of the phases within the network and whether the supply comes through a transformer or directly from a local generator. These questions can be of importance to the engineer concerned with protecting a public supply system, but are of less consequence to the designer of the services within a building. For the designer's purposes the simple procedure described here is adequate and more complicated considerations need not be taken into account in selecting the protection devices to be used within the building.

The prospective current is defined as the RMS value of the alternating component, whereas the cut-off current is defined as the instantaneous current at cut-off. These definitions produce the paradox that the numerical value of the cut-off current may be greater than the numerical value of the prospective current.

The prospective earth fault current is determined by the supply voltage and the impedance of the path taken by the fault current. In Figure 9.12, the path at the remote end of the circuit, is indicated by a–b–c–d–f–g–a. The figure shows diagrammatically the usual situation in urban installations where the consumer's earth point is connected to the sheath of the electricity distribution company's cable, which is earthed at the transformer end as on a TN-S system. If the supply voltage is Uoc and the impedance of this path is Z_s, then the prospective earth fault current is given by $I_f = Uoc/Z_s$. The total impedance Z_s is made up of the impedance of the transformer and the impedance of all the cables in the path. The impedance of a transformer is almost entirely reactive, and is therefore always referred to as reactance. In practice, it is found that the reactance of the transformer sets an upper limit to the fault current that can flow. Thus if a normal 500 kVA transformer is short circuited, the current on the secondary side will be 14 000 A, while the corresponding figure for a 750 kVA transformer is 21 000 A. These are average figures for typical transformers and ignore the impedance of the supply system on the primary side of the transformer. They therefore include a small hidden safety factor. The resistance of the service cable and its sheath is usually quite low, but even a short length of a final circuit cable makes a great reduction in the prospective fault current. For example 20 m of 1.5 mm² cable in an installation supplied from a 750 kVA transformer will limit the fault current to 1000 A.

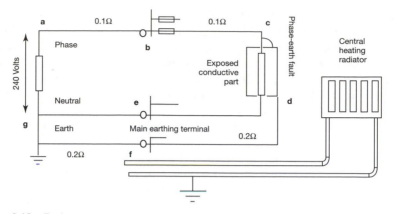

Figure 9.12a Fault currents

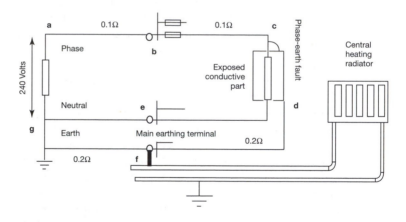

Figure 9.12b Fault currents

Data on cable resistance are given by the manufacturers in their catalogues. Information is also given in the IEE Guidance Note 1, and the On-Site Guide, the leading makers of fuses and CBs provide in their catalogues tables and graphs showing the prospective fault currents with different lengths of cable on the secondary side of standard transformers. The fault itself usually has some impedance, so that the actual fault current is less than the prospective fault current. The prospective earth fault current is calculated on the assumption that the impedance of the fault in Figure 9.12 is zero. The actual fault current could theoretically be calculated by adding the actual impedance of the fault between d and e to the impedance used for calculating the prospective earth fault current, and as the total actual impedance will thus be higher than that of the complete short circuit assumed in calculating the prospective current, the actual fault current will be less than the prospective one.

When a fault occurs on an appliance the cables of the final circuit play an important part in limiting the fault current. Nevertheless, there is always the possibility, even if a small one, of a low impedance fault immediately load side of the fuse or circuit breaker. It is this fault which, however unlikely it may be that it will happen, will produce the highest possible fault current and it is this fault with which the protection must be capable of dealing.

Discrimination

In an installation having the type of distribution described in Chapter 6, there is a series of fuses and circuit breakers between the incoming supply and the final outlet. Ideally, the protective devices should be graded so that when a fault occurs, only the device nearest the fault operates. The others should not react and should remain in circuit to go on supplying other healthy circuits. Discrimination is said to take place when the smaller fuse opens before the larger fuse. This is the desired state of affairs, and when the unwanted converse situation happens it is said that discrimination is lost.

Figure 9.13 shows the time-current characteristic for a CB serving a final circuit and for a 60 A HBC fuse protecting the sub-main leading to the distribution board on which the CB is mounted. If the fault current is less than 1200 A, the CB will open first. If the fault current is greater than this, the HBC fuse will blow before the CB can operate. The resistance of the cables of the final circuit reduces the fault current, so that the further away from the distribution board a fault occurs, the lower will be the fault current. If the fault current at the distribution board is, say, 2000 A, it will fall below this along the final circuit from the board and will drop to 1200 A fairly soon after the board. A fault on the board would blow the board fuse but a fault on the final circuit any distance from the board would leave the board intact and open the CB. The discrimination is said to be acceptable. If the fault current at the supply end of the final circuit is so high that the HBC fuse always opens before the CB, there is no discrimination. If there is discrimination at the load end of the final circuit but not for a fault a short way along of the final circuit, we say the discrimination is not acceptable. With the characteristic curves of Figure 9.13, the discrimination would probably be acceptable even for a fault level at the board of 3000 A. The possibility of a fault at the board is small and the actual fault currents to be cleared will almost certainly be due to faults at appliances. Provided discrimination is maintained for these faults, its loss on the rare occasions when a fault occurs on the permanent wiring close to the board can probably be accepted.

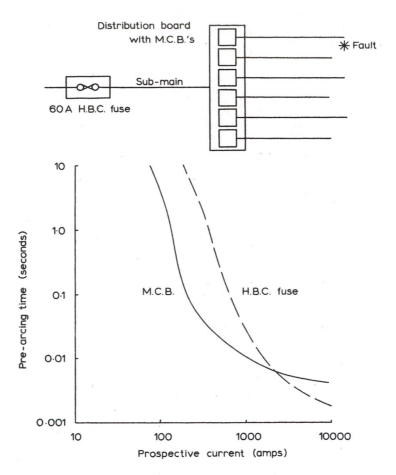

Figure 9.13 Discrimination

In general, discrimination is a problem only when a system uses all the same devices, or an appropriate mixture of CBs and fuses. It can be seen from Figures 9.4 and 9.5 that a fuse will always discriminate against another fuse of a larger rating. A 2:1 rule of thumb for fuses is sometimes used. That is, a fault on a 32 A fused final circuit would cause the 32 A fuse to operate first, if it was backed up on the distribution circuit by a fuse of at least 60 A. Manufacturers produce 'lollipop' or 'bulrush' graphs to compare the relative energies let through by certain devices. As was previously described, there is a time required for a cartridge fuse element to heat up and start to melt. This is termed the pre-arcing time. When the fuse element begins to melt, the overcurrent, being interrupted, will cause an arc across the melting element. The overcurrent will eventually be interrupted. The total operating I^2t of the

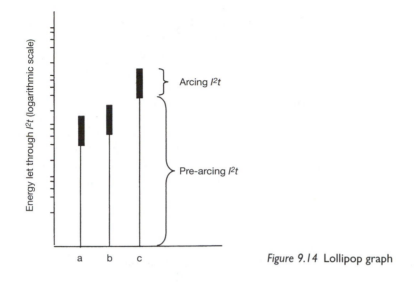

Figure 9.14 Lollipop graph

fuse is the sum of the pre-arcing I^2t and the arcing I^2t. For proper discrimination to occur the total operating I^2t of the fuse required to operate must not be greater than the pre-arcing I^2t of the upstream fuse. If fuse 'b' in Figure 9.14 was used to supply a fuseboard in which fuse 'a' was fitted, a fault on the circuit supplied by 'a' would cause fuse 'a' to operate, but the total energy let through would cause fuse 'b' to be in its arcing sector, thus weakening the fuse 'b'. If fuse 'c' was used to supply a fuseboard, in which either fuse 'a' or 'b' was fitted, a fault on either circuit would cause the lesser fuse to operate without being in the arcing sector I^2t of fuse 'c'. These lollipop graphs must be consulted on high fault currents where the fuse will operate in 0.1 s or less.

Breaking capacity and back-up protection

A certain amount of energy is released when a circuit is broken, whether by a fuse or by a circuit breaker. This energy must be absorbed by the device breaking the circuit, and the capacity to do so limits the current which the device can safely break. The breaking capacity is defined as the maximum current that can be broken at a rated voltage. In switchgear practice, it is common to refer to breaking capacity in MVA, but for the fuses and circuit breakers used in building services, it is usual to refer to breaking capacity in amperes. However, whether MVA or amperes are used, the statement of breaking capacity is incomplete unless it contains the voltage and power factor at which it applies.

In building services, in practice faults are invariably so close to unity power factor that it is hardly necessary to specify power factor. Fuses and circuit breakers are rated at the voltage of the supply which in the UK is either 230 V or 400 V, and therefore the statement of voltage can be taken for granted. Thus in spite of what has been said in the last paragraph breaking capacity is often quoted in amperes only, without further statement.

The cut-off current depends not only on the characteristics of the fuse but also on the nature of the fault current and the point in the alternating supply cycle at which the fault occurs and the fuse starts to act. Although in the majority of cases the maximum prospective fault current will not in fact be reached, for safety the fuse or circuit breaker must have a breaking capacity at least equal to the maximum prospective fault current. The breaking capacity of the various devices used in protection is of some importance and must be taken into account when a selection has to be made between different devices and schemes of protection.

It is not easy to give an exact figure for the breaking capacity of a rewireable fuse, because it depends on the type of fuse carrier or fuse holder used and the exact composition of the fuse cable and also because it is liable to vary with the age of the fuse cable. As an approximation it can be taken to be of the order of 3000 to 4000 A for the largest types of rewireable fuse.

HRC fuses to BS 1361:1971 have a breaking capacity of 16 500 A at 0.3 power factor when rated at 240 V and of 33 000 A at 0.3 power factor when rated at 415 V. HRC fuses to BS EN 88 have a maximum breaking capacity of 80 KA.

CBs to BS EN 60898 used on distribution boards to protect final circuits generally have a two breaking capacities. The higher capacity breaking capacity Icn means that the device will only interrupt that current once, and will no longer be serviceable. At the lower value Ics the device will break that current as many times as is stated in the specification for the device.

It may often be convenient to use a breaking device which has breaking capacity less than the maximum prospective fault current. As an example, with the arrangement of Figure 9.13, it could be that the fault current for a dead short circuit on an appliance at the end of a final circuit is, say, 1500 A, whilst the fault current for a short circuit on the wiring within a short distance of the board is 4000 A. The former is the only fault which is probable, and a CB with a breaking capacity of 3000 A (Ics 3.0), might well be considered a suitable form of protection. If this were installed and the possible fault of 4000 A occurred and the CB were left to clear it, the CB would suffer damage and the wiring might also be damaged before the circuit was fully broken. In such a case back-up protection is required, and is provided by the HBC fuse at the supply end of the sub-main distribution circuit. The fuse limits the maximum fault energy: if the fault current and, therefore, the fault energy is greater than the CB can handle the back-up fuse blows. If on the other hand the fault current is within the capacity of the CB the back-up fuse does not act.

Back-up protection and discrimination are closely connected, but they are not the same thing. Even if the breaking capacity of the final circuit fuse is such that no back-up protection is needed, the final circuit fuse must still discriminate against the sub-main fuse. In other words, discrimination is still needed even when back-up protection is not. Since discrimination is always needed it must also accompany back-up protection, but it does not follow that the provision of back-up protection will automatically give discrimination. It is quite possible to choose the back-up fuse so that it blows, before the distribution sub-circuit fuse, however small the fault current, and this would be back-up protection without discrimination. It is of course to be avoided.

Summing up, we can say that fuses and CBs must be so chosen that back-up protection is provided if it is needed and that discrimination is always provided.

We have described the equipment that is in practice available to give protection to electrical installations and we have considered the nature and magnitude of fault currents and the interaction of fuses and circuit breakers in series with each other. Knowing the probable faults and the equipment available we can now turn to consider how this equipment can be used to give satisfactory protection against the faults that may arise.

Overload protection

Fuses and CBs react to short circuits and thus provide protection against their consequences. However, their time-current characteristics are such that they do not provide real protection against sustained low-level overloads. For example, a 30 A HBC fuse will carry 40 A for a long period. This may harm the cables of the permanent wiring if they have been sized closely to the protective device rating. An electric motor overloaded to this extent would however burn out.

The IEE Regulations require overload protection which will operate before the current exceeds 1.45 times the current-carrying capacity of the smallest conductor in the circuit. If protection against smaller overloads than this is needed it has to be supplied with the equipment which needs the protection. The most usual case is that of an electric motor which is protected against overload by an overload relay in the motor starter. The usual type of overload relay contains a heater element and a bi-metal strip in each motor line conductor. An excessive current causes the bi-metal strip to deflect, the amount of deflection depending on the magnitude of the current and the time for which it flows. When the deflection reaches a predetermined amount the bi-metal operates the tripping mechanism, which opens the coil circuit, and this in turn causes the main contacts to open.

Such an overload protection has a time-current characteristic of the form shown in Figure 9.15. It will be seen that the starter with this overload device

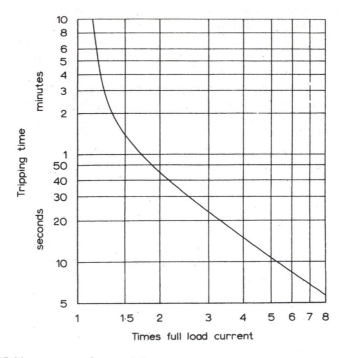

Figure 9.15 Motor starter characteristics

will carry a starting current eight times the full load current for 6 s. A fuse of the same rating would not do this.

A motor starter must be capable of operating several thousand times in its working life. A design which enables it to do so places a limit on the magnitude of the current it can break. Thus while it can deal with overloads it cannot safely break a short circuit. For this reason, the starter which protects the motor against overloads must itself be protected by a fuse to deal with short circuits. The fuse will at the same time protect the permanent wiring against short circuits.

Now a fuse of the same rating as the motor will not carry the starting current for long enough for the motor to run up to speed. The fuse backing up the starter must, therefore, have a rating higher than the normal full load running current of the motor. Motor manufacturers and starter manufacturers provide information which enables the fuse to be correctly chosen. Table 9.1 is a selection from such data. It is also now common practice for manufacturers to quote a motor rating for fuses; this is the running current for which the fuse should be used.

The arrangement of fuse, starter and motor is shown in single line diagrammatic form in Figure 9.16. Logically, cables ab and cd are protected against

Table 9.1 Fuse ratings for motor circuits

Type of starter	Overload release rating-amps	Fusing rating amps
Direct on	0.6 to 1.2	5
	1.0 to 2.0	10
	1.5 to 3.0	10
	2.0 to 4.0	15
	3.0 to 6.0	20
	5.6 to 10.0	30
	9.0 to 15.0	40
	13.0 to 17.0	50
Star-delta	4.0 to 7.0	15
	6.0 to 10.0	20
	9.0 to 17.0	30
	16.0 to 26.0	40
	22.0 to 28.0	50

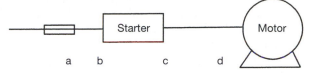

Figure 9.16 Motor protection

overload by the overload device in the circuit. For example, we can see from Table 9.1 that a motor with a running current of 3 A and a starter overload set at 3 A will need a back-up fuse of 15 A. The cable is protected against short circuit by the fuse. The time to raise the temperature of the cable to its limit is given by $t = K^2 S^2 / I^2$. Therefore we can use the formula to determine if the cable is protected against short circuit, and to determine if the starting current and starting time will raise the temperature of the cable above the limit value.

One can, however, take advantage of the fact that the starter protects the cable as well as the motor. In theory, if a very high resistance fault developed on the cable between a and b neither the fuse nor the starter would open the circuit, and damage might result. In practice, the chances of this happening are so small that they may be neglected. The usual practice is to make cables ab and cd such that their current rating is equal to the maximum setting of the overload protection device fitted in the starter. This is probably one of the few cases in which it is in order for the cable to have a rating less than that of the fuse protecting it, and it may be done only where there is a motor starter incorporating an overload relay. One other case is where an overload cannot occur, such as on an immersion heater circuit, where the heater is working or it is not. The circuit must however be protected against short circuit.

Protection of persons

People using the building have to be protected against electric shock. They would get a shock if they came into contact with live parts, and in considering protection a distinction is made between direct and indirect contact. Direct contact is contact by a person with a live conductor which is intended to carry current in normal operation. The normal protection against this is the provision of insulation on all current-carrying cables, and enclosing terminals and connections

Indirect contact is contact with exposed conductive parts which are not intended to carry current but have become live as a result of a fault. Such a fault is indicated in Figure 9.12a. When it occurs, the metal case of an appliance which a person is likely to handle is raised towards line potential and will cause a shock if it is touched by someone using the appliance. Protection is provided by the fact that the case is earthed and that a protective device will disconnect the circuit as soon as a fault current flows to earth.

It is possible that a fault of this type will occur while a person is holding an appliance. In that case he will be subjected to a dangerous potential during the time it takes for the protective device to operate and disconnect the supply. For this reason BS 7671 stipulates the time in which the device must operate, which is 0.4 s for 230 V circuits serving socket outlets and 5 s for circuits serving only fixed equipment. The reason for the difference is that a person is likely to have a firmer grip on a portable appliance plugged into a socket outlet than on a fixed appliance which he is only likely to touch casually. There is a circumstance where the time to disconnect a socket circuit may be increased to 5 s.

A current would also flow through a person if he came into contact with two separate pieces of metal at different potentials. In the event of a fault such a potential difference could exist between the exposed metal case of an electrical appliance and earthed metalwork which is not part of the electrical system, termed extraneous conductive parts, such as structural steelwork, or a central heating radiator. To avoid danger arising in this way all extraneous conductive parts must be linked (bonded) to the main earthing terminal of the installation. The conductors by which this is done are known as main equipotential bonding conductors and methods for determining its size are given in the *IEE Regulations*. This causes all extraneous conductive parts connected to the main earthing terminal to raise in potential, when a fault occurs on a circuit, creating an equipotential zone.

Earth protection

As we have seen, fuses and CBs react to short circuits. If they are to provide protection against faults to exposed conductive parts, the wiring must be such that the fault produces the same conditions as a short circuit, namely a large excess current in the line conductor. This will happen only if the impedance of the path taken by the fault current is low enough. The path is indicated by a–b–c–d–f–g–a in Figure 9.12a/b and is known as the earth fault loop path; its impedance is known as the earth fault loop impedance.

An earth fault occurs when a phase conductor touches exposed metalwork of an installation termed an exposed conductive part, and so raises the metal to a dangerous potential. If a fuse or CB is to be used to clear a fault of this nature, then the fault must immediately produce a current large enough to operate the fuse or breaker quickly. To achieve this, all exposed metalwork which, in the event of some fault, could conceivably become live, is earthed and the earth path is designed to have low impedance. When a fault occurs, current flows through circuit protective conductors to earth, and because of the low impedance in the earth fault loop path, the current is large enough to operate the protective device. It must also be large enough to operate the device within the time stipulated above. The Regulations give details of the maximum earth fault loop impedance which can be allowed to ensure operation within the required times for fuses, CBs and RCBOs.

Since an earth fault raises exposed conductive parts above earth potential it creates the possibility of a voltage existing between such metal, and nearby metalwork such as structural metalwork , which introduces earth potential, and is not part of the electrical installation, and is termed an extraneous-conductive-part, and not affected by the fault and therefore still at earth potential. Although the fuse or CB will clear the fault, that is to say remove it, the operating time of the fuse or CB may be long enough to cause danger of electric shock. One way to prevent danger is to bond the two sets of metalwork together. We have already mentioned this in Chapter 6. In any event the IEE Regulations require the main earth terminal at the incoming supply intake to be bonded to the metalwork as shown in Figure 9.12b, of any gas or water services as near as possible to the point at which those services enter the building.

The policy of protecting against earth faults by making sure that they produce a short circuit and, therefore, operate the fuse or circuit breaker has been described as 'chasing the ampere'. With ever-increasing demand for electricity, circuit ratings and their fuse ratings are becoming ever higher and the short circuit current needed to operate the fuse or circuit breaker becomes higher. Thus ever-lower values are required for earth loop impedances and the fault currents which the fuses have to break become higher. The opinion has been expressed that this method of protection will not be able to keep pace with the consequences of increasing electrical loading.

However, at the present time in urban areas where the electricity company provides an effective earth to the sheath of the service cable (TN-S), or by connecting the main earthing terminal to the supply neutral (TN-C-S) there is no difficulty in achieving an earth loop impedance of less than 1.0 ohm. It may perhaps not be possible to do this as long as steel conduit is relied on as the earth return path, but it can certainly be done by the use of a separate circuit protective conductor. Because of the need for low earth impedances separate protective conductors should nowadays always be used on new installations. Although not strictly necessary, since the cross-sectional area of conduit is more than adequate to satisfy the regulations.

If for any reason the earth loop impedance cannot be made low enough it becomes necessary to use a residual current circuit breaker. An RCD which will operate on an earth fault current of 30 mA will react on a 230 V circuit even if the earth loop impedance is 480 ohms and it is inconceivable that values anything like as high as this would ever be found on a practical installation.

Temporary installations are likely to have higher earth loop impedance paths than permanent ones, and it is very common to use earth leakage protection for the temporary wiring on building sites, particularly in rural areas.

It should be noticed that earthing of exposed metalwork is still necessary when an RCD is used. This can be shown by reference to Figure 9.12a/b. Suppose the earth return path f–g did not exist, then normal current would flow through a–b–c–e–g–a and there would be no imbalance between line and neutral for a current operated CB to detect. Nevertheless the exposed metalwork, connected through the fault to the conductor at d, would be at a potential given by

$$\frac{\text{impedance of abc}}{\text{impedance of abcdega}} \times \text{line voltage}$$

and depending on the relative impedances of the various parts of the earth fault loop impedance path, this could be anything up to almost full line voltage.

We refer yet again to Figure 9.12a. If we assume that the impedance of the transformer winding is negligible, the value of the earth fault loop path Z_s, is $0.1 + 0.1 + 0.2 + 0.2 = 0.6\,\Omega$.

$$I_f = Uoc/Z_s$$

where Uoc is the open circuit voltage of the transformer, the fault current would be

$$I_f = 240/0.6 = 400\,\text{A}$$

and the potential drop from a to c is

$$Ua\text{--}c = I_f \times Za\text{--}c$$
$$Ua\text{--}c = 400 \times (0.1 + 0.1) = 80\,V$$

The voltage of the exposed conductive part will be

$$240 - 80 = 160\,V \text{ above earth}$$

If the faulted piece of equipment is touched by a person simultaneously with the central heating radiator, the person would receive a 160 V shock.

Now consider Figure 9.12b, with the main equipotential bonding in place. Assuming the earth fault current remained the same as without bonding, the volts drop d–f would be

$$Ud\text{--}f = I_f \times Zd\text{--}f$$
$$Ud\text{--}f = 400 \times 0.2 = 80\,V$$

The potential of the main earthing terminal will be

$$Uoc - (Ua\text{--}c + Ud\text{--}f)$$
$$240 - (80 + 80) = 80\,V \text{ above earth potential}$$

Now with the main equipotential bonding in place, the voltage of the central heating radiator will be the same as the main earthing terminal, that is 80 V. Therefore anyone in contact with the faulted piece of equipment and the central heating radiator would receive a shock voltage equal to the potential difference between the faulted piece of the equipment and the radiator, which is 160 V – 80 V = 80 V. Bonding has reduced this from a value without bonding of 160 V. The reason for equipotential bonding is to create an equipotential zone. Exposed conductive parts are earthed to cause rapid disconnection. It is important to differentiate between earthing and equipotential bonding. It would be counter-productive to bond plastic pipework and items of metalwork such as aluminium window frames that do not introduce a potential in the worst case.

The values of impedance of the earth fault loop path are for explanation only and are not meant to be typical.

If the conditions prevent the use of fuses and circuits breakers, for shock protection, such as high earth loop impedances, is possible to use RCDs since these devices do not require a high current to operate quickly. BS 7671 require an RCD to be used to protect a socket outlet which is intended for portable equipment to be used outside the building. This is for additional direct contact protection They also require all socket outlets to be protected by RCDs when earthing is provided by the user's own electrode (a TT system) and not by connection to an earth provided at the supply authorities' transformer. It is left to the designer's discretion whether a separate RCD is provided for each socket outlet, whether each circuit is protected by an RCD or whether all circuits on a distribution board are protected by an RCD on the supply side of the board. Although BS 7671 requires that due account be taken of the operation of a single protective device, an RCD on the main supply of a distribution board would trip the whole board should a fault occur on one circuit.

It is the designer's responsibility to use experience and professional judgement in selecting the scheme of protection.

Earth monitoring

Protection through earthing of exposed metalwork will fail if there is a break in the earth continuity conductor. It is possible to add an extra cable which will monitor the earth continuity conductor and break the main circuit if the earth continuity fails. The basic scheme of such a circuit is shown in Figure 9.17.

The monitoring circuit incorporates a low-voltage transformer, a relay, and a protective circuit breaker. An additional pilot lead is required to the appliance or portable tool. The low voltage is used to drive a current round the loop formed by the earth conductor, a section of the metallic housing of the appliance, the pilot conductor and the relay coil. This current holds in the relay and thus keeps the coil of the circuit breaker energized.

If there is a break in the earth continuity conductor, or indeed anywhere in the pilot circuit, the low-voltage current fails, the relay is de-energized, the main contactor coil becomes de-energized and the circuit breaker opens

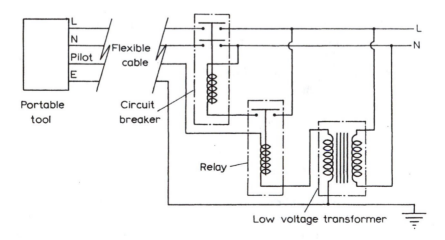

Figure 9.17 Monitored earth leakage protection

the main circuit and cuts off the supply to the appliance. It will be noticed that this monitoring circuit merely checks that the earth continuity conductor is sound; it does not add to the basic earth leakage protection.

Earth electrodes

In normal earthing, the earth and the neutral are quite separate. The load current flowing through the neutral must cause a potential difference between the two ends of the neutral. Since the end at the supply transformer is earthed, the end at the consumer's service terminal must inevitably be at some potential above earth. It cannot, therefore, be used as an earth point.

Nevertheless, an effective earth has to be found for the earth continuity conductors of the permanent installation in a building. In urban areas the sheath of the electricity company's service cable is normally used for this purpose, but there is no obligation on the company to provide an earth, and in rural areas where the supply may be by overhead cable, it may not be possible for them to do so. In such cases, the consumers must provide their own earth electrodes and the design of these become part of the design of the building installation.

An earth electrode is a metal rod, which makes effective contact with the general mass of earth. A common type consists of a small diameter copper rod which can be easily driven to a depth of 6m or more into ground reasonably free of stones or rock. The soil remains practically undisturbed and in very close contact with the electrode surface. Since resistivity is lower in the deeper strata of earth and not very affected by seasonal conditions, deep driving gives a good earth. Rods of this type are practically incorrodible. Also it is easy to get access to the connection at the top of the electrode. A typical arrangement is illustrated in Figure 9.18.

Where the ground is shallow but has low resistivity near the surface, a plate electrode, either of copper or, of cast iron, can be used. When the soil resistivity is high, a cast iron plate can be used with a coke surround. This method is illustrated in Figure 9.19.

Standard cast iron plates are made for use as earth electrodes. They are complete with terminals for the earth continuity conductor. These terminals consist of two copper sockets each secured by a drift-pin, the two being joined by a tinned copper strand to which the earth conductor is bound and soldered. The completed connection is sealed and covered in bitumen before the electrode is buried. It is, therefore, not as accessible as the connection of the rod type electrode.

Long copper strip can also be used as an earth electrode, and the method of doing this is shown in Figure 9.20. It will be seen from this that the strip is a useful type of electrode for shallow soil overlying rock. Strip may be arranged in single lengths, parallel lengths or in radial groups. Standard strip is commercially available for use as earth electrodes.

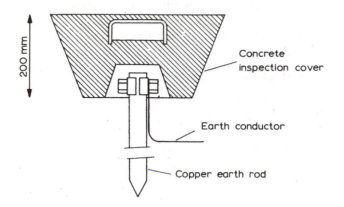

200 mm

Concrete inspection cover

Earth conductor

Copper earth rod

Figure 9.18 Copper rod electrode

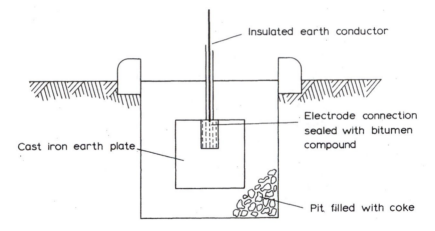

Insulated earth conductor

Electrode connection sealed with bitumen compound

Cast iron earth plate

Pit filled with coke

Figure 9.19 Cast iron plate electrode

When current flows from the electrode into the soil, it has to overcome the resistance of the soil immediately adjacent to the electrode. The path of the current is shown in Figure 9.20. The effect is equivalent to a resistance between the electrode and the general mass of earth, and this resistance is the resistance of the electrode. Furthermore, the surface of the ground near the electrode becomes live when current flows from the electrode to earth and Figure 9.21 shows a typical surface distribution near a rod electrode. It can be seen that an animal standing near such an electrode could have a substantial voltage applied between its fore and hind legs, and in fact fatal accidents to livestock from this cause have been known. The earth electrode should, therefore, be positioned well out of harm's way. It should

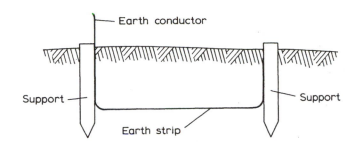

Figure 9.20 Copper strip electrode

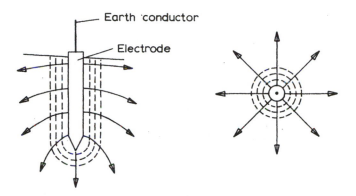

Figure 9.21 Current from electrode into earth

perhaps be noted that the deeper the electrode is below the ground, the smaller will be the voltage gradient at the surface.

The effectiveness of earth protection depends on the low resistance of the electrode when current flows through the electrode into the soil. This resistance cannot be accurately predicted in advance and must be checked by testing. After installation, the electrode should be periodically examined and tested to ensure that its initial low resistance is being maintained. The scheme for testing an electrode is shown in Figure 9.23. The electrode under test is indicated by X; two auxiliary electrodes, Y and Z are driven in for the test. Y must be placed sufficiently far from X for the resistance areas not to overlap, and Z is placed approximately halfway between X and Y. The test electrode X is disconnected from its normal continuity conductor and connected to the test instrument as shown in Figure 9.23. A low-voltage alternating current is passed between X and Y. The current is measured and so is the potential between X and Z. The resistance of the earth electrode is given by the dividend of voltage and current. Check readings are taken with the electrode Z nearer to and further from electrode X, and the results are

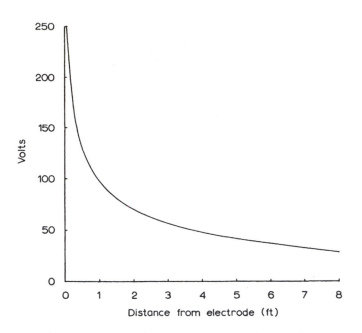

Figure 9.22 Voltage at surface of ground due to rod electrode

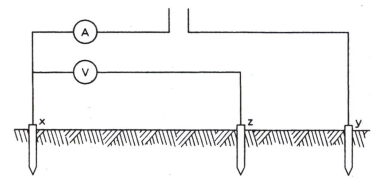

Figure 9.23 Earth electrode resistance test

accepted only if all three readings are substantially the same. If they are not, the test must be repeated with a greater distance between X and Y.

Protective multiple earthing

This is an alternative method of earthing in which the neutral of the incoming supply also forms the earth return path. In other words, instead of the neutral and earth of the incoming supply being separate, they are combined to form a TN-C-S system (definitions in BS 7671 explains the systems in use). The supply authority is required to maintain the resistance between the neutral conductor and earth to a maximum of 10 Ω. To do this the supply authority earth the supply neutral at various multiple points, protective multiple earthing (PME).

The installation within the building is carried out in exactly the same way as for any other system, and separate earth continuity conductors are used. The main earthing terminal at the intake is not, however, connected to a separate earth return, but connected to the neutral of the incoming service cable.

Because with this system the neutral is relied on as the earth, there must be no fuses, cut-outs, circuit breakers or switches anywhere in the neutral. In the UK an area electricity company may not adopt PME without the permission of the Secretary of State for the Environment, and stringent requirements are made to ensure that the neutral conductor is adequate to carry earth fault currents, that it is truly kept at earth potential and that it is protected against breaks in continuity. The permission of British Telecom is also required. This is because the currents into and through the ground at the points of multiple earthing could cause interference to adjacent telephone and telegraph cables in the ground.

After early hesitations, PME is becoming increasingly widespread in the UK. Experience has shown that it is in practice as safe in certain conditions as previously used methods and it has important advantages. In rural areas it makes it unnecessary for consumers to have their own earth electrodes and therefore removes the risks of earth electrodes in the care of unqualified persons. In urban areas it makes the electricity companies' distribution network cheaper. This system however must not be offered to boat or caravan supplies, since there is a small risk of the neutral becoming disconnected. This would cause the shell of the caravan to become live under earth fault conditions. It is also not to be used on petrol station supplies.

Double insulation

Electrical appliances connected to the permanent wiring of a building, whether through plugs into socket outlets or by means of permanent connections, must themselves be protected against faults. There is need for protection against a fault developing on the appliance itself.

When protection of the permanent wiring depends on earthing, the same principle can be used for the appliance. The previous discussion has assumed this, and has proceeded on the basis that the metal casing of an appliance is effectively connected through the earth pin of the plug to the earth connection in the socket. There is, however, an alternative method of achieving safety of appliances which does not depend on earthing the appliances, and this is known as double insulation. For purposes of exposition appliances of the class known as all insulated may be considered as special cases of double insulation.

Double insulation consists of two separate sets of insulation. The first is the *functional* insulation, which is the ordinary insulation of the conductors needed to confine the current to the conductors and to prevent electrical contact between the conductors and parts not forming part of the circuit. The *supplementary* insulation is additional to and independent of the functional insulation. It is an entirely separate insulation which provides protection against shock in the event of the functional insulation's breaking down.

Another term which we have to explain is *reinforced insulation*. This is an improved functional insulation with such mechanical and electrical properties that it gives the same degree of protection against shock as does double insulation.

An all-insulated appliance is one which has the entire enclosure made of substantial and durable insulating material. In effect, it is a double-insulated appliance in which the supplementary insulation forms the enclosure.

Both earthing and double insulation provide protection against the breakdown of the primary functional insulation. Earthing depends, in the ways already described, on ensuring that if the functional insulation fails, exposed metalwork will be prevented from rising significantly above earth potential. If the case of the appliance can be made of insulating material which is robust enough to withstand all conditions in which it is to be used, then there is no danger of shock even if the functional insulation fails. Such an appliance is an all-insulated one, and this form of construction gives adequate safety, but some appliances must have exposed metal; for example, hedge clippers and portable drills. Other appliances are so large that it is impracticable to make an insulating case strong enough to withstand ordinary usage without making the whole appliance too heavy and cumbersome; for example, a vacuum cleaner. In these cases, double insulation can be used. It provides a second barrier of insulating material between conductors and exposed metal parts. The presence of this additional barrier is a protection against the failure of the functional insulation and makes it unnecessary to earth the exposed metal. Double-insulated equipment is designed so that in general two independent sections of insulation must both fail before any exposed metal can become live. The functional and protective insulation must be so arranged that a failure of either is unlikely to spread to the other. They ought, therefore, to be mechanically distinct, so that there is a surface of discontinuity between them.

The principle of double insulation is illustrated in Figure 9.24, in which the phase and neutral conductors each consist of a cable with ordinary functional insulation. The casing is itself of insulating material and forms the supplementary insulation. If a fault develops on the functional insulation, a

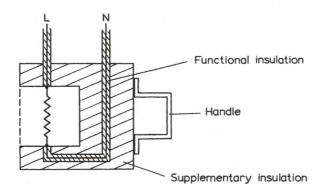

Figure 9.24 Double insulation

short circuit may develop between the live and neutral conductors but the supplementary insulation will prevent the metal handle on the outside from becoming live.

An appliance which is double insulated by the use of either supplementary or reinforced insulation should not be earthed and is not provided with an earth terminal. When it is connected to a standard three-pin plug the earth pin of the plug is left unconnected. Double insulation gives the same degree of protection against shocks as earthing, and makes that protection independent of the earth loop impedance. It also gives protection against high impedance faults to earth on the appliance itself, and thus guards against fires caused by local overheating at the appliance.

Double insulation is a means of making an appliance safe. It cannot give protection against faults on the permanent wiring in the fabric of a building. Thus, if there are any metal parts used in the wiring installation, they must still be earthed. Such parts would be conduit, switches, distribution boards, control panels and so on. It is hardly practicable to carry out an installation of any size without the use of some metal components so that the principle of double insulation cannot be applied to the permanent wiring. Moreover, the designer and erector of the services in a building cannot control what appliances may be connected to the service during the life of the building. Even if all the appliances in a building when it is first put into use are of the double-insulated pattern, so long as appliances depending on earth protection (and all electric kettles do) remain in existence, one of them could at some time be connected to the system. Therefore, the system must have an effective earth for the appliances to be linked to.

One of the strongest arguments for the use of double-insulated and all-insulated appliances is that it makes the safety of the portable appliance independent of the installation to which it is connected. The manufacturer knows that the user is protected by the design of the appliance and this safety is given without reliance on the earthing system of the building in which the appliance is to be used, over which the appliance manufacturer has, of course, no control. The manufacturer has thus gone a long way towards protecting the user against the latter's own ignorance of the safe way of connecting an appliance to a defective system, which could happen either through ignorance or through inadvertence.

At the same time, if all appliances were known to be double insulated, the designer of the electrical services could concentrate on protective devices for the system being designed without having to consider what protection to leave for appliances which the occupants will bring along later. Unfortunately, this is not the case, and the designer must consider the inter-action of other people's appliances and the system. In particular, designers should perhaps reflect on what kind of flexible cords and extension flexes are likely to bridge the gap between their system and a well-made and safe appliance.

The *IEE Regulations* do not allow the designer to assume that equipment connected to socket outlets will be double insulated and they must therefore be provided with earth continuity conductors.

Portable tools

We shall conclude this chapter by considering the special problems of portable tools. These are a very important class of appliances, especially in some factories which use them in large numbers, and they are subject to certain difficulties of their own. When a tool stalls, it is likely to blow a fuse, and after this has happened a few times the operator or maintenance engineer decides that to avoid replacing the fuse every time the tool is momentarily overloaded, a larger fuse will be substituted, capable of carrying the overload. Unfortunately, it is also capable of carrying a substantial earth fault current, for an increased length of time, and the operator can be electrocuted before the oversize fuse clears the fault.

The flexible cables of portable tools come in for exceptionally rough usage and are therefore particularly liable to develop faults. At the same time people using a portable tool in a factory are likely to be either standing on, or else touching or close to, substantial metal parts, so that they have a low impedance to earth. Thus an earth fault is more probable on a portable tool and its effects are more likely to be immediate and serious than on almost any other kind of appliance. It ought, therefore, to receive extra care in protection but in fact may receive less than average attention.

To overcome these difficulties, factories which use portable tools in large numbers often install a special low-voltage supply to serve them. Typical voltages used are 110 V and 55 V to earth. Of course, the tools have to be wound for this supply and it is a disadvantage that the motors are bulkier and heavier.

Another solution is to provide protection against sustained overload by means of circuit breakers with time-delay characteristics such that they will not operate on temporary overloads, and separate protection against earth faults by residual current circuit breakers. A fuse is then needed only for back-up protection, if at all, and can be large enough not to blow when the tool temporarily stalls. It is also advisable to use earth monitoring on the earth conductors to portable tools. This makes it necessary for the flexible cables to have an extra conductor and for the tools themselves to have an extra connection.

None of these precautions is very suitable for the home handyman, who may not have enough understanding of electrical theory to appreciate the need for them. It is probably better for portable tools to be protected by double insulation rather than by reliance on effective earthing. A similar case can be argued for making domestic appliances double insulated. Many modern appliances, of which we may quote vacuum cleaners and hairdryers as examples, are nowadays made with double insulation.

Standards relevant to this chapter are:

BS 88	Cartridge fuses for voltages up to and including 1000 V a.c. and 1500 V d.c.
BS 2950	Specification for cartridge fuse links for tele-communications and light current applications
BS 1361	Cartridge fuses for a.c. circuits in domestic and similar premises
BS 1362	General purpose fuse links for domestic and similar purposes (primarily for use in plugs)
BS 3036	Semi-enclosed electric fuses (ratings up to 100 A and 240 V)
BS 3535/BS EN 60742	Safety isolating transformers
BS 4293/BS EN 61008–1	Residual current operated circuit breakers
BS 4752	Switchgear and controlgear up to 1000 V a.c. and 1200 V d.c.
BS 5486	Factory built assemblies of switchgear and con-trolgear

Chapter 10

Fire alarms

Introduction

A fire alarm circuit, as its name implies, sounds an alarm in the event of a fire. There can be one or several alarms throughout a building, and there can be several alarm points which activate the warning. The alarm points can be operated manually or automatically; in the latter case they may be sensitive to heat, smoke or ionization. There are clearly many combinations possible, and we shall try in this chapter to give some systematic account of the way they are built up. The external circuitry is similar whether the control panel consists of electronic components or electromechanical relays.

Circuits

The simplest scheme is shown in Figure 10.1. Several alarm points are connected in parallel, and whenever one of them is actuated the circuit is completed and the alarm sounds. This is described as an open circuit, and it will be seen that it is not fail-safe, because if there is a failure of supply, the fire alarm cannot work. Another characteristic of this circuit is that every

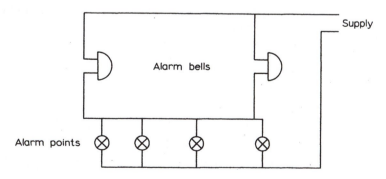

Figure 10.1 Fire alarm open circuit

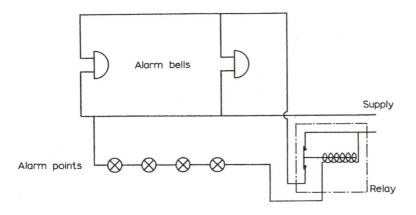

Figure 10.2 Fire alarm closed circuit

alarm point must be capable of carrying the full current taken by all the bells or hooters working together. An end-of-line resistor placed at the remote end of the break-glass points or detectors allows a monitoring current to flow so that any breaks in the wiring can be detected by the cessation of a current flow.

A slightly more elaborate scheme is shown in Figure 10.2. The alarm points are connected in series with each other and with a relay coil. The relay is normally closed when de-energized, and opens when the coil is energized. Thus when an alarm point is activated the relay coil is de-energized, the relay closes and the alarm sounds. The system fails safe to the extent that if the coil circuit fails the main circuit operates the alarm. It is not of course safe against total failure of the supply because in that event there is no supply available to work the bells. The alarm points do not have to carry the operating current of the bells or hooters. This arrangement is called a closed circuit in contrast to the open circuit of Figure 10.1. We can notice that in an open circuit the alarm points are cabled in parallel and are normally open, while in a closed circuit they are cabled in series and are normally closed.

When an alarm has been given it is often desirable to silence the audible alarm before the operating point which actuated the alarm is replaced or reset. An alarm stop/reset unit is made commercially which diverts the current from the general alarm to a supervisory buzzer or indicator but restores the current to its normal condition when the alarm initiating point has been reset. An open circuit including this unit is shown in Figure 10.3.

In a large building it may be desirable to have an indicator at some central position to show which warning point in the building has caused the alarm to sound. Figure 10.4 shows a closed scheme in which each pair of points is connected to a separate signal on an indicator board. The board can have either flags or luminous signs. The circuit can easily be adapted so that each

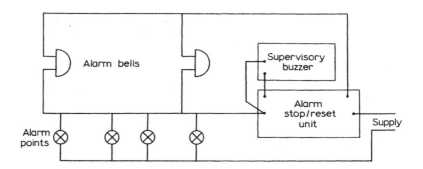

Figure 10.3 Fire alarm with relay unit

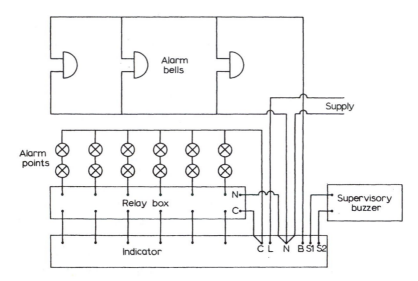

Figure 10.4 Fire alarm with indicator

individual point has its own signal or so that a larger number of points is grouped together to one signal. All the points so grouped are cabled in series and are connected to their own operating relay in the relay box. The alarm contacts are closed when any one of the relays is energized. The bells can be silenced when required, but neither the supervisory buzzer nor the indicator can be reset until the alarm initiating point has been restored to its normal position.

Other refinements can be made for more complicated schemes in large buildings. The exact circuit arrangement must depend largely on the features of the equipment used, and in practice a satisfactory scheme can only be designed round a chosen manufacturer's equipment and with the aid of data from the relevant catalogue.

Electronic systems

Solid state electronics, printed circuit boards and microprocessors have made it possible to include more facilities within fire alarm systems.

The simplest development is for the inputs from the fire detectors to be fed into a microprocessor which is programmed for various functions. These would include the operation of audible alarms and visual indicators and could also include output signals to remote repeater panels and relays which in turn could activate fire-fighting services. It may for example be useful to operate automatic door closers or door releasers, and stop, start or even reverse some of the ventilation fans. Both detectors and audible alarms can be arranged in zones. The programme can be such that a signal from one zone activates the alarms in that zone and in some but not all of the other zones.

A further possibility is circuits which monitor the state of every detecting sensor. In some systems it is possible to distinguish between normal, fire alarm and fault conditions and illuminate indicator lights on the control panel accordingly. It is possible to detect deterioration of heat, smoke or ionization detectors and indicate that maintenance or replacement is necessary. The monitoring is usually done by checking each part of the system in turn in a sequence which is repeated every two or three seconds. These are termed 'addressable systems'.

For large systems, the monitoring process can be displayed on a visual display unit and a permanent record provided by a printer. The addition of a keyboard with the appropriate circuitry enables an operator or supervisor to interrupt the automatic monitoring sequence and test parts of the system at will. The central panel of such a system is shown in Figure 10.5.

These systems can also be combined with burglar or intruder alarms. In factories it may be useful to have detection and warning of particularly important plant failures, and even further extensions are possible. One manufacturer offers a system which combines fire detection, sprinkler supervision, security, plant monitoring and control and air-conditioning monitoring and control, as well as incorporating voice communication.

For sites covering many acres with several buildings it becomes necessary to have an independent alarm system in each building with the output information of each repeated in a central security or management office. This can be done economically by telecommunication multiplexing techniques which allow a large number of panels of many types to be connected together with only three cables and be able to send signals between each other in both directions.

With this type of equipment it is essential that all the components are compatible with each other. In the language of electronics, the designer must

Figure 10.5 Fire detection central station (Courtesy of Gent & Co. Ltd)

ensure that the right interfaces are provided. In practice it is necessary for the building services designer to work with a selected system manufacturer to ensure that all components are compatible with each other.

Wiring

The wiring of a fire alarm installation follows exactly the same principles as any other wiring, but greater consideration has to be given to the protection of the cables and to their ability to withstand fire damage. Cables used in fire alarm systems fall into two general categories. In group 1, cables are not required to operate after the fire has been detected; in group 2, cables are required to operate after the fire has been detected. It is obviously necessary for a fire alarm to go on working for quite some time after a fire has started. The wiring of group 2 must, therefore, be entirely separate from any other wiring. In conduit or trunking systems, it should be segregated from all other services and run in conduit or trunking of its own. It must be able to withstand high temperature, which in practice means that it is MICC to BS 6207 part 1, to BS 6387 categories AWX, SWX, A or S. Other types of cable may be used if they are embedded in 12 mm of plaster or equivalent, protecting them from significant fire risk for half-an-hour. In any case, BS 5839 specifies a number of requirements on the cables used in fire-alarm circuits. For electronic systems the cable may need to be a coaxial or screened type, and the manufacturer's requirements must be checked to ascertain this. The supply to the fire alarm must also be separate from any other supply, and this at the very least means that it must be fed from its own circuit breaker or switch at the main service entry into the building. Some authorities go further and think that the fire-alarm system should be at extra low voltage, and to satisfy this requirement fire alarm equipment is made for 24 V a.c. and 12, 24 or 48 V d.c. operation as well as for mains voltage operation. BS 5839 requires that a risk formal assessment forms the basis of design.

A system working on 24 V a.c. has to be fed from a transformer. The primary of the transformer is fed from its own circuit breaker or switch at the main service entry. D.c. systems are fed from batteries of the accumulator type, which are kept charged by a charger unit connected to the mains. As the battery will operate the system for a considerable period before losing all its charge, this method provides a fire alarm which is independent not only of the mains within the building, but also of all electrical services into the building. For this reason, some factory inspectors and fire-pevention officers insist that a battery system be used. However, when the system voltage is low the currents required to operate the equipment are higher and the voltage drops which can be tolerated are much smaller. We can see this by reflecting that a motor wound for 240 V will work without noticeable diminution of speed or performance if the voltage at its terminals drops by 6 V to 234 V, which is a reduction of 21.5 per cent, whereas a 24 V bell may not sound at all if a potential of 18 V is applied to it. In this case a drop of 6 V in the line is a reduction of 25 per cent. At the same time for a given sound output a 24 V bell needs ten times the current that a 240 V bell does.

Thus voltage drop becomes a very serious factor in the design of any extra-low voltage system. The equipment to be used must be carefully checked to see what voltage drop it can accept and the cables sized to keep the drops very low. This usually results in large cables having to be used. There is a great deal to be said for obviating these difficulties as far as possible by not using systems at less than 48 V. Electronic systems operate with much smaller currents so that for most of the system, voltage drop is not a critical consideration. But the bells or horns still require appreciable power and voltage drop should not be overlooked, particularly in discussion with electronics specialists who are not normally concerned with it.

In the author's opinion, there is very little to be said for a 24 V transformer system. It has all the voltage drop problems of a d.c. system without the independence of the incoming service that batteries give. In other words it appears to have the disadvantages of both mains and battery systems without the advantage of either.

The current carrying capacity of each component has to be taken into account in the design and layout of the installation. It may happen, for example, that the total current of all the alarm signals sounding together exceeds the current which can be taken by the contacts of the alarm initiating points. The closed circuit of the type shown in Figure 10.2 overcomes this problem because the current to the alarm bells does not go through the initiating points. This is a considerable advantage of the closed system, and can be a deciding factor in choosing it in preference to the open system. Even with closed systems, however, the total current of the alarm signals may exceed the capacity of the contacts in the indicator panel. If this happens, a further relay must be interposed between the indicator and the alarm signals.

Fire-alarm points

A typical manually operated fire-alarm point is shown in Figure 10.6. It is contained in a robust red plastic case with a glass cover. The material is chosen for its fire-resisting properties. The case has knock-outs for conduit entries at top and bottom but the material can be sufficiently easily cut for the site electrician to make an entry in the back if needed. Alternative terminals are provided for circuits in which the contacts have to close when the glass is smashed (as in Figure 10.1) and for circuits in which the contacts have to open when the glass is smashed (as in Figure 10.2). In the former case, there is a test switch which can be reached when the whole front is opened with an Allen Key. In the latter case, the test push is omitted because the circuit is in any case of the fail-safe type.

The alarm point illustrated is suitable for surface mounting. Similar ones are available for flush fixing and in weatherproof versions. The current carrying capacity of the contacts should always be checked with the maker's catalogue.

Automatic detectors can respond to heat, smoke or ionization, and in the first case they can respond either at a fixed temperature or to a given rate of rise in temperature. A thermally operated detector for use with power-type systems is shown in Figure 10.7. It consists of a bi-metal strip which deflects

Figure 10.6 Fire alarm point (Courtesy of Gent & Co. Ltd)

Figure 10.7 Heat detector (Courtesy of Gent & Co. Ltd)

when the temperature rises, and thereby tilts a tube half-full of mercury. When the tube tilts, the mercury flows into the other half of the tube where it completes the circuit between two contacts previously separated by air. Alternatively, the arrangement within the tube can be such that the mercury breaks the circuit when the tube is tilted. The casing of the detector illustrated is of stainless steel, and it would be suitable for use in places such as boiler houses. For other areas similar detectors are available with the working parts within aesthetically more pleasing enclosures. They are usually set to operate at 65 °C.

Smoke detectors can be of the optical type. In this a small lamp shines a light across to a photoelectric cell. When smoke enters the detector the light beam is interrupted and the output of the photoelectric cell changes, which initiates the alarm. In modern units the light source can be an LED which requires little space and consumes negligible power. When first introduced smoke detectors often caused nuisance operation of the alarm by reacting to small quantities of smoke which had not been caused by a fire; on some occasions they sounded the alarm as a result of cigarette smoke in an office. Modern ones have adjustable sensitivity so that they can be set to avoid nuisance operation.

Detectors of the ionization type are also referred to as smoke detectors, but they will respond to ionization, which is normally caused by a fire, even if there is no visible smoke. An ionization detector contains a chamber which houses some low-strength radioactive material and a pair of electrodes. The radioactive material makes the air in the chamber conductive so that a small current flows between the electrodes. The size of the current varies with the nature of the gas in the chamber and as soon as any combustion products are added to the air there is a sudden change in the current flowing. The

Figure 10.8 Automatic fire detectors (Courtesy of Gent & Co. Ltd)

detector also has a second chamber which is permanently sealed so that the current through it never changes. As long as the currents through the two chambers are equal there is no output; as soon as they become unbalanced there is a net output which is used to operate a transistor switch in the detection circuit.

Various types of detector which are suitable for use with a monitoring electronic system are illustrated in Figure 10.8. This manufacturer provides a common base which will accept any of the detector heads, so that at any location the means of detection can be very easily changed.

Bells

Any bell could, of course, be used to sound an alarm. However, the voltage at which it operates must be that of the system and the current consumption must be taken into account in the design of the system. Most manufacturers of fire-alarm equipment make bells intended for use with their systems, and it is clearly advantageous to design a system making use of only one maker's equipment. Typical bells have power consumptions of between 1 and 6 W.

Sirens

Electrically operated sirens can be used as an alternative to bells. They are much louder and can be heard at a distance of half to three quarters of a mile. This makes them very suitable for factories in which there may be a lot of background noise. A typical rating is 60 W and we see that a siren takes a much bigger current than a bell. As a consequence, there is a bigger voltage drop in the circuit feeding it. In extra-low voltage circuits, the drop can be sufficiently serious to prevent the sirens from sounding at all, and it becomes especially important to check the layout for voltage drop.

Horns

A horn is an alternative to both bell and siren, and because of its penetrating, raucous note it is particularly suitable where a distinctive sound is needed. Its volume is easily adjustable and its power consumption is intermediate between that of a bell and that of a siren.

The manufacturers of fire-alarm equipment also provide standard indicators, relays and reset units for use with the various circuits which we have described in this chapter. Typical indicators for use with power systems are illustrated in Figure 10.9. The appropriate indicator light is illuminated, or

Figure 10.9 Fire alarm indicators (Courtesy of Gent & Co. Ltd)

a mechanical flag dropped, by a relay which may be either normally energized or normally de-energized. In the first case, the relay holds the signal off and the signal comes on when the activation of the fire alarm point interrupts the circuit. In the second case, the action of the alarm point energizes the relay and brings the signal on. In either case, the indicator must be such that the relay cannot be reset until the alarm point has been returned to its normal position. Indicators for use with electronic systems have already been described.

Self-contained battery and charger units are also available for low-voltage d.c. systems. Alternatively, separate batteries and constant potential chargers can be used. In either case, the designer should check that the ampere-hour capacity of the battery is sufficient for the load it will have to supply. This is of particular importance in those systems which have a current permanently flowing through the alarm initiating points.

Standards relevant to this chapter are:

BS 2740	Simple smoke alarms and alarm metering devices
BS EN 54–1	Fire detection and fire-alarm systems; introduction
BS EN 54–2	Fire detection and fire-alarm systems; control and indicating equipment
BS EN 54–4	Fire detection and fire-alarm systems; power supply equipment
BS 5446–1	Fire detection and fire-alarm devices for dwellings; spec. for smoke/heat alarms
BS 5839	Fire detection and alarm systems in buildings CoP for system design, installation, commissioning and maintenance
BS 6387	Specification for performance requirements for cables required to maintain circuit integrity under fire conditions
BS 6004	Electric cables; single-core unsheathed heat-resisting cables for voltages up to and including 450/750 V, for internal wiring
BS 6007	Electric cables; single-core unsheathed heat-resisting cables for voltages up to and including 450/750 V, for internal wiring
BS 6346	Specification for 600/1000 V and 1900/3300 V armoured electric cables having PVC insulation
BS 5467	Specification for 600/1000 V and 1900/3300 V armoured electric cables having thermosetting insulation
BS 2316	Specification for radio-frequency cables; general requirements and tests; British Government Services requirements

IEE Wiring Regulations particularly applicable to this chapter are:

Part   4
Section   531
Section   533
Section   537
Chapter   54
Appendix   3

Chapter 11

Call and computer systems, telephone and public address systems

Introduction

In many buildings, it is necessary to have a system of calling staff who are on duty in an office or staff room to go to rooms elsewhere in the building. This happens, for example, in hotels, hospitals and retirement homes. In the case of hospitals, patients wish to call a nurse who is in the ward office to their own beds, and in hotels guests may wish to call staff to their rooms. In retirement homes, a resident may wish to summon either domestic or nursing staff. All such systems can be arranged electrically and form part of the electrical services in a building.

Hospital call systems

In hospitals, it is desirable for each patient to be able to call a nurse to his/her bed. Figure 11.1 is a wiring diagram of a simple circuit for achieving this. There is a call unit at each bed which contains a push button, a relay and an illuminated reset lamp push. When the patient pushes the button, the relay is energized and holds itself in until it is released by the reset lamp push. While the relay is energized, a lamp is illuminated; it can be either next to the patient's bed or over the door of the room. At the same time, a buzzer and light are operated in the ward office or wherever else the nurse is to be called from. The buzzer can be silenced by a muting switch, but the light can only be cancelled by the resetting push on the patient's unit. Secondary or pilot lamps and buzzers can be placed elsewhere so that a nurse's attention can be attracted in more than one place or so that a nurse can supervise the activity of his/her staff.

When the call is made, the duty nurse has no indication from where it is coming and must, therefore, walk around all the places on the system until s/he sees the individual lamp which has been illuminated. The system is therefore limited to small areas. An extended version which does not have such a limitation is shown in Figure 11.2. A call unit is provided at each bed and also in each toilet; the toilet unit differs from the bed unit by being

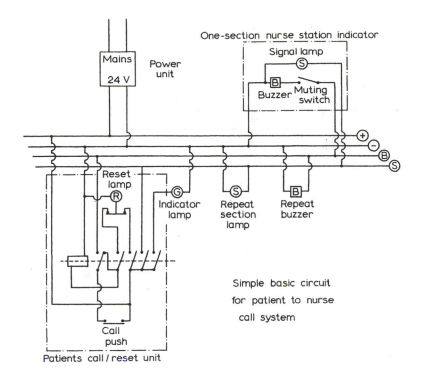

Figure 11.1 Hospital call system

operated by external push buttons instead of by buttons within it. There is a button in each WC compartment and in each bath compartment, all of them being cabled in parallel with each other to the operating contacts of the single toilet unit. Each call unit illuminates a lamp over the door of the room in which that unit is. Thus all the units in a ward illuminate the same lamp over the ward door. Several rooms are grouped in a section and when any unit in one section is energized a signal lamp for that section is illuminated in the nurse's office. There can also be a parallel signal lamp at a suitable position in the corridor.

When the duty nurse receives a call, the indicator in his/her office shows which section the call is coming from. When s/he gets to that section of corridor, s/he will see which door has a light over it, and once inside the room she can see which call unit has the reset lamp alight. Further central stations can be added in parallel with the main one in case staff have to be called from more than one area or in case supervision of staff activities from another office is necessary.

It will have been noticed that the reset button on the call unit is in the form of a lamp which stays alight until it has been pushed to reset the unit. One

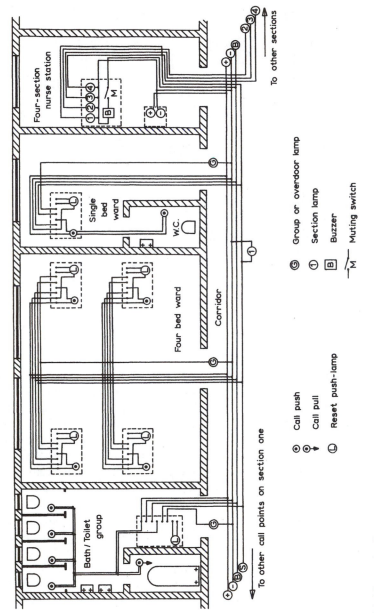

Figure 11.2 Hospital call system

reason for this is to show which unit in a ward of several beds has been operated, but the presence of the light also helps to reassure a nervous or frightened patient that assistance is on the way. It is simpler and cheaper to make the reset push contain the light than to install a separate button and lamp.

The call units and central station can also incorporate a combined microphone and loudspeaker so that the nurse can speak to the patient from her office. The diagram of Figure 11.2 is repeated with this facility added in Figure 11.3.

The indicator units and signal lamps are all made for extra-low voltage so that there is no possibility of electrical shock to the users if any faults occur. Another reason for using extra-low voltage is that it would be unnecessarily expensive to have mains voltage signal lamps. It is, therefore, usual to make the whole system an extra-low voltage one and to size the cables accordingly. The design of the wiring thus becomes similar to that for fire alarms discussed in Chapter 10, but it is not so essential to protect the wiring from fire damage. Ordinary PVC cables may be used and there is not the same objection to the use of a transformer from the main building supply. In fact, call-system equipment is normally made for a 24 V d.c. supply, and the manufacturers also make a power unit consisting of a transformer and rectifier. A 250 V a.c. is supplied to the primary of the power unit and 24 V d.c. is taken from the secondary or output side. The cables must obviously be sized to keep the voltage drop to an absolute minimum, and in a large building it may be necessary to have several independent systems in order that the cables are sufficiently short.

Electronic circuits enable relays to be replaced by transistor switches and lamps to be replaced by light emitting diodes. This reduces the power consumption drastically and, because currents are reduced to the order of milliamps, voltage drop ceases to be a major consideration. Bells and buzzers still require appreciable power but can be operated through amplifiers and relays from sources close to them. The operating principles are the same as for the power-operated systems described and the methods of connection are similar but, because of the small currents, telephone-type cables can be used. In some cases it may be convenient to use multicore cable.

A typical indicator to receive the calls in the central office is shown in Figure 11.4. An indicating lamp suitable for mounting over a room door is shown in Figure 11.5. It has a cast-iron or steel box with a lampholder to take a low-wattage sign-type lamp or a LED and an overlapping brass cover with a ruby glass dome. The box is built into the wall so that the cover is flush with the face of the wall.

A single call button is shown in Figure 11.6. This is contained in a box and is suitable for fixing in a wall within reach of a bath or toilet. An example of a complete call unit is shown in Figure 11.7. It contains the push button, reset light and also controls for the patient's bedside radio outlet. The call

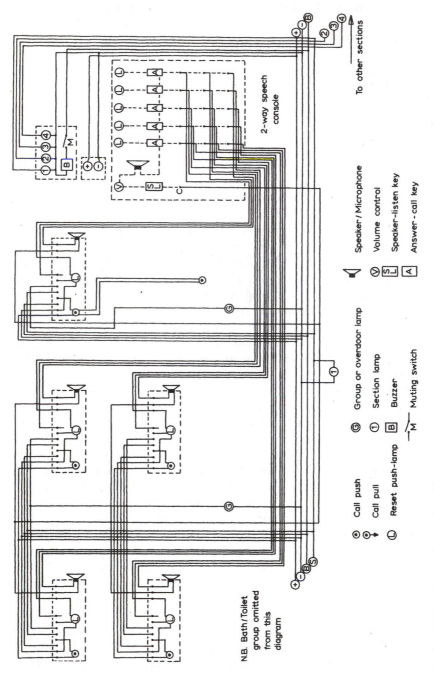

2-way speech console

To other sections

⊙ Call push   Ⓖ Group or overdoor lamp   ▼ Speaker / Microphone

⊙→ Call pull   ① Section lamp   Ⓥ Volume control

Ⓛ Reset push-lamp   Ⓑ Buzzer   Ⓢ Ⓛ Speaker-listen key

       ⌐M Muting switch   Ⓐ Answer-call key

Figure 11.3 Call system with speech facility

Figure 11.4 Alarm indicator (Courtesy of Gent & Co. Ltd)

Figure 11.5 Indicator lamp (Courtesy of Edison Telecom Ltd)

Figure 11.6 Call button (Courtesy of Edison Telecom Ltd)

Figure 11.7 Call unit (Courtesy of Edison Telecom Ltd)

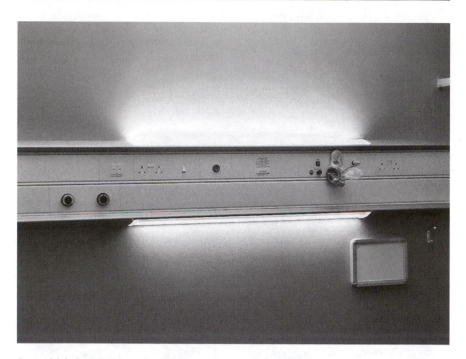

Figure 11.8 Bedhead trunking (Courtesy of Cableflow Ltd)

unit also contains a switch for a bedside lamp and the microphone for a speech system. They are on the end of a wander lead and are designed so that they can be held comfortably in the patient's hand. The wander lead ends in a multiway connector plug which fits into a mating socket in the bedhead trunking shown in Figure 11.8. The permanent wiring of the installation ends in this the trunking.

Door indicators

A call system which is being increasingly installed is the door indicator. This is an illuminated sign, with or without a buzzer, fixed outside an office door and operated by a push at the desk in the office. The sign can be 'Enter', 'Engaged', 'Next Patient' or any other message such as 'Keep Out'. An enter sign is shown in Figure 11.9, together with its wiring diagram. A transformer is contained in the same box as the sign and the system operates at extra low voltage. The table push energizes a relay, which is also contained in the sign box, and this connects the lamp behind the sign to the low-voltage supply. The equipment can be arranged so that the light stays on until reset by the table push. Standard equipment for these applications is made by a number of manufacturers. The particular one shown is suitable for surface mounting,

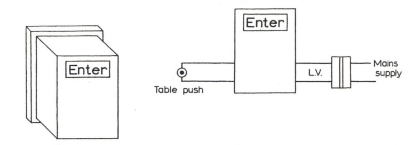

Figure 11.9 Door sign

but they are also made for flush fixing, and clearly for a new building this would be preferable.

The sign could be relay controlled, such as outside an X-ray room at a hospital. When the X-ray equipment is about to be operated the relay automatically activates a ' Keep Out', or other warning sign.

Telephone systems

The design of telephone systems is beyond the scope of this book, but we must consider the provision that has to be made for them within a building. In many cases all that is needed is a route by which the public telephone service, which in the UK is British Telecom, can bring a telephone cable to an instrument. British Telecom telephones are operated by batteries at the telephone exchanges and need no source of power within the buildings they serve. Telephone cable is quite small and if the position of the outlet for the telephone receiver is known it is sufficient to install a 20 mm conduit from outside the building to the outlet, with the same number and spacing of draw-in points as are used for any other conduit system. It is usual for the electrical installer to fix the conduit and leave draw cable in it, which the telephone engineers subsequently use for pulling their cable in after the building is finished and occupied.

The most common procedure used in the UK is for British Telecom or other cable network supplier, to supply plastic ducts which the builder puts in the ground from the telephone main in the road to a point just within the building, and for the electrical contractor to supply and install metal conduit from the end of the plastic duct to the final telephone outlet position. A conduit box is provided where the plastic duct meets the metal conduit, and the electrical contractor puts draw cable into both the duct and the conduit.

If the telephone cable is to come in overhead, as is likely to happen in rural areas, then British Telecom will do all the outside work, including the fixing of a terminal on the wall of the building. The electrical installer then has only to provide conduit with draw cable from the entry point, which in this case will be at high level, to the final telephone outlet position.

Some buildings have an internal telephone system which may consist of extensions to the public telephones or may be an entirely separate installation. Here again the essential matter for the electrical services designer is to agree the outlet positions with the customer and to arrange for them to be linked to each other by conduit or trunking. Trunking can be a useful alternative to conduit when the system is a complex one needing many cables with a large number of junctions. Telephone cables do not have a protective sheathing and therefore need the mechanical protection of conduit or trunking. They can, however, be run exposed on surfaces and this is often done, but in a new building it makes it rather apparent that the designers forgot about the telephones until it was too late.

An internal telephone installation which is independent of the public telephones must receive power from somewhere. All telephones work on extra-low voltage and this is provided either by a battery or by an electronic power pack. A battery needs to be kept charged by a battery charger which in turn has to be supplied by mains power. A power pack usually contains its own transformer but this must then be fed from the mains. In whichever way the telephone works, mains power has to be provided somewhere, usually at the central exchange of the system. The power required is very small and can be supplied from a socket outlet or fused connection unit on the nearest convenient general-purpose power circuit.

Most British Telecom telephones take their power from batteries at the Telephone Exchange, and do not need power from the consumer's supply. Some of the British Telecom private branch exchange systems do however include a power pack which requires a supply from the subscriber's premises. The electrical designer should therefore discuss the system to be used with British Telecom and make sure that any necessary power outlets are provided. They can again be ordinary socket outlets or fused connection units taken from a convenient power circuit at a point adjacent to the telephone equipment. The more modern of telephone sets are connected to the permanent wiring by a jack plug, which inserts into a telephone outlet socket. This socket forms part of a lid which screws onto a standard conduit box.

Public address systems

Public address and loudspeaker systems are somewhat similar to telephones. The details of the equipment to be used can be settled only with manufacturers' catalogues and by discussion with the manufacturers. Once the equipment and its location have been selected, provision must be made for running cables from the announcing station to the loudspeakers. Because these cables are likely to be put in after all other building work is finished a conduit system is the almost inevitable choice. Loudspeaker cables are like telephone cables in that they are small and do not have an outer sheath; this also makes it difficult to find any alternative to putting them inside conduit.

Closed-circuit television systems

There is no real technical difference between the pictures we see at home on television, and those delivered by a CCTV camera and monitor. The real difference is in the cost of the equipment. Therefore we cannot expect to have the same quality of picture from equipment bought for the sums of money a client is prepared to spend, compared with broadcasting company equipment.

Closed-circuit television is used in many circumstances, including surveillance of vehicular, and people traffic, entering and leaving a premises. The CCTV standard is phase alternate line (PAL), also used in normal TV transmissions in Europe with the exception of France, who use PAL only for CCTV.

The typical types of cable are: (a) coaxial, which is unbalanced, meaning that the signal is a voltage with reference to ground. The video signal is between 0.3 to 1.0 V above ground; (b) twisted pair balanced, meaning that the video signal has been converted for transmission along a medium other than coaxial. The signal level is the voltage difference between each conductor; (c) fibre optics, which are immune to outside interference and signals without needing amplification.

External interference is picked up en route by all types of cable, with the exception of fibre optics. Unless suitably screened, power and signal cables should be kept well apart. The longer the length of cables, the greater the losses. Unlike fibre cables, copper cables will have a voltage drop over the length resulting in a lower signal level at the receiving end than that processed by the camera. Provision of cable routes for CCTV is similar to that discussed in telephone systems.

Computer systems

Computer networks are used extensively in organisations to utilise the storage space of a server. To connect the workstations to the server, a network is used. The network wiring provides a transmission path between the workstations and the server. Copper cable can meet most demands at a relatively low cost. The data is transmitted in the form of low-voltage electrical signals, which are unfortunately subject to interference. The cables must, therefore, be run in situations where interference will not be a problem. Fibre optic cables can transmit data over longer distances than copper cable, and the fibre optic cable is not subject to interference. With fibre optic cables the data is converted into light by a transducer and sent through the fibre optic cable. A second transducer converts the light signals back into low-voltage signals at the server. Fibre optic cables are used for higher bandwidth applications.

They allow more information to be transmitted faster but, however, are more expensive to install. Wireless networks use radio signals to transmit data. They tend to be lower bandwidth than wired networks. The building services engineer must liase with specialist installation companies to determine the requirements of the company with regard to cable runs required.

The electrical mains supply to computer systems requires special consideration. Information technology equipment inherently gives relatively high leakage current to earth. To ensure that the circuit protective conductors remain secure in circuits supplying IT equipment, BS 7671 Section 607 Earthing Requirements for the Installation of Equipment having High Protective Conductor Currents sets out the special measures required. For distribution and final circuits where the total protective conductor current exceeds 10 mA, the protective conductor must comply with the regulations with respect to protective conductors and be not less than 10 mm², or 4 mm² if mechanically protected, or two protective conductors may be used which may be of different types, e.g. copper, and steel conduit.

For final circuits only, where the total protective conductor current will exceed 10 mA, the protective conductor is run in the form of a ring, irrespective of whether the circuit is a ring or radial one. Alternatively, a connection is made between the remote end of the copper protective conductor and the steel enclosure, if used. If two or more identical radial circuits are used, a connection can be made between the remote ends of the protective conductors, on each circuit. This gives a parallel path to earth, for each circuit.

The building service engineers may consider using more final circuits in computer suites, etc., than would normally be installed in other parts of the building. Using more final circuits would reduce the leakage current on each final circuit. However, the leakage current on each final circuit, is cumulative on the associated distribution circuits, and therefore must be addressed.

Standards relevant to this chapter are:

BS EN 50134–7   Social alarm systems
BS 5839   Fire detection and alarm systems in buildings
BS 6259   Code of practice for sound systems
BS EN 50132–7   Alarm systems; CCTV surveillance systems for use in security applications
BS 8220   Guide for security of buildings against crime
BS 7671   Section 607

Chapter 12

Reduced-voltage systems

The use of extra-low-voltage wiring for fire alarms and call systems has been discussed in the previous two chapters. Other applications occur in laboratories, where permanently installed reduced-voltage outlets are required for various experiments. Permanent outlets are easier for the staff than the use of accumulator batteries which have to be carried from preparation room stores and set up on the laboratory benches for each experiment. Reduced-voltage supplies are also needed for microscopes which have a built-in light for illuminating the slide.

The requirements for any particular laboratory must, of course, be agreed by the electrical designer with the staff who will be using the laboratory. In some cases, as for example illuminating microscope slides, the supply is needed at a constant voltage. Such a supply can be provided by a transformer. Usually, this is comparatively small and can be mounted on a bracket fixed to the wall either of the laboratory or of an adjacent store. For a given power, the current on a reduced-voltage service is higher than on a mains-voltage circuit and, therefore, the cable sizes soon become substantial. To prevent the use of excessively large cables, it is convenient to keep down the number of outlets on one circuit and to use a separate transformer for each secondary circuit.

It would be possible to take the secondary of the transformer to a reduced-voltage distribution board and split there to several reduced-voltage circuits. The cable from the transformer to the distribution board would, however, be very large to take the necessary current, and it is better to use a separate transformer for each secondary circuit. The kVA rating required is calculated from the secondary voltage and total output power needed. As usual in this kind of design, it is advisable to allow ample spare capacity so that the transformer rating should be somewhat above the calculated requirement.

The voltage on the primary of the transformer is known, being the ordinary mains supply voltage in the building, and this determines the transformer ratio. The ratio determines the primary current and thus provides all the information necessary to design the mains circuit feeding the transformer. A fuse can, if desired, be provided on .the secondary of the transformer, but an overload on the secondary would draw an overload on the primary so that the fuse in the supply to the transformer will also protect the secondary. This will not, however, be the case if the primary has been oversized while the secondary has not. The exact carrying capacities of the primary and secondary sides should be carefully compared before the fusing arrangements are finally decided on.

In other cases, a laboratory needs a variable reduced-voltage output. This makes it possible to set up experiments with a choice of voltage. Reduced-voltage laboratory units are made which contain a transformer, a rectifier and variable tappings on the output switches. The one illustrated in Figure 12.1 gives a choice of outputs ranging from 6 V to 24 V a.c. and from 6 V to 24 V d.c. It can, therefore, be set to give the output required for whatever experiment is in hand.

The wiring arrangements are exactly the same as for a fixed output transformer. The cables must, of course, be sized for the largest current which will be taken, which will correspond to the lowest voltage. It is also at the lowest voltage that voltage drop along the cable is most serious.

Figure 12.1 Reduced-voltage unit

A number of accessories is available for terminating the reduced-voltage wiring at the benches, and some of these have been described in Chapter 1. For laboratory work, the type described is most suitable because the cables used for setting up the bench experiment can be readily connected to these terminals. Microscopes or other permanent equipment requiring a reduced-voltage supply will usually have a trailing flexible lead with a plug at the end of it. For these, a socket outlet is clearly more convenient than a laboratory type of terminal, but it should not be possible to plug a reduced-voltage piece of equipment into a mains voltage socket. Reduced-voltage wiring for such applications should, therefore, terminate in 5 A two, or three-pin socket outlets which should be clearly labelled with the voltage. Two, or three-pin plugs can then be supplied and fixed to the equipment, and it will not be possible for anyone to push these into ordinary socket outlets.

Intrinsically safe circuits

Equipment for hazardous areas is discussed in Chapter 1. One technique in areas where there is a risk of fire is the use of intrinsically safe circuits. The principle of these is that the energy of any spark which occurs shall be limited so that it is not sufficient to ignite the vapour. This is achieved by using reduced voltages and equipment which does not take high currents at these voltages. The power in the circuit is thus low and there is not enough energy available to initiate combustion.

Not all equipment can be designed on this basis, but it is often possible to have intrinsically safe circuits within a hazardous area operating relays which control normal equipment outside the danger zone. This may be cheaper than installing flameproof equipment within the zone.

Standards relevant to this chapter are:

BS 1259   Intrinsically safe electrical apparatus and circuits

IEE Wiring Regulations particularly applicable to this chapter are:

Section   411
Regulation   553–3

Chapter 13

Communal and closed-circuit TV systems

If all the tenants in a block of flats had their own TV aerial on the roof of the building, the result would be very unsightly. In the case of a 24-storey tower block having 4 flats on each floor, the roof would probably not be large enough to accommodate 96 separate aerials. Even a low-rise development looks ugly if every house has its own aerial; sometimes a four-storey development consists of two flats and a maisonette above each other so that each 'house' would need three aerials. In fringe reception areas, one needs large aerials mounted very high up. This makes it difficult to equip each dwelling with its own aerial. In built up areas, large buildings shield smaller ones, so that if an estate consists of a number of small blocks and one or two towers, occupants of the small blocks left to provide their own aerials might find it desirable to put them on masts rising as high as the top of the tower block.

For these reasons, it is an advantage to receive television and radio signals at one suitably sited aerial array and relay them to individual dwellings by cables or transmission lines. Very large relay systems exist, serving whole towns, sometimes from a mast receiver several miles away. The building services engineer is more likely to be concerned with community systems serving a single block of flats or one small estate of houses and maisonettes. In this book, we confine our attention to such community systems.

Radio signals are electro-magnetic waves in space. They cover a range of frequencies which are classified as shown in Table 13.1. Since the product of frequency and wavelength is always equal to the velocity of light, which is constant, the frequency is inversely proportional to the wavelength. Radio broadcasts have in the past usually been identified by the wavelength, but at the frequencies used for television the wavelength becomes so small that it is more convenient to use the frequency. The properties of aerials and transmission lines depend very much on frequency and different types have to be used for different frequencies. It is convenient to subdivide the VHF and UHF frequencies into five bands, which makes it possible for commercial equipment to be manufactured for one or two selected bands only. This subdivision is shown in Table 13.2.

Table 13.1 Frequency bands

Designation	Abbreviation	Frequency range
Low frequency	LF	30 kHz–300 kHz
Medium frequency	MF	300 mHz–3 MHz
High frequency	HF	3 MHz–30 MHz
Very high frequency	VHF	30 MHz–300 MHz
Ultra high frequency	UHF	300 MHz–3 000 MHz
Super high frequency	SHF	3 000 MHz–30 000 MHz

Table 13.2 Broadcasting services

Range	Band	Channel numbers	Frequency	Service
LF	–	–	150–285 kHz	AM sound long wave
MF	–	–	535–1605 kHz	AM sound medium wave
HF	–	–	2.3–26.1 MHz	AM sound short wave
VHF	I	1–5	41–68 MHz	TV Band I
	II	–	87.5–100 MHz	FM sound (VHF)
	III	6–13	175–215 MHz	TV band III
UHF	IV	21–34	470–582 MHz	TV band IV
	V	39–68	614–854 MHz	TV band V

If a signal consists of one frequency only, the only way it can convey information is by varying in amplitude. As soon as several adjacent frequencies are present, they can combine to form complicated waveshapes and the total number of distinguishable patterns increases rapidly. This is a simplified explanation of why the band of frequencies required for a transmission increases as the amount of information to be conveyed increases. Television provides much more information than sound broadcasting, and therefore each service requires a large band-width. For sound broadcasting, each station needs a bandwidth of only 10 kHz. A station broadcasting on 1500 m (which corresponds to 200 kHz) actually uses all wavelengths between 1457 m and 1543 m. Provided the next station has a nominal wavelength of 1587 m or more there will be no interference between them; it is obvious that there is no difficulty about keeping stations separate from each other under these conditions.

A 625 line TV picture, on the other hand, requires a bandwidth of 5.5 MHz. It is immediately obvious from Table 13.1 that this cannot be transmitted at less than HE and that the HF range would only accommodate five different stations. This is the reason that TV is transmitted in the VHF and UHF ranges. Even within these, care has to be taken about separation of stations. The five bands of frequency are, therefore, further divided into a number of channels each of which covers a bandwidth of 6 MHz. These channels are also indicated in Table 13.2. Each station is allocated one channel, and neighbouring stations are thus prevented from interfering with each other.

Since the distance over which VHF and UHF waves can be propagated is quite limited, two stations more than a certain minimum geographical distance apart can safely use the same channel.

Aerials

If an e.m.f. is placed in the centre of a short cable (Figure 13.1), the two halves of the cable act as capacitor plates, one becoming positively charged and the other negatively. Each charge produces an electric field. Suppose now that the e.m.f. is alternating; there is then an alternating charging current in the cable. When the current is a maximum the positive and negative charges occupy the same place and produce equal and opposite fields. When the current is zero the positive and negative charges are at opposite ends of the cable and produce a resultant electric field. Thus there is an electric field which alternates with the charging current in the cable.

The current also produces a magnetic field which spreads out from the cable with the velocity of light. The motion of this magnetic field induces a further electric field.

Now the oscillating charges in the cable have not only a velocity, but also an acceleration. This acceleration is propagated outwards in the electric field at a finite velocity and, therefore, the field further out is moving with a lower velocity than that closer in. Since the charges oscillate the acceleration is alternately forward and backward, and the result is that the complete field radiated forms closed loops which travel out from the cable and expand (Figure 13.2). It can be shown that this radiated field is appreciable only if the length of the cable is of the same order as the wavelength.

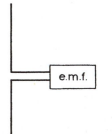

Figure 13.1 Principle of dipole

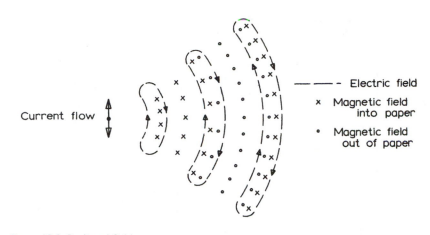

Current flow

------- Electric field

×   Magnetic field
    into paper

•   Magnetic field
    out of paper

Figure 13.2 Radiated field

The total electric field thus contains three terms. The first two are the induction fields and the third is the radiation field. Near the aerial the induction fields predominate, but they become negligible at a distance greater than about five wavelengths. At larger distances, the radiation field is the only important one.

By a converse mechanism, a cable placed in an alternating electric field and suitably orientated to that field will have an e.m.f. induced in it. In fact, it turns out that receiving aerials are identical to transmitting aerials. In practice, receiving aerials can be made simpler than transmitting aerials because high efficiency is not so important when receiving as when transmitting.

The simple aerial of the type shown in Figure 13.1 is known as a dipole and its total length is half the wavelength radiated or received. The description given above is an attempt to explain in simple physical terms how a dipole radiates and receives. Any electric current is associated with a magnetic and an electric field, the relationship always satisfying Maxwell's equations. The field radiated by an aerial is thus the solution of Maxwell's equations for the boundary conditions given by the current distribution in the aerial and the geometry of the aerial. The mathematical difficulties of calculating such solutions are so great that theoretical solutions are not given in even the most advanced textbooks on radio propagation, and aerials are designed on the result of experimental investigations. The general principle remains that the dimensions of the aerial are approximately equal to the wavelength. It follows from this that different aerials are required for different frequency bands.

Aerials are used for services ranging from telegraphy through navigation, broadcasting and telephony to radar and space communications. There is a very large number of types of aerial in use to cover the wide range of

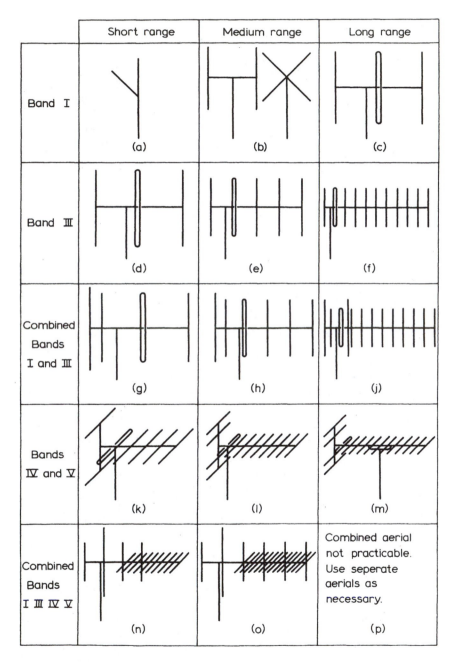

Figure 13.3 TV aerials

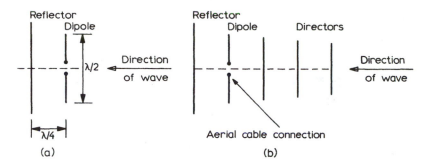

Figure 13.4 Strengthening elements

applications and frequencies employed, but the following are the types most likely to be encountered by the building services engineer. They are all simple variations of the basic dipole described above.

For band I, a single dipole as shown in Figure 13.3a can be used for reception at a short range from the transmitter. If the receiver is some distance from the transmitter a modification is introduced to increase the strength of the dipole. It has been found that the addition of elements not connected to the receiver cable can strengthen the signal at the dipole. An element slightly longer than the dipole and spaced about a quarter of a wavelength behind it has the effect of reflecting waves onto the dipole and thus strengthening the signal to it. This is illustrated in Figure 13.4 and results in the well known H aerial shown in Figure 13.3b. A modification of this is the X aerial, also shown in Figure 13.3b. The principle is illustrated in Figure 13.5 from which it is seen that the dipole and reflector are partially folded on themselves. It has been found that they then operate like a straight pair of elements occupying the mean positions shown dotted in Figure 13.5.

Further improvement in reception can be obtained by adding directors in front of the dipole at distances of about a quarter of a wavelength, and progressively shorter than the dipole (Figure 13.4). It is found that the effect of these is to increase the sensitivity of the dipole to radiation from the direction in which the array is pointing. An arrangement such as that of Figure 13.4 is known as a Yagi array.

For long-range reception on band I, an aerial consisting of dipole, reflector and director (Figure 13.3c) is used.

As explained later in this chapter, maximum power is transferred from a source to a load when their impedances are equal. The half wave dipole has an impedance of about 75 ohms, which matches the characteristic impedance of the coaxial aerial cable used. When other elements, that is to say reflectors and directors, are added the impedance of the aerial is reduced, and much of the power received is lost at the mismatch between aerial and cable. This can

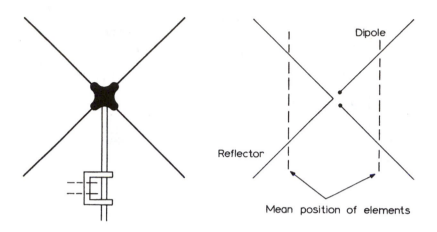

Figure 13.5 Aerial

be overcome by folding the dipole, as shown in Figure 13.6. It is still half a wavelength long but its impedance is higher, and when it is used in an array its impedance matches that of the cable. Yagi arrays, therefore, generally use a folded dipole.

Similar aerials are used for the reception of FM radio on band II, but they are put horizontally instead of vertically. This is simply because the radiation broadcast for this service is polarized in the horizontal plane whereas that for television services is polarized in the vertical plane. The same types of aerials are used for band III, but because of the shorter wavelengths the strength of the signal decreases more rapidly and, therefore, a larger number of elements is used in the array. Typical arrays are shown in Figure 13.3d, e and f, and combined band I and band II aerials are shown in Figure 13.3g, h and j.

At UHF the range of transmitters becomes much less, although there is less interference between neighbouring stations. Therefore, the receiving aerials have a larger number of elements. These are readily accommodated because as a result of the smaller wavelength they are shorter and more closely spaced. In fact a six-element UHF array can present a neater and more compact appearance than a single dipole for band I. Also as a consequence of the shorter wavelength, the reflector can more effectively take the form of a square mesh. Typical arrays are shown in Figure 13.3k, l and m.

Figure 13.6 Folded dipole

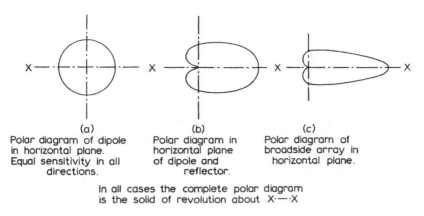

(a)
Polar diagram of dipole
in horizontal plane.
Equal sensitivity in all
directions.

(b)
Polar diagram in
horizontal plane
of dipole and
reflector.

(c)
Polar diagram of
broadside array in
horizontal plane.

In all cases the complete polar diagram
is the solid of revolution about X·—·X

Figure 13.7 Polar diagrams

All the aerials we have described are directional. The voltage induced in them depends on the angle between the axis of the array and the plane of the wave of radiation. It is a maximum when the axis of the array is perpendicular to the wavefront and is zero when the axis of the array is parallel to the wavefront. The sensitivity can be represented by the length of a line drawn in the direction of the advancing wavefront. The locus of the ends of all such lines forms the polar diagram. This is illustrated in Figure 13.7.

Greater sensitivity in the axial direction can be obtained by altering the shape of the polar diagram as shown in Figure 13.7c. One way of achieving this is to have a pair of Yagi arrays mounted side by side in a broadside arrangement, as shown in Figure 13.8. It will be appreciated that in all cases

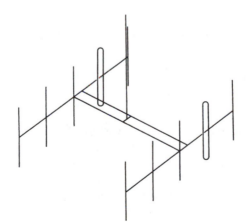

Figure 13.8 Twin arrays

the axis of the aerial array must point as closely as possible towards the transmitter.

Transmission lines

The signal received by the aerial is sent to the television outlets along an aerial cable or television transmission line. The design of the line is an important part of the design of a communal TV system, and we must learn something about transmission engineering to understand it. Transmission engineers are very much concerned with loss of power, which is usually measured in decibels. A decibel is one-tenth of a bel, and a bel is the logarithm to base 10 of the ratio of two powers. If the power at the sending end is P_s and that at the receiving end is P_r the loss of the line is

$$\mathrm{Log}_{10}\left(\frac{P_s}{P_r}\right) = 10\,\log_{10}\left(\frac{P_s}{P_r}\right) \text{ decibels}$$

The decibel is convenient because of the very large losses and amplifications encountered in communications engineering; for example, if an amplifier has an output 10 000 times the input it is more convenient to say that is has a gain of 40 dB. Since the gain, or loss, in decibels is a ratio, the input level should also be stated.

Power ratios are proportional to the square of the voltage or current ratios. Therefore:

$$\log 10\left(\frac{P_s}{P_r}\right) = 2\,\log_{10}\left(\frac{V_s}{V_r}\right) = 2\,\log_{10}\left(\frac{I_s}{I_r}\right)$$

Thus when measurements are made in volts or amps the loss is

$$20\,\log_{10}\left(\frac{V_s}{V_r}\right) \text{ dB or } \log_{10}\left(\frac{I_s}{I_r}\right) \text{ dB}$$

If the logarithms to base 'e' are used instead of to base 10, the unit is the neper instead of the bel. This is not used so often, but it is sometimes convenient because the attenuation of a transmission line per unit length is always a power of 'e'.

There is a loss of power in all transmission lines. At very low frequencies this is largely due to the resistance of the line, although inductance and capacitance are important for exact calculation of long power lines. At high frequencies inductance and capacitance become much more important, and it can readily be shown that the losses increase rapidly with frequency. At frequencies above 3000 MHz the losses in cables are so high that transmission by cables is no longer possible and the only way of conveying energy at these frequencies is by waveguides.

The power engineer distributing power at 50 Hz is interested in supplying the power taken by the load with the minimum loss in the line. The communications engineer sending signals to a receiver has a rather different outlook. Here much smaller quantities of energy are being handled, and amplifiers can be installed along the line which feed in energy from an independent source without distorting the wave shape of the signal. The main concern is to provide a strong enough signal to the receiver at the end of the line. It can be shown that maximum power is taken by a load when that power equals the power lost in the generator. Although at this condition maximum power is taken by the load, the efficiency of the transmission is only 50 per cent. This is clearly uneconomic for power transmission but is practicable in telecommunications where the magnitude of the signal is much more important than transmission efficiency. The difference between the operating points of power and communications systems is shown in Figure 13.9.

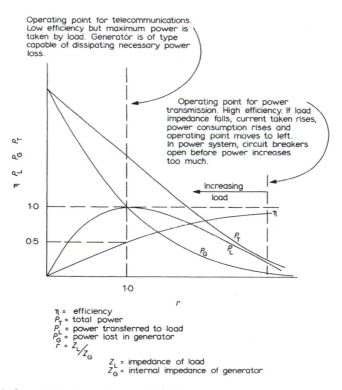

Figure 13.9 Operating points of transmission lines

When an alternating voltage is applied to the sending end of an infinite line, a finite current flows because of the capacitance and leakage inductance between the two cables forming the line. The ratio of voltage applied to current flowing is the input impedance. The input impedance for an infinite length of line is known as the *characteristic impedance* and is denoted by Z_o. It should be noted that the characteristic impedance varies with frequency.

Since the line is infinite, no current waves reach the far end. Therefore, there is no reflection and no reflected waves return to the sending end. For the same reason, the current flowing depends only on the characteristic impedance (Z_o) and is not affected by the terminating or load impedance (Z_r) at the far end. Although an infinite line is obviously a purely hypothetical object, in practice the state of affairs we have just described is approximately fulfilled by many long lines. Furthermore, a short line terminating in a load impedance equal to the characteristic impedance of the line (i.e. $Z_r = Z_o$) behaves electrically as if it were an infinite line.

The characteristic impedance is the ratio of voltage to current at any point in an infinite line or in a correctly terminated line. However, the current and voltage are not the same at all points; because of the ordinary impedance of the line, they become progressively less along the line.

Let

I_s = current at sending end
I_1 = current one kilometre down line

Then $\dfrac{I_1}{I_s} = e^{-y}$ where y = propagation constant per kilometre of line.

y is a complex quantity so that I_1 is both less than I_s and also different in phase. In general,

$I_n = I_s e^{-ny}$ where I_n = current n kilometres along the line.

Similarly, $E_n = E_s e^{-ny}$

y is a complex quantity which can be written $y = \alpha + j\beta$ where α is the attenuation constant and β is the phase constant.

The four quantities:

Z_o = characteristic impedance
y = propagation constant
α = attenuation constant
β = phase constant

are characteristic of the particular cable being used. They are known as the secondary line constants and can be calculated theoretically from the four primary line constants which are

R = resistance per kilometre (ohms)
G = leakage per kilometre (mhos)
L = inductance per kilometre (henries)
C = capacitance per kilometre (farads)

Whilst the primary constants are independent of frequency the secondary constants in general vary with frequency.

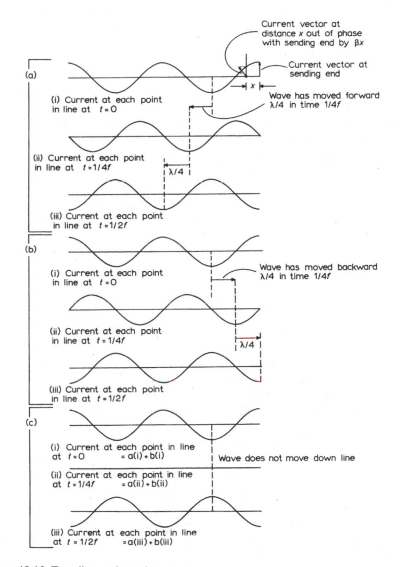

Figure 13.10 Travelling and standing waves

Now a communication signal carries information in its waveshape. It is most important to preserve this shape while the signal is being sent along the line. There are three main causes of distortion:

1   Characteristic impedance varies with frequency. If the line is terminated in an impedance that does not vary with frequency in the same manner as that of the line, distortion will result.
2   Attenuation varies with frequency.
3   The velocity at which the wave shape travels along the line varies with frequency, so that waves of different frequencies arrive at different times.

It can be shown that the condition for minimum attenuation is $LG = CR$. It can also be shown that this condition makes Z_o independent of frequency. This is called the distortionless condition. On some communication lines the inductance is artificially increased to bring the line nearer to this condition, but this is not found necessary on communal TV systems.

If a line of characteristic impedance Z_o is joined to an impedance having a value other than Z_o part of the wave travelling down the line will be reflected back at the point of discontinuity. The reflection is a maximum when the line is either open circuited or short circuited ($Z_r = \infty$ or $Z_r = 0$) and is zero when $Z_r = Z_o$. The current in the line is always the sum of the incident wave and the reflected wave.

This way of looking at matters will seem unfamiliar to power engineers. The rigorous mathematics of transmission lines is the same for power lines as for communication lines, but differences arise from differences in the frequencies at which they are operated. At 50 Hz a line 500 km long is less than one-tenth of a wavelength. Although the stationary distribution of current along it is mathematically equal to the sum of two waves travelling in opposite directions, this fact is of only academic interest to the power engineer. At 3000 MHz, however, the wavelength is only a few metres and the two travelling waves have a physical meaning which is easily visualized.

At the sending end, the current can be represented by a phasor of length I_{smax} rotating at an angular frequency w where $w = 2\pi f$ and f is the frequency of the applied voltage. At a point x down the line, the current I_x differs from I_s because of the attenuation of the cable and can be represented by a vector of length $I_{smax} = I_{smax} \cdot \mathrm{eu}2^{-\propto x}$ at an angle of βx to the original phasor, but still rotating at an angular frequency of w. The instantaneous current along the line at successive intervals is then as shown in Figure 13.10a. For simplicity in drawing this figure $\propto$ has been taken as zero, so that the current is the same in magnitude along the line. It will be seen that at all times the envelope of instantaneous current along the line is a sine wave. Moreover, the sine wave moves down the line. The wavelength is that length at which $\beta x = 2\pi$

$$\therefore \beta\lambda = 2\pi$$

$$\therefore \lambda = 2\frac{\pi}{\beta}$$

Since velocity = frequency $\times$ wavelength

$$v = f\lambda$$

$$= f.2\frac{\pi}{\beta} = 2\frac{\pi}{\beta}$$

$$= w\beta$$

This is the velocity at which the signal travels down the line. It is not the same as the velocity at which energy is transferred.

A wave travelling in the opposite direction will be as shown in Figure 13.10b. When the incident and reflected waves are equal in magnitude they combine as shown in Figure 13.10c. We can see that there is a wave on the line of frequency f and wavelength $\lambda = w/\beta$ but it does not travel along the line. Whereas with the travelling wave the rotating phasor has the same magnitude along the line and varies only in phase along the line, in this case the vector changes in magnitude along the line. As a result there are nodes where the current is always zero and anti-nodes where there is a maximum. This type of wave is called a standing wave, and is produced by the combination of equal incident and reflected waves. If only part of the incident wave is reflected then there is a standing wave with a travelling wave superimposed on it. Power is transferred only by the forward travelling wave, so that standing waves represent a loss. Reflected waves also originate at junctions where one cable branches into two or three.

Complete reflection occurs when a line is either open circuited or short circuited. Under these conditions, there is no forward travelling wave, and no power is transferred. This is readily understandable, because neither an open circuited nor a short circuited line feeds a load.

For maximum transfer of power the internal impedance of the generator must be matched to the characteristic impedance of the line and this must in turn be matched to the input impedance of the load. In the case of the communal TV system, the generator is the aerial. If the matching is not correct, standing waves are formed in the line, and power is dissipated in the line. Some of this dissipation takes the form of radiation which causes interference to neighbouring aerials.

In general, the impedance of the generator is not the same as that of the line, and that of the line is not the same as that of the receiver. Therefore, at each of these points of discontinuity some form of impedance transformer is required. Such a transformer can be made from a four pole network which

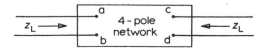

Figure 13.11 Impedance transformer

has different input impedances between the two pairs of terminals. In Figure 13.11, the line with characteristic impedance Z_l sees the impedance Z_l between terminals a and b and is therefore, correctly terminated. The load with impedance Z_r sees itself supplied from an impedance Z_r between terminals c and d and is, therefore, also correctly matched. There is a small loss of power in the four pole network, but this is preferable to the large losses that would occur in the line if the mismatching were permitted to remain.

A similar problem has to be solved where there is a branch. In Figure 13.12a, the input cable sees the continuation and branch cables in parallel and is in effect terminated by an impedance of $Z_l/2$. A network has to be provided as in Figure 13.12b, so that each of the three cables sees an impedance of Z_l. There are a number of devices which have the necessary characteristics, but many of them are sensitive to frequency and operate correctly only over a limited band of frequencies. In communal TV practice, a simple arrangement of resistances is used, as shown in Figure 13.13. These junction boxes also perform another function which we shall come to later in this chapter.

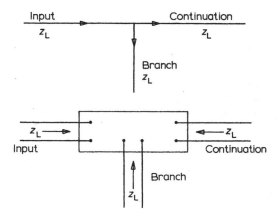

Figure 13.12 Branch network

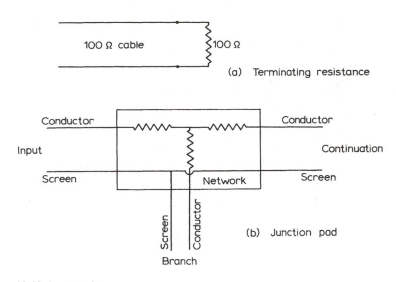

(a) Terminating resistance

(b) Junction pad

Figure 13.13 Junction box

Cables

Having discussed the theory of a transmission line, we are now in a position to say something about the cable which actually forms the line. We start by noting that any cable carrying current tends to act as a radiating aerial. At low frequencies the power radiated from an ordinary cable is so small that it can hardly be detected, but at high frequencies it can become significant. Not only is there a loss of power from the line itself, but the radiation will cause interference in neighbouring receivers. Similarly, any cable acts as a receiving aerial, and a line feeding a television or radio set can pick up unwanted high-frequency radiations. Both these effects can be suppressed by efficient screening, and radio and TV services therefore always use screened cable.

A line may be a single conductor using the earth as a return. This has capacitance to the earth and is termed an unbalanced line. If a conductor is provided for the return, it can be arranged so that either the two conductors have different capacitances to earth or that they have the same capacitance to earth. The former arrangement is termed unbalanced and the latter balanced. Typical arrangements are shown in Figure 13.14.

The energy conveyed by a transmission line is in fact held in the electric and magnetic fields associated with the current and voltage. In the case of open lines, these fields extend infinitely into space. At high frequencies the energy is rapidly dissipated into space, and the losses from the transmission system become unbearably high. If a screen is placed round the conductors,

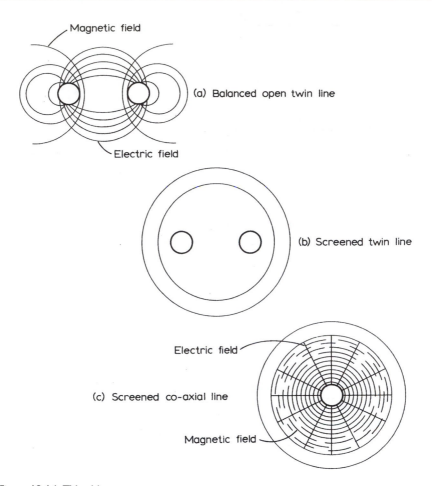

Figure 13.14 TV cables

the fields are confined within the screen and the losses are reduced. Typical forms of radio frequency cable are shown in Figure 13.15. The cable of Figure 13.15a has an inner conductor of copper cable and an outer conductor of seamless lead tube. It is suitable for high frequency transmission and high power aerial feeders. Figure 13.15b shows a cable with the inner conductors supported in the centre of a tube of polyethylene and an outer conductor of cable braid with PVC or lead alloy sheath. Figure 13.15d is a screened and balanced twin feeder. Figure 13.15e shows a coaxial cable relying mainly on air as the insulation between the conductors with an insulating helical thread supporting the inner conductor. Figure 13.15f is similar to Figure 13.15d, but does not have the two conductors wound over each other; it is often used in radio relay systems.

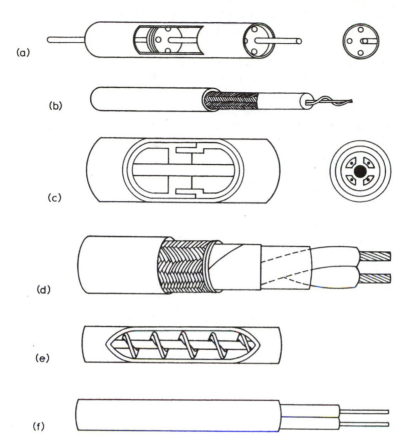

Figure 13.15 Radio frequency cables

As the frequency increases the losses in the dielectric become more important than the resistance loss, and for high frequency cables the properties of the dielectric must be carefully considered. The best performance can be obtained by air-spaced cables, but cables with good solid dielectrics are used where economics outweigh purely technical considerations. Communal TV systems normally employ screened coaxial cable with polyethylene dielectric.

Frequency translation

In communications, information is contained in a complete waveform covering a band of frequencies. This band of frequencies is evenly spaced about the carrier frequency, but the wave can be transferred to any other band of frequencies of equal width, without any loss of information. It can be transmitted in this form and later transferred back to its original frequency band, or the information can be read out in the new band.

The losses in a line increase with frequency and in the early days of communal TV systems it was impracticable to send signals along cables at UHF frequencies because the losses were too high. UHF broadcasts were therefore translated near the aerial masthead to suitable channels in the VHF range and transmitted along the communal distribution system in this form. They were not translated back at the receiving points and the receiving sets had to be adjusted accordingly. The tuner in a TV set contains a number of pre-cabled tuning or filter circuits, each set to a particular channel. The station selector switch connects the appropriate filter, leaving the others out of circuit. All that was necessary therefore was for a service technician to take out one pre-cabled circuit and replace it with another pre-cabled to the new channel. This was a very simple operation.

The frequency changing equipment accepted the broadcast signals and translated them to the required channels by reference to high-stability local oscillators.

Modern amplifiers have made it possible to send UHF signals along aerial distribution cables so that frequency translation is no longer necessary, but it may still be encountered on some existing systems.

Mixers and splitters

Because the signal received by the aerial is attenuated as it travels along the cable, it must be amplified. There are difficulties in designing amplifiers which work equally well over a large range of frequencies and, therefore, two or more amplifiers are used, each operating on a particular band of frequencies. The output impedance of each amplifier must be matched to the characteristic impedance of the cable. Also the output of one amplifier must not feed back into another amplifier to distort the output of that one. It is, therefore, necessary to insert a mixer unit between the amplifiers and the line. The mixer unit has to accept two or more different frequencies and combine them, but at the same time isolate their sources one from another. It achieves this by suitable filtering networks of inductances and capacitances.

The layout of a scheme sometimes makes it necessary to take two cables away from one amplifier. The output impedance of one amplifier must then be matched to the characteristic impedances of two cables working in parallel. This is done by a splitter unit which divides the output from an amplifier and distributes it between two or more lines. The splitter is a network of resistances, inductances and capacitances chosen according to the conditions under which the division is to be made.

Power loss and amplification

As we have already said, because of losses in the transmission system, the signal received at the aerial has to be amplified either at the aerial or along the line or both. Now as the gain of an amplifier is increased the noise it introduces also increases, and this sets a limit to the gain which can be used. In practice, amplifiers with a gain of 30 to 60 dB are used. If a 30 dB amplifier is used, then the distribution system can be allowed to attenuate the signal by 30 dB before a repeater amplifier has to be installed. Similarly a 60 dB amplifier permits losses of 60 dB to be incurred before a repeater is necessary.

Attenuation occurs at a uniform rate along the length of the cable, but at each branch there is a sharp loss in the junction unit. Consequently, the graph of signal strength against cable run appears as in Figure 13.16. It will be seen that the signal level at each branch decreases as one goes along the cable. A TV set must receive a signal not less than about 1 mV but will distort the picture if the signal is more than about 6 dB higher than this minimum. The signal level at a junction must be high enough to accommodate the losses

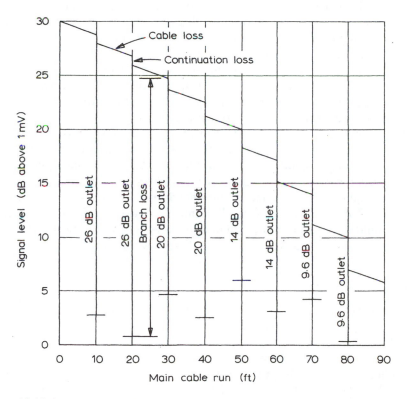

Figure 13.16 Attenuation graph

Table 13.3 Standard junction attenuators

Reduction of outlet signal relative to input		Reduction of continuation signal relative to input	
Ratio	*dB*	*dB*	*Ratio*
100 to 1	40	0.1	1.01 to 1
50 to 1	34	0.2	1.02 to 1
20 to 1	26	0.46	1.05 to 1
10 to 1	20	0.9	11.11 to 1
5 to 1	14	1.9	1.25 to 1
3 to 1	9.6	3.5	1.50 to 1

in the length of line continuing from the junction to the next amplifier. The attenuation in the shortest branch from the junction must be large enough to bring the signal strength down from that at the junction to less than the maximum acceptable to the receiving set at the end of the short branch. The branch cable is quite short and in any case its length cannot be adjusted to yield the required attenuation. It is, therefore, necessary to build in some extra attenuation, and this is done in the junction unit itself. The junction unit attenuates the signal to the branch outlet terminals by a given amount whilst keeping the attenuation to the line continuation terminals as low as possible. This is the second function of the junction unit which we referred to above and it is achieved by a suitable network of resistors.

It will be seen from Figure 13.16 that the attenuation required to produce a given output signal level is different at each junction. It would be most inconvenient to make a special unit for every junction, but fortunately this is not necessary. A good TV set has a certain tolerance in the input voltage it can accept, so that a standard attenuator can be used for several successive junctions giving a small range of outputs within the limits acceptable to the receivers. Table 13.3 shows a standard range of ratios which have in practice been found adequate in a large number of cases. The resulting signals available at the outlets in a typical case are also shown in Figure 13.16.

Typical systems

It is generally found that up to about 50 dwellings can be served from one repeater amplifier. Two typical schemes are shown in Figures 13.17 and 13.18.

Figure 13.17 indicates a housing development consisting of two blocks of dwellings. Each block has 17 single storey flats on the ground floor (intended for old people) and three layers of maisonettes above them. Each of these layers consists of three floor levels; the entrance to all maisonettes is on the

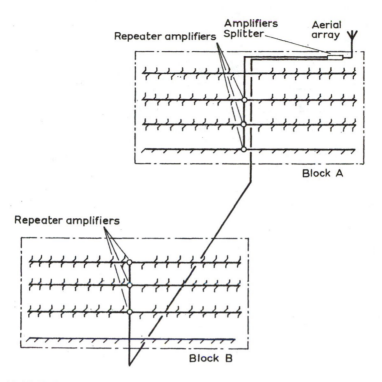

Figure 13.17 Typical scheme

middle layer, and alternate maisonettes have the bedrooms below and above the entrance and living rooms. Access corridors thus occur only on the ground floor and floors 3, 6 and 9, the other floors containing rooms reached by internal stairs within the maisonettes. All services follow the same distribution pattern, that is to say, they run in the ceiling of the access corridors and rise and drop into alternate maisonettes.

There is an aerial array which can receive three existing television channels and which also has provision for the reception of future services on three other channels. The array is mounted on the tank room on the roof of one of the blocks. The receiving equipment is fixed inside the tank room and consists of amplifiers and splitters. Two cables are taken from this main station, one to serve each block. They run along a duct in the roof and then drop in a duct alongside the main stairs. One cable drops to the ground and then continues inside a 50 mm plastic conduit under an open space to the other block where it rises in a duct alongside the main stairs. The other cable drops in the same duct of the first block, but has a junction box at level 9. From this two branches run along the ceilings of the access corridors with further junction boxes outside each front door. A third branch from the

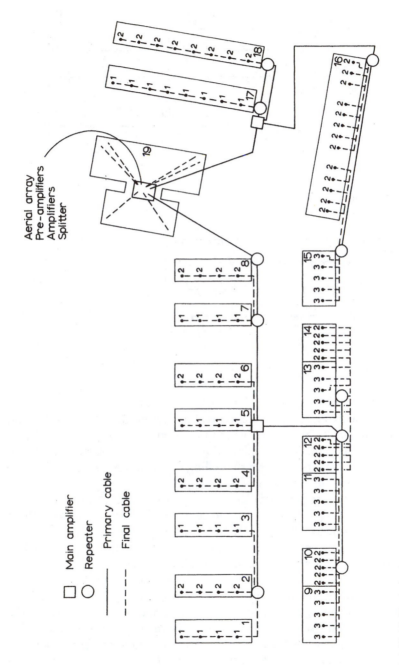

Aerial array
Pre-amplifiers
Amplifiers
Splitter

□ Main amplifier
○ Repeater

——— Primary cable
– – – Final cable

Figure 13.18 Typical scheme

junction box continues down the duct and feeds repeater amplifiers at levels 6, 3 and 1. From each of these, outgoing cables run along the ceilings of the access corridors feeding junction boxes outside each flat.

The cable entering the second block serves that block in an identical manner except that it works from the bottom up instead of from the top down. The reapeaters are therefore at levels 3, 6 and 9, whilst the ground floor is served directly from the main mast-head amplifier.

Figure 13.18 illustrates an estate consisting of one 24-storey tower block and 18 low blocks. Of the low blocks, numbers 1–8 and 17–18 are built on top of a podium covering a ground-level car park. They are of two storeys and alternate blocks contain maisonettes and a pair of single-floor flats. Blocks 9–16 start at ground level and are four storeys high. Here alternate blocks contain one maisonette and two flats above each other and two maisonettes above each other. Each floor of the tower block has four flats.

The aerial array is on the tank room of the tower block. The receiving equipment is just inside the tank room and consists of amplifiers and splitters together with a power unit. Eight of the outgoing cables cross the roof and drop inside conduit in the corners of the tower block. In each corner one cable serves the living rooms in the upper half of the block with a junction box at each level from which a short stub cable leads to the aerial outlet. The other cable in each corner drops past these levels without junctions and then serves the living rooms in that corner in the lower half of the block in a similar manner.

Two other cables from the receiving equipment drop in trunking in the central service duct of the tower block and then continue underground in 25 mm polythene conduit. One of them runs along blocks 8–2 receiving amplification at points in blocks 8, 7 and 5 and terminating in a final amplifier in block 2. From each of these amplifiers a final outlet cable runs at high level in the car park under each block. Under each living room there is a branch going to the living room above.

From the amplifier at block 5 there is another branch taking the main cable to further amplifiers in blocks 10, 12 and 13. From each of these there is a cable running within a polythene conduit outside the block. There is a junction box in the wall of each bay of these blocks from which an aerial cable runs to each living room outlet. Where there are two or three living rooms above each other two or three branches come off next to each other and run in separate 20 mm conduit to the several outlets. This arrangement makes it unnecessary to enter the lower flat if the cable to one of the upper flats has to be renewed.

The other cable from the tower block goes to block 17 where it feeds an amplifier. The cable branches at this amplifier; one branch goes to amplifiers in blocks 17 and 18 and the other to an amplifier in block 16. Blocks 17 and 18 are fed from their amplifiers in the same way as blocks 1–8 and block 16 is fed in the same way as blocks 10–13.

On the whole scheme all the junction units are contained in conduit boxes accessible from outside so that any repairs or replacements can be done without technicians having to enter flats. This is an important consideration because it is always difficult to get workmen to a job at a time when all the tenants are there to let them in.

The power to the amplifiers is supplied from the receiving power unit and is fed at mains frequency along the aerial cable itself. This method of line-feeding the amplifiers makes it unnecessary to provide power points at each amplifier position and this results in a significant saving in cost.

A smaller scheme requiring no repeater amplifiers is shown in Figure 13.19. This development consisted of a four-storey block A of four maisonettes and four blocks of terraced town houses B, C, D and E. The aerial was mounted on the roof of block A and there was an amplifier with a splitter and a power unit in a cupboard at high level on the common staircase of this block. Four cables ran through 20 mm conduit within this block to serve the four living rooms in it.

Two other cables dropped in 20 mm conduit in the block and continued in 20 mm polythene conduit in the ground outside. One ran along blocks C, D and E whilst the other ran along block B. In both cases there was a junction

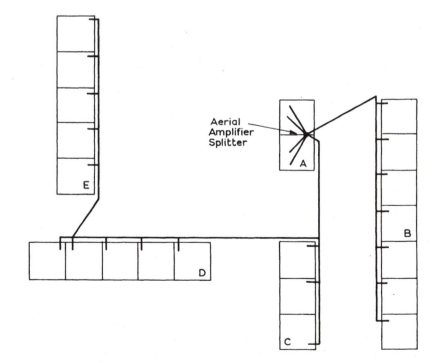

Figure 13.19 Small scheme

box in the wall of each house from which a short stub aerial cable ran in conduit to the outlet in the living room. The longest cable on this scheme served only 13 dwellings and it was therefore possible to avoid the use of repeater amplifiers altogether. On a small scheme it is better to have a splitter at the masthead with several distributing cables than to run a single cable round the whole site with several repeater amplifiers along it.

Standards relevant to this chapter are:

BS 3041   Radio frequency connectors
BS 6259   Code of practice for the design, planning, installation, testing and maintenance of sound systems
BS 6330   Code of practice for reception of sound and television broadcasting

Chapter 14

Lightning protection

Lightning strokes can be of two kinds. In the first, a charged cloud induces a charge of opposite sign in nearby tall objects, such as towers, chimneys and trees. The electrostatic stress at the upper ends of these objects is sufficiently great to ionize the air in the immediate neighbourhood, which lowers the resistance of the path between the cloud and the object. Ultimately, the resistance is lowered sufficiently for a disruptive discharge to occur between them. This type of discharge is characterized by the time taken to produce it, and by the fact that it usually strikes against the highest and most pointed object in the area.

The second kind of stroke is a discharge which occurs suddenly when a potential difference between a cloud and the earth is established almost instantly. It is generally induced by a previous stroke of the first kind; thus if a stroke of this kind takes place between clouds 1 and 2 (Figure 14.1), cloud 3 may be suddenly left with a greater potential gradient immediately adjacent to it than the air can withstand, and a stroke to earth suddenly occurs. This type of stroke occurs suddenly and is not necessarily directed to tall sharp objects like the first kind of stroke. It may miss tall objects and strike the ground nearby. Figure 14.2 shows other ways in which this. kind of stroke may be induced. In each case, A is a stroke of the first kind and B is the second type of stroke induced by A. In each case the first stroke from cloud 1 changes the potential gradient at cloud 2 and thus produces the second stroke.

The current in a discharge is uni-directional and consists of impulses with very steep wave fronts. The equivalent frequency of these impulses varies from 10 kHz to 100 kHz. While some lightning discharges consist of a single stroke, others consist of a series of strokes following each other along the same path in rapid succession. The current in a single stroke can vary from about 2000 A to a maximum of about 200 000 A, with a statistical average of 20 000 A. It rises to a peak value in a few microseconds. When a discharge consists of several successive strokes, each stroke rises and falls in a time and to an amplitude of this order so that the whole discharge can last up to a second.

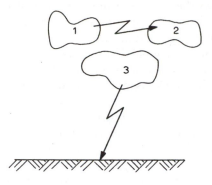

Figure 14.1 Induced lightning stroke

The effects of a discharge on a structure are electrical, thermal and mechanical.

As the current passes through the structure to earth it produces a voltage drop which momentarily raises the potential of part of the structure to a high value above earth. One function of a lightning conductor is to keep this potential as low as possible by providing a very low resistance path to earth. It is recommended in the British Standard Code of Practice (BS 6651:1999) that the resistance to earth of the protective system should not exceed 10 ohms. The sharp wave front of the discharge is equivalent to a high-frequency current and, therefore, there is also an inductive voltage drop which has to be added phasorially to the resistive drop. Part of the lightning conductor is thus inevitably raised to a high potential. This brings with it a risk of flashover from the conductor to other metal in the structure, such as water and gas pipes and electrical cables. These in turn would then be raised to high potential which could bring danger to occupants of the building, and it is necessary to guard against such flashovers. Bonding the lightning

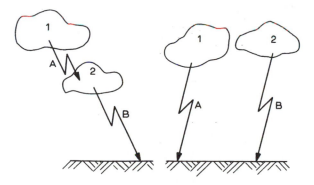

Figure 14.2 Induced lightning strokes

protection system to the main earthing terminal of the installation does this. The discharge of the lightning stroke to earth can also produce a high potential gradient in the ground around the earthing electrode, which can be lethal to people and to animals. The resistance to earth of each earthing electrode should be kept as low as is practicable.

The duration of a lightning discharge is so short that its thermal effect can in practice be ignored.

When a large current of high frequency flows through a conductor which is close to another conductor, large mechanical forces are produced. A lightning conductor must, therefore, be very securely fixed.

A lightning conductor works by diverting to itself a stroke which might otherwise strike part of the building being protected. The zone of protection is the space within which a lightning conductor provides protection by attracting the stroke to itself. It has been found that a single vertical conductor attracts to itself strokes of average or above average intensity which in the absence of the conductor would have struck the ground within a circle, having its centre at the conductor and a radius equal to twice the height of the conductor. For weaker than average discharges the protected area becomes smaller. For practical design it is therefore assumed that statistically satisfactory protection can be given to a zone consisting of a cone with its apex at the top of the vertical conductor and a base of radius equal to the height of the conductor. This is illustrated in Figure 14.3. For structure of a complicated nature a 'rolling sphere' of 6 m diameter method is used.

A horizontal conductor can be regarded as a series of apexes coalesced into a line, and the zone of protection thus becomes a tent-like space (Figure 14.4). When there are several parallel horizontal conductors the area between them has been found by experience to be better protected than one would expect from the above considerations only. On the basis of experience the recommended design criterion is that no part of the roof should be more than 5 m from the nearest horizontal conductor except that an additional 1.0 m may be added for each 1.0 m by which the part to be protected is below the nearest conductor.

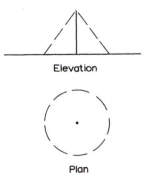

Elevation

Plan

Figure 14.3 Protected zone

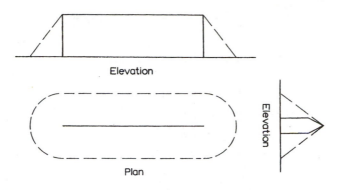

Figure 14.4 Protected zone – horizontal conductor

Whether or not a building needs protection against lightning is a matter of judgement. It obviously depends on the risk of a lightning stroke and also on the consequence of a stroke. Thus a higher risk of a strike can probably be accepted for an isolated small bungalow than for, say, a children's hospital. While no exact rules can be laid down that would eliminate the designer's judgement entirely, some steps can be taken to objectify the assessment of risk and of the magnitude of the consequences. The method recommended in BS 6651:1999 is to determine the probable number of strikes per year, apply a weighting factor to this, and see if the result is more or less than an acceptable level of risk. The weighting factor is the product of individual factors which take into account the use of the structure, the type of construction, the consequential effects of a strike, the degree of isolation and the type of country.

The probable number of strikes is given by

$$P = A_c \times N_g \times 10^{-16}$$

where

P = probable number of strikes per year
A_c = area protected by conductor, m^2
N_g = *lightning* flash density, i.e. the number of flashes to ground per km^2 per year.

A map showing values of N_g for different parts of the UK is shown in Figure 14.5. This and other extracts from BS 6651 are reproduced here by permission of the British Standards Institution (BSI). Complete copies can be obtained from BSI at Linford Wood, Milton Keynes, MK14 6LE. It should be noted that the area protected depends on the height of the conductor,

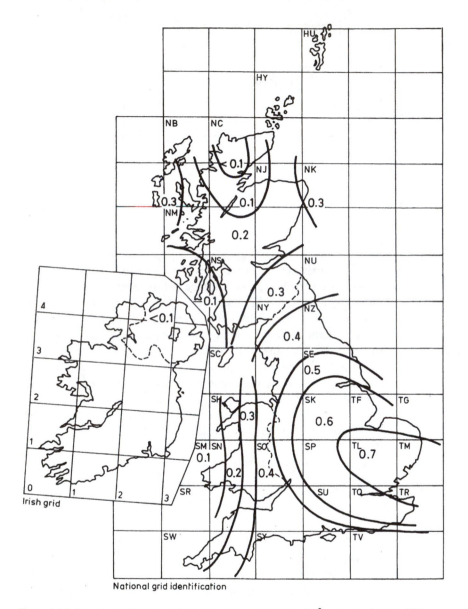

Figure 14.5 Number of lightning flashes to the ground per km² per year for the UK

which is normally the height of the building, and the latter is thus allowed for in the calculation of P.

The individual weighting factors are reproduced from BS 6651 in Table 14.1. The previously calculated value of P is multiplied by the product of

Table 14.1 Need for lightning protection

Weighting factor	Factor
A Use of structure	
Houses and similar buildings	0.3
Houses and similar buildings with outside aerial	0.7
Factories, workshops, laboratories	1.0
Offices, hotels, blocks of flats	1.2
Places of assembly, churches, halls, theatres, museums, department stores, post offices, stations, airports, stadiums	1.3
Schools, hospitals, children's and other homes	1.7
B Type of construction	
Steel framed encased with non-metal roof	0.2
Reinforced concrete with non-metal roof	0.4
Steel framed encased or reinforced concrete with metal roof	0.8
Brick, plain concrete, or masonry with non-metal roof	1.0
Timber framed or clad with roof other than metal or thatch	1.4
Brick, plain concrete masonry, timber framed, with metal roof	1.7
Any building with a thatched roof	2.0
C Contents or effects	
Contents or type of building	
Ordinary domestic or office building, factories and workshops not containing valuable materials	0.3
Industrial and agricultural buildings with specially susceptible contents	0.8
Power stations, gas installations, telephone exchanges, radio stations	1.0
Industrial key plants, ancient monuments, historic buildings, museums, art galleries	1.3
Schools, hospitals, children's and other homes, places of assembly	1.7
D Degree of isolation	
Structure in a large area of structures or trees of same height or greater height, e.g. town or forest	0.4
Structure in area with few other structures or trees of similar height	1.0
Structure completely isolated or twice the height of surrounding structures of trees	2.0
E Type of country	
Flat country at any level	0.3
Hill country	1.0
Mountain country between 300 m and 900 m	1.3
Mountain country above 900 m	1.7

all the individual factors to give an overall risk factor, P_o. The standard recommends that protection is needed if P_o is greater than 1×10^{-5} per year.

A complete lightning protective system consists of an air termination network, a down conductor and an earth termination. The air termination network is that part which is intended to intercept lightning discharges. It consists of vertical and horizontal conductors arranged to protect the required area in accordance with the empirical rules which we have given above. Typical arrangements are shown in Figure 14.6.

The earth termination is that part which discharges the current into the general mass of the earth. In other words, it is one or more earth electrodes. These have already been discussed in Chapter 9; earth electrodes for lightning protection are no different from earth electrodes for short-circuit protection systems. The total resistance of an earthing system, with all electrodes in parallel, should not exceed 10 ohms. It is clearly safer to ensure that the resistance of each electrode is less than 10 ohms. It is also recommended that the same earth termination system should be used for lightning protection as for all other services. The electrodes should be the rod or strip type, and should be either beneath or as near as possible to, the building being protected. Plate electrodes are expensive and come into their own only when large current-carrying capacity is important. Because of the short duration of a lightning stroke, this is not a consideration for lightning electrodes. The practice sometimes adopted of putting the electrode some distance away from the building is both unnecessary and uneconomical, and may increase the danger of voltage gradients in the ground.

The down conductor is the conductor which runs from the air termination to the earth termination. There should be one down conductor for every 20 m of perimeter. For buildings higher than 20 m there should be one down conductor for every 10 m of perimeter. A tall non-conducting chimney should have two down conductors equally spaced, with metal conductors joining the two down conductors round the top and bottom of the chimney and at intervals along its height. The down conductors should preferably be distributed round the outside walls of the building. If this is for any reason not practicable a down conductor can be contained inside a non-metallic and non-combustible duct. It can, for example, run inside a service duct provided the service duct does not contain any non-metal-sheathed cables. Sharp bends, as for example at the edge of a roof, do not matter, but re-entrant loops can be dangerous. A re-entrant loop produces a high inductive voltage drop which can cause the lightning discharge to jump across the loop. The discharge can, for example, go through the masonry of a parapet rather than around it. On the basis of experience it can be said that this danger may arise when the perimeter of the loop is more than eight times the length of the open side. This is illustrated in Figure 14.7. If a parapet is very narrow the problem can be solved by taking the conductor through a hole in the parapet as shown in Figure 14.8.

Sometimes a building is cantilevered out at a level above the ground. If the down conductor followed the contour of the building, there would be a real risk of flashover under the overhang, which could be lethal to anyone standing there. In such a building the down conductor must be taken straight

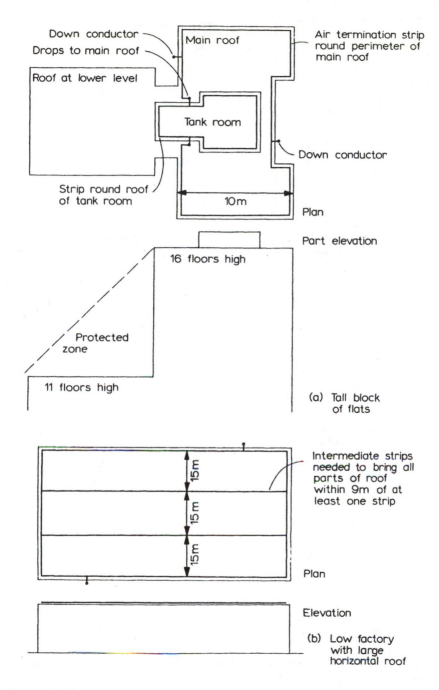

Down conductor
Drops to main roof

Main roof

Air termination strip
round perimeter of
main roof

Roof at lower level

Tank room

Down conductor

Strip round roof
of tank room

10m

Plan

Part elevation

16 floors high

Protected
zone

11 floors high

(a) Tall block
of flats

Intermediate strips
needed to bring all
parts of roof
within 9m of at
least one strip

15m

15m

15m

Plan

Elevation

(b) Low factory
with large
horizontal roof

Figure 14.6 Typical lightning conductors

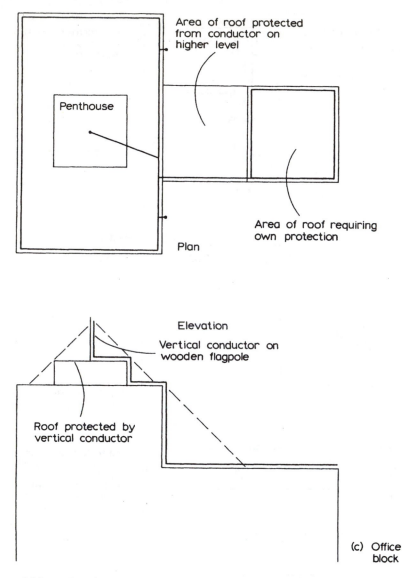

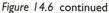

Figure 14.6 continued

down inside the ducts within the building. This problem and its solution are illustrated in Figure 14.9.

The material used for lightning conductors is normally aluminium or copper. The criterion for design is to keep the resistance from air termination to earth to a minimum. Since the bulk of resistance is likely to occur at the

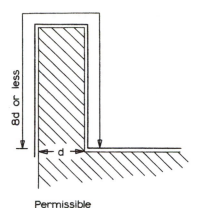
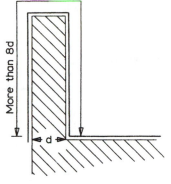

Permissible   Not permissible

Figure 14.7 Re-entrant loops

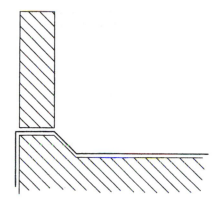

Figure 14.8 Parapet

earth electrode the resistance, and therefore the size, of the down conductor would not appear to be critical. Recommended dimensions are given in Table 14.2. Larger conductors should be used if the system is unlikely to receive regular inspection and maintenance.

External metal on a building should be bonded to the lightning conductor with bonds at least as large as the conductor.

When a lightning conductor carries a stroke to earth, it is temporarily raised to a considerable potential above earth. There is, therefore, a risk that the discharge will flash over to nearby metal and cause damage to the intervening structure or occupants. This can be prevented either by providing sufficient clearance between conductor and other metal or by bonding them to ensure that there can be no potential difference between them. The clearance required depends on the voltage to which the lightning system rises, which in turn depends on the current and the impedance. The impedance has

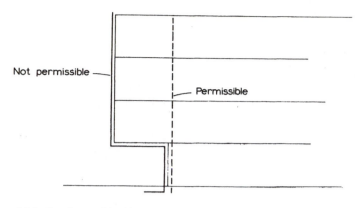

Figure 14.9 Cantilevered building

Table 14.2 Lightning conductors

Components	Minimum dimensions
Air terminations	*mm*
Aluminium and copper strip	20 × 3
Aluminium, aluminium alloy, copper and phosphor bronze rods	10 diam.
Stranded aluminium conductors	19/2.50
Stranded copper conductors	19/1.80
Down conductors	
Aluminium and copper strip	20 × 3
Aluminium, aluminium alloy and copper rods	10 diam.
Earth terminations	
Hard drawn copper rods for driving into soft ground	12 diam.
Hard drawn or annealed copper rods for indirect driving or laying in ground	10 diam.
Phosphor bronze for hard ground	12 diam.
Copper clad steel for hard ground	10 diam.

a resistive component and an inductive one; in the worst case, which is the one which should be designed for, the two components add linearly. The induced voltage arises in a loop formed by the down conductor and other metalwork so that the coupling is generated by the self inductance minus the mutual inductance to this metal work. This quantity is termed the transfer inductance and is given by the expression

$$M_{\mathrm{T}} = 0.46 \log_{10} \frac{S}{r_{\mathrm{e}}}$$

where

M_T = transfer inductance, μH m^{-1}
S = distance between centre of down conductor and centre of nearest vertical metal component, m
r_e = equivalent radius of down conductor, m.

For a circular down conductor r_e is the actual radius. For the more usual case of a rectangular strip down conductor,

$$r_e \frac{w+t}{3.5}$$

where

w = width, m
t = thickness, m.

The inductive voltage is proportional to the rate of change of current, and for design purposes this must be taken as the maximum likely to occur, which is 200 kA s^{-1}. The voltage is therefore calculated from the formula

$$V_L = 200 \frac{lM_T}{n}$$

where

V_L = inductive voltage, kV
l = length of inductive loop, m
M_T = transfer inductance μH m^{-1}
n = number of down conductors.

The length of the loop is the distance over which the down conductor and other metal run in parallel. The number of down conductors is brought into the formula because the total current is assumed to be shared between all of them, and if the peak current reached in one down conductor is $1/n$ times the total peak current, then the rate of change of current in one conductor is also $1/n$ times the maximum rate of change assumed. This assumption is not entirely valid, but it can be corrected for by the addition of 30 per cent to the calculated voltage for the down conductor at a corner of a rectangular or square building which has more than four down conductors, and a corresponding deduction of 30 per cent from the calculated voltage for a down conductor in the central area of such a building.

The resistive voltage is the total maximum current, assumed to be 200 kA, divided by the number of down conductors and multiplied by the permitted resistance to earth of the down conductor. The latter is the combined resistance of all down conductors, which is allowed to be 10 ohms, times the number of down conductors, so that the number of down conductors in fact cancels out the equation.

The sum of the inductive and resistive voltages is the voltage which could occur between the down conductor and the adjacent metalwork. Figure 14.10 shows the spacing required to avoid flashover for a given voltage. If the distance between the down conductor and the adjacent metalwork is less than this, the metalwork should be bonded to the down conductor. It will be found that the critical factors determining whether or not bonding is required are usually the number of down conductors and the resistance to earth.

Metal services entering the building should be bonded as directly as possible to the earth termination. Large masses of metal, such as a bell frame in a church tower, should be bonded to the nearest down conductor as directly as possible. Short isolated pieces of metal like window frames may be ignored and do not have to be bonded. Similarly, metal reinforcement in a structure which cannot easily be bonded and which cannot itself form

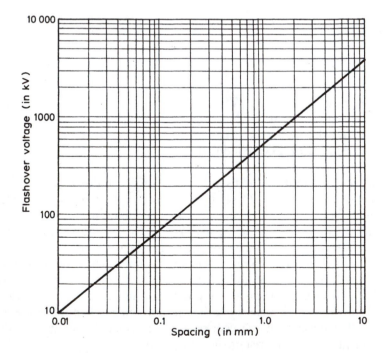

Figure 14.10 Flashover voltage in air as a function of spacing

part of a down conductor can also be ignored. The danger from such metal is best minimized by keeping it entirely separate from the lightning protection system.

It is perfectly in order for metal cladding or curtain walling which has a continuous conducting path in all directions to be used as part of a lightning protection system. In the extreme case, a structure which is itself a complete metal frame, such as a steel chimney, needs no lightning conductor other than itself. It is enough to earth it effectively.

A structure having reinforcement or cladding forming a close metal mesh in the form of internal reinforcement or screen approaches the conditions of a Faraday Cage, in which any internal metal assumes the same potential as the cage itself. The risk of side flashing is thereby reduced and the recommendations for bonding need not be so strictly adhered to.

The metal bars of concrete reinforcement are tied together by binding cable. Both the bars and the binding cable are usually rusty, so that one does not expect a good electrical contact. Nevertheless, because there are so many of these joints in parallel the total resistance to earth is very low, and experience has shown that it is quite safe to use the reinforcement as a down conductor. Naturally the resistance from air termination to earth must be checked after the structure is complete and if it is too high a separate down conductor must after all be installed.

A building containing explosive or highly flammable materials may need more thorough protection. An air termination network should be suspended above the building or area to be protected, and the conductors should be spaced so that each protects a space formed by a cone having an apex angle of 30°, i.e. a smaller zone than is adopted for less hazardous buildings. The height of the network should be such that there is no risk of flashover from the network to the building, and the down conductors and earth terminations should be well away from the building. All the earth terminations should be interconnected by a ring conductor buried in the ground. All major metal inside or on the surface of the building should be effectively bonded to the lightning protection system.

It may be difficult to put a radio or television aerial on a roof so that it is within the space protected by the air termination network, and this may present something of a problem. If the down lead is concentric or twin screened, protection can be obtained by connecting the metallic sheath of the cable to the lightning conductor. With a single or twin down lead it is necessary to insert a discharge device between the conductors and an earth lead. In either case metal masts, crossarms and parasitic elements should be bonded to the lightning conductor.

As an example of the calculations described in this chapter consider a large factory in a built-up area within Greater London. It is assumed to be 80 m long by 15 m wide and to be 6 m high. Vertical rods on the roof to give protection over such an area would be impractically high, so the air termination

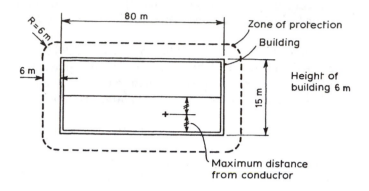

Figure 14.11 Zone of protection and spacing of air termination

must be a network of conductors on the roof. One strip will run round the perimeter, and an additional lengthwise strip down the centre of the roof will ensure compliance with the requirement that no part of the roof is more than 5 m from the nearest horizontal conductor. This is shown in Figure 14.11 which also shows the area protected; the latter extends outside the building by a distance equal to the height.

This amount of preliminary design had to be done to establish the area protected, which is needed to determine whether or not protection is necessary. The protected area A_c is $(80 + 6 + 6) \times (15 + 6 + 6) + \pi 6^2 = 2600\,m^2$. From Figure 14.5 it is seen that for Greater London $N_s = 0.6$.

$$P = 2600 \times 0.6 \times 10^{-6} = 1560 \times 10^{-6}$$

The weighting factors are as follows:

A:	factory	1.0
B:	steel frame encased with non-metal roof	0.2
C:	normal factory, no special contents	0.3
D:	structure in large area of structures of same height	0.4
E:	flat country	0.3

$$P_o = 1560 \times 10^{-6} \times 1.0 \times 0.2 \times 0.3 \times 0.4 \times 0.3 = 11 \times 10^{-6} = 1.1 \times 10^{-5}$$

This is greater than 1.0×10^{-5} and therefore protection is needed. The building perimeter is $(2 \times 80) + (2 \times 15) = 190\,m$ and the number of down conductors required will therefore be $190/20 = 10$. Each will terminate in a rod type earth electrode.

There are metal rainwater pipes running down the building, and it is necessary to consider whether they should be bonded to the down conductors. The down conductors may be 20 mm × 3 mm

$$\therefore r_{\mathrm{e}} = \frac{0.02 + 0.003}{3.5} = 0.00657\,\mathrm{m}$$

Suppose there is a rainwater pipe 1.5 m from a down conductor. Then

$$M = 0.46 \log_{10} \frac{1.5}{0.00657} = 1.08$$

Since both rainwater pipe and down conductor run the full height of the building, $l = 6$ and the number of down conductors is 10. Then

$$V_{\mathrm{L}} = 200 \times \frac{6 \times 1.08}{10} = 130\,\mathrm{kV}$$

The down conductor is not at a corner, so this figure can be reduced by 30 per cent.

$$V_{\mathrm{L}} = 130 \times 0.7 = 90.7\,\mathrm{kV}$$

The resistive voltage V_{R} is $200 \times 10 = 2000\,\mathrm{kV}$.
The flashover voltage $V_{\mathrm{L}} + V_{\mathrm{R}} = 90.7 + 2000 = 2100\,\mathrm{kV}$.

From Figure 14.10 the safe spacing for 2100 kV is 5 m. The rainwater pipe is less than this distance from the down conductor and therefore bonding is required. Without bonding, the flashover voltage arises almost completely from the resistive component and in order to eliminate this along the whole length of the pipe bonding is required at both top and bottom.

Standards relevant to this chapter are:

BS 6651   Code of practice for protection of structures against lightning

Chapter 15

Emergency supplies

Introduction

There are rare occasions when the public electricity supply fails and a building is left without electricity. In some buildings, the risk of being totally without electricity cannot be taken, and some provision must be made for an alternative supply to be used in an emergency. What form this provision should take is an economic matter which depends on the magnitude of the risk of failure and the seriousness of the consequences of failure. In this chapter, we shall say something about the available methods of providing an alternative supply.

Standby service cable

The Electricity Supply Authority can be asked to bring two separate service cables into the building. They will normally make a charge for this, but it provides security against a fault in one of the cables. It does not, of course, give security against a failure of the public supply altogether.

In heavily built up areas, such as London and other large cities, the public distribution system is in the form of a network and each distribution cable in the streets is fed from a sub-station at each end. The supply system itself thus contains its own standby provision. The only addition the building developer can make is to duplicate the short length of cable from the distributor in the road into the building, and it may be doubted whether the risk of this cable failing is sufficiently great to justify the cost of duplicating it. In rural areas the service cable to individual buildings may be quite long, and may take the form of an overhead line rather than an underground cable. The risk of damage is thus greater than in urban areas and there is much more reason for installing a duplicate cable.

Battery systems

Central battery and individual battery systems have been discussed in Chapter 7 as means of providing emergency lighting. A central battery system can also provide d.c. power. An alternative is for the battery to feed a thyristor inverter which then gives a.c. power.

It is difficult to install and keep charged a battery large enough to give the quantities of power needed in a whole building. In building services, in practice, batteries are used for emergency lighting but seldom for emergency power.

A battery system will give an emergency supply only for as long as the battery charge lasts. It then becomes dependent on a restoration of the mains supply for long enough to recharge the battery. Thus we can see that this system does not protect against long interruptions of the public supply.

Standby generators

A diesel or gas turbine generator set can be installed in a building to provide electricity when the public supply fails. This is a complete form of protection against all possible interruptions of the main supply. The generator can be large enough to supply all the needs of the building and its output can be connected to the ordinary mains immediately after the supply authority's meters and it then provides standby facilities for the entire building. It is cheaper, and may be adequate for the risk to be guarded against, to have a smaller generator serving only the more important outlets. In this case, the distribution must be arranged so that these outlets can be switched from main to emergency supply at one point and so that there is no unintentional path from the emergency generator to outlets not meant to be served by it. In effect the building is divided at the main intake into two distribution systems and only one of them is connected to the emergency changeover switch. It is also possible to install a completely separate system of wiring from the emergency generator to outlets quite distinct from the normal ones. This may be the simplest thing to do in a small building or when the emergency supply is required to serve only one or two outlets. It has the disadvantage that individual pieces of equipment have to be disconnected from one outlet and reconnected to another. Whilst this may not be acceptable in a hospital it may be quite in order in a large residence or hostel to have one or two emergency power points into which vacuum cleaners and other domestic equipment can be plugged when the main power supply is interrupted.

Buildings in which standby generators have been installed include poultry farms, chemical process plants, hospitals, telephone exchanges, computer rooms and prisons.

An emergency generator can be started either manually or automatically. A manual start is simple, but it involves a delay during which the building is without power. This delay can be avoided by automatic starting, initiated by a sensing unit which detects a drop in the mains voltage. Figure 15.1 shows the circuit of a typical mains failure control panel.

When the mains fail, relay 1CC/6 is de-energized and opens the main circuit breaker. It also completes the circuit to the operating coil of relay 2CC/6, thus preparing the circuit for shut down when the mains are restored. Relays VS1, VS2 and VS3 are separately operated by each of the three phases, and each has the effect of de-energizing the main relay ICC/6, so that the system is brought into operation on the failure of any one phase.

When the mains fail, relay VS 1/2 is also de-energized and its contacts then bring into operation relays T1, R1, R2 and R3. Relay R1 starts the run solenoid of the diesel engine, relay R2 energizes the starter motor and relay R3 temporarily disconnects the battery charger. If the engine has not started after 10 s, relay T1 de-energizes relays R1, R2 and R3 and lights a fail-to-start warning lamp. It also energizes relay R4, one of whose contacts breaks the circuit of relay R1 which has the effect of making a restart impossible. Thus, if the engine does not start within 10 s it locks out and nothing further can happen until it receives some manual attention.

If, or perhaps we should say when, the engine starts, relay VS4/1 is energized. This interrupts the operating coil circuits of relays R2 and R3 and prevents relay Ti from energizing relay R4. The starting sequence is thus brought to an end, the battery charger is reconnected and the starter motor stopped.

Relay T2 is now energized and in turn energizes relay R5 which completes the circuit to the operating coil of relay 2CC/6. The latter closes the standby generator. At the same time, it lights the indicator to show that the standby generator is on load and puts a break in the operating coil circuit of relay 1CC/6. This ensures that the mains circuit breaker will not close while the standby circuit breaker is closed. The plant is now running on standby.

When the mains are restored relays VS2 and VS3 are energized and in turn energize relay VS1. The circuit to complete the supply to relay ICC/6 is thus prepared. Also the circuits to relays T1 and R1 are broken. Relay Ti then breaks the circuit to relay R4 and energizes relays R2 and R3. The starter circuit is kept open by relay R1 which is kept de-energized by relay VS1.

With R1 de-energized the run solenoid is de-energized and the standby set stops. As soon as it shuts down relays VS4 and T2 open. The latter breaks the circuit to relay R5 and the normally open contact of R5 breaks the circuit to relay 2CC/6. This opens the standby circuit breaker and simultaneously completes the circuit to relay 1CC/6, which then closes the main circuit breaker. The standby set is now shut down and the load is back on the mains.

It takes 8 to 10 s for a diesel generator to come to full speed. With the system just described this period is needed to bring the emergency supply into action after the mains have failed and, therefore, during this period there is no supply to the load. In some applications an interruption even of this short

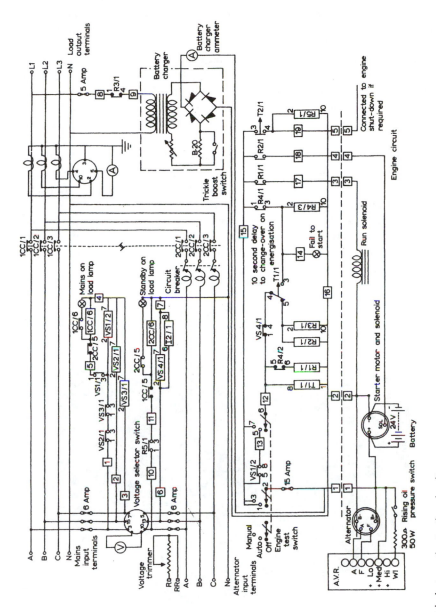

Figure 15.1 Automatic starting circuit

duration is not acceptable, and a more complex arrangement is necessary. In one system the diesel engine is coupled to a clutch the other side of which is connected to a squirrel cage induction motor. The induction motor drives an alternator through a flywheel, and the alternator supplies the load. Under normal conditions the induction motor is connected to the mains and the set operates as a motor alternator supplied from the mains. When the mains fail the motor is disconnected from the mains and the diesel engine is started. As soon as it reaches its running speed, the clutch operates and the alternator is driven through the shaft of the motor by the diesel engine. During the time it takes for the engine to come up to speed the alternator is kept going by the flywheel. The automatic controls required for this arrangement are similar to those already described.

Clearly this scheme is much more expensive and involves some permanent losses in the motor alternator set. It is used only for comparatively small power outputs for special purposes, such as telecommunications and power for aircraft landing systems.

Standby generators are normally supplied as complete units on a stand. Figure 15.2 is a picture of a typical set. The diesel engine is a normal engine with a governor, and it would be outside the scope of this book to enter on

Figure 15.2 Standby generator

a description of diesel engines. The alternator is directly coupled to the engine and has an automatic voltage regulator. The commonest type of alternator used is the screen protected, provided with brushless excitation. It is directly coupled to the engine and in smaller sizes may be overhung. In larger sizes it is supported at both ends from the set base plate. A separate exciter is mounted within the casing on the main shaft. In most modern sets the automatic voltage regulator is one of the static types. Finally, there is a control panel with voltmeters, ammeters, battery charger, incoming and outgoing terminals and the relays and circuits for the automatic start and stop control. A fuel tank is needed for the diesel engine, but this is normally supplied as a separate item and fixed independently of the generator set, with a short fuel pipe between them.

Diesel engines are noisy and it is prudent to arrange some form of sound-attenuating enclosure. The enclosure must have openings for fresh air to the engine and for the engine exhaust, and these openings will be found to limit the degree of silencing that can be achieved. Several manufacturers supply diesel generator sets complete in an enclosure which provides silencing and is also weatherproof, so that the set can be installed outdoors.

Similar generating sets can, of course, be used to supply power to a building under normal conditions. In the UK it is not economic for consumers to generate their own power, but there are still parts of the world where it is a reasonable proposition.

There are, however, cases in industrial countries where it is economic for consumers to use their own generating plant to supply peak loads. Many factories are supplied on a tariff which includes a charge for the peak instantaneous load. A factory may have a process which takes a fairly steady load during most of the day with a high peak for one or two hours. It may then be economic to limit the power taken from the public supply to rather less than the maximum needed and to make up the deficiency at peak times with the factory's own plant. Figure 15.3 shows a load diagram to illustrate this. The public mains are used at all times and are used by themselves so long as the load is less than 300 kVA. As soon as the load exceeds this figure the factory's own generating plant is started and is run in parallel with the public mains. The power taken from the public mains is limited to a maximum of 300 kVA at all times.

The same type of diesel generator is used for this application as for standby purposes. The start up and shut down sequences are initiated automatically by a kVA meter instead of by a voltage detector, but are otherwise similar to those already described.

Uninterruptible power supplies

The requirements of computers have led to the development of uninterruptible power supply units, generally referred to as UPS. In essence they

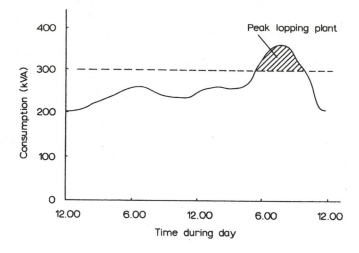

Figure 15.3 Load diagram

depend on a battery and inverter to provide an emergency supply. Because computers are sensitive to voltage and frequency fluctuations it is useful to feed them through a network which smoothes out fluctuations in the supply and suppresses surges caused by switching of other equipment connected to the same supply. A UPS generally incorporates such a circuit and therefore the complete unit contains a battery, charger, inverter, changeover switch and smoothing circuit. In another arrangement, shown in block diagram form in Figure 15.4, the mains supply is rectified and then inverted, with the battery connected between the rectifier and inverter. This avoids a separate charger and eliminates the changeover switch. The battery is automatically kept charged and any drop in mains voltage results in current being taken from the battery with no effect on the output. The capacity of the UPS will depend on the application. For a general office application the capacity may supply the computer for one hour. In large offices such as in an insurance company head office, the inverter is supplied from a very large battery bank giving many hours of back-up.

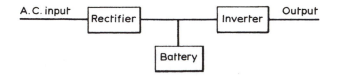

Figure 15.4 Scheme of UPS unit

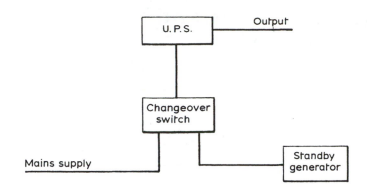

Figure 15.5 Standby system

Most UPS have batteries which will maintain the output for at least an hour. Insurance companies and the like are likely to have very large UPS systems because of the large number of computers they use on their premises. The one-hour UPS may be adequate for a small computer in an industrialized country with a very reliable public electricity supply. An interruption in supply is not likely to last for long, and there is adequate time to complete work in hand, save data on disc and switch off in an orderly way before the battery runs down. If this is not considered sufficient protection, the UPS can be combined with a standby generator as shown in Figure 15.5. The UPS battery provides the supply while the generator set runs up to speed. This arrangement ensures secure supply to the computer without the mechanical complication and losses of the motor alternator system described previously. Standards relevant to this chapter are:

BS 5266 Code of practice for the emergency lighting of premises

Chapter 16

Lifts, escalators and paternosters

Introduction

The general design of lifts is very well established, and in this country at least, nearly all the reputable lift manufacturers will design and supply a satisfactory lift as a matter of routine if given the details and the size of building. Nevertheless, the designer of the building electrical services must be able to advise the client about the lifts, to negotiate with the lift suppliers and to compare competing tenders. The designer must, therefore, know something about the technical details of lifts and we shall accordingly devote this chapter to a brief outline of the subject.

First, we can note that there are three categories of lifts. Passenger lifts are designed primarily for passenger use; goods lifts are mainly for goods but can on occasion carry passengers; and service lifts are for goods only and are of such a size that passengers cannot enter into the car. Lift speeds are determined by the number of floors served and the quality of service required. They vary from $0.5\,\mathrm{ms}^{-1}$ to $10\,\mathrm{ms}^{-1}$ in high office blocks.

In deciding the size of car one can allow $0.2\,\mathrm{m}^2$ for each passenger, and when determining the load the average weight of a passenger can be taken as 75 kg. It must, however, be remembered that in many buildings the lift will be used for moving in furniture and the car must be big enough for the bulkiest piece of furniture likely to be needed. The author has made measurements of domestic furniture and has concluded that the most awkward item to manoeuvre is a double bed, which can be up to 1670 mm wide by 1900 mm long and 360 mm high. In flats it is unfortunately also necessary to make sure that stretchers and coffins can be carried in the lift. To accommodate these, a depth of 2.5 m is required. The whole car can be made this depth or it can be shallower but have a collapsible extension which can be opened out at the back when the need arises. The lift well must, of course, be deep enough to allow the extension to be opened. In hospitals some of the lifts must take stretchers on trolleys and also hospital beds and these lifts must be the full depth of a complete bed.

Grade of service

The quality of service is a measure of the speed with which passengers can be taken to their destination. It is the sum of the time which the average passenger has to wait for a lift and of the travelling time once in the lift. The maximum time a person may have to wait is called the waiting time (WI) and is the interval between the arrival of successive cars. It depends on the round trip time (RTT) of each lift and on the number of lifts.

The average time a person has to wait is WI/2. The average time travelling is RTT/4. The sum of these, WI/2 = RTT/4, is called the grade of service. If there are N lifts, then WI=RTT/N, and grade of service becomes WI(2 + N)/4.

It is usual to classify the grade of service as excellent if WI(2 + N)/4 is less than 45 s, good if it is between 45 and 55 s, fair if it is between 55 and 65 s and casual if it is more than 65 s.

The use of a building will often enable a designer to estimate the probable number of stops during each trip. If this is difficult, then a formula can be developed by probability theory, and is:

$$S_n = n - \left[\left(\frac{P - P_a}{P} \right)^N + \left(\frac{P - P_b}{P} \right)^N + \ldots + \left(\frac{P - P_n}{P} \right)^N \right]$$

where

$S_n =$	probable number of stops
$n =$	number of floors served above ground floor
$N =$	number of passengers entering lift at ground floor on each trip
$P =$	total population on all floors
$P_a, P_b, \ldots P_n =$	population on 1st, 2nd ... nth floor.

Three to four seconds must be allowed for opening and closing the doors at each stop. A further 1 to 11.5 s have to be allowed for each passenger to enter the lift and 1 to 2 s for each passenger to leave.

The travelling time is made up of periods of acceleration, constant speed and retardation. Figure 16.1 gives the time versus distance curves for the acceleration normally associated with various lift speeds. On each curve, the point marked X indicates the end of acceleration and start of constant velocity. The retardation is generally taken to be equal in magnitude to the acceleration. Providing the distance between stops is long enough for the lift to reach steady speed before starting to slow, the total travelling time of a round trip is given by:

$$t = \frac{2}{V}(d S_n + D + d)$$

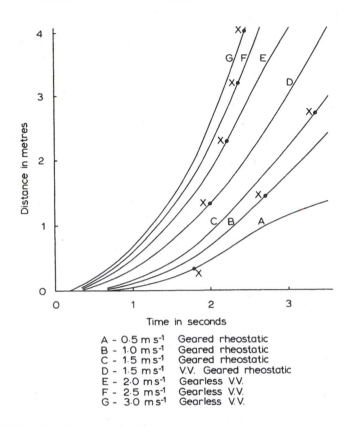

A - 0·5 m s⁻¹   Geared rheostatic
B - 1·0 m s⁻¹   Geared rheostatic
C - 1·5 m s⁻¹   Geared rheostatic
D - 1·5 m s⁻¹   V.V. Geared rheostatic
E - 2·0 m s⁻¹   Gearless V.V.
F - 2·5 m s⁻¹   Gearless V.V.
G - 3·0 m s⁻¹   Gearless V.V.

Figure 16.1 Acceleration curves for lifts

where

> t = total travelling time
> d = distance during which acceleration takes place
> D = distance between ground and top floors
> S_n = number of stops between ground and top floors
> V = lift speed.

The best way of showing how all this data is used to assess the grade of service is by means of an example. Let us assume we are dealing with an office block with eight floors. The heaviest traffic will occur in the morning when people are arriving at work, and we shall assume that we know enough about the occupancy of the building to have been able to estimate that 75 per cent of the work force will arrive in one particular half hour. For estimating the probable number of stops, traffic to the first floor can be ignored and we can set out the number of people requiring service as follows:

Table 16.1 Lift service comparison

	A	B	C	D
Load persons	10	20	10	15
Speed ms^{-1}	1.5	1.5	2.0	2.0
Probable no. of stops per trip (S_n)	5.23	6.35	5.23	5.99
Accelerating distance (d) m	2.60	2.60	2.20	2.20
$d \times S_n$	13.60	16.50	11.50	13.20
Distance between ground and top floors (D) m	25.00	25.00	25.00	25.00
$(dS_n + D + d)$	41.20	44.10	38.70	40.40
$\dfrac{2(dS_n + D + d)}{2 \times \text{speed}}$ = travelling time (s)	55.00	59.00	38.00	40.00
Door opening time (s)	21.00	28.00	21.00	24.00
Passengers entering and leaving (s)	25.00	50.00	25.00	37.00
Total travelling time	101	137	84	101
10% margin	10	13	8	10
RTT(s)	111	150	92	111
No. of lifts	4	3	4	3
No. of trips per lift in 30 min	16	12	19	16
No. of persons per lift in 30 min	160	240	190	240
Total no. of persons carried in 30 min	640	720	760	720
WI(s)	28	50	23	37
$\dfrac{\text{WI}}{4}(2 + N)$	42	62	35	46
Grade of service	Excellent	Fair	Excellent	Good

Calculation of S_n $S_n = n - \displaystyle\sum_{i=2}^{i=8}\left(\dfrac{P - P_i}{P}\right)^N$ $P = 662$ $n = 7$

i	Pi	$P - Pi$	$\left(\dfrac{P = P_i}{P}\right)$	$\left(\dfrac{P = P_i}{P}\right)^{10}$	$\left(\dfrac{P = P_i}{P}\right)^{15}$	$\left(\dfrac{P = P_i}{P}\right)^{20}$
2	36	626	0.95	0.60	0.46	0.36
3	93	569	0.86	0.22	0.10	0.05
4	160	502	0.76	0.06	0.01	0.00
5	85	577	0.58	0.22	0.10	0.05
6	120	542	0.82	0.12	0.04	0.02
7	105	557	0.84	0.18	0.08	0.03
8	63	599	0.905	0.37	0.22	0.14
			Σ 1.77	1.01		0.65
			$S_n = 7 - \Sigma$ 5.23	5.99		6.35

Floor	2	3	4	5	6	7	8	Total
No. of persons requiring service	36	93	160	85	120	105	63	662

The figures in the second line are 75 per cent of the floor populations, which we assume we have either been given or can guess. The distance between the ground and eighth floor is 25 m.

The round trip time can be calculated and hence it is possible to calculate the number of lifts needed to carry 662 people in 30 mm. From this, the grade of service can be obtained. If the calculation is set out in tabular form, different combinations can be easily compared. This has been done in Table 16.1. A 10 per cent margin is added to the calculated total time to allow for irregularities in the time interval between different lifts in the bank of lifts.

It can be seen that in this example the most satisfactory arrangement is four lifts each taking 10 persons at a speed of $1.5 \, ms^{-1}$. A speed of $2.0 \, ms^{-1}$ would be unnecessarily extravagant.

It will be found that where the service is not so concentrated lower speeds are sufficient. For this reason, it should not be necessary to use speeds of more than 0.75 or $1.0 \, ms^{-1}$ in blocks of flats.

Accommodation

The machine room for the lifting gear is normally at the top of the lift shaft or well. It can be at the bottom or even beside the well, and in the latter case it can be at any height, but from these positions the ropes must pass over more pulleys so that the overall arrangement becomes more complicated. It is, therefore, better to provide space for the machine room at the top of the well. Room must also be left for buffers and for inspection at the bottom, or pit, of the well. The sizes of the machine and pit rooms must ultimately be agreed with the lift manufacturers, but for preliminary planning before a manufacturer has submitted a quotation the dimensions in Table 16.2 may be taken as a guide.

Drive

Nearly all lifts use a traction drive. In this, the ropes pass from the lift car around a cast iron or steel grooved sheave and then to the counterweight. The sheave is secured to a steel shaft which is turned by the driving motor. The drive from the motor to the shaft is usually through a worm gear. The force needed to raise or lower the lift car is provided by the friction between the ropes and the sheave grooves. The main advantage of the traction drive is that if either the car or counterweight comes into contact with the buffers the drive ceases and there is no danger of the car being wound into the overhead structure. Other advantages are cheapness and simplicity.

Table 16.2 Lift dimensions

Passenger lifts

Load persons	Speed (ms⁻¹)	Well Width (m)	Depth (m)	Machine room Width (m)	Length (m)	Height (m)	Top landing to M/C room floor (m)	Pit depth (m)
General purpose passenger lifts								
8	1.0	1.80	1.90	3.10	4.80	2.60	4.00	1.60
10	0.75	2.00	1.90	3.10	5.00	2.60	4.00	1.60
10	1.0	2.00	1.90	3.10	5.00	2.60	4.00	1.70
10	1.5	2.00	1.90	3.10	5.00	2.60	4.20	1.70
16	0.75	2.60	2.20	3.50	5.30	2.70	4.10	1.70
16	1.00	2.60	2.20	3.50	5.30	2.70	4.20	1.90
16	1.50	2.60	2.20	3.50	5.30	2.70	4.30	1.90
20	0.75	2.60	2.50	3.50	5.60	2.70	4.10	1.70
20	1.00	2.60	2.50	3.50	5.60	2.70	4.20	1.90
20	1.50	2.60	2.50	3.50	5.60	2.70	4.30	1.90
High speed passenger lifts								
12	2.5	2.20	2.20	3.20	7.50	2.70	6.80	2.80
16	2.5	2.60	2.30	3.20	8.00	2.70	6.80	2.80
16	3.5	2.60	2.30	3.20	8.00	3.50	6.90	3.40
20	2.5	2.60	2.60	3.20	8.30	3.50	6.20	2.80
20	3.5	2.60	2.60	3.20	8.30	3.50	7.10	3.40
20	5.0	2.60	2.60	3.20	8.30	3.50	8.20	5.10

Goods lifts

Load (kg)	Speed (ms⁻¹)	Well Width (m)	Depth (m)	Machine room Width (m)	Length (m)	Height (m)	Top landing to M/C room floor (m)	Pit depth (m)
General purpose goods lifts								
500	0.5	1.80	1.50	2.00	3.70	2.40	3.80	1.40
1000	0.25	2.10	2.10	2.10	4.30	2.40	3.80	1.50
1000	0.50	2.10	2.10	2.10	4.30	2.40	3.80	1.50
1000	0.75	2.10	2.10	2.10	4.30	2.40	3.80	1.50
1500	0.25	2.50	2.30	2.50	4.50	2.70	4.00	1.50
1500	0.75	2.50	2.30	2.50	4.50	2.70	4.20	1.80
1500	1.00	2.50	2.30	2.50	4.50	2.70	4.20	1.80
2000	0.25	2.80	2.40	2.80	4.70	2.90	4.10	1.50
2000	0.75	2.80	2.40	2.80	4.70	2.90	4.50	1.80
2000	1.00	2.80	2.40	2.80	4.70	2.90	4.50	1.80
3000	0.25	3.50	2.70	3.50	5.00	2.90	4.20	1.50
3000	0.50	3.50	2.70	3.50	5.00	2.90	4.40	1.70
3000	0.75	3.50	2.70	3.50	5.00	2.90	4.50	1.80

Table 16.2 continued

Load (kg)	Speed (ms⁻¹)	Well		Machine room			Top landing to M/C room floor (m)	Pit depth (m)
		Width (m)	Depth (m)	Width (m)	Length (m)	Height (m)		
Heavy duty goods lift								
1500	0.50	2.60	2.40	2.60	4.80	2.70	4.80	1.70
1500	0.75	2.60	2.40	2.60	4.80	2.70	4.80	1.80
1500	1.00	2.60	2.40	2.60	4.80	2.70	4.80	1.80
2000	0.50	2.90	2.50	2.90	5.00	2.90	4.80	1.70
2000	0.75	2.90	2.50	2.90	5.00	2.90	4.80	1.80
2000	1.00	2.90	2.50	2.90	5.00	2.90	4.80	1.80
3000	0.50	3.50	2.80	3.50	5.30	2.90	4.80	1.70
3000	0.75	3.50	2.80	3.50	5.30	2.90	4.80	1.80
3000	1.00	3.50	2.80	3.50	5.30	2.90	4.80	1.80
4000	0.50	3.50	3.40	4.00	6.20	2.90	5.20	1.70
4000	0.75	3.50	3.40	4.00	6.20	2.90	5.20	1.80
5000	0.50	3.60	4.00	4.00	6.80	2.90	5.20	1.70
5000	0.75	3.60	4.00	4.00	6.80	2.90	5.20	1.80

Figure 16.2 shows a geared traction unit has a drive motor permanently coupled to the gear by a vee rope drive. There is a brake working on a brake disc on the end of the worm shaft and the grooved sheave is easily discernible at the side of the machine. The control panel is in the foreground

The only other kind of drive is the drum drive. In this case, one end of the car ropes and one end of the counterweight ropes are securely fastened by

Figure 16.2 Geared drive unit
(Courtesy of Schindler Lifts Ltd)

clamps on the inside of a cast iron or steel drum, the other ends being fastened to the car and counterweight respectively. One set of ropes is wrapped clockwise around the drum and the other set anti-clockwise, so that one set is winding up as the other set is unwinding from the drum. As the car travels, the ropes move along the drum in spiral grooves on its periphery. The drum drive suffers from the disadvantage that as the height of travel increases the drum becomes large and unwieldy. It has been almost entirely superseded by the traction drive.

Figure 16.3 shows various arrangements of ropes for traction drives. Figure 16.3b shows a double wrap drive, in which each rope passes over the sheave

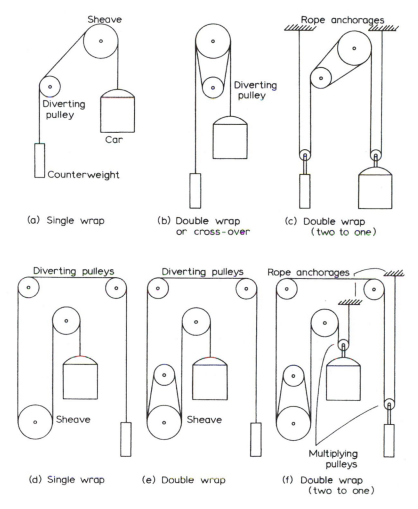

(a) Single wrap

(b) Double wrap or cross-over

(c) Double wrap (two to one)

(d) Single wrap

(e) Double wrap

(f) Double wrap (two to one)

Figure 16.3 Roping systems

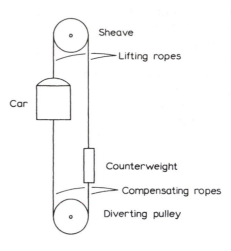

Figure 16.4 Compensating ropes

twice. The increased length of contact between rope and sheave increases the
maximum available lifting force, or alternatively permits a lower coefficient
of friction for the same lifting force. Figure 16.3c shows a double wrap two-
to-one system in which the speed of the car is half the peripheral speed of the
sheave. Figures 16.3d, e and f correspond to Figures 16.3a, b and c but with
the winding machine at the bottom of the well.

Compensating ropes are sometimes fitted on long travel lifts in order to
make the load on the motor constant by eliminating the effect of the weight
of the ropes. A simple method of doing this is shown in Figure 16.4.

Motors

A lift motor should have a starting torque equal to at least twice the full load
torque; it should be quiet and it should have a low kinetic energy. The last
requirement is necessary for rapid acceleration and deceleration and also for
low wear in the brakes. The theoretical power needed can be calculated from
the lifting speed and the greatest difference between the weights of car plus
load and counterweight. The actual power will depend on the mechanical
efficiency of the drive which can be anything from 30 per cent to 60 per cent.
Suitable motor sizes for various lifts are given in Table 16.3. The acceleration
is settled by the torque-speed characteristic of the motor and the ratio of
motor speed to lift speed.

Types of motor

In most cases, in the UK at least, a three phase a.c. supply is available in a
building which is to have a lift installation. For lift speeds up to about $0.5\,\text{ms}^{-1}$
a single-speed squirrel cage motor is suitable, although it has a high starting

Table 16.3 Approximate lift motor ratings (motor ratings in kW)

Low efficiency geared lifts

Car speed (ms⁻¹)	Contract load (kg)					
	250	500	750	1000	1500	2000
0.25	2	3.5	5	5	8	10
0.50	3	5.0	8	10	15	20
0.75	4	8.0	10	15	20	25
1.00	5	10	12	18	25	35
1.25	6	12	15	20	30	45
1.50	7	15	20	25	40	50

High efficiency geared goods lifts

Car speed (ms⁻¹)	Contract load (kg)						
	250	500	750	1000	1500	2000	3000
0.25	1	2.0	3	4.0	6.0	8	10
0.50	3	4.0	6	7.5	10.0	14	20
0.75		5.0	8	10.0	12.5	20	30
1.00		7.5	10	14.0	20.0	25	

High efficiency geared passenger lifts

Car speed (ms⁻¹)	No. of passengers					
	4	6	8	10	15	20
0.50	3	3	4.0	5.0		
0.75		5	7.5	7.5	12	15
1.0			10	10	15	18
1.5				12	17.5	22

current and tends to overheat on duties requiring more than 100 starts an hour.

For speeds between about 0.5 ms⁻¹ and 1.25 ms⁻¹, it becomes necessary to use a two-speed motor in order to have a low landing speed. The squirrel cage motor can be wound to give two combinations of poles, thus giving two speeds. A two-speed system is not a variable-speed drive; it is variable in the sense that it has two speeds. These systems were used widely in the 1970s and 1980s. They effectively employed direct on-line starting and thus needed flywheels attached to the motor to smooth the movement and reduce jerk. The use of a flywheel makes it inefficient

DC silicon-controlled rectifier (SCR)

Using power electronics, a DC motor can be used to vary the speed of the lift by varying the armature voltage. This method is the most widely used in DC drives, in the form of a controlled three-phase rectifier. This can be implemented in two forms. One form is a fully controlled bridge rectifier, which allows two-quadrant operation.

The other form uses two bridges in parallel, each connected to drive the motor in the opposite direction of the other. By using both bridges, the motor can be operated in both driving and braking modes, in forward and reverse directions (i.e. four-quadrant operation).

AC variable voltage (ACVV)

These systems were widely used in the mid-1980s and early 1990s. They are very simple in the method of operation. They rely on three pairs of back-to-back thyristors for varying the stator AC voltage on a double-cage squirrel cage motor. By varying the firing angle, the stator voltage is varied and a new speed torque curve results.

Variable voltage variable frequency (VVVF)

The most widely used system today is the VVVF system, usually referred to as an inverter drive. The principle of operation relies on a rectifier to produce DC into the so-called DC link and an inverter, which produces sinusoidal current into the windings. By changing the frequency of the inverted signal, the synchronous frequency and hence the speed torque curve is moved to the desired profile. The supply is fed to a servo motor.

Servo motors can be programmed to give the required S curve profile for travel between floors.

For speeds above $1.5\,\mathrm{ms^{-1}}$ the same types of motor could be used as for the lower speeds, but in fact they very rarely are. At the higher speeds, it is possible to design a d.c. motor to run at a speed which makes reduction gearing to the drive unnecessary. The a.c. supply is therefore used to drive a variable voltage motor generator set which supplies the d.c. to the lift driving motor.

If only a single phase supply is available, a repulsion-induction motor can be used for speeds up to $0.5\,\mathrm{ms^{-1}}$. For higher speeds it is better to use the a.c. to drive a motor generator and have a d.c. lift machine.

When d.c. is used for speeds less than $0.5\,\mathrm{ms^{-1}}$, a single speed shunt or compound wound motor is employed. When the lift is decelerating the machine runs as a generator, and in the case of a compound wound motor this makes special arrangements necessary. For speeds between $0.5\,\mathrm{ms^{-1}}$ and $1.25\,\mathrm{ms^{-1}}$ two-speed shunt motors are used, so that a lower speed is available

Figure 16.5 Gearless drive unit
(Courtesy of Schindler Lifts Ltd)

for good levelling at the landings. The increase from low to high speed is obtained by the insertion of resistance in the shunt field. For speeds of 1.5 ms⁻¹ and above, a d.c. shunt wound motor running at between 50 and 120 rpm is employed. At these speeds the motor can be coupled directly to the driving sheave without any gearing. Because of the size of the motor it is not possible to vary the speed by more than 1.5 to 1 by field control, and speed was usually controlled by the Ward Leonard method. The absence of gearing increases the overall efficiency, improves acceleration and results in smoother travelling. A picture of a gearless machine is shown in Figure 16.5.

External set value systems

The more modern approach has been to integrate a logic controller and the drive system. This has the advantage that the precise speed can be selected at any point in the journey, levelling speed can be eliminated, and different speeds can be selected depending on the expected length of journey.

This integration has taken the form of feeding the required speed value directly into the variable speed drive from the logic controller. Thus, the logic controller, which is monitoring the position of the lift car and its destination and its exact position with respect to the floor and landings, generates the required speed profile and sends it either as an analogue signal or a digital signal to the drive. The analogue signal is usually sent to the drive via an isolation amplifier, in order to eliminate any interference or faults in one system affecting the other. If sent in a digital format, an opto-coupler is usually used to isolate the two systems.

The set value generator in this case will reside inside the lift logic controller, which is invariably implemented using a microprocessor-based system. The logic controller would receive pulses from the shaft encoder or the motor indicating the exact position of the lift car in the shaft. Based on this information, a value in a table is provided, giving the required value of speed at that point. This value is sent to the variable-speed drive, which then controls the speed accordingly. These systems are always position-dependent systems, as the speed always follows the position, regardless of time

Brakes

Lift brakes are usually electromagnetic. In the majority of cases, they are placed between the motor and the gearbox; in a gearless machine the brake is keyed to the sheave. The shoes are cperated by springs and released by an electromagnet the armature of which acts either directly or through a system of links. A typical brake is shown in Figure 16.6. The brake is used only when the car is parked. To slow the car down, several methods are employed. Plugging is reversing the phase sequence as the motor is running; the synchronous magnetic field reverses direction, causing the motor to slow

Figure 16.6 Lift brake

down rapidly. Eddy current braking uses an aluminium disc on the end of the drive motor shaft. A magnetic field is applied to the disc and currents are induced in the disc which act to slow the shaft down. The braking effect is proportional to the speed of rotation of the shaft. Another method is to inject a DC current into the motor winding. Injecting DC in a motor winding will tend to try to stall the rotor. This is because the magnetic field set up inside the motor is a stationary constant field always pointing in one direction.

Lift cars

Passenger cars should be at least 2.00 m high, and preferably 2.15 m or more. They can be made to almost any specification, but most manufacturers have certain standard finishes from which the client should choose.

Lift cars consist of two separate units, namely the sling and the car proper. The sling is constructed of steel angles or channels and the car is held within the sling. The sling also carries the guide shoes and the safety gear. The car is sometimes insulated from the sling frame by anti-vibration mountings. Goods cars are of rougher construction than passenger cars but otherwise follow the same principles.

Except for very small installations it is now almost universal practice to have an emergency telephone in the car. It can be connected either as a direct line to the public telephone network or as an extension of the private branch exchange in the building. It is generally fitted in a recess in the wall of the car with a hinged door over it.

All electrical connections to a car are made through a multi-core hanging flexible cable. One end of this is connected to a terminal box under the car, and the other end to a terminal box on the wall of the well approximately half-way down. A separate hanging cable may be needed for the telephone.

Counterweights

A counterweight is provided to balance the load being carried. As the load carried varies, the counterweight cannot always balance it exactly; it is usual for the counterweight to balance the weight of the car plus 50 per cent of the maximum load to be taken in the car. A typical counterweight frame is shown in Figure 16.7. It contains cast-iron sections held in the steel framework and rigidly bolted together by tie rods. The lifting ropes are attached to eye bolts which pass through the top piece of the frame.

Guides

Both the car and the counterweight must be guided in the well so that they do not swing about as they travel up and down. Continuous vertical guides are provided for this purpose. They are most commonly made of steel tees,

Figure 16.7 Counterweight frame

and there are standard tees made especially for use as lift guides. The guides are fastened to steel plates by iron clamps at intervals of about 2 m and these plates are secured to the sides of the well. They may be secured by bolts passing through the wall of the well and held by back plates on the other side or by being attached to angle irons or channels which are in turn built into the wall. The latter is the usual practice with concrete building construction.

Guide shoes are fitted on the car and on the counterweight and run smoothly on the guides. Figure 16.8 shows a shoe on a guide. For smooth

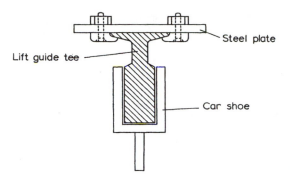

Figure 16.8 Shoe of lift guide

running, the guides must be lubricated and various types of automatic lubricators have been designed for lift guides. The commonest kind makes use of travelling lubricators mounted on the car and counterweight. More recently unlubricated guides have been used with shoes lined with carbon or PTFE.

Doors

Solid doors have now entirely superseded collapsible mesh gates. They are quieter, stronger and safer. It is usual now for the car and landing doors to be operated together. If the entrance to the car is not to be much narrower than the car itself then in the open position the door must overlap the car. To accommodate this, the well must be wider than the car. This will be clear from the plan of a typical lift installation shown in Figure 16.9.

Doors can be opened and closed manually, but it is more usual to have them power operated. In order not to injure passengers caught by closing doors, the drive has to be arranged to slip or reverse if the doors meet an obstruction. Every lift car door must have an interlock which cuts off the supply to the lift controller when the door is open. This can be a contactor which is pushed closed by the door and falls open by gravity or spring action when the door opens.

The landing door must be locked so that it cannot be opened unless the car is in line with the landing. The most usual way of doing this is by means of a lock which combines a mechanical lock and an electrical interlock. The electrical interlock ensures that there is no supply to the controller unless the gate is locked. The mechanical part can be unlocked only when a cam on the car presses a roller arm on the lock; thus the landing door can only be opened when the car is at the landing. The controls withdraw the cam when the car is in motion and return it only as the car approaches a floor at which it is to stop. This makes it impossible for anyone to open a landing door as the car passes the landing if the car is not stopping there.

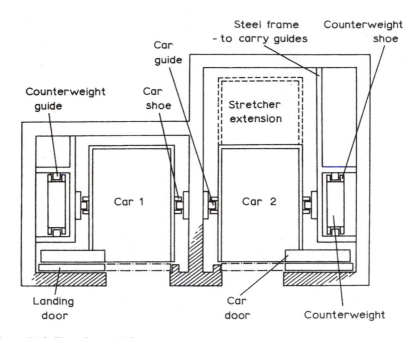

Figure 16.9 Plan of typical lift arrangement

Indicators

Indicators are available for showing when the car is in motion, the direction of travel and the position of the car in the well. A position indicator may be installed in the car, and in many cases also at each landing. Direction indicators are provided at the landings, and a common arrangement is to have a position an direction indicator in the car and at the ground floor with direction indicators at the other landings.

The car positional controllers previously described may be interfaced with an electronic system which then sends the car positional information to LCD displays at each floor level and in the car itself. It would be beyond the scope of this book to describe the circuitry required to do this.

Safety devices

Every lift car must have a safety gear which will stop it if its speed increases above a safe level. The motor and brake circuits should be opened at the same time as the safety gear operates. If the lift travel is more than about 9 m the safety gear should be operated by an overspeed governor in the machine room.

For speeds up to $0.8\,\mathrm{ms^{-1}}$ instantaneous gear is generally used. This consists of a pair of cams just clear of each guide, one on each side of the guide. The cams have serrated edges and are held away from the guide by springs. A safety flyrope passes from the safety gear over a top idler wheel to the counterweight. Tension on the safety rope causes the cams to come into instantaneous contact with the guides and they then clamp the car to the guides. The safety rope comes into tension if the lifting ropes break. Alternatively, it can be connected to an overspeed governor. One type of governor is shown in Figure 16.10. It has a pulley driven from the car by a steel rope. Flyweights are mounted on the pulley and linked together to ensure that they move simultaneously and equally. The flyweights move against a spring which can be adjusted to give the required tripping speed. As the speed increases, the weights move out against the spring force and at the tripping speed they cause a jaw to grip the rope, which produces the tension necessary to operate the cams.

For lifts at higher speeds, gradual wedge clamp safety gear is used. This also works by clamping the car to the guides, but the clamps are forced against the guides gradually and so bring the car to rest more smoothly. The clamps can be brought into play by screw motion or by a spring.

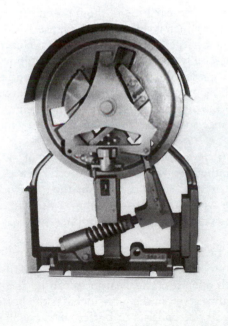

Figure 16.10 Lift governor

Figure 16.11 Flexible guide clamp

Another type of safety gear used on high speed lifts is the flexible guide clamp, an example of which is illustrated in Figure 16.11. It consists of two jaw assemblies, one for each guide, mounted on a common channel under the car. The jaw assembly has a pair of jaws with a gib in each jaw. Tension on the governor rope resulting from operation of the governor pulls the operating lever and causes the gibs to move up the jaws. The consequent wedging action of the gibs between the jaws and the guides compresses the jaw spring to produce a gripping force on the guides which gives a constant retardation.

A lift must also have upper and lower terminal switches to stop the car if it overruns either the top or bottom floor. These can take the form of a switch on the car worked by a ramp in the well, or they may consist of a switch in the well worked by a ramp on the car. There should be a normal stopping switch and a fixed stopping switch at each end of the travel.

Clearance must be allowed for the car at the top and bottom of the well to give it room to stop if the normal terminal switch fails and is passed and the terminal switch operates. The clearances can be as given in Table 16.5. The bottom clearance given in the table includes the buffer compression.

The final safety device consists of buffers in the well under the car and under the counterweight. For low speed lifts they can be made as volute or helical springs, but for high speed lifts oil buffers are used.

Table 16.4 Lift clearances

Lift speed (ms−1)	Bottom clearance (m)	Top clearance (m)
0–0.5	0.330	0.455
0.5–1.0	0.410	0.610
1.0–1.5	0.510	0.760

Landing

As it stops, the car must be brought to the exact level of the landing. With an automatic lift, this depends on the accuracy with which the slowing and stopping devices cut off the motor current and apply the brake. Levelling is affected by the load being carried; a full load travels further than a light load when coming to rest from a given speed on the downward trip and less far on the upward trip. To overcome this, it is desirable that the car should travel faster when carrying a full load up than when travelling up empty. A motor with a rising characteristic would be unstable, but the desired effect can be easily achieved with variable voltage control. The rising characteristic is needed only at the levelling speed, which is from about 1/6 to 1/20 of the maximum speed.

Type of control

An automatic control system has a single call button at each landing and a button for each floor in the car. A passenger presses the car button for the desired floor and the lift automatically travels there. Calls made from landings while the car is in motion are stored in the controller memory. With Automatic Collective Control, each landing has both an UP and a DOWN button, and there is a set of floor buttons in the car. Every button pressed registers a call, and up and down calls are answered during up and down journeys respectively, in the order in which the floors are reached. The order in which the buttons are pressed does not affect the sequence in which the car stops at the various floors, and all calls made are stored in the system until they have been answered. Down calls made while the lift is travelling up are kept until after the up journey is finished, and up calls made while the lift is moving down are similarly kept until that trip is finished.

The system can be modified to work as a collective system in the down direction and as a simple automatic system in the up direction. It is then known as Down Collective. This version is sometimes used in blocks of flats and is based on the assumption that occupants and their visitors travelling up like to go straight to their own floors, but that everyone going down wants to get off at the ground floor. Thus upward travellers should be able to go straight to their own floor without interference, while downward travellers are less likely to be irritated by intermediate stops to pick up other passengers going to the same destination. This reasoning ignores milkmen, postmen and other delivery workers, and the author of this book finds it unconvincing. Nevertheless, it appears to be popular with many authorities.

Duplex control is used when two lifts are installed in adjacent wells. The landing buttons serve both lifts. Landing calls are stored and allotted to the cars one at a time as the cars finish journeys already in progress. For three lifts working together Triplex Control is used.

It is also possible to arrange lifts with dual control so that they can be used either with or without an attendant.

Electronic systems have made more sophisticated forms of control possible and these have proved particularly valuable in tall office buildings with a group of three or more lifts in each service core. The term 'home floor' is used to designate the floor to which a car returns when it is not in use. It is not necessary for all the cars in a group to have the same home floor. Programmed control of groups of high speed lifts is a system in which cars are despatched from their home floor in a predetermined sequence so that even if they are not in use they are already moving through the building when the first call is made. Providing the programme is suitable for the pattern of traffic, this will ensure that when a call is made there is a car nearer than the home floor to the floor at which the call was made.

In a 'Balanced' programme cars are dispatched at set intervals from both terminal floors and each car makes a complete round trip. An 'Up Peak' programme dispatches cars from the lower terminal only and reverses each car when it is empty. A 'Down Peak' programme despatches them from the upper terminal at set intervals and returns each car from the lower terminal as soon as it is empty. In an 'Intermittent' programme cars can be taken out of service in a pre-arranged sequence.

When there is traffic in both directions but more going up than down a 'Heavier Up' programme will dispatch cars from both terminals at intervals which are automatically adjusted so that the cars are equally spaced. In the reverse situation cars stop more frequently when going down and a 'Heavier Down' programme adjusts the dispatch times accordingly.

A traffic analyser measures the rate at which calls are made and answered and in doing so distinguishes between up and down calls. It can be used to change operation from one control scheme to another. This is valuable in office blocks where the pattern of traffic changes throughout the day. 'Up Peak' and 'Down Peak' programmes are useful at the beginning and end of the working day with the 'Heavier Up' and 'Heavier Down' programmes making a contribution during the lunch period.

Weighing contacts under the car floor can detect the load and this can be used to make a car which is already fully loaded pass a landing without stopping even though there is a call waiting at that landing in the direction in which the car is travelling.

Every lift manufacturing company has its own particular system. This means that the specifier must discuss the scheme with manufacturers and if it is desired to put the lift installation out to competitive tender the description of the controls must be loose enough to allow some variation.

Controllers

The conventional lift motors are started, stopped and reversed by contactors. The operating coils of the contactors are energized at the appropriate times by relays which are connected in a circuit to give the required scheme of operation. The assembly of contactors, relays and associated wiring forms the controller, which is usually placed in the motor room, which may be the physical size of the panel shown in Figure 16.5. Sufficient space must be left round the controller for maintenance, and it must also be placed so that a maintenance technician working at it cannot accidentally touch a moving part of the lift machine.

A controller circuit is necessarily complex because it contains many interconnected relays; but each relay performs only one function and they are arranged to energize each other in a logical sequence to achieve the operation required, an also interlocked to prevent up and down functions to be selected at the same time. The resulting wiring diagram may perhaps be described as involved but not complicated. In a book which deals with electrical services as a whole and devotes only one chapter to lifts, it is not practicable to give a full description of circuits for all the possible modes of control, and we shall do no more than explain the working of a simple automatic system. It will have to serve as a model illustrating principles which can be extended and adapted for other systems.

Servo motors are controlled by electronic servo drives, and do not require relay. The motor commands are supplied to the motor from the servo drive. The motor position thus the car position can be controlled to a fraction of a degree of rotation, by utilising the digital encoder fitted to the motor shaft.

Escalators

An electrical services engineer should also know something about escalators. These are moving staircases. They consist essentially of pivoted steps linked to each other and pulled along by an endless chain. The steps have guide pins which move in tracks on either side of the tread arranged so that the steps come out of the concealed section horizontally, are then pulled or pivoted into the shape of a staircase and finally return to the horizontal before returning back into the concealed section. The steps complete their circuit within the concealed section, and on this part of their travel they are flat. This is illustrated in Figure 16.12.

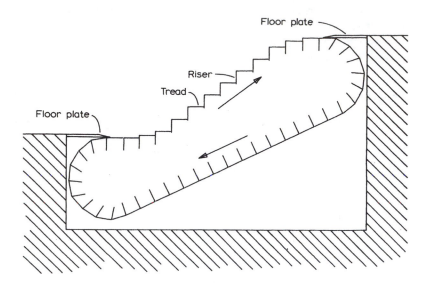

Figure 16.12 Escalator

The surface of each tread has grooves parallel to the direction of motion. The stationary platforms at the top and bottom of the escalator have fixed combs which mesh with the grooves in the treads in order to ensure a smooth run in and out of the treads under the fixed floor. The stationary platform is actually a floor plate over the recess under the moving staircase and covers the working mechanism at the top and bottom landings. It has an extension known as a combplate and the combplate carries the projecting comb teeth.

An escalator also has a balustrade with a handrail, and the handrail moves on an endless chain in step with the stairs. There are separate chains for the handrail and the steps but they are both driven through a gearbox from the same motor. The usual speed of an escalator is $0.5\,\mathrm{ms^{-1}}$ and it ought never to exceed $0.75\,\mathrm{ms^{-1}}$. The inclination varies between 27° and 35° to the horizontal.

The drive and transmission have to carry the total load on the escalator. Since people do not stand at even and regular intervals on the whole staircase the load averaged over the whole length of the escalator is less than the maximum load on individual treads. The peak load on each tread is of concern to the structural designer but the electrical engineer concerned with the power requirements can use the average passenger load taken over the total area of exposed treads. This average can be taken as $290\,\mathrm{kgm^{-2}}$.

An escalator must have a brake which has to fail safe if there is an interruption to the electrical supply. The brake is therefore applied by a spring or a hydraulic force and is held off against the mechanical force by an electrically energized solenoid. As is the case with lifts, there is also provision for releasing the brake manually and handwinding the escalator.

Since an escalator is in continuous operation there are no passenger controls, but there must be an on/off switch which can be worked by a responsible person in charge of the premises. It would be dangerous for the escalator to be started or stopped by someone who could not see the people on it and the switch must be in a place from which the escalator can be seen. Such a place is almost inevitably in reach of the public using the escalator, who ought not to be able to work the switch, and so the switch must be a key operated one. The *British Standard on Escalators* (BS 2655) requires a key operated starting switch to be provided at both ends of the escalator.

Emergency stop switches are provided in the machinery spaces under the escalator and also in positions accessible to the public at the top and bottom of the escalator. The operation of any of these switches disconnects the electrical supply from both the driving machine and the brake. The removal of the supply from the brake allows the mechanical force to apply the brake and bring the escalator to a halt. Some escalators are fitted with a speed governor which similarly disconnects the electrical supply from the drive and brake. There are further safety devices to disconnect the supply if one of the driving chains breaks.

Most escalators are reversible. The driving motor is a squirrel cage induction motor and the drive is reversed by contactors which change the phase sequence of the supply to the motor.

A travellator differs from an escalator in being either horizontal or having a very small slope not exceeding 12°. This makes it unnecessary for it to form steps and passengers are conveyed on a continuous platform. The upper surface of the platform must have grooves parallel to the direction of motion which mesh with the combplates. In other respects a travellator or moving walkway is designed in exactly the same way as an escalator.

Paternosters

Whilst paternosters are a type of lift they also have similarities with escalators and it is more convenient to discuss them after the latter. A paternoster is a lift which has a series of. small cars running continuously in a closed loop. It is difficult to explain this clearly in words but it should be clear from Figure 16.13. The cars are open at the front and move slowly enough for people to step in and out of them whilst they are in motion, just as they step on and off an escalator. In fact a paternoster can perhaps be thought of as a vertical escalator. To make it safe for people to get on and off whilst the cars are in motion the speed must be less than $0.4\,\mathrm{ms}^{-1}$.

The cars are constructed in the same way as ordinary lift cars but do not have doors and are not large enough to take more than one person each. In practice this means that the cars are less than $1.0\,\mathrm{m} \times 1.0\,\mathrm{m}$ in plan. They

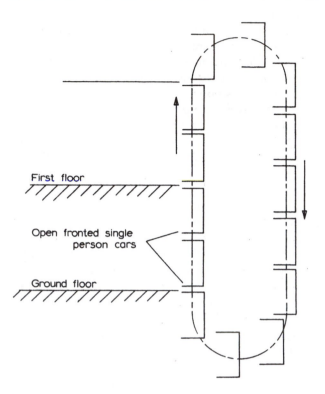

First floor

Open fronted single
person cars

Ground floor

Figure 16.13 Paternoster

must of course be of normal height. The front of the floor of each car is made as a hinged flap. This ensures that if a person has one foot in the car and one on the landing he will not be thrown off balance as the car moves up. Since the cars move in a continuous loop they provide their own counterweight and no additional counterweight is needed. Rigid guides are provided for the cars which have shoes similar to those of ordinary lift cars.

In the space between cars there is a protective screen level with the front of the cars. This prevents people stepping into the shaft in between cars. It is still necessary to make sure that the landings and entrances are well illuminated. The cars are carried on a continuous steel link chain. The driving machinery is similar to that of an escalator and is always placed above the well. It includes a brake which is applied mechanically and held off electrically, so that the paternoster is braked if the electrical supply fails. As in the case of both lifts and escalators there is provision for handwinding.

A paternoster is started by a key-operated switch, either at the ground floor or at the main floor if this is other than the ground floor. There are emergency stop buttons at each floor, in the pit and in the machinery space.

Although they have advantages, paternosters are not used very often. They take up rather less space than escalators but have a lower carrying capacity. We can show this by considering an escalator with a slope of 350 and a vertical rise between treads of 230 mm. The distance along the slope between succeeding steps is 230/sin 35° = 400 mm or 0.4 m. If the speed of the escalator is 0.5 ms^{-1}, the steps follow each other at intervals of 0.4/0.5 = 0.8 s. As each step can take one passenger, the carrying capacity is one person in every 0.8 s, or 75 persons per minute.

The vertical speed of a paternoster is at most 0.4 s^{-1}' and the car height cannot be less than 2.2 m. Neglecting any gap between the cars we see that the cars follow each other at intervals of 2.2/0.4 = 5.5 s, and each car can take only one passenger. The carrying capacity is thus one person every 5.5 s, or 11 persons per minute.

However well constructed and carefully operated it is, a paternoster cannot help being more of a hazard than an escalator to the elderly, the infirm and above all to small children. This practically restricts its applications to industrial premises not needing a high carrying capacity.

Standards relevant to this chapter are:

BS 2655   Lifts, escalators and paternosters
BS 5655   Lifts and service lifts
BS 5656   Safety rules for escalators and passenger conveyors

Chapter 17

Regulations

In most countries the supply of electricity is governed by legislation and we ought not to conclude this book without an account of the rules which apply in the UK. We have to refer to both the Electricity Safety Quality, and Continuity Regulations 2002 and the Electricity at Work Regulations 1989.

The Electricity Safety Quality, and Continuity Regulations 2002 place an obligation on the Distribution Companys to provide a supply of electricity to everyone in their area who asks for it. They naturally charge for the electricity and may make a charge for making the connection to their distribution system. This will depend on how much they have to extend that distribution network in order to reach the new consumer's premises. The Acts also confer power on certain government departments to make further regulations to control the supply of electricity.

These deal chiefly with the standards of service and safety to be met by the distribution companies, and are not of direct concern to the designer of services in a building who is concerned with what happens on the consumer's side of the connection and not with what goes on in the road outside. The Regulations do, however, give the distribution company some powers of supervision over the consumer's installation. The chief of these is that the Company may not connect a consumer's installation to its supply if it is not satisfied that the insulation meets a prescribed value and that the installation has adequate protective devices. If a consumer does not comply with the regulations, the company may refuse to connect a supply, or if it has already been connected may disconnect it.

These Regulations are somewhat general and it is conceivable that there could be doubt about their precise interpretation. In practice, difficulties hardly ever arise, and there are probably two reasons for this. First, distribution companies do not in practice inspect installations and are content with the installer's certificate of completion showing the insulation resistance. Second, and more importantly, installations complying with the Institution of Electrical Engineers' Regulations for the Electrical Equipment of Buildings BS7671 are deemed to comply with the Electricity Safety Quality, and

Continuity Regulations 2002. This brings us to consideration of the IEE Regulations, and we can note a curious, and perhaps typically British, feature about them. They are the most important regulations which in practice have to be observed and yet they are published as a National Standard and have no legal standing of their own. They may however be used in a court of law to claim compliance with a legal requirement. This comes about in the following way.

There is no legal need for an installation to comply with the IEE Regulations. If an installation satisfies the Electricity Safety Quality, and Continuity Regulations 2002 the law does not care whether or not it also satisfies the IEE Regulations. But the law also says that if it happens to satisfy BS 7671 it will be deemed to satisfy the Electricity Safety Quality, and Continuity Regulations 2002, and in practice this is the easiest way of showing that the Electricity Safety Quality, and Continuity Regulations 2002 have been satisfied. As a result everyone in the industry is familiar with the IEE Regulations, but very few people are aware of the curiously roundabout legal sanction behind them.

The sixteenth edition of BS 7671 was issued in 1991 with subsequent amendments to BS7671:2004. References to the Regulations in this book are to this edition.

Part 1 of the Regulations sets out the scope, object, and fundamental principles; Part 2 contains definitions of terms; Part 3, assessment of general characteristics, lists the main features of an installation which have to be taken into account in applying the subsequent parts; Part 4 describes the measures to be taken for protection against the dangers that may arise from the use of electricity and Part 5 deals with the selection of equipment and accessories and with the details of construction and installation. Part 6 deals with special locations. Part 7 is concerned with inspection and testing and there are six appendices giving further need to know information.

Further information is given in a set of Guidance notes published by the IEE, Guidance Note 1 often being referred to in this book, which gives further information on means by which the regulations are complied with.

Chapter 13 of Part 1 of the IEE Regulations states Fundamental Principles. If this chapter is not complied with, it may be taken that the distribution company would be justified in disconnecting the supply. Parts 3 to 6 of the Regulations set out methods and practices which are considered to meet the requirements of Chapter 13. A departure from these parts of the Regulations does not necessarily involve a breach of Chapter 13 but should be given special consideration. In fact the Regulations make clear that they are not intended to discourage invention and that departure from them may be made if it is the subject of a written specification by a competent body or person and results in a degree of safety not less than that obtained by adherence to the Regulations.

If a manufacturer wishes to introduce a new technique which is not envisaged in the current edition of the Regulations, application can be made for a certificate from a qualifying body.

Much of what has been said in previous chapters is based on the methods and practices described in BS 7671 and there seems little point in attempting either an abridgement or a gloss on the Regulations here. The Regulations do not contain instruction in the basic engineering principles on which they are based; they are regulations and not a textbook. Engineers who have followed a suitable course and understood the principles of electrical services should be able to read and understand the regulations without the interposition of a detailed commentary. Designers who follow the principles we have tried to explain in this book ought to find that their schemes almost inevitably comply with the regulations.

The other main source of legislation we have to refer to are the Electricity at Work Regulations 1989. These are concerned with safety in all places of work, but do not themselves contain detailed rules for the use of electricity. Compliance with BS 7671 will almost inevitably satisfy all the requirements of the Electricity at Work Regulations 1989, and the design principles explained in this book take into account the requirements of the Regulations.

Chapter 18

Design example

In order to illustrate the practical application of the principles discussed in previous chapters we shall, in this chapter, describe a typical industrial design. The example chosen is taken from a scheme handled in the previous author's office some years ago. It does embody the criteria in use today, although the design package would yield closer limits. It is appreciated that a building services engineer will now use software design packages. It is useful to see how the design values were arrived at. The buildings of a disused factory were taken over by a chemical manufacturing company which proposed to adapt them as a new works. Electric services were needed for lighting and power to machinery.

The general plan of the buildings is shown in Figures 18.1–18.3, which also show the main part of the lighting layout. As the design of lighting has been excluded from the subject matter of this book it is not proposed to reproduce the lighting calculations here, but it should be noted that after the number of lights needed in each area had been calculated they were positioned with regard to the layout of the machinery as well as to the need to maintain reasonable uniform levels of illumination.

The factory consists of an east building of two storeys with a basement and a three-storey west building with a covered yard between them extending the full height of the east building. There is a walled car park adjacent to the buildings and a new boiler-house was to be built in this area. Since the existing buildings provided more space than was needed for the new works, part of the west building was to left unoccupied: no services were to be installed in this part but the installation as a whole was to be capable of extension into this area.

The bulk of the lighting consisted of twin-tube 1500 mm fluorescent luminaires with some single-tube luminaires in passages and areas requiring lower illumination. A few incandescent luminaires were provided in toilets and on stairs (not all of which are shown in Figures 18.1–18.2). The covered way between the occupied and unoccupied sections of the west building in which materials would be hoisted to the upper levels was lit by three wall-mounted mercury lamps at ground-floor level and three at second-floor level.

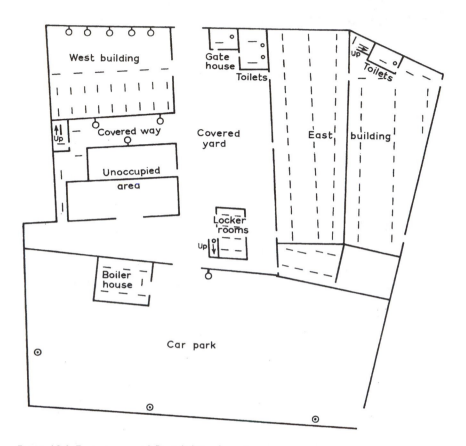

Figure 18.1 Factory ground-floor lighting layout

One end of the west building contained tall machinery on the ground floor and the first-floor slab was not carried across this. An area of double the normal height was thus left and this was lit by wall-mounted mercury lamps at the lower level and high-bay industrial mercury luminaires under the first-floor ceiling. The covered yard was lit by wall-mounted high-pressure sodium floodlights at the level of the first-floor ceilings. Four street-lighting lanterns were provided for the car park, three of them being mounted on columns on the roadway from the building and one on a bracket on the wall of the building.

The first stage in the design was to arrange the lights in circuits and to arrange the circuits in convenient groups to be served from several distribution boards. The lighting would have to be divided in a suitable manner between the three phases to give as nearly as possible the same loading on all three phases and this had to be borne in mind when the lights were

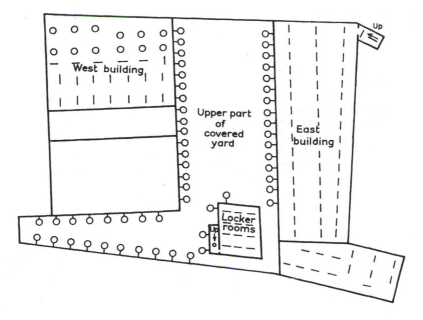

Figure 18.2 Factory first-floor lighting layout

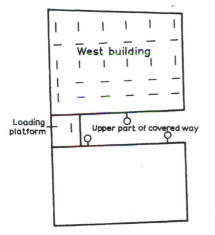

Figure 18.3 Factory second-floor lighting layout

Table 18.1 Types of lighting

Ref.	Type	Current (amps)
A	1500 mm twin fluorescent	0.92
B	1500 mm single fluorescent	0.46
C	Wall-mounted 125 W MBF	1.15
D	Tungsten bulkhead	0.42
E	High-bay industrial mercury with 250 W MBF lamp	2.15
F	Wall-mounted area floodlight with 250 W SON lamp	3.0
G	Bulkhead luminaire with 50 W MBF/U lamp	0.6
H	Side-entry street-lighting lantern with 35 W SOX lamp	0.6

arranged into circuits. For convenience, the different types of luminaire used were listed, as shown in Table 18.1.

It was decided that in this type of factory the lighting could be run in 2.5 mm² cable fused at 15 A. To allow a margin for safety and small alterations the circuits would be designed to carry not more than 12 A each. Although it was intended to use three different sizes of mercury lamp it was felt that there was a possibility that at some time in the future a works manager might change the luminaires without checking the capacity of the wiring and it was therefore decided to design all the circuits serving luminaires with mercury lamps to be capable of taking 250 W lamps. Similarly, circuits serving single-tube fluorescent luminaires would, where appropriate, be designed to take twin-tube luminaires so that the luminaires could at any time be replaced without alterations to the wiring. Hence, a maximum number of luminaires on a circuit would be:

$$\frac{12}{0.92} = 13, \text{ but say 12 fluorescent luminaires or}$$

$$\frac{12}{3.0} = 4 \text{ sodium luminaires or}$$

$$\frac{12}{2.15} = 5.6, \text{ but say 4 mercury luminaires}$$

It was clearly going to be desirable to control more than this number of lights from one switch and it was decided to do so by switching the lights through contactors. One switch would operate a multi-pole contactor controlling several lighting circuits.

At this stage a check was made on the voltage drop in the lighting circuits. Probable positions of distribution boards were guessed and from the drawings the average length of a lighting circuit was estimated as 35 m. At the time when this design was produced, the maximum volt drop allowed on

230 V was 9 V, it was decided to build in a factor of safety and allow a maximum of 6 V, and it seemed reasonable to allow half of this in the sub-mains and half in the final circuits, that is to say 3 V. The single phase volt drop of 2.5 mm² cable is 18 mV per ampere per metre.

$$3000\,(\mathrm{mV}) = 18 \times I \times 35 \left(\frac{\mathrm{mV}}{\mathrm{A/m}} \times \mathrm{A} \times \mathrm{m} \right)$$

$$\therefore I = 4.76\,\mathrm{A}$$

This is a pessimistic value since the current in the circuit will reduce as current is 'dropped off' at each luminaire, and the design current Ib will not flow in the whole length of the circuit. The designer may decide to average. However we took this value as true.

Clearly the need to reduce voltage drop was more critical than the current rating of the cable and the number of luminaires per circuit would have to be reduced. Acceptable figures would be six fluorescent luminaires or two sodium (slightly over the design value) or two mercury luminaires per circuit.

The loadings were now estimated for each area in a convenient tabulated form as shown in Table 18.2.

This formed a preliminary guide. The number of circuits in each area was decided by referring to the maximum number of luminaires per circuit as determined above and also with an eye to convenient switching arrangements. At the same time, some margins were allowed to make it possible to adjust the circuit arrangements later without major modifications to the distribution scheme. It will be noted for example that the car-park lights are not included in the table. This was because the design had to proceed before the client had taken final decisions on all his requirements. The fact that last-minute alterations would certainly be made had therefore to be kept constantly in mind.

The total load from Table 18.2 was 460.94 A. It should therefore be distributed to give about 150 A per phase. An ideally equal distribution could not be hoped for but each phase should carry between 140 and 160 A and at the same time each phase should be contained within a reasonably clear zone of the building. As a first step towards achieving this the loads for each area were summarized from Table 18.2, as shown in Table 18.3. They were then arranged in three groups for the three phases. After two attempts the results shown in Table 18.4 were obtained.

This was not as good as had been hoped for. However, the process of manipulating the figures had given the designer a feel for them and he realized that he was not likely to achieve any further improvement at this stage. It would be possible to make some adjustment after the distribution boards were scheduled and this was done next.

Table 18.2 Loading estimates for each area

| Area | Luminaire | | | | |
	Ref.	No. off	Amps each	Amps total	No. of circuits needed
Gate-house	A	1	0.92	0.92	
	B	2	0.46	0.92	
	D	3	0.42	1.26	
				3.10	1
Pump house	A	8	0.92	7.36	2
Boiler house	A	7	0.92	6.44	2
Covered way	C	6	2.15	12.9	3 controlled by 1 contactor
W bldg Grd flr	A	24	0.92	21.00	3:1 switched directly, 2 controlled by 1 contactor
	G	5	2.15	4.30	2
E bldg Stores	A	48	0.92	44.2	8 controlled by 4 contactors
Ovens	A	33	0.92	30.36	6 controlled by 4 contactors
Toilet area	A	1	0.92	0.92	
	B	3	0.46	1.38	
	D	1	0.42	0.42	
				2.72	1
Maintenance	A	8	0.92	7.36	2
Lockers	A	8	0.92	7.36	2
Stairs	D	1	0.42	0.42	1
1st Floor Covered yard	F	34	3.0	102.0	16 controlled by 8 contactors
Side yard	F	20	3.0	60.0	10 controlled by 4 contactors
Lockers	B	12	0.46	5.52	1
W bldg 1st flr	A	20	0.92	22.08	6 controlled by 2 contactors
	E	12	2.15	25.80	6 controlled by 2 contactors
E bldg 1st flr	A	48	0.92	44.2	8 controlled by 4 contactors
1st flr Maintenance	A	7	0.92	6.44	2
1st flr Pump house	A	7	0.92	6.44	2
E bldg Cellar	A	12	0.92	11.04	2
W bldg 2nd flr	A	30	0.92	27.6	6 controlled by 2 contactors
W bldg 3rd flr	B	5	0.46	2.30	1

Table 18.3 Load summaries

Area	Load in amps
W bldg grd flr	25.30
Pump house	7.36
Gate-house	3.10
Covered way	12.90
	48.66
Boiler house	6.44
W bldg 1st flr	47.88
Covered yard (main area)	102.00
Covered yard (side area)	60.00
W bldg 2nd flr	27.6
W bldg 3rd flr	2.3
E bldg grd flr	44.20
E bldg grd flr	30.36
E bldg Toilet area	2.72
Maintenance	7.36
Lockers	7.36
Stairs	0.42
	92.42
E bldg 1st flr	44.20
E bldg Maintenance	6.44
E bldg Pump house	6.44
Lockers	5.52
	62.60
E bldg cellar	11.04

Table 18.4 Distribution of load across phases (provisional)

	Amps
Brown (Red) phase	
W bldg 2nd flr	27.6
W bldg 3rd flr	2.3
Covered yard main area	102.0
Boiler house	6.4
	138.3
Black (Yellow) phase	
W bldg grd flr	48.66
W bldg 1st flr	47.88
East cellar	11.04
Covered yard site area	60.00
	167.58
Grey (Blue) phase	
E bldg grd flr	92.42
E bldg 1st flr	62.60
	155.02

The lights and switching were shown on drawings. In each area, the luminaires were grouped into circuits in accordance with the maximum number of luminaires per circuit previously determined. Clearly the luminaires on any one circuit must be in a reasonably compact group. Also, although the luminaires on one circuit can be controlled by more than one switch, the converse is not true: one switch cannot control luminaires on several circuits unless a multi-pole contactor is used. The most practicable way of settling these matters is to mark the circuits and switching groups on drawings of an adequately large scale.

Standard distribution boards are available with 12 and 16 ways. Suitable positions were chosen on the drawings for distribution boards to serve groups of 7 to 12 circuits to allow a reasonable number of spare ways on each board. The positions were chosen to keep the final circuits reasonably short and so that as far as possible each board would be in the 'load centre' of the area it was serving. It became evident in. this process that the second and third floors of the west building should be served from a single board, that the gate-house would need its own board, that three distribution boards would conveniently handle both parts of the covered yard, that the ground and first floors of the east building would each need two distribution boards and that the cellar of the east building would be most conveniently served from the gate-house. The information from the drawings was then summarized in distribution-board schedules which are reproduced in Table 18.5. A further table was then made in order to decide on which phase each of these boards should be and this is given in Table 18.6.

The figures in the three right-hand columns were entered in pencil, rubbed out and moved from column to column until by a process of trial and error quite a good balance over the phases was obtained. The first attempt

Table 18.5 Lighting distribution boards

Board no. 1   E bldg maintenance area 1st flr Phase Black (Yellow) sub-main 35 mm²

Circuit no.	No. and location of lights		Fuse (A)	Cable (mm²)
1	4	Pump house and changing rooms grd flr	15	2.5
2	4	Changing rooms grd flr	15	2.5
3	5	1st flr maintenance area	15	2.5
4	5	1st flr maintenance and sub-station	15	2.5
5	6	Pump house	15	2.5
6	6	Changing rooms 1st flr	15	2.5
7	5	Changing rooms 1st flr and stairs	15	2.5
8	4	Car park lights	15	2.5
9				
10				
11				
12				

Table 18.5 continued

Board no. 2	W bldg grd flr Phase Black (Yellow) sub-main 35 mm^2			
Circuit no.	No. and location of lights		Fuse (A)	Cable (mm^2)
1	5	Bulkheads on wall	15	2.5
2	3	Production area	15	2.5
3	3	Production area	15	2.5
4	4	Production area	15	2.5
5	3	Production area	15	2.5
6	4	Production area	15	2.5
7	4	Production area	15	2.5
8	3	Hoist yard, low level	15	2.5
9	3	Hoist yard, high level	15	2.5
10	5	Rear entrance	15	2.5
11	4	Stairs	15	2.5
12				
13				
14				
15				
16				

Board no. 3	W bldg 1st flr Phase Black (Yellow) sub-main 35 mm^2			
Circuit no.	No. and location of lights		Fuse (A)	Cable (mm^2)
1	2	Mercury over vats	15	2.5
2	2	Mercury over vats	15	2.5
3	2	Mercury over vats	15	2.5
4	2	Mercury over vats	15	2.5
5	2	Mercury over vats	15	2.5
6	2	Mercury over vats	15	2.5
7	3	Fluorescent production area	15	2.5
8	4	Fluorescent production area	15	2.5
9	4	Fluorescent production area	15	2.5
10	3	Fluorescent production area	15	2.5
11	4	Fluorescent production area	15	2.5
12	4	Fluorescent production area	15	2.5
13				
14				
15				
16				

Table 18.5 continued

Board no. 4   *Phase Brown (Red) sub-main 35 mm^2*

Circuit no.	No. and location of lights		Fuse (A)	Cable (mm^2)
1	4	Production area	15	2.5
2	5	Production area	15	2.5
3	5	Production area	15	2.5
4	4	Production area	15	2.5
5	5	Production area	15	2.5
6	5	Production area	15	2.5
7	3	Laboratory and landing	15	2.5
8	5	Third floor	15	2.5
9				
10				
11				
12				

Board no. 5   *E bldg grd flr stores Phase Grey (Blue) sub-main 35 mm^2*

Circuit no.	No. and location of lights		Fuse (A)	Cable (mm^2)
1	4	Stores	15	2.5
2	4	Stores	15	2.5
3	4	Stores	15	2.5
4	4	Stores	15	2.5
5	4	Stores	15	2.5
6	4	Stores	15	2.5
7	4	Stores	15	2.5
8	4	Stores	15	2.5
9	4	Stores	15	2.5
10	4	Stores	15	2.5
11	4	Stores	15	2.5
12	4	Stores	15	2.5
13				
14				
15				
16				

Table 18.5 continued

Board no. 6   *E bldg grd flr oven area Phase Grey (Blue) sub-main 35 mm²*

Circuit no.	No. and location of lights		Fuse (A)	Cable (mm²)
1	5	Circulation area	15	2.5
2	4	Ovens	15	2.5
3	4	Ovens	15	2.5
4	4	Ovens	15	2.5
5	4	Ovens	15	2.5
6	6	Ovens	15	2.5
7	6	Ovens	15	2.5
8	5	Maintenance area	15	2.5
9	4	Maintenance area	15	2.5
10	5	Toilets and stairs	15	2.5
11				
12				
13				
14				
15				
16				

Board no. 7   *E bldg 1st flr stores Phase Grey (Blue) sub-main 35 mm²*

Circuit no.	No. and location of lights		Fuse (A)	Cable (mm²)
1	4	Stores	15	2.5
2	4	Stores	15	2.5
3	4	Stores	15	2.5
4	4	Stores	15	2.5
5	4	Stores	15	2.5
6	4	Stores	15	2.5
7	4	Stores	15	2.5
8	4	Stores	15	2.5
9	4	Stores	15	2.5
10	4	Stores	15	2.5
11	4	Stores	15	2.5
12	4	Stores	15	2.5
13				
14				
15				
16				

Board no. 8   *Gate-house Phase Black (Yellow) sub-main 16 mm²*

Circuit no.	No. and location of lights		Fuse (A)	Cable (mm²)
1	6	Lodge and toilets	15	2.5
2	6	E bldg cellar	15	2.5
3	6	E bldg cellar	15	2.5
4				

Table 18.5 continued

Board no. 9   Covered yard Phase Brown (Red) sub-main 35 mm²

Circuit no.	No. and location of lights		Fuse (A)	Cable (mm²)
1	2	Covered yard	15	2.5
2	2	Covered yard	15	2.5
3	1	Covered yard	15	2.5
4	2	Covered yard	15	2.5
5	2	Covered yard	15	2.5
6	1	Covered yard	15	2.5
7	2	Covered yard	15	2.5
8	2	Covered yard	15	2.5
9	2	Covered yard	15	2.5
10				
11				
12				

Board no. 10   Covered yard Phase Brown (Red) sub-main 35 mm²

Circuit no.	No. and location of lights		Fuse (A)	Cable (mm²)
1	2	Covered yard	15	2.5
2	2	Covered yard	15	2.5
3	2	Covered yard	15	2.5
4	2	Covered yard	15	2.5
5	2	Covered yard	15	2.5
6	2	Covered yard	15	2.5
7	2	Covered yard	15	2.5
8	2	Covered yard	15	2.5
9	3	Covered yard	15	2.5
10	3	Covered yard	15	2.5
11				
12				

Board no. 11   Covered yard Phase Black (Yellow) sub-main 35 mm²

Circuit no.	No. and location of lights		Fuse (A)	Cable (mm²)
1	2	Covered yard	15	2.5
2	2	Covered yard	15	2.5
3	2	Covered yard	15	2.5
4	2	Covered yard	15	2.5
5	2	Covered yard	15	2.5
6	2	Covered yard	15	2.5
7	2	Covered yard	15	2.5
8	2	Covered yard	15	2.5
9				
10				
11				
12				

Table 18.6 Distribution of load across phases (final)

Board no.	Area	Amps	Brown (Red)	Black (Yellow)	Grey (Blue)
				Phase	
1	E and W bldgs grd flr	24		24	
2	W grd flr	32		32	
3	W lst flr	30		30	
4	W 2nd and 3rd flr	31	31		
5	E grd flr	48			48
6	E grd flr	45			45
7	E lst flr	48			45
8	Gate-house	15	15		
9	Covered yard	48	48		
10	Covered yard	66	66		
11	Covered yard	48		48	
	Total	145		149	138

was made on the basis of the provisional phasing decided on before the distribution boards had been scheduled.

The size of sub-main necessary to serve these boards was next calculated. The necessary current rating was evident from Table 18.6 but it was also necessary to calculate the size of cable needed to give an acceptable voltage drop. The distance from the intake to the furthest board was measured on the drawings and found to be 98 m. This was rounded off to 100 m for the purpose of calculation. The current taken by the most distant board was 31 A and for the calculation this was rounded off to 30 A. It had previously been assumed that 3 V would be lost in the final circuits and it was now decided to allow a 2 V drop in the sub-main. This would make the total well less than the permissible maximum but there is no restriction on how low the voltage drop is and it seemed prudent to allow a margin for future extensions and also for possible alterations in the final positions of distribution boards and routes of cables.

$$2\,V = 2000\,mV$$

Permissible drop is given by

$$2000 = \frac{mV}{A/m} \times 30 \times 100 = 3000 \times \frac{mV}{A/m}$$

$$\therefore \frac{mV}{A/m} = \frac{2000}{3000} = 0.67$$

35 mm^2 cable has a voltage drop of 1.25 mV/A/m and is rated at 145 A, when run singly. For a 30 A current we could suffer a correction factor of 30/145 = 0.2. We could run 12 or more multicore PVC steel wire armoured cable on cable tray single-layer clipped touching each other, and the correction factor would be 0.7. A larger sub-main would seem unreasonable for the loads involved. Although the volt drop of 35 mm^2 cable is higher than the calculated figure, the calculation was on the safe side and was carried out only for the longest sub-main. The next size of cable is 50 mm^2 which is considerably harder to handle and therefore more expensive to install. It would be rather unusual to use such large cable for lighting distribution and it was therefore decided that 35 mm^2 cable would be acceptable. Each of these cables would be served from a 60 A switch fuse. An exception was made for board no. 8 which would carry only 15 A. By inspection and without any calculation, it was decided that a 16 mm^2 cable rated at 85 A clipped direct or 94 A clipped to cable tray, run singly, with a volt drop of 2.8 mV/A/m would be adequate for this. It would be served from a 30 A switch fuse.

Attention was now turned to the design of the power distribution. A list of the machinery to be installed was obtained from the client and written out as shown in Table 18.7. The locations of the equipment were also obtained and are shown in Figures 18.4–18.5. It should be noted that all power equipment was to be three-phase except for FHP motors on rotary valves.

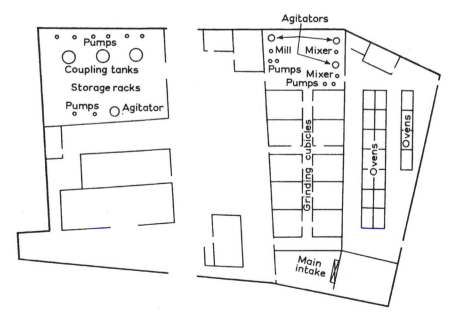

Figure 18.4 Factory ground-floor equipment layout

Table 18.7 Machinery, assumed current demand

			Running current (amps per phase)		
Item	No. of	kW each	Each	Total	Allow for diversity
'A' Agitator	4	3.73	8	32	16
Type 1 mill	1	37.3	70	70	35
Type 2 mill	1	18.65	36	36	–
'A' Mixers	2	3.73	8	16	8
Shakers	3	2.24	5	15	10
Extractor	13	3.73	8	104	52
'B' Mixers	2	11.19	22	44	22
'G' Mixers	10	14.92	30	300	200
'G' Mills	10	7.83	16	160	
Rotary valves	20	0.19	3	60	15
Single-phase motors					
'A' Pumps	1	5.60	11	11	–
'B' Pumps	1	3.73	8	8	8
'C' Pumps	3	2.98	6	18	9
'D' Pumps	1	3.73	8	8	8
'E' Pumps	3	5.60	11	33	11
'F' Pumps	3	5.60	11	33	11
Ovens	18	3.73	8	144	96
Hoist	1	3.73	8	8	–
'A' Fans	3	5.60	11	33	22
Conveyors	1	7.46	15	15	15
Dissolver	5	5.60	11	55	33
Coupling tanks	3	11.19	22	66	44
Lift	1	0.75	2	2	–
'B' Agitators	1	1.49	3	3	3
'G' Pump	1	2.24	5	5	–
'B' Fans	1	22.38	40	40	–
Boiler burner	1	7.46	15	15	15
'H' Pumps	1	11.19	22	22	22
'C' Fans	1	5.60	11	11	11
Burner auxiliary motor	1	2.24	5	5	5
'J' Pumps	1	3.73	5	5	5
		Total amps per phase		1369	676
		KvA over 3 phases		982	486

Most of it was accounted for by motors driving pumps, agitators and other mechanical equipment: the running currents per phase were taken from standard motor performance tables.

The allowance for diversity was based on the designer's previous industrial experience and his assessment of what equipment might normally be in use simultaneously. The lighting load on the most heavily loaded phase was 149 A and in view of the nature of the building it seemed reasonable to apply

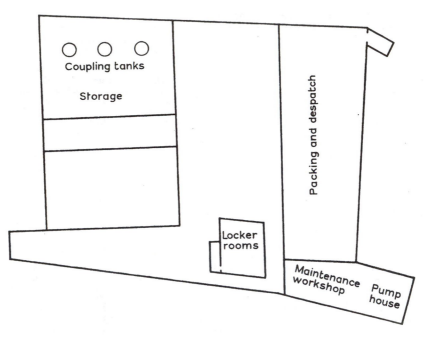

Figure 18.5 Factory first-floor equipment layout

a diversity factor of 0.6 to this, giving an after-diversity lighting load of 90 A. Addition of this to the power load gave a total after-diversity load of 766 A per phase which is 570 kVA over all three phases. This could conveniently be catered for by 800 A busbars at the main intake.

A difficulty arose over this figure. The supply to the existing board came from a 315 kVA transformer. If the electricity company were to be asked for a bigger supply they would make a substantial charge which the factory owner wished to avoid. The client also thought the calculated load was high but could not dispute the total installed load. He told the designer that at an older but similar works belonging to the same company measurements showed that the actual maximum demand was 27 per cent of the total installed load. If the same figure were applied to the new factory the maximum demand would be 0.27 × (982 kVA power load + 120 kVA lighting load) = 298 kVA which would be within the capacity of the existing supply. The client therefore wanted this figure to be used. Whilst unable to challenge the client's measurements the designer felt that a diversity factor of 27 per cent was surprisingly low. He pointed out that if the distribution was designed on this figure and it turned out to be low it would be very difficult and expensive subsequently to increase the capacity of the installation. He was reluctant to work on this basis. After discussion it was agreed that 800 A

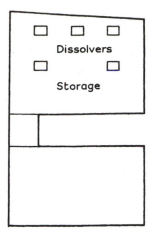

Figure 18.6 Factory second-floor equipment layout

busbars would be installed at the main intake but would be served through a 400 A switch fuse from the existing 315 kVA (equivalent to 440 A per phase) supply. This would make it possible to cater for a larger load if the need arose without expensive alterations but would not increase the initial cost very much. It therefore satisfied both points of view.

A description such as this inevitably makes the design process seem very precise whereas in practice at each stage there are many unknown facts for which the designer has to make a guessed allowance. In the present case the plant design was proceeding at the same time as the electrical design and neither the ratings nor the positions of all the equipment were finally settled. Table 18.7 is in fact based on the third attempt to draw up such a list; it would be an unnecessary waste of space to reproduce the earlier tables which differed only in detail. However, the element of uncertainty led to two important decisions about the general scheme.

First, it was decided to use busbars with separately mounted switch fuses rather than a cubicle-type switchboard. This would give excellent flexibility for future extensions and also for changes and additions which might become necessary before the installation was completed. It seemed quite likely that this would be necessary because of the uncertainty of the final plant layout.

Second, it was decided that the design of the power installation would go only as far as the final distribution boards. The final circuits from these to the various motors would be settled on site after the machines were installed. In areas where there was to be a lot of equipment horizontal busbars could be run along the building walls with tap-off boxes spaced as required.

With these considerations in mind the load was listed again but this time area by area. The load was summed for each area and a decision made on the size and rating of the distribution board to serve that area, This list is

Table 18.8 Distribution of load across phases

| Area | Item | No. of | Running current (amps per phase) | | |
			Each	Total	After diversity
1	'A' Agitators	2	8	16	
E bldg N end	Type 1 mills	1	70	70	
	'B' Pumps	1	8	8	
	'C' Pumps	1	6	6	
	Shaker	1	5	5	
		6		115	100
2	'A' Agitator	2	8	16	16
E bldg N end	'B' Mixer	2	22	44	44
	Type 2 mill	1	36	36	
	'A' mixer	2	2	16	
	'C' Pump	2	6	12	41
	Shaker	2	5	10	
	Extractor	1	8	8	
		12		142	101
3	Per cubicle				
E bldg Grinding	'C' Mixer	1	30		
cubicles	'C' Mill	1	16		
	Rotary valve	2	6		
	Extractor	1	8		
		5	60		
4	Ovens	18	8	144	
E bldg Ovens	Extractors	2	8	16	
				160	
5	Hoist	1	8	8	
W bldg 3rd flr	'A' Fans	3	11	33	
	Conveyors	1	15	15	
	'D' Pump	1	8	8	
		6		64	45
6	Dissolver	5	11	55	33
W bldg 2nd flr					
7	Coupling tanks	3	22	66	22
W bldg 1st flr					
8	'E' Pump	3	11	33	
W bldg Grd flr	'F' Pump	3	11	33	
	Lift	1	2	2	
	'B' Agitator	1	3	3	
	'A' Pump	1	11	11	
	'G' Pump	1	5	5	
		10		87	40
9	'B' Fan	1	40		
Boiler room	Burner	1	15		
	'M' Pump	1	22		
	'C' Fan	1	11		
	Auxiliary motor	1	5		
	Pump	1	5		
		6	98		

shown in Table 18.8, It will be noticed that some additional items not listed in the previous table were added at this stage.

The load in areas 1 and 2 could be catered for by a 24-way 300 A TPN distribution board served from a 200 A switch fuse.

A check with manufacturers' catalogues showed that it would not be possible to get a standard board with outgoing fuse-ways in the wide range of sizes needed, that is to say from 5 A to the 100 A needed for the mills. It would therefore be necessary to use two separate boards, one with fuse-ways from 2 to 30 A and one with fuse-ways from 20 to 100 A. The former would have fourteen items with an installed load of 97 A giving about 58 A after diversity and the latter would serve four items with an installed load of 150 A giving about 90 A after diversity. A 20-way 60 A TPN board and a 6-way 100 A TPN board would meet these requirements.

In area 3, the equipment in one cubicle only is listed. The mixer and the mill do not run at the same time. The rotary valves run intermittently, therefore the maximum simultaneous demand can be assessed as 30 + 3 + 8 = 41 A. There are ten such cubicles making the installed load 10 × 60 = 600 A. After diversity this will be say 400 A.

In this area there is a total of 10 × 5 = 50 pieces of equipment. To allow spare capacity 65 ways on a distribution board are needed.

Each bay is approximately six metres long. A busbar would have not more than six tap-off points along this length but each bay contains two cubicles with ten pieces of equipment. Therefore a busbar is not the most practicable method and distribution boards should be used.

The distribution boards will be mounted on a wall. As there is a central gang-way midway between the two facing walls the arrangement will have to be symmetrical so that either two or four distribution boards will have to be used. This gives the possibility of either 2 of 36-way 300 A TPN boards from 200 A switch fuses or 4 of 18-way 200 A TPN boards from 150 switch fuses.

At first sight the first alternative appeared cheaper but on checking with the manufacturers it was revealed that standard boards are not made as large as this so the second alternative had to be adopted.

Area 4 can be conveniently served by 200 A TPN busbars fed by a 200 A isolator at the busbars which can in turn be served from a 150 A switch fuse on the main panel.

At this stage it had been decided that the east building would require six distribution boards and one set of busbars. All this could conveniently come from a subsidiary distribution centre in the building. The sum of the after-diversity loads calculated for this was 741 A but allowing for diversity between the boards the maximum load on the busbars would be less. To allow for adequate short-circuit strength and also for future extensions it was decided to use 800 A busbars for the subsidiary centre. It had already been decided, as explained above, that the main intake would have 800 A busbars with a 400 A incoming switch fuse. To give discrimination, the outgoing switch fuse could not be larger than 300 A. The after-diversity load was probably still being over-estimated but whereas switch fuses and if necessary cables can be changed later it would be very expensive to replace the busbars. Therefore the local busbars can still be 800 A but should have an incoming isolator of a lower rating. There is a fuse at the outgoing end of the cable from the main intake and there is no need for another fuse at its other end. As the fuse is 300 A the isolator which is protected by the fuse should have a higher rating, say 400 A.

Reference was made in the last paragraph to short-circuit strength. In fact no separate calculation was made for this design but the results of calculations on other projects were made use of.

The busbars are rectangular copper bars supported at regular intervals. The dimensions of the bars and the spacing of supports are given in the manufacturer's catalogue. If the length between two successive supports is treated as a simply-supported beam the maximum permissible bending moment can be calculated from the bending stress formula:

$$\frac{M}{I} = \frac{p}{y}$$

where

M = bending moment (Nm)
I = second moment of area (m^4)
p = stress (Nm^{-2})
y = distance from neutral axis to outermost fibre (m).

I and y are easily calculated for a rectangular section, p is the maximum allowable working stress of pure copper, and M is the moment to be calculated.

The bending moment for a simply-supported beam with uniform loading is

$$M = \frac{wL^2}{8}$$

where

M = bending moment (Nm)
w = load per unit length (Nm^{-1})
L = distance between supports (m).

As M has been established and L is known, this enables w to be calculated to give the maximum permissible uniform load on each bar.

When a current flows in two parallel rectangular bars the resulting mechanical force between them is given by

$$w = \frac{(120\, i^2 \times 10^{-8})}{s}$$

where

w = force per unit length (Nm^{-1})
i = current (A)
s = spacing between bars (m).

If the force per unit length is taken as the maximum permissible uniform load which has just been calculated, and the spacing between the bars is known from the manufacturer's catalogue, this formula allows the maximum allowable value of the current to be calculated. This value is then the maximum current which the bars will be just strong enough to withstand and they should not be exposed to a possible short-circuit current higher than this.

Perhaps this seems a lengthy and somewhat circuitous piece of reasoning. It is, however, a typical example of the way in which the various requirements for a distribution system have to be fitted together. It has not been written as a description of the final scheme but rather to show the process by which the scheme was arrived at.

The subsequent distribution centre in the east building could also serve a distribution board in the maintenance area and the unit heaters for the space heating. No information was available at this stage of the equipment which would be installed in the maintenance workshop but a 12-way 60 A TPN board would certainly be adequate. The area would have ten heaters which could be served from a 12-way SPN board.

At this stage there was still some uncertainty about the exact positions of the equipment in the lower part of the west building and indeed about how much of the equipment planned would be installed initially and how much left for the future.

Partly for this reason and partly to give the greatest possible flexibility for the final connections, it was decided after discussion with the client to provide a busbar under the first floor ceiling of the west building to serve the first and ground floors. It will be remembered that part of the first-floor slab was omitted to give a two-storey height to part of the ground floor. This made it possible to serve the ground floor from a busbar at high level on the first floor. Indeed in view of the lack of information available to the electrical designer about the height of the motors on the machinery to be installed this seemed the only reasonable thing to do.

From Table 18.8 the total amps per phase on the ground and first floors were 153 installed and 62 after diversity. Some 200 A busbars served by a

Table 18.9 Summary for W building

| Floor | Running current (amps per phase) | |
	Total installed	After diversity
Grd	87	40
1st	66	22
2nd	55	33
3rd	64	45
	272	140

200 A switch fuse would be ample for this load (this is the lowest standard rating for busbars).

The second floor needed an 8-way 60 A TPN distribution board served from a 60 A switch fuse.

The third floor needed an 8-way 60 A TPN distribution board served from a 60 amp switch fuse.

The loading for the various areas of the west building was then summarized as shown in Table 18.9. It became evident that the whole of this could conveniently come from a subsidiary distribution centre within the west building. Adequate margins and provision for future additions suggested that a suitable size would be 400 A busbars served from a 200 A switch fuse.

The space heating of the west building was to be provided by four unit heaters on the second floor and four on the first floor which all required a supply for fans and thermostats. Much of this equipment could be conveniently served from a six-way SPN distribution board on its own floor and these two boards could also be served from the subsidiary distribution centre.

The only remaining area to be dealt with was the boiler room. This is Item 9 in Table 18.8. There would be little diversity here and it was therefore decided to provide a 150 A TPN distribution board served from a 150 A switch fuse.

To save a multiplicity of sub-mains cables, it was decided that in the west building the lighting distribution boards would be served from the subsidiary distribution centre. The east building was nearer the main intake so that it would not be so cumbersome and expensive to run several cables between them. Also the number of switch fuses required on the east building distribution centre for the power boards alone was already quite high. It was therefore decided that the east building lighting boards would be served directly from the main intake.

The distribution scheme was now sketched, as shown in Figure 18.7. This is the most convenient method of summarizing the decisions taken so far and checking for any inconsistencies or omissions. In its final form it is also the

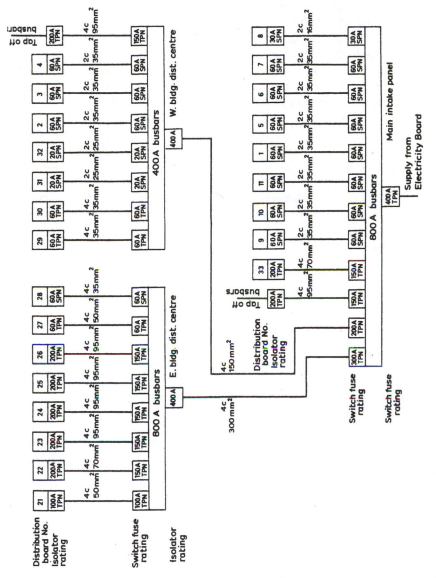

Figure 18.7 Factory distribution diagram

clearest way of explaining the scheme to be installed to contractors and suppliers.

It now remained to decide the sizes of the various sub-main distribution cables which, at this stage, had not been written into the scheme of Figure 18.7. The necessary current ratings were clear from the switch fuse ratings needed on the scheme but the cables also had to be calculated for voltage drop. It is only necessary to make sure that the voltage drop is not excessive and one of a limited number of standard-size cables must be chosen. The calculation was therefore simplified by taking 100 m as the longest run of a sub-main cable and using the same length in calculating all of them. It had earlier been assumed that, of the total permissible voltage drop, half would be in the final circuit and half in the sub-mains. To keep to this assumption the sub-mains had to be calculated for a drop of 4.6 V (4 per cent of the Nominal Voltage/2), to take into account future extensions the volts drop would be restricted to 3 V.

In view of the number of sub-mains involved the calculation was again set out in a tabular form as shown in Table 18.10. Column 2 gives the current rating for reference method 11 single layer clipped to cable tray. In column 3 the drop in millivolts per amp metre to give a drop of 1 V over the assumed total length of 100 m has been calculated. This figure was then multiplied by

Table 18.10 Sizing of sub-main distribution cables

1	2	3	4	5	6	7
		mV/A/m for 1 volt drop = (1000) / (amps × 100)	mV/A/m for 3 volt drop	Cable		
Board no.	Amps			mm²	Amps	mV/A/m
21	60	0.17	0.50	50	125	0.81
22	100	0.10	0.30	70	155	0.57
23	150	0.07	0.20	95	190	0.43
24	150	0.07	0.20	95	190	0.43
25	150	0.07	0.20	95	190	0.43
26	150	0.07	0.20	95	190	0.43
27	60	0.17	0.50	50	125	0.81
28	30	0.33	1.00	35	72	1.1
29	45	0.22	0.67	35	72	1.1
30	25	0.40	1.20	35	72	1.1
31	12	0.83	2.50	25	62	1.5
32	12	0.83	2.50	25	62	1.5
33	100	0.10	0.30	70	155	0.57
W. busbars	100	0.10	0.30	70	155	0.57
Oven busbars	150	0.07	0.20	95	190	0.43
E. sub-centre	300	0.03	0.10	300	390	0.185
W. sub-centre	120	0.08	0.25	150	250	0.35

three and rounded off in column 4 to give the millivolts per amp metre for a 3 V drop. Columns 2 and 4 thus showed the minimum requirements of the cable: the cable chosen to match this was then entered in columns 5, 6 and 7. The cable sizes were then entered on the scheme which is reproduced in Figure 18.7 and this completed the design.

In this example the designer's freedom was restricted by the limitations of an existing building. In principle, where a new building is being designed, the designer of the electrical services can be called in early enough to suggest arrangements which would result in a more economical services installation. The effect of voltage drop or cable sizes makes it desirable to have the spaces allocated for intake panels and distribution boards as near as possible to the centre of the area being served, load centres. The provision of false ceilings, and horizontal and vertical ducts influences the type of wiring system to be employed. The thickness of plaster may determine whether or not cables can be buried within it. If walls are built of a single thickness of brick it will not be practicable to chase them for cables or conduits, and the electrical installation may have to be run on the surface.

All these matters can be discussed by the electrical services designer and the architect at a very early stage and should in theory influence the building design. In practice it seems that since it is always possible to adapt the electrical installation to any building, purely architectural considerations always override the engineering ones. Many architects have no objection to conduit on the surface of walls even in a completely new building, and if this is accepted the type of construction no longer matters.

In the early stages of design the architect's ideas are very fluid and it is difficult for the electrical designer to make suggestions which are more than vague generalities. By the time he receives drawings on which he can start design work of his own the shape and style of the building have been settled and can no longer be altered to accommodate or simplify the services.

Thus the engineering designer's influence on the overall design of the building tends to exist more in theory than in practice.

When the work is to be put out to competitive tender it is necessary to draw up a specification describing the quality and standard of the equipment to be used and the standard of workmanship expected. The specification which was used for the scheme described in this chapter is reproduced in the following pages.

It is often prudent to include in a specification descriptions of equipment which may not be needed for the scheme as designed. Variations are frequently made during construction, and they could introduce a piece of equipment not originally needed. If it has not been described in the speci-fication a short variation instruction can give rise to different interpretations which could result in a contractual dispute.

For example, the original scheme may not require any isolators as opposed to fuse switches and switch fuses. If an isolator is subsequently required and there is no clause in the specification covering isolators, the variation instruction must include a complete description or there is the possibility that an unsuitable type will be supplied. Since there is invariably less time available for drafting variations than for the original specification, it is better to have a few extra clauses in the specification than to risk contractual difficulties later on.

Specification of electrical works

Cubicle panels

Main and distribution switchboards as listed in the schedules shall be purpose-made and shall consist of a sheet-steel cubicle designed for access from front only or from front and rear according to site position, containing distribution busbars, all cable terminations and interconnections. All items. of switch and fusegear are to be flush-mounted on the front of the cubicle which is to be finished grey stoved enamel.

Switchboards shall be suitable for controlling reduced voltage supplies and shall be comprehensively tested before dispatch from the manufacturer's works to ensure satisfactory operation of all component parts. The tests shall include continuity and 2 kV flash tests. Busbar systems in switchboard shall be tested at 50 kA for 1 s.

Full protection shall be provided by means of mechanical interlocks with the covers and operating levers, The switchboard shall have an earthing terminal and earthing bar.

External connections shall be provided to allow all outgoing cables to terminate at either top or bottom of the switchboard.

Busbars

Busbar panels as shown on the drawings and listed in the schedules are to be of the ratings indicated and are to be of high-conductivity copper mounted on robust vitreous porcelain insulators complete with all necessary clamps. The busbars are to be enclosed in a stove-enamelled sheet-steel casing with cast-iron frame members and detachable top, bottom and side plates. The covers are to be of the screw-on type. The panels are to be provided with all necessary holes and bushes for incoming and outgoing cables.

Incoming and outgoing switch fuses of the types and ratings shown on the drawings and schedules shall be provided and installed adjacent to the busbar chamber. All necessary interconnections between switch fuses and busbars shall be made and all the equipment shall be fixed on a common angle-iron frame which is to be supplied as part of the electrical contract. The frame is to be painted one coat primer and two coats grey finish.

Where necessary, trunking shall be supplied and installed from busbars to meter positions.

Fuse switches

Fuse switches shall be heavy-duty pattern fitted with HRC fuse links. They shall have heavy-gauge steel enclosures with cast-iron frame members, rust-protected and finished grey stoved enamel. Front access doors shall be fitted with dust-excluding gaskets and shall be interlocked so that they cannot be opened when the switch is 'on'. Operating handles shall be lockable in both the on and off positions. The top and bottom endplates shall be removable.

Each fuse switch shall be supplied complete with the correct HRC fuse links.

Each fuse switch shall have flag on-off indication.

Fuse switches shall be 500 V rating and shall be clearly marked with their current rating, and the items of equipment that they serve.

Switch fuses

Switch fuses shall be industrial pattern dust-proof type with HRC fuse links. They shall have enclosures fabricated from sheet steel finished grey stoved enamel with removable top and bottom endplates and shall have doors fitted with dust-proof gaskets. They shall have front-operated handles with visible on-off indication.

The interiors shall have vitreous porcelain bases fitted with plated non-ferrous conducting components. Switches shall be of the quick make-and-break type and have removable shields over the fixed contacts and removable moving contact bars.

Each switch fuse shall be supplied complete with the correct HRC fuse links.

Switch fuses shall be 500 V rating and shall be clearly marked with their current rating, and the items of equipment that they serve.

Isolators

Isolators shall be heavy-duty pattern with steel enclosures having cast-iron frame members, rust-protected and finished grey stoved enamel. Front access doors shall be fitted with dust-excluding gaskets and shall be interlocked so that they cannot be opened when the switch is 'on'. Operating handles shall be lockable in both the on and off positions and shall have visible on-off indication.

Isolators shall be 500 V rating and shall be clearly marked with their current rating.

The moving contact assemblies are to be removable for inspection and maintenance.

Distribution boards

All distribution boards shall be single-pole or triple-pole with neutral bar, and with fuseways/CBs 20 or 30 A or above as specified.

All distribution boards shall be of the surface pattern in heavy sheet-steel cases of the 500 V range with HRC fuse carriers.

On all triple-pole and neutral distribution boards the number of neutral terminals to be provided shall be the same as the total number of fuseways/CBs in the board. This information must be given to the manufacturers when ordering, together with information with regard to composite boards having a multiplicity of fuse ratings as specified.

In the case of flush installations, the distribution boards shall be mounted over flush adaptable iron boxes into which the conduits and wiring of the system will terminate. The boxes shall be of a size to be agreed on site with the consulting engineer.

Doors of all distribution boards shall be lockable either by means of a barrel-type lock with detachable key or by means of a modified door-fixing screw, bracket and padlock.

Ample clearance shall be provided between 'live' parts and the sheet-steel protection to allow cables to be brought to their respective terminals in a neat and workmanlike manner.

To separate opposite poles a fillet of hard incombustible insulating material shall be provided of sufficient depth to reach the inside of the door.

In each distribution board spare fuse carriers shall be provided and held in place by a suitable clip so that the carrier cannot be inadvertently dislodged.

Distribution boards shall be fixed at a height to give easy access, and be provided with a schedule complying with 514–09–01 of BS 7671.

Starters

A starter shall be provided for each motor as indicated on the drawings and schedules.

The starters shall be surface-mounted with a sheet-steel case containing a triple-pole contactor with vertical double break per pole having silver-faced contacts. They are to have continuously rated operating coils with inherent undervoltage release. Operating coils are to be supplied from phase to neutral. The starters shall have magnetic-type overload relays with adjustable oil dashpot time lags and stop/reset push-buttons in the front cover. The cover is also to contain the start push-button.

Starters are to have single-pole auxiliary switches and shall incorporate single-phase protection.

Star-delta starters shall have a time-delay device complete with all main and control wiring and terminal block for incoming and outgoing cables. The time-delay device shall be of the pneumatic pattern with an instantaneous reset allowing restarting immediately after a star-delta switching operation. The star and delta contactors are to be mechanically and electrically inter-locked.

The overload relays are to be correctly set to ensure adequate protection without nuisance tripping.

Steel conduit

All steel Class 'B' conduits and conduit fittings throughout the whole of this installation shall comply in all respects with British Standard Specification BS 31:1940. All PVC insulated cables, other than flexibles, shall be protected throughout their length with heavy-gauge screwed welded conduit (enamelled or galvanized as required) with the necessary malleable iron loop-in, draw-in, angle and outlet boxes. No type of 'elbow' or 'tee' will be allowed on works under this Specification.

Where adaptable boxes are used they shall be of cast iron or heavy-gauge sheet steel of not less than 12-gauge.

No conduit of less than 20 mm diameter shall be used.

A solid coupling shall be inserted in every flush conduit run at the point where it leaves a ceiling, wall or floor for ease of dismantling if required.

Except where otherwise stated conduit is to be finished black enamel.

No conduit shall be installed with more than two right-angle bends without draw-in boxes and draw-in boxes shall not be more than 8 m apart.

All conduits, except where otherwise specified, shall drop not rise to the respective points. In no circumstances shall the conduit be erected in such a manner as to form a U without outlet, or in any other way that would provide a trap for condensed moisture.

Provision shall be made for draining all conduits or fixtures by a method approved by the consulting engineer.

No ceiling looping-in point box shall be used as a draw-in box for any other circuit than that for which such point box is intended.

Ceiling point boxes are to be of medium pattern malleable iron, with fixing holes at 50 mm centres and conforming to BS Specification.

Flush ceiling point boxes which do not finish flush with the finished surface of the ceiling, etc., shall be fitted with malleable iron extension rings.

Horizontal or diagonal runs of flush conduit on structural or partition walls will not be permitted. All flush conduits shall drop or rise vertically to their respective points.

Connections between conduits and trunking and conduit and steel boxes, or between conduit and steel cases of distribution gear or equipment, shall be made by means of a flanged coupling and brass smooth-bore entry bush. The lead washer shall be fitted on the inside of the trunking or box, etc.

All lids for draw-in boxes, etc., whether of the BS or adaptable type, shall be of heavy cast-iron or 12-gauge sheet steel, and shall be fixed (overlapping for flush work) by means of two or four M6 round-headed brass screws as required.

Conduits set through walls will not be permitted. When change of direction is required after passing through a wall an appropriate back outlet box is to be fitted.

All joints between lengths of conduit, or between conduit and fittings, etc., are to be threaded home and butted.

Sets and bends are to be made without indentation, and the bore must be full and free throughout. All screw-cutting oil must be carefully wiped off before joining up.

Conduit runs, as far as possible, are to be symmetrical and equally spaced.

The electrical contractor must take all precautions in situations likely to be damp to see that all conduits and boxes in the vicinity are rendered watertight.

During the progress of the work all exposed ends of conduits shall be fitted with suitable plastic or metal plugs. Plugs of wood, paper and the like will not be acceptable as sufficient protection.

Lighting, heating, power and any other types of circuit shall be run in separate conduits and no circuit of any one system shall be installed in any conduit or box of any other system.

The proposed runs shall be submitted to the consulting engineer for approval before work is commenced.

Conduit fittings

All conduit fittings shall be of malleable iron which shall conform to the British Standards Specification BS 31:1940.

All fittings shall be of the screwed pattern, and no solid or inspection elbows, tees or bends shall be installed. Generally, all conduit fittings shall be stove-enamelled black or other approved finish inside and out, but where galvanized conduit is installed, all fittings shall be galvanized by the hot process both inside and out. Such fittings shall be of Class B pattern.

All conduit fittings not carrying lighting or other fittings shall be supplied with suitable cast-iron covers with round-head brass screws. Where flush boxes are installed the covers shall be of the overlapping rustproof pattern.

All ceiling point boxes, except in the case of surface conduits, shall finish flush with the underside of the ceiling, extension rings being used where necessary.

Every flush ceiling point box to which a luminaire is to be attached shall be fitted with a break-joint ring of approved type.

Where surface conduit is used in conjunction with distance saddles, special boxes shall be used, to obviate the setting of conduit when it enters or leaves the boxes.

All conduit boxes, including boxes on and in which fittings, switches and socket outlets are mounted, shall be securely fixed to the walls and ceilings by means of not less than two countersunk screws, correctly spaced, and the fixing holes shall be countersunk, so that the screw heads do not project into the box.

Flexible conduit

Connections to individual motors and heating equipment run in conduit shall be made using a minimum of 300 mm of watertight flexible conduit. The conduit shall be Kopex LS/2.

Flexible conduit connecting to heating equipment shall employ butyl rubber insulated CSP sheathed cables and suitable terminal blocks shall be used in all boxes where a change in cable type is involved.

Earth continuity of all flexible conduits shall be maintained by 4 mm^2 minimum copper conductors forming one of the cores of the cable.

Flexible conduits shall be terminated with the Kopex couplings and connectors specially made for the purpose.

Cable trunking

Cable trunking shall be supplied and installed complete with fittings and accessories and shall be of an approved manufacture. It shall be manufactured from zinc or lead-coated sheet steel finished stove enamelled grey or galvanized and shall be of 18 swg for sizes up to and including 75 mm × 75 mm section and 16 swg for sizes above.

All bends, tees, reducers, couplings, etc., shall be of standard pattern: where it is necessary for a special fitment to be used, it is to be fabricated by the manufacturers.

Where it is necessary to provide additional trunking over fixings, these shall be supplied by the manufacturer and shall be applied with the manufacturer's special tools.

Where holes or apertures are formed in the trunking for cable entry, they shall be bushed with brass smooth-bore entry bushes, or PVC grommet strips. Cable supports are to be inserted in vertical runs of trunking and cables are to be laced thereto in their respective groups.

Fire barriers of hard insulating material shall be provided in vertical runs of trunking where they pass through floors.

Where more than one service is involved multi-compartment trunking shall be employed to separate the services.

Cable tray

Cable tray is to be made of 16-gauge perforated mild-steel sheet and is to be complete with all coupling pieces and bends, offsets and fixing brackets, to enable the tray to fit the structure accurately.

Where cables are taken over the edge of the tray they shall be protected by rubber grommets.

MICC cable

Mineral-insulated metal-sheathed cables shall be high-conducting copper conductors embedded in magnesium oxide and sheathed with copper with an overall covering of PVC.

All cable terminations shall be protected and sealed with ring-type glands with screw-on pot-type seals utilizing cold plastic compound and neoprene sleeving all of an approved pattern, and applied with the special tools recommended by the cable manufacturers.

Cold screw-on pot-type seals shall be used except where the ambient temperature in which the cable will operate will exceed 170°F, where the hot-type seal shall be used.

Four-core MICC cables shall not be used for ring circuits.

Vibration-absorbing loops shall be formed in MICC cables connected to motors and other vibrating equipment.

Connections and joints in MICC cables shall only be made at the terminals of switches, ceiling roses, or at connector blocks housed in outlet boxes. Connector blocks shall have a minimum of two screws per conductor.

Where entry is made into equipment which does not have a spouted entry, the cable shall be made off by means of coupling, male bush, and compression washer.

MICC cables shall be neatly installed and shall be clipped by means of copper saddles secured by two brass screws. Where two, three or four cables are run together multiple saddles shall be used.

MICC cables shall be delivered to the site with the manufacturers' seals and identification labels intact and shall be installed in accordance with the manufacturers' recommendations and using the specialized tools recommended by the manufacturer. They shall be tested when installed before being sealed and again at the end of the contract.

They shall be sealed against the ingress of moisture at all times during the contract.

PVC cable

Cable PVC-insulated only, and PVC-insulated PVC-sheathed cable shall be 600/1000 V grade to BS 6004:1969.

The cable shall be delivered to site on reels, with seals and labels intact and shall be of one manufacturer throughout the installation.

The cable shall be installed direct from the reels and any cable which has become kinked, twisted or damaged in any way shall be rejected. The installation shall be cabled on the loop-in system, i.e. wiring shall terminate at definite points (switch positions, lighting points, etc.) and no intermediate connections or joints will be permitted. Cables shall not pass through or terminate in lighting fittings.

Where it is necessary to make direct connection between the hard wiring and flexible cord, this shall be done by means of porcelain-shielded connectors with twin screws. No luminaire shall be connected directly to the hard wiring.

The terminations shall be suitable for the type of terminal provided and shall be either sweated lugs of appropriate size, or eyelet or crimped type cable terminations, all of reputable manufacture. Shakeproof washers shall be used where electric motors are connected.

Where cable cores are larger than terminal holes, the cables shall be fitted with thimbles. For all single connections, they shall be doubled or twisted back on themselves and pinching screws shall not be permitted to cut the conductors. Cables shall be firmly twisted together before the connection is made.

In no circumstances shall cables be trapped under plain washers as a termination.

Cables shall be coloured in accordance with IEE Regulations BS 7671.

Only two cables shall generally be bunched together at one terminal. In exceptional cases three cables may be bunched together at one terminal with the authority of the engineer given on site.

Flexible cords

All flexible cords shall comply with British Standard Specification BS 6500:1969, and shall consist of high-conductivity tinned copper conductors of the required cross-sectional area insulated and sheathed as detailed hereunder:

Lighting pendants

Two-core 0.75 mm^2 heat-resisting circular flexible cord EP rubber-insulated CSP-sheathed. Colour of sheath, white.

Heating apparatus and equipment requiring flexible
cable connection

Heat-resisting circular flexible cable. EP rubber-insulated CSP-sheathed having the number of cores with cross-sectional areas as specified.

Apparatus and equipment, other than heating, requiring
flexible cable connection

Circular flexible cable PVC-insulated PVC-sheathed having the number of cores with cross-sectional areas specified.

The cores of all flexible cords shall be coloured throughout their length and colour-coded to comply with the British Standard Specification.

PVC SWA cable

PVC-insulated single-cable armoured cables shall be 500/1000 V grade and shall comply with BS 6346:1969.

The cable shall comprise round or shaped conductors, of equal cross-sectional area, composed of high-conductivity plain annealed copper cable insulated with PVC, coloured for identification. The cores to be laid up circular and sheathed with PVC. The cable shall be served with one layer of steel-cable armour and sheathed overall with PVC.

The cable shall be manufactured and supplied in one length on a suitable drum. No through joints will be allowed. All cables shall be of one manufacture.

Where individual cables are run on the surface suitable supports shall be fitted to give a minimum clearance of 15 mm between cables and face of structure. Where cables are installed vertically, the cable shall be gripped firmly by clamps of an approved pattern.

Where cables are grouped and run on the surface they shall be carried on wrought-iron brackets or purpose-made clips of approved design, fixed at not more than 600 mm centres.

All PVC SWA cables run on the surface shall be adequately protected to a height of 2 m from the ground.

Where PVC-insulated SWA cables are laid in the ground they shall be laid on not less than 75 mm of sand, covered by a further 75 mm of sand and protected by means of continuous interlocking warning tiles of approved pattern.

All cable trenches shall be excavated to a depth of 0.5 m in unmade ground and 0.7 m where crossing roadways and backfilled by the builder who will also provide and install all necessary cable ducts and earthenware pipes for cable entry into buildings, but the electrical contractor shall be responsible for correctly marking out all cable routes, supplying and installing waring tiles and marker posts, and generally supervising all work in connection with the cable-laying requirements.

Cable joints

All cable runs between one definite terminal point and another throughout the whole of the installation shall be installed without intermediate joints.

Luminaires

All luminaires shown and listed on the drawings and schedules shall be provided and installed. Luminaires with non-standard suspension lengths shall be ordered to the correct lengths to suit mounting height as indicated on the drawings and schedules. The installation of luminaires shall include all necessary assembling, wiring and erection.

Terminations to non-pendant luminaires shall be in heat-resisting flexible cord with porcelain-insulated terminal block connectors for connection to PVC-insulated cable or PVC-insulated PVC-sheathed cable.

Fluorescent luminaires shall be mounted either directly or on suspensions from two BS conduit boxes installed at the spacing required to suit the fitting.

Ceiling roses

Ceiling roses shall be white of reputable manufacture in accordance with BS 67. They shall be of porcelain, or of plastic with porcelain interiors and shall be fitted with plastic backplates or plastic mounting blocks semi-recessed where necessary to comply with the IEE Regulations.

Where they are of the three-plate type the phase terminal shall be shrouded so as to prevent accidental contact if the cover is removed.

Lamp holders

Lamp holders shall be of the bayonet-cap type for tungsten lamps up to and including 150 W, and of the Edison screw type for larger lamps.

Where they are integral with lighting luminaires, they shall be brass with porcelain interiors. For use with flexible pendants, they shall be of white plastic with compression glands. Where batten lamp holders are installed the lamp holders shall be of white plastic. In damp situations they shall be fitted with Home Office skirts.

Lamp holders for fluorescent tubes shall be of the heavy pattern bi-pin type of white plastic construction.

All lampholders shall be lubricated with molybdenum disulphide to ensure easy removal of threaded rings and lamps.

Lamps

Lamps shall be supplied and fitted to all points and luminaires shown and listed on the drawings and schedules.

Tungsten filament lamps of 40–100 W (inclusive) shall be of the coiled coil type. Generally they shall be energy saving types. Lamps shall be pearl-finished when fitted in open shades or in globes which are unobscured and shall be of the clear type when fitted in closed units of opalescent glassware or any other type of luminaire elected where the filament is not under direct vision.

The colour of all fluorescent lamps shall be the new white, 3500 K.

Lighting circuits

Lighting circuits shall be installed on the loop-in system with three terminal-type ceiling roses with shrouded live terminal, integral backplate, earth terminal and break-joint ring. Looping shall not be carried out at switch positions.

No luminaire shall be connected directly to the hard wiring or have circuit wiring passing through it.

Cables on one circuit are not to run through the BS boxes behind ceiling roses or luminaires on other circuits.

Light switches

Flush switches shall be rocker-operated with white flush plastic plates of the single-switch or grid-switch type.

Surface switches shall be heavy-gauge steel with conduit entries and shall have rocker-operated mechanisms. They shall have steel front plates of the single-switch or grid-switch type.

Switches outdoors or otherwise exposed to damp conditions shall be of industrial pattern watertight type with galvanized steel, or thermoplastic boxes and waterproof gaskets.

Socket outlets

All socket outlets shall be of the switched type with rocker-operated switch mechanisms.

Flush socket outlets shall be of the insulated pattern with white or ivory finish.

Surface socket outlets shall be metal clad type with steel front plate.

Connections to space heaters

The circuit to each unit heater, fan convector and other similiar piece of heating equipment shall terminate in a double-pole isolator from which the final connection shall be made in heat-resisting rubber insulated cable in flexible conduit. The casing of the heater shall be bonded to the earth continuity conductor.

Connections to motors and machinery

The circuit to each machine shall terminate in an isolator as near the machine as possible. Where a motor starter is required it shall be placed adjacent to and immediately after the isolator. The final connection from the isolator or starter to the machine shall be in PVC-insulated cable in conduit. The rigid conduit shall terminate in a box approximately 300 mm from the machine terminals and the final section from this point to the machine shall be in flexible conduit. The metalwork of the machine shall be bonded to the earth continuity conductor.

Regulations

The installation shall comply with Electricity at Work Regulations, Electricity Safety Quality, and Continuity Regulations 2002 and any other applicable statutory regulations. It shall conform with the Institution of Electrical Engineers' Regulations for the Electrical Equipment of Buildings BS 7671.

The installation and all material used shall comply with all relevant British Standards and Codes of Practice.

Clearance from other services

All electric conduit and equipment shall be installed at least 150 mm clear of any other metalwork, and in particular of any water, gas, steam or chemical pipes.

Bonding and earthing

All conduit connections, boards, fittings, trunking, etc., shall be properly screwed together so as to ensure proper mechanical and electrical continuity throughout.

Great care is to be taken in bonding and earthing the installation and tests are to be carried out as the work progresses to check the electrical continuity of all metalwork, conduits, etc., and earth continuity conductors. This is particularly important where work is built into the fabric of the building.

For the purpose of estimating the electrical contractor may assume that he can earth to the supply authority's earthing terminal.

The electrical contractor shall contact the supply authority at an early stage in the works to ensure that a suitable earthing terminal will be provided.

The electrical contractor shall be responsible for the bonding and earthing of all exposed metalwork, structural or otherwise, and of the metalwork of any gas or water service, to the earthing termination at the intake position, in accordance with IEE Regulations BS 7671.

No earth continuity conductor shall be less than 1.5 mm^2 copper cable insulated and coloured green and yellow.

The steel cable armouring of the sub-main cables shall be efficiently bonded together and to the respective switchboard, distribution board, sealing chamber and conduits at which they terminate and to all adjacent metalwork.

The frames of all electric motors and starting panels, etc., are to be efficiently earthed. Where flexible metallic conduit is used, a stranded insulated and coloured green and yellow copper cable of not less than 6 mm^2 is to be run from the terminal box through the flexible metallic conduit to terminate in the first cast metal box in the conduit run.

The circuit protective conductor shall be attached at each end by means of a crimped socket, brass screw and spring washer.

Pipelines, tanks, vessels and all other equipment associated with the piping or storage of highly inflammable materials shall be statically bonded to an effective earth continuity conductor by means of 30 mm $\times$ 10 mm hard drawn tinned copper tape, secured by means of the flange bolts. The earth continuity conductor shall be taken to an earth electrode and bonded to it.

Earth electrode

Where an earth electrode is required it shall take the form of extensible copper earth rods driven into the ground at suitable spacing. The number of rods and the depth to which they are driven shall be determined according to the soil resistivity at the site to give an earth resistance not exceeding 0.5 ohms.

Concrete inspection covers shall be provided over every earth electrode and a means shall be provided for disconnecting the bonding cable from every earth electrode.

Connection to and between electrodes shall be carried out in insulated stranded cable.

Testing

Continuity and insulation tests shall be carried out during installation.

At completion polarity, bonding, earth loop impedance, continuity and insulation tests shall be carried out on the entire installation and in each part of it. The tests shall be witnessed by the consulting engineer and shall be carried out in accordance with the requirements of the Institution of Electrical Engineers' Regulations BS 7671. A completion certificate schedule of inspection, and schedule of test results as prescribed by BS 7671 shall be provided.

Circuit lists and labels

At each distribution board a circuit schedule complying with BS 7671 IEE Wiring Regulations shall be supplied and fixed on the inside of the distribution board door.

The schedule shall state clearly the position, number and wattage of lamps, socket outlets, etc., which the fuseways/CBs control. A sample circuit schedule shall be submitted for approval before installation.

On the cover of each distribution board, fuse switch, switch fuse, isolating switch and starter a 45 mm × 20 mm traffolyte label (white-black-white) shall be fixed and engraved in 5 mm characters, giving details of the service position and phase, etc. In addition, traffolyte (white-red-white) labels engraved in 8 mm characters '400 V' shall be fixed to all TPN distribution boards.

All labels shall be fixed by means of four 6 mm round-headed brass screws.

Identification of cables

All power, instrument, control and indication cables shall be provided with indestructable cable marking collars which shall bear the cable number. The marking collars shall be fitted at every cable termination.

The individual cores of cables shall be numbered to indicate which terminal they are connected to.

Fuses

HCR fuse links of the current rating shall be supplied and installed in all fuse carriers.

Bibliography

Amongst the many books published on this and related topics, the following are suggested for readers at this level.

Francis, T.G., *Electrical Installation Work*
Lewis, M.L., *Electrical Installation Technology: Advanced Work*
Linsley, T., *Basic Electrical Installation Work*
Scaddon, B., *Electrical Installation Work*

Index